HISTORY

IN THEIR

HANDS

To Marcia Volpert,

May you be strengthened in the future so that you may continne -- as you have in the past -- to strengthen our hard-won Jewish name.

כל הכבוד,

Harvey Lutske

פסח 1996

HISTORY IN THEIR HANDS

A Book of JEWISH AUTOGRAPHS

Harvey Lutske

JASON ARONSON INC.
Northvale, New Jersey
London

Design by Pamela Roth.

For credits, see credits section at end of book.

This book was set in 12 pt. Palatino.

10 9 8 7 6 5 4 3 2 1

Library of Congress Cataloging-in-Publication Data
Lutske, Harvey.
History in their hands : a book of Jewish autographs / Harvey Lutske.
p. cm.
ISBN 1-56821-290-9
1. Jews—Autographs—Facsimiles. 2. Jews—Biography. 3. Rabbis—Autographs—Facsimiles. 4. Rabbis—Biography. I. Title.
Z42.3.J48L88 1996
929.8'8089'924—dc20 94-19626

Manufactured in the United States of America. Jason Aronson Inc. offers books and cassettes. For information and catalog write to Jason Aronson Inc., 230 Livingston Street, Northvale, New Jersey 07647.

Because autographs are the history of generations,
this book is dedicated to:

My father of blessed memory, Morris Lutske;

My mother, may her light continue to shine, Maxine W. Lutske;

My sons Eli, Ethan, and Seth.

CONTENTS

Yes, I am a Jew, and when the right honorable gentleman's ancestors were savages on a primitive island, mine were priests in the Temple of Solomon.

—Benjamin Disraeli

ACKNOWLEDGMENTS

A book like this is not written without the assistance and encouragement of many people and institutions. I would be both negligent and irresponsible to not mention those who aided me from start to finish.

First and foremost, I thank my wife, Sharon, and my sons, Eli, Ethan, and Seth. Family acknowledgments are usually left to the end, but family members are the very first who are affected when any project is undertaken. Without their patience, understanding, and occasional interruptions, this book would not have been written.

My mentor, adviser, and compatriot Jon D. "Iggy" Shannon of Chillicothe, Missouri, has been a constant source of support to me. I thank him heartily for all his help and wish him that his personal collection never be sullied by a forgery.

Editors, too, are usually left until the end, but Arthur Kurzweil's enthusiasm and support of this work were tremendously encouraging to me. His discerning sense of criticism is rare. He is a gentleman of the first order, to boot. Fortunate is the writer who has an editor like him.

Many thanks to David and Claudia Schulson of David Schulson Autographs, Inc., New York City, who so graciously shared with me a number of the items found herein. They are amiable, personal, knowledgeable, and insightful people in a business where all too much is glitz and the dollar. The time and materials they shared with me are strongly represented in this book.

The Aron-Ettenberg families of Los Angeles and New York, notably Dr. Isa Aron and Sylvia Ettenberg, were very supportive. Mrs. Ettenberg's advice and referrals, in particular, are beyond acknowledgment. I look forward to our storming through Zabar's together.

A hearty *Yaasher Koach*, may you all be strengthened, to David Lilly of Brookline, Massachusetts, who shared with me his personal collection; Sholom Katz, Esq., son of the late Rabbi Samuel Katz, chief rabbi of the Rabbinic Court in Los Angeles, who allowed me to review his father's correspondence; Avraham Yaakov Finkel of Boro Park, New York, who shared his sources and library with me; and Charles Hamilton, *doyen* of American autograph dealers.

A number of people helped me with translations, through a variety of scribbled, scrawled, and almost cuneiformlike scratches ranging from Hebrew to French to German to Yiddish to English to Russian. I appreciatively say todah, merci, a dahnk, and thank you to my mother- and father-in-law, Hilde and Irving Korr, of Oakland, California; to Rabbi Abraham Kin; to Dr. Saul Newman; and to Ahoova Gol Zeffren.

I trust the following institutions will forgive me for listing individuals first, for without their assistance this book would not have been possible. Repositories of information, such institutions bring together donors, scholars, and researchers, all with the same goal in mind—to preserve and share knowledge: the Central Zionist Archives in Jerusalem, which proved to be a gold mine, one with attentive, cooperative workers; the same must be said of the Schwadron Collection of the Jew-

ish National University Library; Kevin Proffitt, archivist of the American Jewish Archives in Cincinnati, whose knowledge and speed in helping me completely restored my faith in institutions; Jane Levy, librarian of the Blumenthal Rare Book and Manuscript Library of the Jewish Museum of the West in Berkeley, California, whose let-me-sit-down-beside-you-and-explain-how-most-archives-work explanation made me feel perfectly at home and comfortable; Harvey Horowitz, head librarian of the Hebrew Union College Library, Los Angeles, and staff librarian Yaffa Weisman, who were always there whenever I felt lost and misguided and in over my head; Dr. Adaire Klein and Cheryl Miller of the Los Angeles–based Simon Wiesenthal Center, whose strength in working daily with the gruesome Holocaust materials is something I completely envy; and Cecile Kuznitz, assistant archivist, and other members of the YIVO Institute for Jewish Research staff, who oversee more than 22 million items.

Last, but by no means least, let me acknowledge and thank Rabbi Jerry Schwarzbard and his staff of the Henry R. and Miriam Ripps Schnitzer Special Collections Library of the Jewish Theological Seminary of New York. The Seminary's library is recognized worldwide as second to none.

These acknowledgments would not be complete without my thanking Dr. Alex Grobman, director of the Los Angeles Martyrs Memorial and Museum of the Holocaust, for his assistance, encouragement, insights, and review of the manuscript.

I apologize to anyone whose name I have inadvertently excluded.

INTRODUCTION

In the Academy Award–winning movie *Norma Rae,* a small-town southern mill worker meets, for the first time in her life, a Jew. A labor organizer, one Reuben Warshafsky, is in town to help unionize the local textile mill. Watching him unpack in his motel room, Norma Rae engages him in her first-ever conversation with a real, live Jew, in a voice as thick as syrup: "Yuu a Juuu?" When the labor organizer responds in the affirmative, she asks, "Whut makes you different?" For a brief moment he pauses, then, continuing his unpacking, he answers: "History."

Jews have always been making history. Through Jewish ideas, thought, and action, through just the very fact of *being,* Jews have been actively in the maelstrom of history. From the beginning of recorded history, Jews have been on the scene. If the ancient city of Ur, with its famed ziggurat, stands at the base of archaeology, so does Abraham, the forefather of Judaism, Christianity, and Islam. If ancient Egypt is viewed as one of the cradles of civilization, then an early Egyptian stele records the nation of Israel as one of the infants in the cradle. Surely Joseph, the viceroy of Pharaoh, was there. Whether through intellect, action, or even victimization, Jews have integrally been making history.

The people in this book are all history makers. They are men and women, children and the aged. They made history in Palestine, in Israel (indeed some *created* the State of Israel), and in the Diaspora. Their history is part of war and peace, politics and entertainment. Some made history in science, others in the humanities. Some made recent history; others go back a thousand years. Through their hands, through their acts, history has been created, altered, and advanced.

As long as history is recorded, many of these people will live forever. The Rambam will live forever. Dr. Jonas Salk will live forever. David Ben-Gurion will live forever. Without overaggrandizing, these people are an integral part of the continuum of the story of humanity.

Some have changed the world irrevocably. Never again will childhood be a time of fear of withered and crippled limbs caused by poliomyelitis; Jonas Salk saw to that. As Isaac Newton changed forever knowledge about gravity, so Einstein transformed the science of physics. The history of international relations has been altered dramatically by Theodor Herzl, Chaim Weizmann, David Ben-Gurion, and Golda Meir. And the human soul has been touched forever by Anne Frank.

Why a book of Jewish autographs? What's in a signature? As a Jew and an American, I am part of a dual continuum and, like many others, I feel history. Like most Americans, I am terribly impressed when I see the actual handwriting of Abraham Lincoln, Benjamin Franklin, George Washington, Patrick Henry. In museums in Washington, Los Ange-

les, Springfield, Illinois, or anywhere else their letters, diaries, and journals have been preserved, I witness history. I feel a thrill when I see an actual letter in Abraham Lincoln's own hand. Ben Franklin impresses me. So does George Washington Carver. Robert E. Lee evokes in me a tremendous feeling of character, stature, and nobility. Jack London and Teddy Roosevelt convey a unique American vitality and robustness. In these letters, manuscripts, and documents I touch history, and, in turn, it touches me. Such is part and parcel of my American heritage and fabric.

How must a Frenchman feel when he sees documents penned by Napoleon? How does a Pole feel when he sees records of Copernicus and Madame Curie? How does an Englishman feel when he sees leaves from Roger Bacon, letters by Winston Churchill? How do any of us feel when we see the actual words and notebooks of great leaders, thinkers, or dreamers, citizens of the world like DaVinci or Galileo?

Why a book of Jewish autographs? What's in a signature? The ultimate signature comes from the Bible: "And the tables were the work of God, and the writing was the writing of God, graven upon the tables." That, however, remains in a different realm. In a more immediate vein, to be a Jew and see an actual writing by the legendary Maimonides is an incredible feeling. A thousand years old, it is a direct transmission of the Mesorah, the Tradition. For any Jew who affiliates, it is Judaism transmitted through the generations, through the centuries, from Sinai to *Medinat Yisrael*—the State of Israel. For a scientist, the papers of Einstein or Salk are the manifestations of a mind probing the wonders and secrets of the universe. For a nationalist, the signatures of Ben-Gurion and Golda Meir reveal the identities of founders of a new world. For the twentieth-century Jew, it is through the signature of Elie Wiesel or Simon Wiesenthal that the horror of anti-Semitism is experienced. To see the Israeli Declaration of Independence is to see a modern miracle wrought from the dreams of Theodor Herzl and the ashes of Auschwitz. It is the same as viewing the Declaration of Independence, with John Hancock's bold flourish, and recognizing as an American that here is a document challenging the centuries-old belief in the "divine" right of kings and the oppression of others.

A signature is a mark in time. Manuscript collectors are time travelers. Letters and documents put people, places, and events in perspective. Handwritten documents have much in common with cemeteries and battlefields, where we latecomers upon the scene hear the conversations, both whispers and shouts, of what has been.

There is history to be witnessed.

I know a woman who is an avid Abraham Lincoln collector and expert. Among the many letters and documents she has of Lincoln's, she also owns a verified stovepipe hat. When I first saw it, I was considerably impressed. "This," I thought, "belonged to Abraham Lincoln!" But the more I looked at it, the more I realized it was simply a hat. After a while, one hat is the same as any other. This one just happened to have been worn by a president. After some introspection, the hat lost its glamour. It was somehow impersonal. A hat is, after all, a hat.

But a signature is a piece of one's self. Who else but Abraham Lincoln could produce an Abraham Lincoln signature? What is more personal than one's own handwriting?

As Jews, not all the people presented here were or are religious. Far from it. Nor were all ardent Zionists. Many were ardent Frenchmen, Americans, Englishmen, Germans, and members of a dozen other nationalities. The names here represent Jews who have advanced the Jewish name, the Jewish people, the Jewish cause.

What most emerges from this collection is the wonderful and overabiding sense of

peoplehood, nation. A phrase from the Pledge of Allegiance is ever so accurate: "One nation, under God . . ." How true! Across centuries and nations and cultures and politics and race and injustice and justice, Jews have always been and remain "one nation, under God," holding in a life-and-death grip the sense of peoplehood. Uniquely, the last 150 years have seen a veritable explosion of Jewish history makers. Ghettos, the *Haskalah*, May Laws, pogroms, mass immigrations, the Dreyfus Affair, Herzl, political Zionism, world wars, the Nazi infamy, the birth of the State of Israel, have all occurred in a historical "twinkling of an eye."

What's in a signature? *"September 22, 1895. . . . Condemned on the evidence of handwriting, it will soon be a year since I asked for justice; and the justice I demand is the unmasking of the wretch who wrote that infamous letter."* Thus wrote the condemned Alfred Dreyfus. Researching this book was a great deal more difficult than I thought it would be. The records of the lives of the people here brought out a host of emotions: depression, pride, sadness, joy, wonder, incredulity, melancholia, envy, dignity, amazement. There were biographies I read that—I openly admit—brought tears to my eyes and a lump in my throat. There were other biographies I read that made me want to audibly say "Yes!" with pride and honor. My emotions were far ranging.

For several days after researching Anne Frank and Dr. Janusz Korczak, I was in an emotional funk. What sense can be made out of the Nazi madness? And madness it was. To read Simon Wiesenthal's account of his conversation with the semisympathetic Nazi *Rottenfuhrer* (Corporal) Merz is to shake one's head in complete disbelief. We are all so beaten upon with the ongoing issues of the Holocaust, we have become inured to the horror. But if we stop and think, if we stop and *feel*, what answer can possibly be applied to murdering children in an orphanage?

And then to dwell on Anne Frank and see her actual letters and learn she died from starvation and typhus within weeks of her concentration camp's liberation . . . weeks! It brought an overwhelming sadness to me. To the dead, a few weeks is as limitless as two galaxies. It is forever.

When celluloid Reuben Warshafsky told Norma Rae that what made Jews different was history, he didn't tell her everything. Because for Jews, history is not behind us.

It's in us.

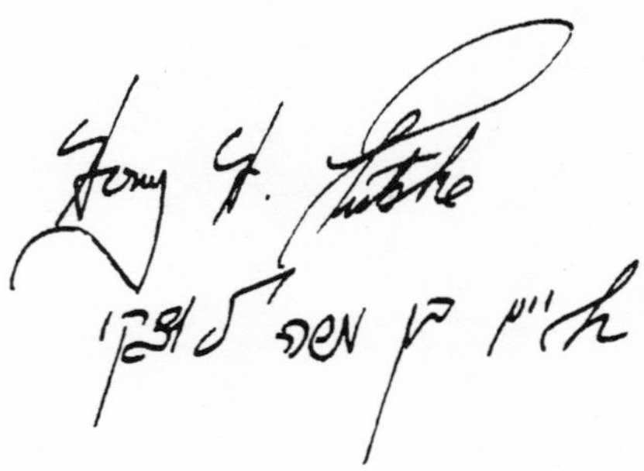

A BRIEF WORD ON AUTOGRAPHS

The first question asked of me by one friend of this project was, "How come you didn't include Rashi's autograph?" (Rabbi Shlomo ben Yitzchaki of France, the greatest biblical commentator in Jewish history). And the answer was simple: Because there is none. History being what it is—the recording of time as it passes—many documents either have been lost forever or have still not been discovered. Documents are lost in two ways: intentional destruction (the reason, for example, that paper shredders were invented) and accidental loss through fire, aging, parasitic infestation, or secreting to preserve them. In the latter case, items have been hidden for group safety (like the Dead Sea Scrolls of Qumran) or personal possession (because the signature of a scholar, for example, or a mystic, was often vested with special properties by the owner.

Politics can also play a role. Currently under way are strong lobbying efforts seeking full disclosure from the Vatican of their acknowledged Judaica library holdings. The same applies to various local governments of the recently defunct Soviet Union. Treasures galore exchange hands during wars: gold, art, paintings, religious icons, and documents. And European history is awash in war.

Of the many autographs in this book, few involve documents of tremendous significance. To be sure, there are some, such as those in the Israeli Declaration of Independence, or the manuscripts of the Rambam (Maimonides) and Yehudah Ha-Levi. But most are routine and involve either commercial or personal matters. This is due to several reasons: some items have not withstood the test of time and have been lost; dramatic moments were not always recorded by the participants; events at the time did not seem important and thus were not recorded. For instance, Abraham Lincoln thought little of his very brief speech at Gettysburg, and handwritten copies were made only because it was a quick "few words." Mr. Lincoln did not write in his diary: "Today I gave the Gettysburg Address." While not completely absent from the historical record, such diary notes are rare. (Herzl's diary, among a handful of others, was a wonderful exception.)

Likewise, accessibility is a major problem. Unfortunately, dealing with institutions, as any researcher knows, can be difficult at best. The signature of Maimonides, for example, is in only three or four institutional collections worldwide, including Jerusalem, New York, and Leningrad, and getting a response from Jerusalem is not always any easier than getting a response from Leningrad.

The selection of individuals may bother some readers, who wonder why one person

was included and not another. Availability of some autographs is again an answer. A second answer is that one man's saint is another's despot. The majority of people who make history also make enemies. Even the most beloved of leaders have been vilified, and the most vilified had their followers. Perspective changes according to the individual.

The autographs, letters, and manuscripts here are in several languages: Hebrew, English, Yiddish, French, German, Russian, among others. Insofar as Jews historically have been minimally bilingual and commonly literate in four or five languages, many used the language of their country in correspondence. Thus, some people are represented in more than one language, again depending upon availability.

For the individual interested in collecting autographs, many (but as mentioned above, not all) readily abound. Availability and economics are *the* key factors. The common ways of getting a current autograph are by writing to the individual or by purchasing it. In today's documents and manuscripts market, auction houses devoted to autographs and professional, well-established, reputable dealers are the novice's best and safest sources for authentic autographs. I cannot stress too strongly the word *reputable.* In the past ten years, autograph dealers have multiplied exponentially, and anybody wishing to call himself or herself a dealer can. *Caveat emptor*—let the buyer beware. Less-than-reputable dealers are not the only worry; autographs can be expensive, and the lengthy history of forgery is a fascinating one.

Athletic and musical/entertainment personalities as separate categories have not been included in this volume. This is not because Jews were not instrumental in these fields but because I chose not to include them at this time. Perhaps in a future volume I will address these other special Jews.

I

SAGES AND SAINTS

A pious elder recognizing the end of his days prayed that he might have a preview glimpse of the World-to-Come. His prayer was heard and his request granted; an angel came and advised him that he would accompany the *tzaddik* for a brief look into *Olam Ha-Ba*. Upon their arrival, the elder saw a number of men, sages and scholars, sitting at long tables, studying the Holy Books as they had on earth. "Is this it?" asked the surprised elder. "Is this Heaven?" "Aah," exclaimed the *malach*, "you're not seeing what you see correctly. It is not that the men are not in Heaven: Heaven is in the men."

—from the tradition

ISRAEL BEN ELIEZER—THE BAAL SHEM TOV

"I can sing a prayer as well as say it."

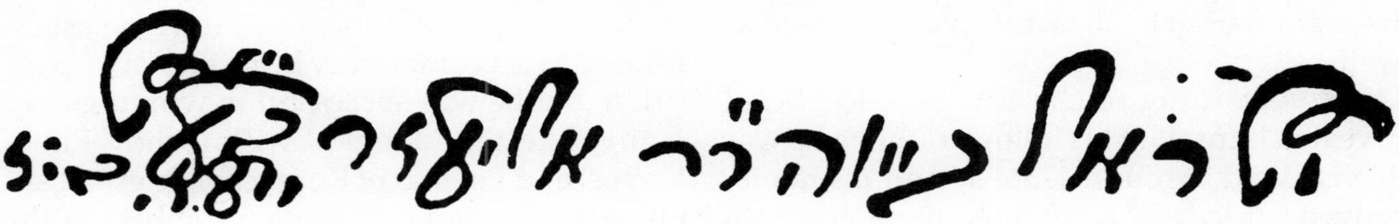

Israel ben Eliezer, also known as the Baal Shem Tov ("The Master of the Good Name") and the Besht (an acronym derived from the Hebrew *B*aal *Sh*em *T*ov), was the legendary founder of the renewal movement in Judaism known as Chasidism, or *Chasidut*. His teachings and philosophies have strengthened and injected new life into Judaism over the last 200 years.

Like most legendary figures, the Baal Shem Tov's life is obscured in truths and myths. The first book about him (he himself left no writings other than a few letters) was published in 1815, fifty-five years after his death, by which time the number of people who had actually known him was quickly dwindling. He was born about 1700 to elderly and poor parents in the small village of Okop, Podalia (currently the western Ukraine), and was orphaned as a young child. He was cared for communally by the townspeople and civic leaders, and it was seen to that he received a

Jewish education. As a teenager, he earned his keep as a teacher to young children and as an assistant to the village beadle and ritual slaughterer. His preference, however, was to spend time in the adjacent fields and woods. He was perceived as good-natured but unremarkable, certainly no scholar. Married at about age 18, his wife died within a few weeks. He later left Okop and went to the village of Tlust, where he supported himself as the teacher at the *cheder*.

Ben Eliezer remarried, but he and his new wife were disowned by her brother. The couple lived quietly for a number of years in a small village in the Carpathian Mountains. In effect, ben Eliezer went into seclusion. Eking out a livelihood by digging lime, the Baal Shem Tov prepared himself for his later life.

It was at this time that ben Eliezer began developing for himself a name as a Baal Shem, a master of the name, a healer and miracle worker. It is said he had learned from the farmers and peasants many of the natural properties of herbs, plants, and roots. It is documented he made amulets and gave advice for monetary payment. He was sought out not just by peasants, but by the wealthy and learned as well.

According to chasidic lore, the Besht revealed himself to his followers when he was 36 years old. Around 1736, he and his family moved to Medziboz, where he remained until his death. He spoke to the people in simple, lay Yiddish and explained how there was an alternate approach to worshiping God, observing the *mitzvot*, and finding, seeking, and connecting with the Master of the World. The Jews and Judaism of the Besht's time were sorely strained and welcomed him. The Besht's generation had inherited the recent mantle of the past hundred years of bitter disappointment of false messiahs and widespread pogroms. The 1600s saw the Chmielnitzki massacres, in which an estimated 100,000 Jews were slaughtered. Judaism had fragmented into two classes: the wealthy and/or learned and the unlettered and poor. Religion was hierarchical and stagnant. Many leading rabbis dealt with fine academic subtleties of the Talmud, *pilpul* (casuistry and hairsplitting), leaving the common, working Jew with real, everyday problems.

The Besht taught that man should seek attachment (*devekut*) or cleave to God, not just in prayer but in all aspects of everyday activity. Prayer, he taught, must be done with complete devotion (*kavanah*) and, like Torah study, which also brings man closer to God, not done as an intellectual activity or as a fixed routine. The Besht emphasized emotional precedence over rational faith, joy over asceticism, and devotion over discipline. To the masses, as well as to many educated, intellectual Jews, his teachings were a whirlwind of revelation. One need not be a scholar to know God; the way to God did not require great learning. Spiritual fulfillment was attainable. The uneducated, in particular, were taken by this tender, catering, offering approach of God.

The Baal Shem Tov's reputation as miracle worker changed to religious leader, philosopher, ethical mentor. From the established Jewish community he faced stern opposition, but he was successful in winning over many, like the Maggid of Zlotochov Rabbi Yechiel and Pinchas of Koretz, while establishing disciples and eventually establishing the concept of the chasidic *tzaddik*.

The Besht taught through simple stories, parables, and examples. His opponents, or the *mitnaggdim*, ridiculed and vigorously attacked his simple approach and reduced emphasis on traditional talmudic scholarship. But the Besht's teachings of God were popular, not cerebral. And they were eminently successful. By the time of his death in 1760, it was estimated there were more than 10,000 followers of the Baal Shem Tov.

The movement that the Baal Shem Tov gave rise to has not yet seen its peak. Today

there are such well-known sects as the Lubavitch, Bobover, Gerer, and Satmer *chasidim* and a host of others. These groups collectively are sometimes referred to as the Ultra-Orthodox. Following World War II, the *chasidim* and the remnants of Europe's *mitnaggdim* took upon themselves the responsibility of rebuilding the lost world and reestablishing Eastern European Jewry. It is not an understatement to say that the Baal Shem Tov was responsible for one of the major movements in all of Judaism.

LEVI YITZCHAK OF BERDITCHEV— THE BERDITCHEVER

"The tailor said, 'I declared to God: You wish me to repent of my sins, but I have committed only minor offenses. I may have kept leftover cloth, or I may have eaten in a non-Jewish home, where I worked, without washing my hands. But Thou, O Lord, hast committed grievous sins: Thou hast taken away babies from their mothers, and mothers from their babies. So let us be quits. If Thou wilt forgive me, I shall forgive thee.'"

"Said the Berditchever: 'Why did you let God off so easily? You might have forced Him to forgive all of Israel!'"

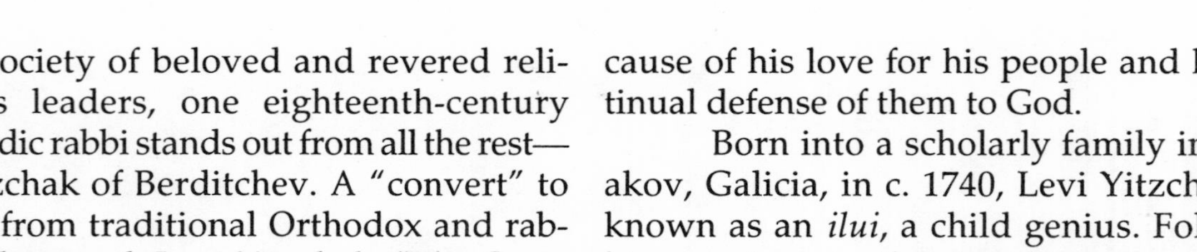

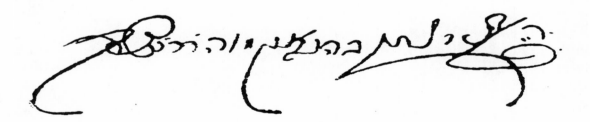

In a society of beloved and revered religious leaders, one eighteenth-century chasidic rabbi stands out from all the rest—Levi Yitzchak of Berditchev. A "convert" to *Chasidut* from traditional Orthodox and rabbinic background, Levi Yitzchak, "The Compassionate," has come down over the centuries to be one of the most beloved of all rebbes because of his love for his people and his continual defense of them to God.

Born into a scholarly family in Hoshakov, Galicia, in c. 1740, Levi Yitzchak was known as an *ilui*, a child genius. Following his marriage to the daughter of a wealthy contractor, Levi Yitzchak continued his religious studies. In 1766, just six years after the

death of the Baal Shem Tov, he went to study *Chasidut* under Dov Baer, the Maggid (preacher) of Mezhirech and the leading disciple of the Besht. Levi Yitzchak was won over to Chasidism and by 1774 was publicly accepted and acknowledged as a chasidic rebbe.

Until his permanent move to Berditchev in 1785, Levi Yitzchak faced intense opposition in concentrated Jewish areas of Lithuania and twice was forced from rabbinical positions by the opponents of Chasidism, called the *mitnaggdim* (literally, "opponents"). Upon his move to Berditchev, where he remained until his death in 1810, he enjoyed a relatively antagonistic-free environment, where he was at liberty to write (producing his two-volume *Kedushat Levi,* "The Holiness of Levi," a Torah and rabbinic legend commentary) and to teach his followers.

Levi Yitzchak has been called one of the best-loved figures in Jewish popular imagination. Unlike many *tzaddikim,* he was lenient and loving, recognizing human frailty and the difficulties life forced upon his followers. He called God to account on this, and numerous folktales tell of him defending the Jewish people to God, whom Levi Yitzchak questions and criticizes and accuses of being too stern. With faith, love, compassion, and accountability, in the famous "*Kaddish* of Levi Yitzchak" he demands *A Din Toyre Mit Gott* ("Calling God to a Rabbinical Court"):

Good morning to You, Master of the World.
I, Levi Yitzchak, son of Sarah of Berditchev,
Have come to You in an official legal matter
On behalf of Your people Israel.
What do You have against Your people Israel?
And why do You oppress Your people Israel?
No matter what happens, it is "Command the children of Israel!"
No matter what happens, it is "Say to the children of Israel!"
No matter what happens, it is "Speak to the children of Israel!"
Dear Father! How many other peoples are there in the world?!
Babylonians, Persians, Edomites!
The Germans, what do they say?
"Our King is a King!"
The English, what do they say?
"Our Royalty is Royalty!"
And I, Levi Yitzchak, son of Sarah of Berditchev, say,
"*Lo ozuz mimkomo!* I will not move from here!
There must be an end to this—it must finally stop!
Greatened and Sanctified be the Majestic Name!"

Levi Yitzchak's beauty was, and remains, his defense of the children of Israel. To him, each Jew was pure and blameless. He exuded a love and sweetness for his people, which was returned to him through their affection. Most defenders of Israel stood up to kings, noblemen, anti-Semites, soldiers, even governments. Levi Yitzchak stood up to God.

NAFTALI TZVI YEHUDA BERLIN—THE N'TZIV

"Before his death, my father told me about his . . . not allowing any secular studies in the yeshivah *of Volozhin. Over this issue the* yeshivah *closed down, and this led to his final illness from which he never recovered. He maintained, 'Therefore, my son, do not feel bad that this matter was the cause of my leaving the world and closing the* yeshivah, *for this great issue is important enough for people to give their lives for it.'"*

—Rabbi Chaim Berlin, the N'tziv's son

Talmudist, rabbi, halachist, and commentator, Rabbi Naftali Tzvi Berlin was for almost forty years head of one of the most influential *yeshivot* in all of Eastern Europe.

He was born in Mir, Poland, in 1817. It has been said that the N'tziv was a student of but average intelligence, and not a child prodigy. Through diligence and application, he achieved the absolutely highest levels of scholarship and, subsequently, leadership. In his own devotion to Torah, it has been reported that to fight fatigue while studying, he would immerse his feet in a bowl of cold water. At the age of 14 he married the granddaughter of Rabbi Chaim Volozhin, the founder of the Volozhin *yeshivah,* and succeeded to the leadership of that institution in 1854. Under his guidance, the *yeshivah* eventually had an attendance of more than 400 students. Avoiding the

common method of *pilpul*, or talmudic hair-splitting, the N'tziv taught with an eye toward the plain meaning of the text, and established its authority via parallel texts in legal sources and the Jerusalem Talmud.

The N'tziv was famous not only for his method of study (which followed that of Elijah of Vilna, the famed Vilna Gaon), but also for his brilliance as a scholar and his warmth and personal devotion as a *rosh yeshivah* (dean). As a halachist, he concerned himself actively with the community at large and its needs. He answered questions from all over the world, including from American rabbis. He authored *Meshiv Davar*, a two-volume response, and a popular commentary on the Torah, *Ha-Ameik Davar*. As a scholar, he also conducted a daily lesson, in the Bible portion of the week, something unusual in the *yeshivot* of his time. He was greatly admired and revered by his students. The national Hebrew poet laureate Chaim Nachman Bialik describes the "heart-warming personality" of the N'tziv in his poem *Ha-Matmid*.

Berlin was also a supporter of Zionism, joining the Hibbat Zion movement at its beginning and encouraging observant Jews to move to Palestine. He supported the settlement of Palestine even though it was by nonreligious factions. *"The purpose of establishing Jewish settlements,"* he said, *"is . . . to revive the spirit of our Holy Land; not to upbuild Palestine, but to bring into being the holiness of the Land of Israel."*

In 1879 the N'tziv encountered official difficulties with the Russian government, which, at the request of secular Jews who wanted a "modern" seminary, demanded that secular studies, including Russian, be taught at the *yeshivah*. Berlin was not opposed to secular education, but he was staunch in his opinion that the *yeshivah* was not the place for it. His orientation was that the *yeshivah* was to educate and train scholars of the traditional type. This conflict, including a call for the reduction of the number of students in attendance, continued for over a decade and did not end until 1892, when the government forcibly closed the *yeshivah* and disbanded its students. The N'tziv and his family were officially exiled, moving first to Minsk, then to Warsaw. On August 11, 1893, approximately eighteen months after his forced removal from Volozhin, the N'tziv died.

The Volozhin *yeshivah* was one of the outstanding *yeshivot* of its time. Over the decades, virtually thousands of *talmidim* (students) studied there. Under the N'tziv's personal direction and aegis, the Volozhin *yeshivah* produced educated leaders and laymen alike for forty years. On the strength of his beliefs and scholarship, Berlin developed an orientation of learning Torah that has continued to today.

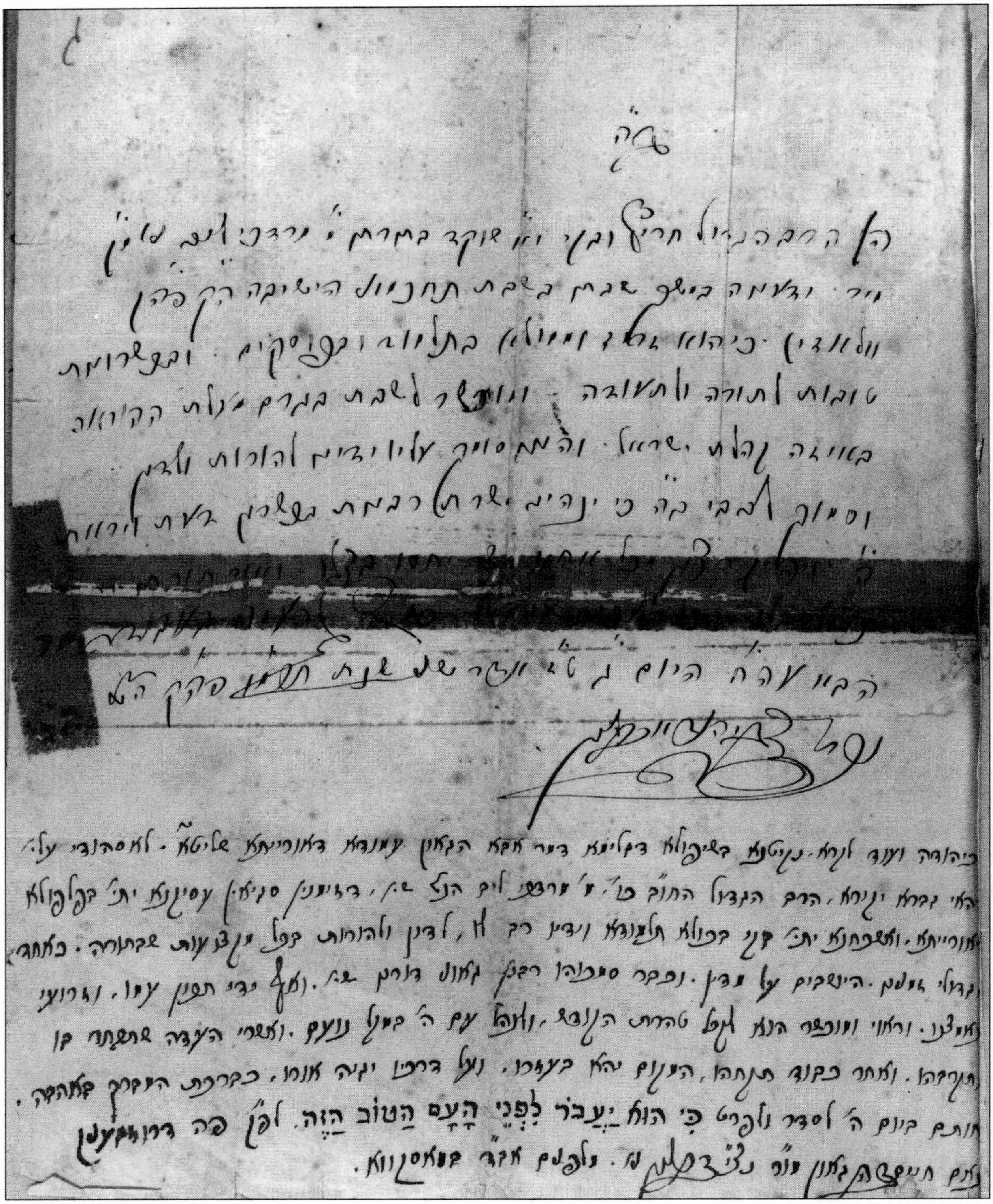

A letter granting one Motkhe Leib of Mir s'michah, *rabbinic ordination and the right to* poskin (*make Jewish legal decisions*), *signed by Rabbi Naftali Tzvi Yehuda Berlin, the N'tziv.* (*Photograph by Suzanne Kaufman.*)

ISRAEL MEIR KAGAN HACOHEN—THE CHOFETZ CHAIM

"A person who is resolved not to speak evil will be free from all other transgressions between man and his fellowman. He will not slander, embarrass, or insult anyone, and he will keep away from feuds. . . . Certainly, he will not cheat others or steal; he is careful not to harm anyone with words, all the more so with actions."

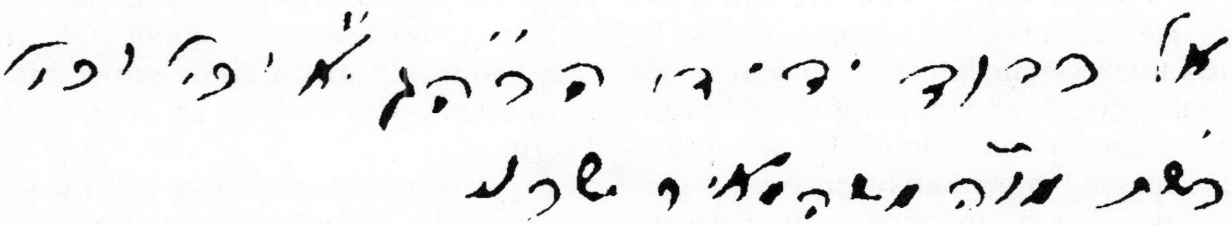

Writing sample.

Saintliness is not a word used much in traditional Judaism. Great men and women, alive or dead, are referred to as *tzaddikim* (righteous people), *gedolim* (outstanding or accomplished people), or, on rare occasion, *chasidim* (the most pious people). But there is one man to whom the appellation of saint (though certainly not in the broad Christian sense) applies: Israel Meir Kagan HaCohen, the Chofetz Chaim.

Rabbi Israel Meir Kagan's universally acknowledged saintliness, and key to his unparalleled name, lies in his perfection of the classical Jewish ethical characteristics (*midot*).

A scholar and pious Jew unsurpassed by any of his generation, he is revered by Jews for his personal perfection and was often referred to as "The Perfect Jew." He was the unexcelled example of conduct in the realm of Jewish ethics known as *ben adam l'chaveiro*, the way an individual should ideally conduct his actions between himself and his fellow man. Not only a scholar for scholars, he was an example for the masses of lay Jews of Eastern Europe.

Born in Zhetel, Poland, on January 26, 1839, the Chofetz Chaim was imbued as a child and youth with the classical principles of Judaism. He married at 17 and moved to the small Polish village of Radun, which became famous because of his presence, and remained there all his long life. He refused to become a professional rabbi and did the bookkeeping in a small village grocery store run by his wife. Eventually he turned to writing and teaching, and in 1869 he founded a small *yeshivah* that was to become one of Eastern Europe's outstanding centers of Talmud study.

The Chofetz Chaim's life is filled with stories of humility and humanity. As a village shopkeeper, his reputation grew and so did his business, until he ordered his wife to open the store only for half days, lest the success of their business reduce that of other village merchants. He never borrowed funds unless he was absolutely certain he could repay them. He personally attended to the comfort and needs of the students in his *yeshivah*. He was punctilious in paying immediately for services performed, whether to a tailor or a wagon driver. He spoke simply, pleasantly, and with words and love straight from his heart. Witnesses testified that when they heard him praying alone, not formalized prayers from the prayer book but when he spoke directly to God, he spoke in simple Yiddish, the everyman's tongue.

Israel Meir's nickname came from the title of his first book, which he chose to publish anonymously; he was not seeking public acknowledgment. The expression *chofetz chaim* is a term from Psalm 34: "Who is the man who desires life (*chofetz chaim*) and longs for many days of happiness?" The thrust of his book was a compilation and explanation of the laws of *lashon ha-ra* and *r'chilut* (harmful speech and gossip, talebearing). The Chofetz Chaim recognized that improper and unguarded speech was dangerously detrimental to society and sought to curb it. People who were meticulous in their ritual observances seemed to disregard this lubrication for societal well-being. (The Book of Psalms observes: *Mavet v'chai b'yad ha-lashon* ("Life and death are in the power of the tongue").

His book and his emphasis on this sorely neglected aspect of human behavior were well accepted. The Chofetz Chaim himself was absolutely perfected in this *mitzvah*; numerous rabbinical and lay testimonies give credence to this. The Chofetz Chaim wrote his *seforim* (religious books) not for personal gain but to highlight aspects of vital Jewish living: *Machaneh Yisrael* ("The Camp of Israel"), a guide for Jewish soldiers in the Polish and Russian armies; *Nidchei Yisrael* ("The Dispersed of Israel"), guidelines for those who had emigrated from Eastern Europe to other lands; *Ahavat Chesed* ("Loving-kindness"), a work about the legal and moral aspects of kindness and love; and seventeen others. Yet, with all these ethical/humanitarian works, his magnum opus is the *Mishnah Berurah*, or "Lucid Learning."

A comprehensive six-volume set, the *Mishnah Berurah* is the Chofetz Chaim's commentary on Rabbi Yosef Karo's *Shulchan Aruch, Orach Chayim*. It took the Chofetz Chaim twenty-three years to complete the work, which covers everyday life and the practices and actions pertaining to it. The *Mishnah Berurah* quickly gained widespread acceptance.

The Chofetz Chaim lived through the turbulence of World War I. He was active in establishing communal organizations for the

Jewish good, all the while spreading his doctrine and personal examples of purity of speech and love for his fellowman. At the end of his life, he decided to immigrate to Palestine, but the pleas of his fellow townspeople were overwhelming and he remained in Radun.

The Chofetz Chaim passed away on September 14, 1933, at the age of 95. Following his death, numerous *yeshivot* and ethical societies were named for him. His impact has been how to actually *live* an ethical life. To say his name today is still to illustrate the classical Jewish ethic of man and his fellowman. Worldwide there are national *Chevrah Shmirat Ha-Lashon* societies: Guarding One's Speech organizations.

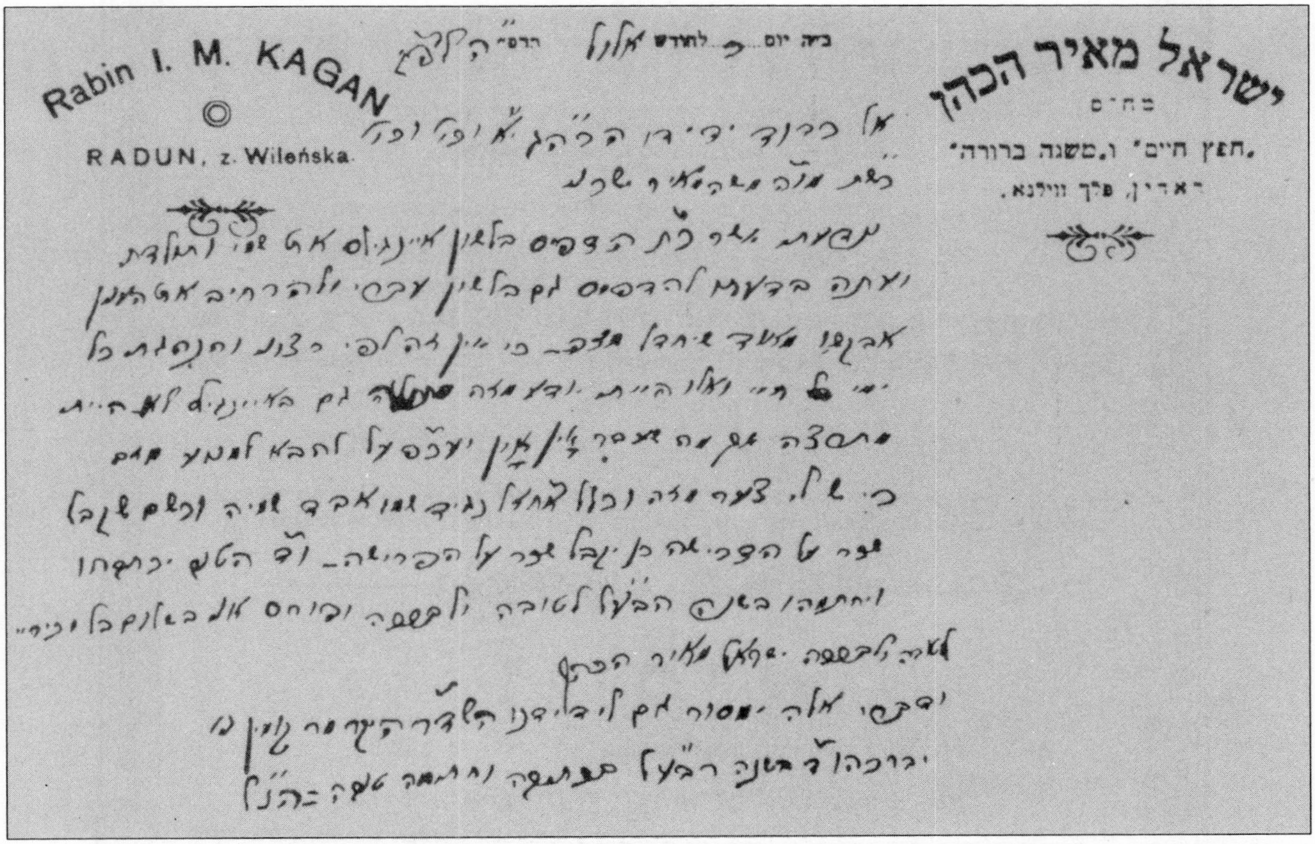
Rabin I. M. KAGAN

RADUN, z. Wileńska

ישראל מאיר הכהן

מח״ס

״חפץ חיים״ ו״משנה ברורה״

ראדין, פלך ווילנא.

A response from Rabbi Israel Meir Kagan, the Chofetz Chaim, to an inquiry regarding having his biography translated into Hebrew. The Chofetz Chaim replies in the negative, saying he prefers it not be done.

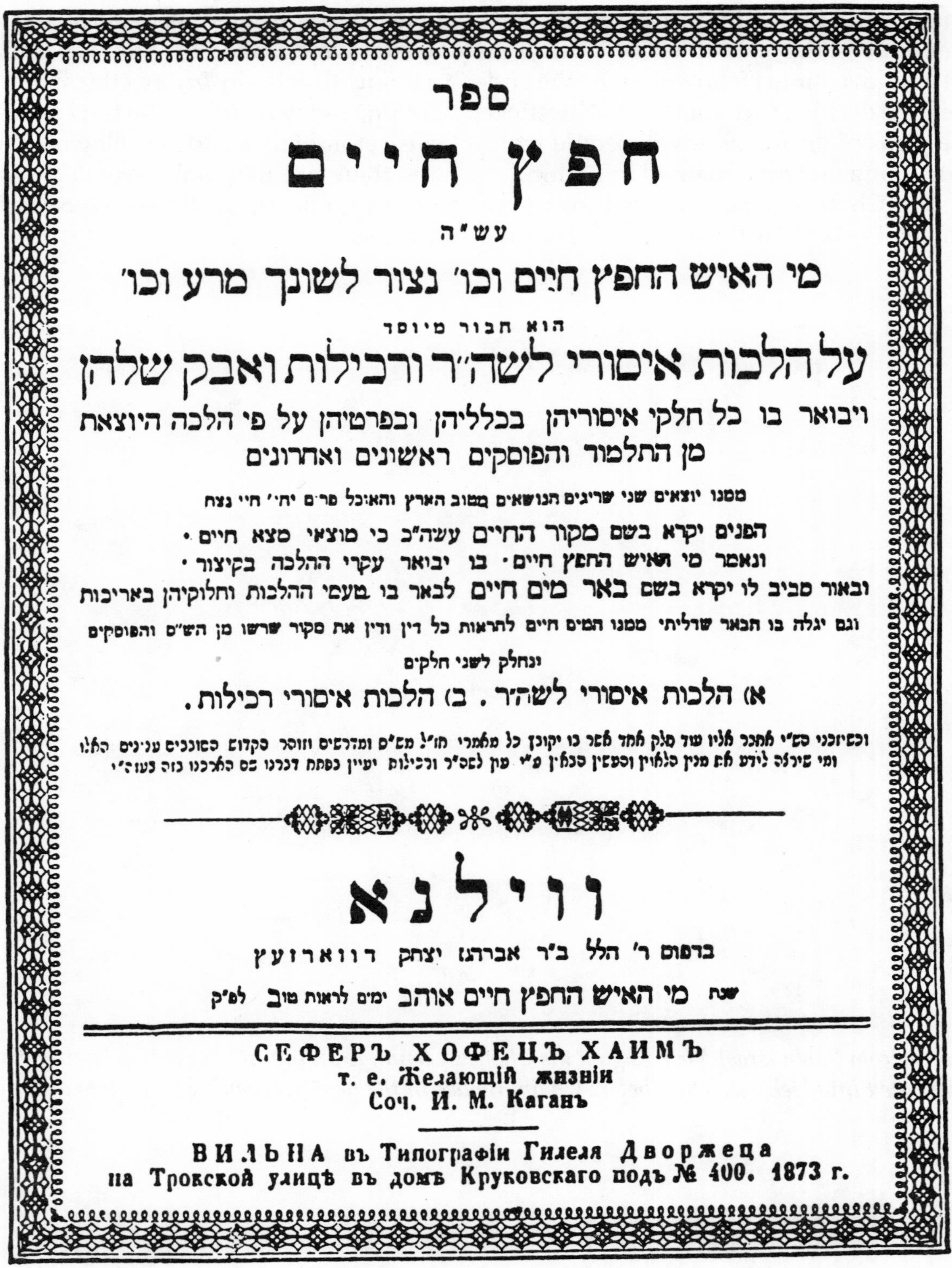

ספר

חפץ חיים

עש״ה

מי האיש החפץ חיים וכו׳ נצור לשונך מרע וכו׳

הוא חבור מיוסד

על הלכות איסורי לשה״ר ורכילות ואבק שלהן

ויבואר בו כל חלקי איסוריהן בכלליהן ובפרטיהן על פי הלכה היוצאת
מן התלמוד והפוסקים ראשונים ואחרונים

ממנו יוצאים שני שריגים הנושאים מטוב הארץ והאוכל פר״ם יחי׳ חיי נצח

הפנים יקרא בשם מקור החיים עשה״כ כי מוצאי מצא חיים ·
ונאמר מי האיש החפץ חיים· בו יבואר עקרי ההלכה בקיצור ·
ובאור סביב לו יקרא בשם באר מים חיים לבאר בו טעמי ההלכות וחלוקיהן באריכות

וגם יגלה בו תבאר שדליתי ממנו המים חיים לתראות כל דין ודין את מקור שרשו מן הש״ס והפוסקים

ונחלק לשני חלקים

א) הלכות איסורי לשה״ר . ב) הלכות איסורי רכילות .

וכשיזכני השי״ת אחבר אליו עוד חלק אחד אשר בו יקובץ כל מאמרי חז״ל מש״ס ומדרשים וזוהר הקדוש המזהירים ענינים האלו
ומי שירצה לידע את ענין האיסור והענשין הנמשכין ע״י עון לה״ר ורכילות יעיין בפתח דברנו שם הארכנו בזה בעזה״י

ווילנא

בדפוס ר׳ הלל ב״ר אברהם יצחק דווארזעץ

שנת מי האיש החפץ חיים אוהב ימים לראות טוב לפ״ק

СЕФЕРЪ ХОФЕЦЪ ХАИМЪ
т. е. Желающій жизни
Соч. И. М. Каганъ

ВИЛЬНА въ Типографіи Гилеля Дворжеца
на Троской улицѣ въ домѣ Круковскаго подъ № 400. 1873 г.

Title page of the first edition of the book Chofetz Chaim, *a compendium on the laws of malicious speech.*

MOSES SOFER (SCHREIBER)—THE CHATAM SOFER

"I admonish you not to alter, God forbid, your Jewish names, language, and manner of dress. Let your watchword be, 'Jacob came whole *to the city of Shechem.'"*
—Ethical Will, November 24, 1836

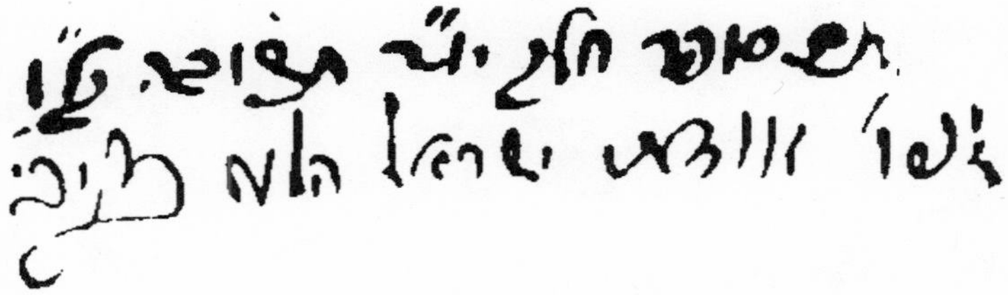

Writing sample.

Although Lithuania in the eighteenth and nineteenth centuries was the leading center of Jewish scholarship, other countries were also producing families of great rabbis and great scholarship. One of the most noted was the Hungarian rabbi Moses Sofer.

A leading rabbi, legal authority, defender of Orthodoxy, and prolific author, the Chatam Sofer—whose name is taken from an abbreviation of his insightful commentary on the Torah—was born in Germany in Frankfurt am Main in 1762. (The surname *sofer*, or "scribe," denotes a family of scholars.) In his childhood he mastered all the traditional and classic Jewish texts, as well as biology, mathematics, engineering, and astronomy.

In 1798 Sofer was appointed the rabbi of Mattersdorff, Hungary, one of the "seven communities" in western Hungary. Judaism flourished there under the liberal policies and

protection of the local royalty. Sofer stayed in Mattersdorff, teaching and leading his congregation for eight years, until 1806, when he was appointed rabbi of Pressburg, at that time the most important community in Hungary. In 1812, after the death of his first wife, Sofer married Sarah Eger, the daughter of the celebrated and distinguished rabbi Akiva Eiger. This marriage and their children established one of the great family lines of rabbinic scholarship and leadership.

The Chatam Sofer made his indelible mark through his writings, his opposition to the Reform movement, and his strong advocacy of the traditional Jewish way of life. His *Chatam Sofer*, or *Chiddushei Torat Moshe* (hence his name, *CHaTaM*), is a seven-volume work of original Torah interpretations and insights. Sofer also wrote sermons, rabbinic legal responses (for communities as far away as Africa and Asia), poems, letters, diaries, and an ethical will. His writings were clear, illustrative, and influential. When the Reform movement began in Germany in 1819, Sofer was one of the first to forcibly contest it. He wrote, argued, and lobbied against the new movement, which he saw as a threat to the Jewish community at large. He argued strongly against prayer in the vernacular. Sofer was convinced of the perfection and superiority of traditional Jewish life over the prevalent culture.

A modest man of small stature, Sofer referred to himself as *Moshe ha-katan mi-Frankfurt*, or "Moses the insignificant of Frankfurt." His selfless consideration underlaid his scholarship and personal charisma, and his reputation was greatly advanced by his many students who were appointed to pulpits and important teaching positions throughout Eastern Europe. The *yeshivah* he founded in Pressburg was said to be the largest since the great Jewish academies of Babylonia.

As a result of his strong efforts against Reform Judaism and in favor of traditional Orthodoxy, Sofer was considered the leading rabbi of that period. He died in Pressburg, Hungary, in 1839. Most of his writings were published by his family following his death.

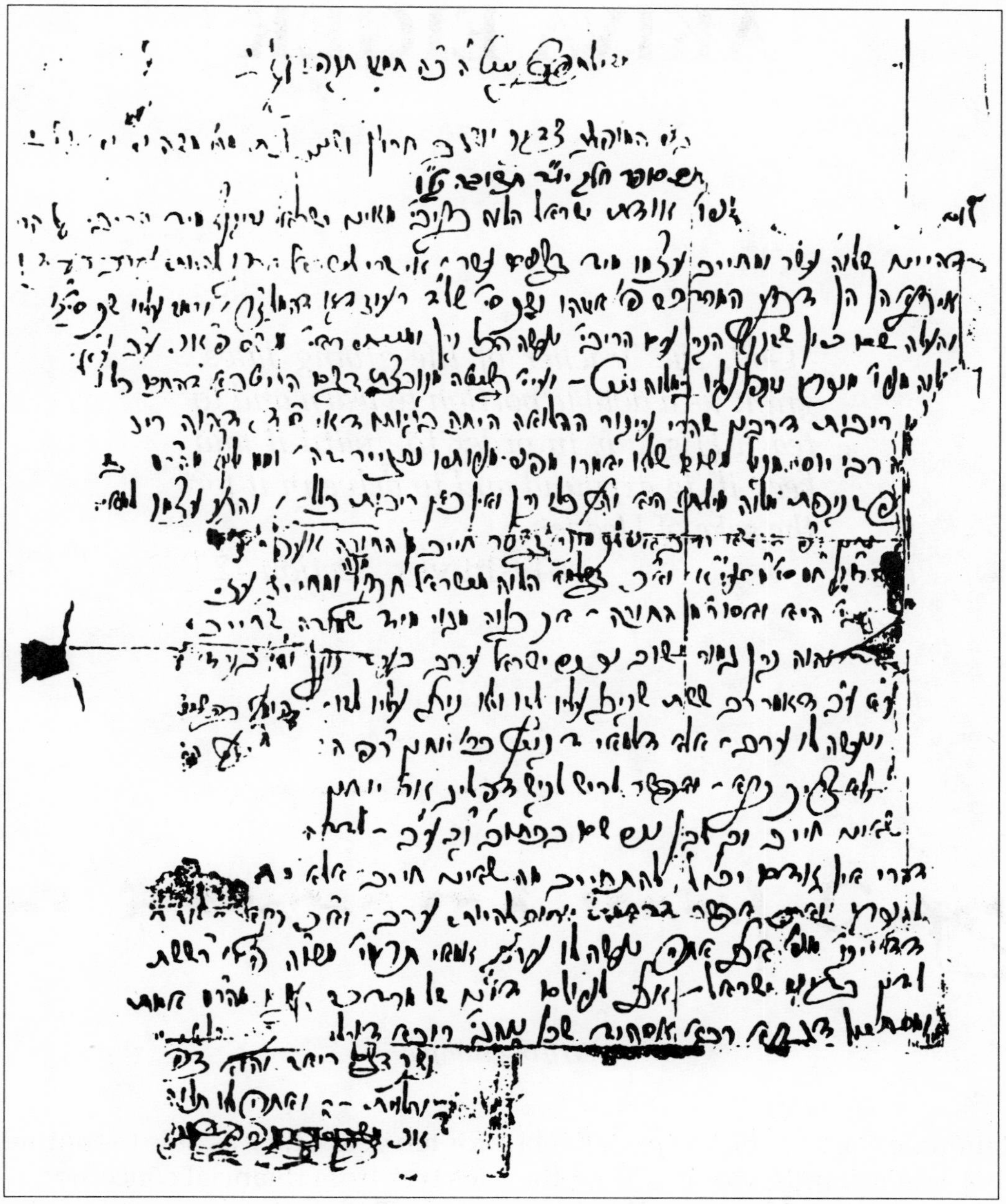

Letter signed by Moses Sofer, the Chatam Sofer.

AKIVA EIGER

"God, the Teacher of life-giving laws, grant us a double portion to learn and to teach His law, in order to guard it and keep it, to expound and to delve in it for the sake of Heaven."

—Teshuvot, *Section 223*

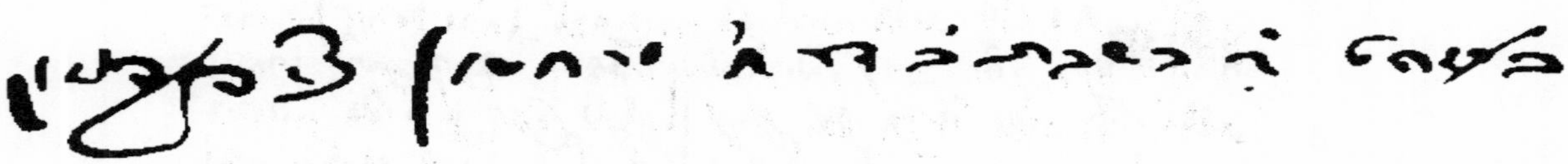

Writing sample.

The talmudic giant, rabbi, and *posek* Rabbi Akiva Eiger stands out as one of the greatest minds and leaders of his time. The author of numerous works, he was a forceful and formidable proponent of Orthodoxy in a changing era.

Born in Eisenstadt, Austria, in 1761, Eiger was another of the superior minds who mastered the Torah and Talmud as a child and teenager. At the age of 13, he wrote a commentary on *Chullin*, the talmudic tractate dealing with the laws on the slaughter of animals and birds. Fortunate to live with his father-in-law for ten years, he was able to continue his studies free from financial concerns.

Following a disastrous fire in 1791, which caused financial loss, Eiger accepted the position of rabbi in Maerkisch-Friedland, Germany, where he established a *yeshivah*. As his rabbinic reputation and influence grew, he fielded many legal questions from rabbis and individuals around the world. In 1807 he led a delegation to meet with French authorities regarding Jewish rights in the newly established duchy of Warsaw. In 1814 Eiger was elected rabbi of Posen, where he encountered strong

opposition from *maskilim*, who feared his reputation and influence. Nonetheless, his appointment was sustained.

Even though he was considered the unofficial chief rabbi of the greater Posen district, Eiger maintained a reputation as a modest man. He strongly disdained titles then popular in rabbinic circles. He recognized the political realities of the *Haskalah* and Reform Judaism and made concessions when necessary (including encouraging the use of German, not Yiddish, as the language of education). Sensitive to the needs of the community, Jews and gentiles alike, Eiger received a royal message of gratitude from Frederick William III for his services during a cholera epidemic in 1831. Eiger established a number of charity organizations that functioned as late as World War II.

His writings include notes on the Babylonian Talmud and the *Mishnah*, original insights on the *Shulchan Aruch*, and legal responses ranging from traditional questions to such "modern" issues as epilepsy, autopsies, and battered wives:

> Question: Over the past ten years a woman periodically came to the *Bet Din* [religious court] to complain about her husband beating her savagely. He threatened her with a knife, and she refused to live with him any longer; but at the urging of the *Bet Din* she then agreed to reconciliation. She received written assurances that if he ever struck her again, even upon her provocation, he must divorce her and pay her an alimony settlement. After four [more] years of continued beatings, she left her husband and went to live with her father. . . .
>
> Last *Nisan* [April] she again appeared before the *Bet Din* crying that her husband beat her constantly, and she showed her arms covered with blue marks. She brought her maid to testify that he struck her three days before she gave birth, that she ran away, that he pursued her, threw a brick at her, and broke a plate on her head so that she fainted. . . .
>
> The husband heard the testimony and did not deny it. . . . He said, "There is no need for witnesses. I admit that I struck her. I only ask that I be given another chance."
>
> Answer: I recognize that a divorce would be extremely difficult since she has eight children, the youngest six months old. But she insists that she does not want to live with him any longer. . . . I ruled that the husband cannot force the wife to live with him, and she cannot be considered a rebellious wife based on conjugal matters. . . . Although he does not deny beating her, he states that she provoked him by humiliating and cursing him. . . . He must pay for her support, but he may pay it in weekly installments. . . . It is impossible to hire an observer to determine who is at fault. Even if an observer should live with them for a few weeks, the husband would refrain from beating her during that time but afterward he would simply resume his practice. Therefore, my ruling is that he cannot force her to live with him under the same roof.
>
> —Avraham Yaakov Finkel,
> *The Responsa Anthology*

Eiger's understanding of the human condition, his realistic approach to life, combined with his superior scholarship, led him to be a foremost figure of his people. When he died in 1837, he was mourned throughout the Jewish world.

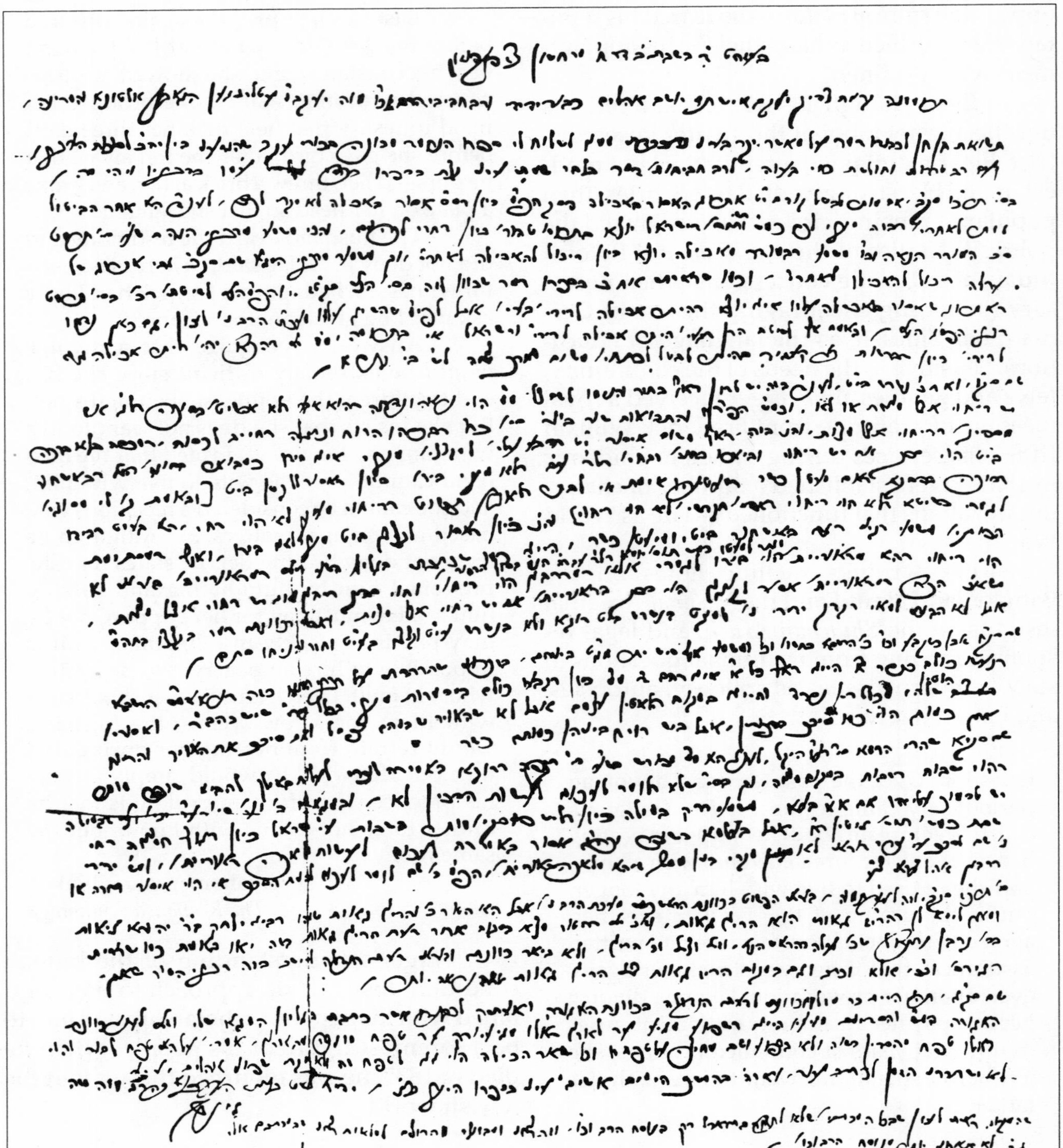

Holograph page by Rabbi Akiva Eiger, dealing with Jewish legal matters.

JACOB EMDEN

"The words of a poor, meager man asking God . . . may He grant me my one request: to remain in the house of the Lord all my days and may all my endeavors be in His holy, beautiful and praiseworthy Torah."
—She'elat Yaavetz, *introduction to Part I*

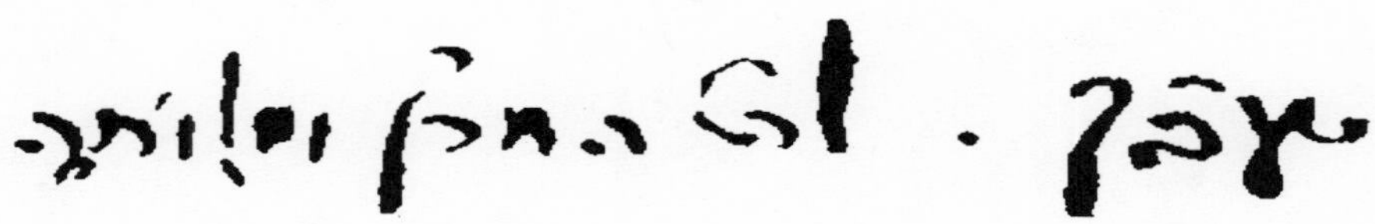

Rabbi Jacob Emden was one of the leading scholars of his time. A legal authority, kabbalist, critic-at-large, fierce individualist, and vocal anti-Shabbatean advocate, Emden has been called stormy, independent, and uncompromising.

Born in Altona, Germany, in 1697, Emden's teacher was his father, Tzvi Hirsch Ashkenazi. Open-minded for that era, Emden not only mastered Jewish classical and legal texts, but was also familiar with nonlegal works and knew German, Dutch, and Latin.

Emden appears to have been a born scholar and rebel. A scholar in his own right, he authored works of responses (*She'lat Yaavetz*), a commentary on the *Mishnah* (*Lechem Shamayim*), a commentary on *Orach Chayim* of the *Shulchan Aruch* (*Mor u-Ketzi'ah*), as well as a prayer book with important commentary. Other than being rabbi of Emden from 1728 to 1733, he held no official position and thus felt free to be a community and social critic. In 1733 he founded his own printing press in Altona, publishing books and essays. He was most critical of the act of *chillul Ha-Shem* (any act that brings into disrepute the name of a Jew—and God, by extension), and of Rabbi Jonathan Eybeschuetz and the Shabbatean controversy.

Emden is remembered best for two passions: his search for the truth through *halachah* and the dictates of his conscience, which embroiled him in a bitter fourteen-year controversy with Rabbi Jonathan Eybeschuetz. World Jewry was suffering from the despairing and disillusioning aftereffects of false messiahs, notably Shabbtai Tzvi. Eybeschuetz was appointed rabbi of the three towns of Altona, Hamburg, and Wandsbek in 1750. Shortly thereafter he distributed several amulets in Hamburg and another adjacent town. Emden interpreted their contents to be Shabbatean and published such a charge. The controversy that ensued caused Emden not only to flee to Amsterdam but to split German Jewry, both in rabbinic and lay circles. Both men were powerful and influential rabbis and scholars, with their own camps. The intensity was so great that civil authorities had to be called in to subdue the acrimony.

Emden was also a writer and grammarian par excellence. He is recognized as a fine literary talent as well as a detailed commentator on the structure of grammar in the *siddur*, correct vocalization, linguistic considerations, and, in one text, the differences between synonyms. He died in 1776.

Jacob Emden's contribution to Jewish history was his passion for Judaism. It caused tremendous controversy and much pain, but it was undertaken as a *kiddush Ha-Shem*, a sanctification of God's name.

זה השער לי״י

זה ספר

מאור עינים

לר׳ עזריה מן האדומי יצ״ו

והוא נחלק לשלשה חלקים

האחד מתואר

קול אלהים אשר בו ידבר על

הרעש׳ שהתחילו בפירירה י״ח

נובימ׳ של״א · והשני מתואר

הדרת זקנים שהוא ספור

מעשה הזקני׳ פותרי התור׳ לתלמי

המלך כנעתק מן היוני לרומיי

וממנו ללשון הקדש׳ ·

והשלישי מתואר

אמרי בינה אשר יפרד והיה

לארבע׳ מאמרי׳ כוללי׳ ששים פרקי׳

על דרושי׳ שונים ככל הנראה

מן הלוח בקצה הספר ·

נדפס פה מנטובה י״ח נובימבר של״ד

Title page of a religious book signed Yaavetz *by Rabbi Jacob Emden. (Photograph by Suzanne Kaufman.)*

MOSHE FEINSTEIN—REB MOSHE

"The Holy Torah said one law for all men. No man is inherently holier than his fellow, except for his greatness in Torah."
—Darash Moshe

Reb Moshe, as he was affectionately called, was this century's leading *posek* of Orthodox Jewry. Until his death, on March 24, 1986, he was considered the foremost halachic authority.

Feinstein was born in the village of Uzda (Minsk area), Russia, on March 3, 1895. A child prodigy, he gave his first talmudic discourse at the age of 12. At the age of 25, he was selected as rabbi of Luban. By 1920, he was fighting against Communist religious persecution. Feinstein stayed in Russia until 1937, when Stalinist forces threatened his life and he migrated to the United States.

Upon his arrival in New York, he was appointed head of the Mesivta Tiferes Yerushalayim *yeshivah*, a position he held until his death. Under his aegis, it became one of the leading *yeshivot* in America. During this time his influence and prestige continued to in-

crease. He was elected to numerous high-ranking positions, including president of the Union of Orthodox Rabbis and chairman of the American branch of the Mo'ezet Gedolei ha-Torah of Agudat Yisrael, the Council of Torah Sages. Upon the passing of Rabbi Aharon Kotler in 1962, Reb Moshe was recognized as the leading figure in the Ashkenazic world. Mayors, governors, and presidents had all sought out and acknowledged him.

Acknowledged as the *Gadol Ha-Dor*, or the preeminent individual of his generation, Feinstein wrote numerous works. His responsa have been published in a six-volume set titled *Igrot Moshe.* Also noteworthy are his talmudic lectures (*Dibrot Moshe*) and his commentary on the Torah (*Darash Moshe*). In these works Feinstein considered all types of current problems: organ transplants, Internal Revenue Service issues, drug use, education, the feminist movement, Holocaust problems:

> Question: A woman and her daughters were kept in hiding with a non-Jewish family during the years of the Holocaust. After they had stayed with them awhile, the non-Jew forced them to convert to Christianity, threatening to betray them to the Germans to be killed if they refused to convert. Unable to face up to this grave challenge, the woman agreed and was accepted into the Christian faith without the services of a cleric. The non-Jew himself sprinkled water on her and took her and the children to church. Immediately after the liberation they proudly returned to Judaism and they are fully observant Jews. Do they have to undergo any special procedures?
>
> Answer: They are not considered apostates; they are not persons who abandoned their faith. . . . If she is in good health, it is recommended that she fast each year on that day, if she remembers the date. If she doesn't, she should fast on any day she wishes. The daughters, who were small at the time, do not have to fast. . . .
>
> —Avraham Yaakov Finkel,
> *The Responsa Anthology*

Reb Moshe was known not only for his unparalleled erudition, but also for his refinement and gentleness. In a period of uncertainty, he led a generation of Jews by his insightful and humane understanding of the issues. Since Reb Moshe's death, no rabbinic figure has been chosen to replace him, and the void has been sorely felt by the Orthodox community.

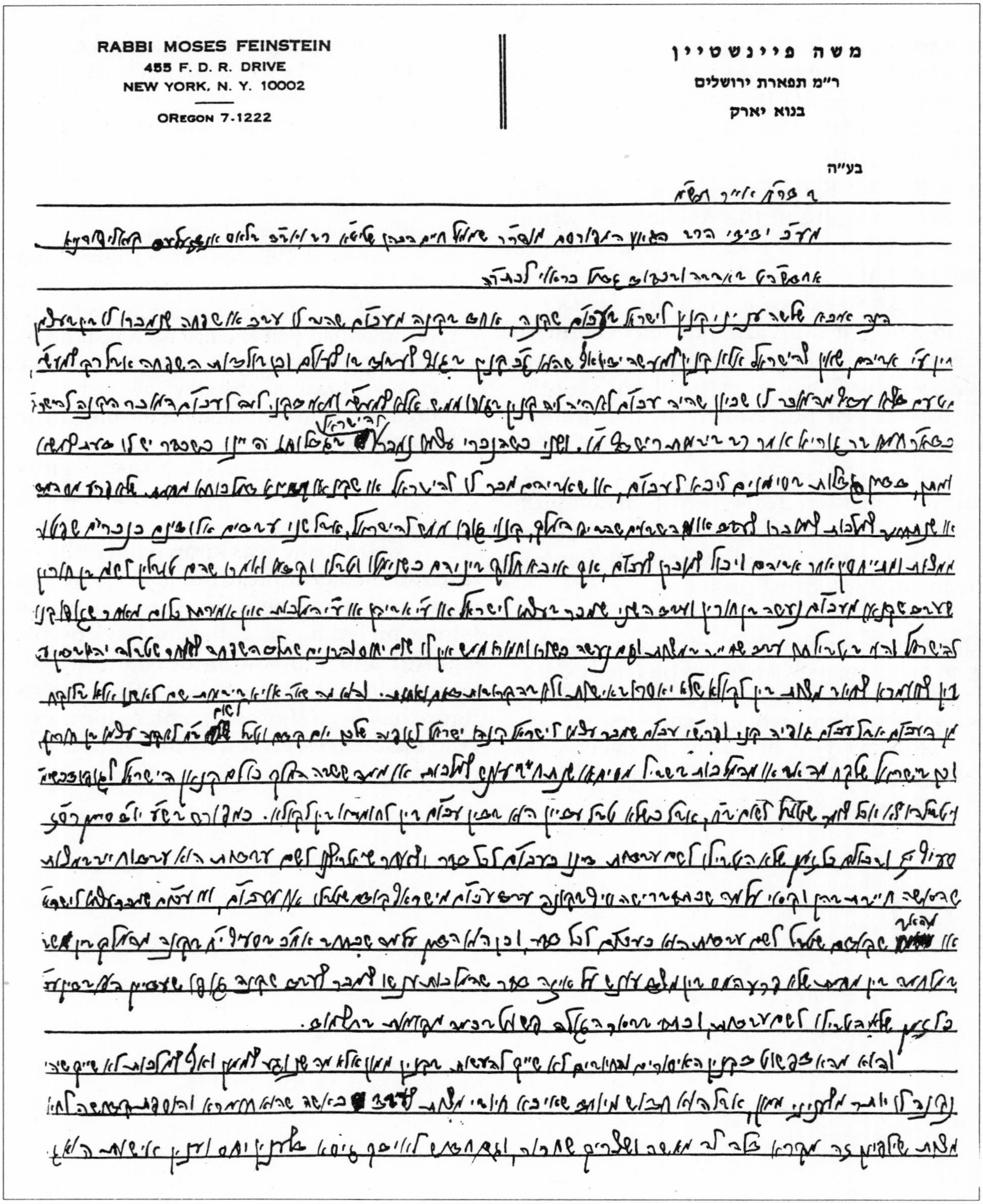

RABBI MOSES FEINSTEIN
455 F. D. R. DRIVE
NEW YORK, N. Y. 10002
OREGON 7-1222

משה פיינשטיין
ר"מ תפארת ירושלים
בנוא יארק

בע"ה

Two-page letter on letterhead by Rabbi Moshe Feinstein to Rabbi Samuel Katz, head of Los Angeles

Rabbinic Court, regarding an inyan *in the Talumd on concept of* Kinyan, *or acquisitions.*

YITZCHAK MEIR ALTER OF GER—THE CHIDUSHEI HARIM—THE GERER REBBE

"The pure Jewish soul is enveloped within an unclean covering, termed klippot, *shells of the fruit. These husks form a barrier that separates the Jewish soul from its holy source. The 613* mitzvot *are the instruments for removing this barrier. They give light and life to the Jewish soul. When you remove the covering by means of* mitzvot, *your soul becomes the chariot of God's* kedushah [*holiness*]*."*

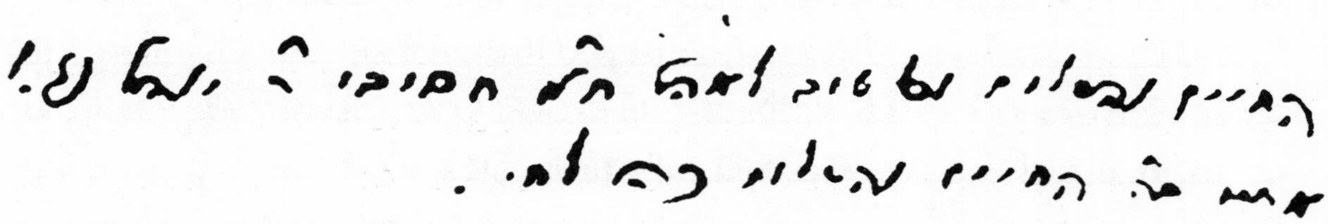

Writing sample.

The chasidic dynasty established by Yitzchak Meir Alter, and carried on after his death, was one of the major influences in Polish *Chasidut*; the influence established by the Alter Rebbe D'Ger lasted from his lifetime through the Holocaust to the present.

Also spelled *Ger* and *Gur*, the founder of the Gerer sect of *Chasidut*, which existed in

Poland from 1859 to World War II, was born in Mognuszew, Poland, in 1799. Yitzchak Meir Alter came from a genealogy and background seminal with importance: he traced his ancestry back to the eminent Rabbi Meir of Rothenburg (1215–1293), and his father was a disciple of the legendary Levi Yitzchak of Berditchev and an intimate of the famed Koznitzer Maggid. Yitzchak Meir distinguished himself at an early age and acquired for himself a reputation as a brilliant young scholar.

Yitzchak Meir did not create Ger *Chasidut*. For himself, he was a disciple of the famous Rabbi Simcha Bunam of Pshis'cha and, following his death, he lent great support to the enigmatic Menachem Mendel of Kotzk. After the Kotzker's death in 1859, Yitzchak Meir was acknowledged by the majority of the Kotzk *chasidim* as their rebbe; the mantel of *tzaddik* was placed upon him. Yitzchak Meir settled in Ger (Gora Kalwaria in Polish), about nineteen miles southeast of Warsaw.

Yitzchak Meir was involved in the conditions of his people and was well versed in the problems Jews faced in Poland. He fought to maintain the traditional way of Jewish life, and taught it as well. He was one of Poland's foremost scholars of his period. His writings are considered classics in the dialectical way of studying (*pilpul*). His halachic work *Chiddushei Ha-Rim* covers both talmudic and *Shulchan Aruch* topics. He wrote novellas, along with responsa and commentaries on the Torah and the Jewish holidays. Although a follower of the Kotzk school, he involved himself in the day-to-day life of his *chasidim*. In his personal life, he had thirteen children, all of whom died during his lifetime.

Above all, Yitzchak Meir stressed the unparalleled importance of Torah study. He also taught the Kotzk philosophy of profundity of thought in seeking out the truth and striving for self-perfection.

The Alter Rebbe led Ger *Chasidut* for only seven years, but those seven years had a formative influence on all chasidic development in Poland. Ger enjoyed a leading spiritual and political position in Polish Jewry until the Holocaust. Yitzchak Meir, the Alter Rebbe, died in Ger in 1866.

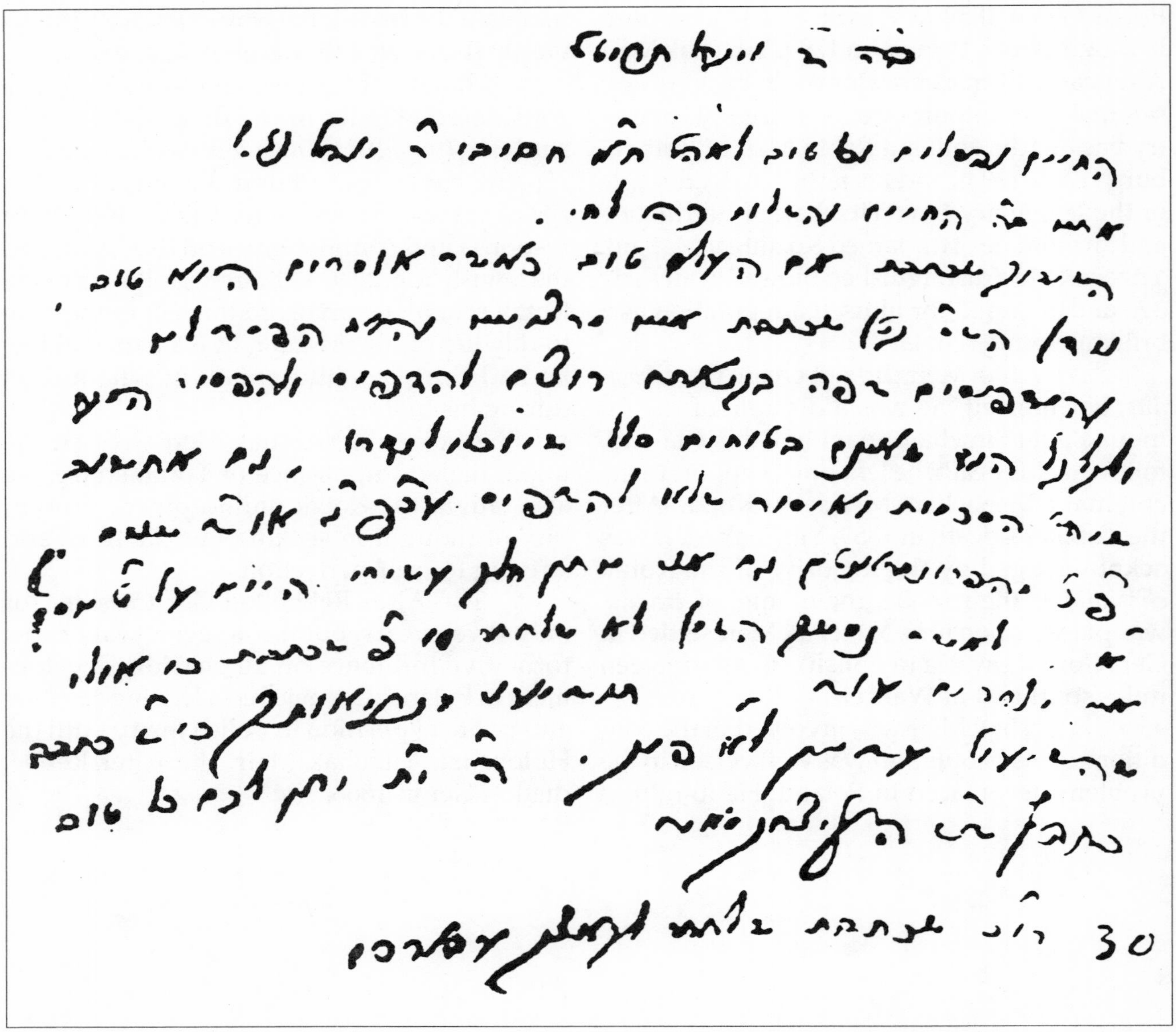

Sample of Rabbi Yitzchak Meir Alter's handwriting dealing with a shiddach, *a marital match, and the* chossen, *the bridegroom.*

ALEXANDER DAVID GOODE

"We are fighting for the new age of brotherhood, the age of brotherhood that will usher in the world democracy we all want; the age when men will admire the freedom and responsibility of the common man in American democracy. Our methods will be imitated and improved upon. Our spirit of tolerance will spread. . . . Justice and righteousness, as dreamed of by the prophets who gave the world the democratic spirit, will cover the earth as a torrent."

—*From a letter to his wife, Theresa*

The biography of Rabbi Alexander Goode is a brief one. He died at the age of 32 that another man might live.

Born in Brooklyn, New York, on May 10, 1911, the firstborn son of a rabbi, Goode grew up in a racially mixed neighborhood of Washington, D.C. Racial fights and religious taunts confronted him and his brothers growing up in an integrated but unenlightened time and place, lessons that deeply affected him. A high school honor student and star athlete (boxing, wrestling, track, and tennis), he was the personification of the all-American boy. With scholarship funds provided by the sisterhood of a Washington synagogue, he attended the University of Cincinnati and received his rabbinical ordination from the Hebrew Union College. In 1937 he accepted the pulpit at Temple Beth Israel in York, Pennsylvania. There, long before the social activism of today's rabbis, Goode was heavily involved in both the interfaith movement and the fight against segregation in Pennsylvania public schools. In 1940 he received his Ph.D. in history from Johns Hopkins University, with his thesis "The Jewish Exilarchate during the Arabic Period, 640–1258."

Goode served as a pulpit rabbi for only a short period. An emotional and intellectual

Jewish and American patriot, in January 1941—eleven months before the Japanese attack at Pearl Harbor—he attempted to join the U.S. Navy chaplaincy, but no vacancies existed. After Pearl Harbor, he applied to the army, took his chaplain's training at Harvard, and was commissioned a first lieutenant in July 1942. Over his protests for a more active duty post, his first orders assigned him to duty in Greenland.

In January 1943, along with hundreds of other soldiers and sailors, he was aboard the freighter-turned-troop transport SS *Dorchester*, heading in a convoy through the German submarine-patrolled waters of the North Atlantic. Goode was one of four chaplains aboard. With him were the Reverend George L. Fox of the Methodist Church of Vermont, the Reverend John P. Washington, a Roman Catholic priest from Arlington, New Jersey, and the Reverend Clark Poling of the Reformed Church of Schenectady, New York.

For several days the convoy made its way across cold and gloomy seas. They had left Massachusetts, sailed to Newfoundland, and after a brief stop, continued on to their destination. On the night of February 4, 1943, the luck of the SS *Dorchester* ran out: she was hit by a torpedo from a Nazi U-boat. Chaos ensued.

Struck in the engine room, the vessel was left powerless, with water gushing in through the hull. Soldiers and sailors alike panicked, rushing for the deck and the lifeboats. In the initial hysteria, lifeboats were launched improperly, men rushed about without their life preservers, and emergency procedures were temporarily forgotten. Engineless, the ship began listing heavily to portside. The *Dorchester* was sinking and the order to abandon ship was given.

It is estimated that a man can survive in the arctic waters of the North Atlantic for eighteen to forty minutes. Survivors of that night told how all four chaplains gave away their life jackets, parkas, and gloves to others who had forgotten their own in the rush from below the deck. Lieutenant John J. Mahoney later recalled how Rabbi Goode heard Mahoney swearing at himself for having forgotten his gloves. "Don't bother, Mahoney. You can have these. I have another pair." Goode pulled off his own gloves and gave them to him. Mahoney, who spent eighty hours in a lifeboat before being rescued, later testified, "I owe my life to those gloves. I landed in a lifeboat that was awash, and for eight hours had to hold on in waters the official temperature of which was thirty degrees. My fingers would have been frozen stiff had it not been for the gloves. I would never have made it without them. As it was, only two of us survived out of the forty that were in the boat."

As the ship went down, the same survivors recounted how the four chaplains stood together on the deck, arms interlocked. In giving away their lifejackets and refusing places in the few remaining lifeboats, the chaplains knew their fates. Of the *Dorchester*'s 1,000 personnel aboard, only 300 survived. Posthumously, Rabbi Goode and his fellow chaplains were awarded the Purple Heart and the Distinguished Service Cross, America's second-highest military honor.

Uncounted Jews, rabbis or not, have died for the sake of Torah. Rabbi Alexander David Goode made the supreme sacrifice by following one of Judaism's basic tenets: *v'ahavta l'rayecha kamocha*, you will love your neighbor as yourself. Numerous memorials have been dedicated to Rabbi Alexander David Goode and his fellow clergymen for making that supreme sacrifice.

YEHUDAH HA-LEVI

"O city of the world, most chastely fair
In the far west, behold, I sigh for thee,
O had I eagle wings, I'd fly to thee,
And with my falling tears make moist thine earth
My heart is in the East, and I am in the uttermost West—"

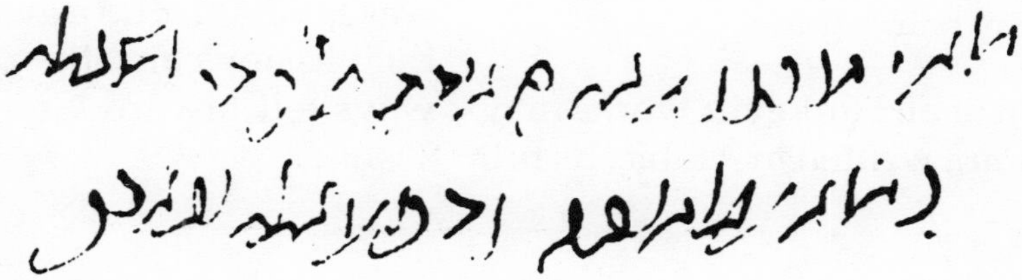

Writing sample.

Rabbi, philosopher, and physician, Yehudah Ha-Levi was also one of the greatest Jewish poets of the Middle Ages. Writer of prose and poetry, religious, secular, and nationalistic works, he was also the author of the *Sefer Ha-Kuzari* ("The Book of the Khazars").

Born into a wealthy family in Spain c. 1075, Yehudah Ha-Levi had the benefits and privileges of the upper class. He received both a secular and religious education, studying rabbinics, Hebrew, Arabic, medicine, and philosophy: the classical education of Spanish Jewry. He practiced medicine in Toledo, a part of Christian Spain, but as anti-Jewish pressures intensified, he moved to Andalusia, which was Muslim dominated. Driven by a personal compulsion and love for the land of *Eretz Yisrael*, he was in his sixties when he left Spain for Palestine, leaving behind his wife and daughter. Romantic legend aside that he was killed by a galloping horseman as he arrived in

Jerusalem and knelt to pray, Ha-Levi never saw the Holy Land. From Spain he arrived in Egypt, where he became immersed in various activities, and died there in 1141.

Ha-Levi's writings are extensive; known to exist are more than 400 secular works dedicated to friendship, love, wine, nature, and beauty. His liturgical works are found throughout the *siddur* and *mahzor*, as well as in collections of religious poetry and penitential prayers. A poet of the people as well as poet of God and Israel, his verses ring with the passions and yearnings of life:

Awake, O my love, from your sleep,
Your face as it wakes let me view,
If you dream someone kissing your lips,
I'll interpret your dreaming for you.

With the same passion he felt for human love, Ha-Levi wrote of his love, even in his old age, for the Land of Israel:

But fairer than all to me is yon gentle maiden,
Ah, time's swift flight would I gladly stay,
Regretting that my hair is gray.

Best known of all Ha-Levi's works may be his *Sefer Ha-Kuzari*, written in Arabic. Its full title—"The Book of Argument and Demonstration in Aid of the Despised Faith"—better describes its thrust. The *Kuzari* is a retelling of the legend of the Khazars, a kingdom in the Crimea ruled by a wise and benevolent king who, seeking the proper religious way of life, held a disputation with Christian, Muslim, and Jewish spokesmen. Following the disputation, the king and his nation converted to Judaism. Through the allegory, Ha-Levi compares Judaism with Christianity and Islam and asserts its superiority. Ha-Levi argues, through the *Kuzari*, against philosophic thought and Aristotelian philosophy and contends that a prophetic religion delivered through direct revelation does not need to authenticate itself by rational proofs.The *Sefer Ha-Kuzari* continued to be a popular work in kabbalistic circles until the fifteenth century, and later had a mark of influence on Chasidism.

Of Ha-Levi's life, little is known. But his works live eternally, memorialized in his prayers, odes, elegies, and poems. He has been called the "romantic singer of Zion." It was Ha-Levi who articulated the great love—the passions and the pinings—Jews have always felt toward God and the land of *Eretz Yisrael*.

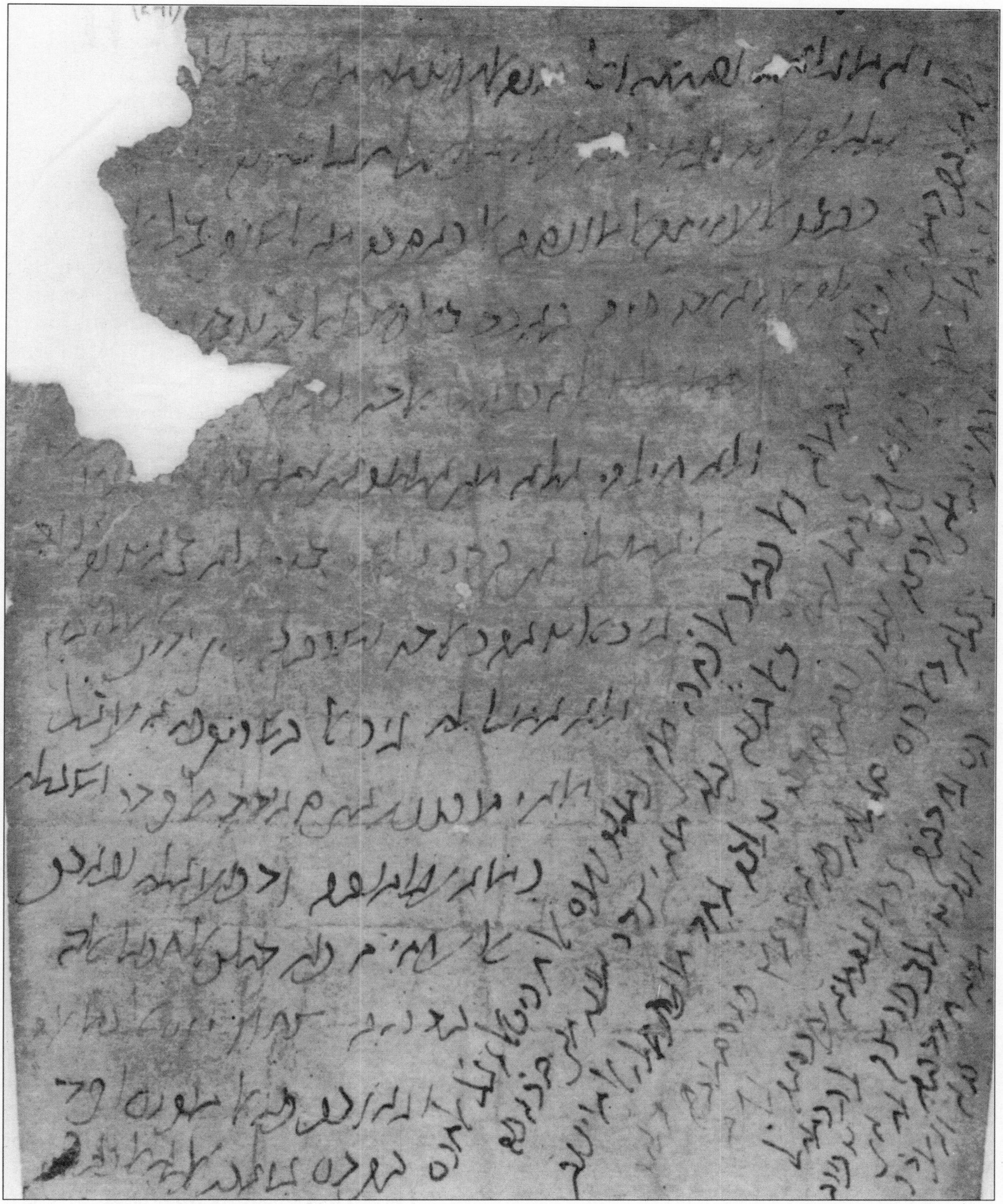

Fragment manuscript by Yehudah Ha-Levi. (Photograph by Suzanne Kaufman.)

SAMSON RAPHAEL HIRSCH

"The reform which Judaism requires is an education of the age up to the Torah, not a leveling down of the Torah to the age. The spirit of the age changes; the Torah remains."

Samson Raphael Hirsch is considered the foremost rabbi of Orthodox Judaism in Germany during the mid to late 1800s. This was the period of the *Haskalah*, a time of much unrest and debate and the rise and advocacy of Reform Judaism. From the 1830s on, Hirsch was in the forefront of maintaining traditional Judaism.

Born in Hamburg in 1808, Hirsch studied with Rabbi Jacob Ettlinger and Rabbi Chacham Isaac Bernays, receiving a traditional education. In 1829 he studied for a year at the University of Bonn, where, while studying philosophy, classical languages, and history, he developed a close relationship with Abraham Geiger, who would go on to become a leading advocate of Reform Judaism. In the 1830s Hirsch assumed the position of chief rabbi of Oldenburg and while there wrote his two classics: *Nineteen Letters on Judaism* (1836) and *Horeb: Essays on the Duties of the Jewish People in the Diaspora* (1837). *Nineteen Letters* made a deep impression in German Jewish circles as a "brilliant intellectual presentation . . . in classical German." Hirsch continued to accept other, increasingly more prestigious rabbinical posts and in 1856 became chief rabbi of Moravia.

Hirsch's philosophy was *Torah im Derech Eretz,* Torah life but with modern secular knowl-

edge. One could be an observant Jew, studying Torah and Talmud, and still acquire knowledge of modern secular society. This concept was called Neo-Orthodoxy, or modern Orthodoxy.

Hirsch believed in progressive trends, such as political emancipation, clerical attire, and a stress on the "basics" of Jewish holy books: the Five Books of Moses, the Prophets, and the Writings. This belief was in opposition to the sentiments of the extreme Orthodox community in Moravia, which held that the Talmud should be the focus of Jewish studies. As a result of this difference, Hirsch moved to Frankfurt in 1851, where he organized an autonomous Orthodox Jewish community, separate from the established and growing Reform community. For thirty-seven years, until his death in 1888, he served as rabbi of Congregation Adass Jeschurun (Israelitische Religiongesellschaft). In 1876 Hirsch was instrumental in obtaining Prussian legislation permitting Jews to secede from the existing state-recognized communities. Thus, there was a legal acknowledgment of separate Orthodox communities.

Hirsch maintained that Judaism was to be understood by its own source, the Torah. The *mitzvot* were designed to bring a Jew to as high a level of perfection as possible. The Torah was given in the abandonment of the desert to show that peoplehood depends upon neither a nation or soil. Jews were singled out for a special mission, which meant not that God loved only the Jews, but that Jews should give all their love and loyalty to God.

Hirsch's writings, stances, and lectures were aimed at those Jews, primarily German, who were abandoning the ways of Judaism. In his time, being a Jew usually barred one from advanced education and business opportunity. Assimilation, via Reform Judaism, was making strong inroads in the lives of the German Jews. Traditional Jewish practices were seen as an embarrassment and impediment to acceptance of Jews into German society. There was a move underfoot, for example, to change the Sabbath to Sunday. The separatism Hirsch espoused distinguished the German Jew from his non-Jewish fellow German. Hirsch believed in a certain level of separatism: "Be a Jew. Be it really and truly; then you will be respected, not in spite of it but because of it."

Hirsch fought German-Jewish assimilation by establishing schools in which a traditional Jewish education was presented along with a general education, including German language, mathematics, geography, and natural sciences. He translated the Five Books of Moses, the Psalms, and the prayer book into German and wrote extensive commentaries on the Five Books that are still actively studied today. He stood up for the dignity of Torah and traditional Judaism for those who were unsure which path to pursue.

By the strength of his character, words, and intellect, Samson Raphael Hirsch helped to preserve Orthodox Judaism in Germany, Europe, and America. His influence is felt to this day.

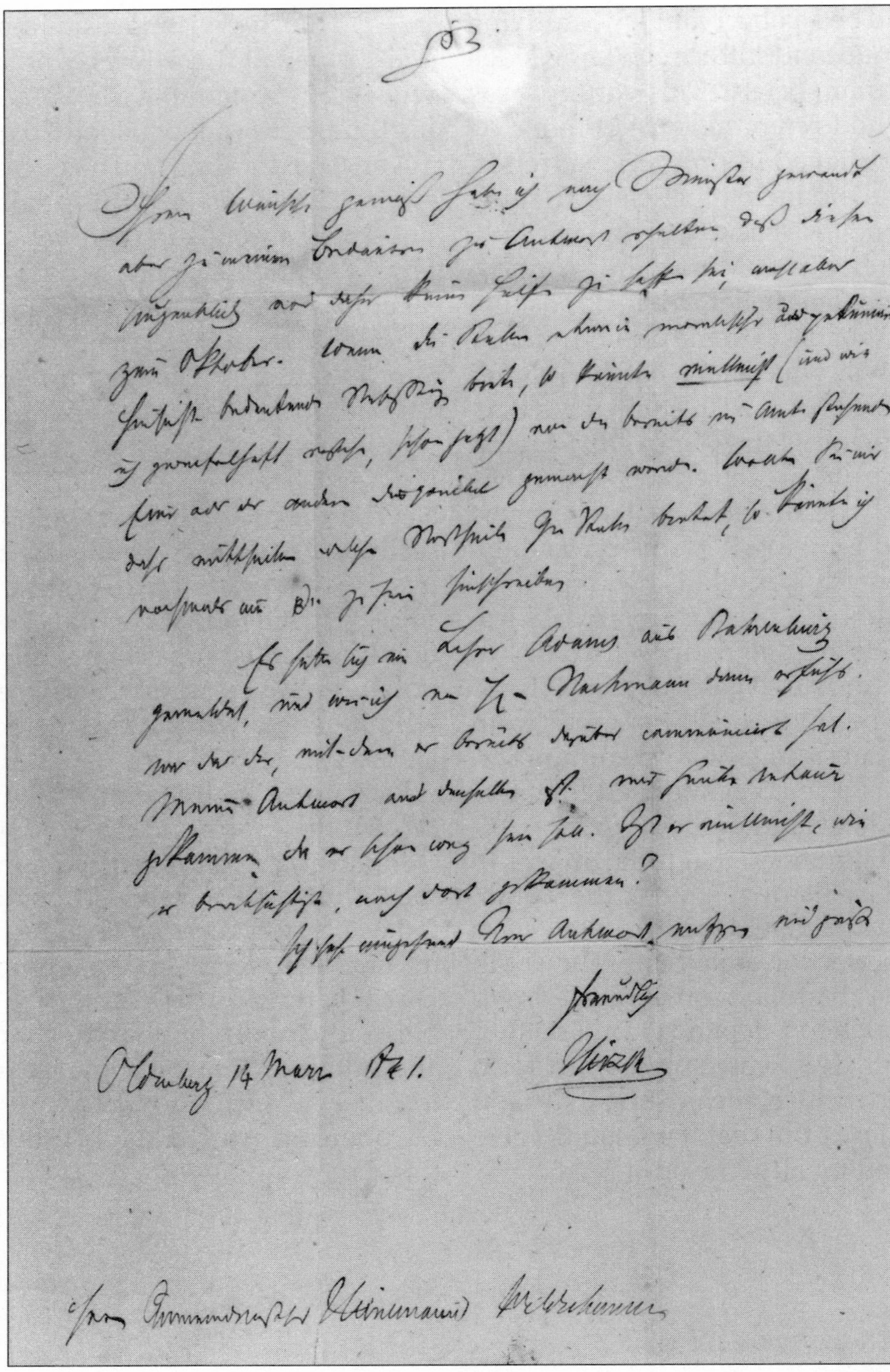

Letter signed by Rabbi Samson Raphael Hirsch. (Photograph by Suzanne Kaufman.)

RABBI JOSEPH KARO

"I am the Mishnah*—Within me is the true wisdom. I am the soul of the* Mishnah, *for I, the* Mishnah, *and you are one. . . . I shall always accompany you, and forsake you neither in this world or the world to come. . . . Let my words be distinct in your mouth."*

—Maggid Mesharim

It is hard to overemphasize Rabbi Joseph Karo's place in Jewish history. His immortality among Jews is guaranteed through his reputation as a mystic and kabbalist and his authorship of the legal works the *Bet Yosef* ("The House of Joseph") and the *Shulchan Aruch* ("The Set Table"), his abbreviated codified compilation of Jewish law. To this day, the *Shulchan Aruch* is the recognized legal authority for daily Jewish life.

Born in Toledo in 1488, Rabbi Joseph Karo came from a distinguished Spanish family that left Spain for Portugal at the time of the Inquisition, then migrated again to Turkey. He spent the majority of his life there, living in Adrianople, Nikopol, and Salonika, the latter being one of the great centers of Jewish mysticism. Karo was heavily influenced by pietists and kabbalists. He became a mystic and while in his twenties established a name for himself as one of the period's foremost scholars. In 1522 in Nikopol, at the age of 34, he began the formidable task of codifying all existing Jewish law.

Jewish law up until that time consisted of a plethora of laws and interpretations; over the centuries and between the various great talmudic academies, authorities had become

numerous and diverse. Over a period of twenty years, employing the previously established codes of Maimonides (the Rambam), Asher ben Yechiel (the Rosh), and Isaac Alfasi (the Rif), along with the opinions of numerous other rabbinic authorities, Rabbi Karo cohesively and definitively codified Jewish law, naming his monumental work the *Bet Yosef* ("The House of Joseph").

The superiority of the *Bet Yosef* to previous legal compositions (such as the Rambam's *Mishneh Torah*) was in its detailed origin and compilation of all the variant views on each Jewish law. Rabbi Karo stated every law, beginning with its source in the Talmud, its development, and even divergent views; all this to be able to discern the authoritative ruling. The *Bet Yosef* was widely accepted, studied, and followed. But it was written primarily for Torah scholars, not for everyday Jews. More influential was the abbreviated digest Rabbi Karo prepared for young students, the *Shulchan Aruch* ("The Set Table").

As a condensation of the *Bet Yosef*, the *Shulchan Aruch*, with its four sections governing daily life—*Orach Chayim* ("The Way of Life"), *Yoreh De'ah* ("The Teacher of Knowledge"), *Even Ha-Ezer* ("The Stone of Help"), and *Choshen Mishpat* ("The Breastplate of Judgment")—was to prove to be the definitive halachic authority. With additional commentaries by Rabbi Moses Isserles, it was accepted by the Jewish world.

Mystic, kabbalist, and ascetic that he was, Karo believed he was visited nightly by a divine spirit or mentor, whom he called the Maggid, or narrator. The Maggid revealed divine mysteries and the appropriate conduct becoming to an ascetic and served as an inspiration to Rabbi Karo in his daily life. This ecclesiastic manifestation Rabbi Karo defined as the personification of the *Mishnah*. Rabbi Karo kept a diary of all this, which was published as *Maggid Mesharim* ("Narrator of Righteousness").

Regarding his magnum opus, the *Bet Yosef*, the *Encyclopaedia Judaica* notes that "for encyclopedic knowledge and complete mastery of the subject, for thoroughness of research, and for keen critical insight this work is unmatched in the whole of rabbinic literature. To this day it is an indispensable guide for anyone desirous of following the development of any individual law of the Talmud from its source to the stage of its development in the sixteenth century."

Joseph Karo died in Safed, Israel—the city of mystics—in 1575, at the age of 87.

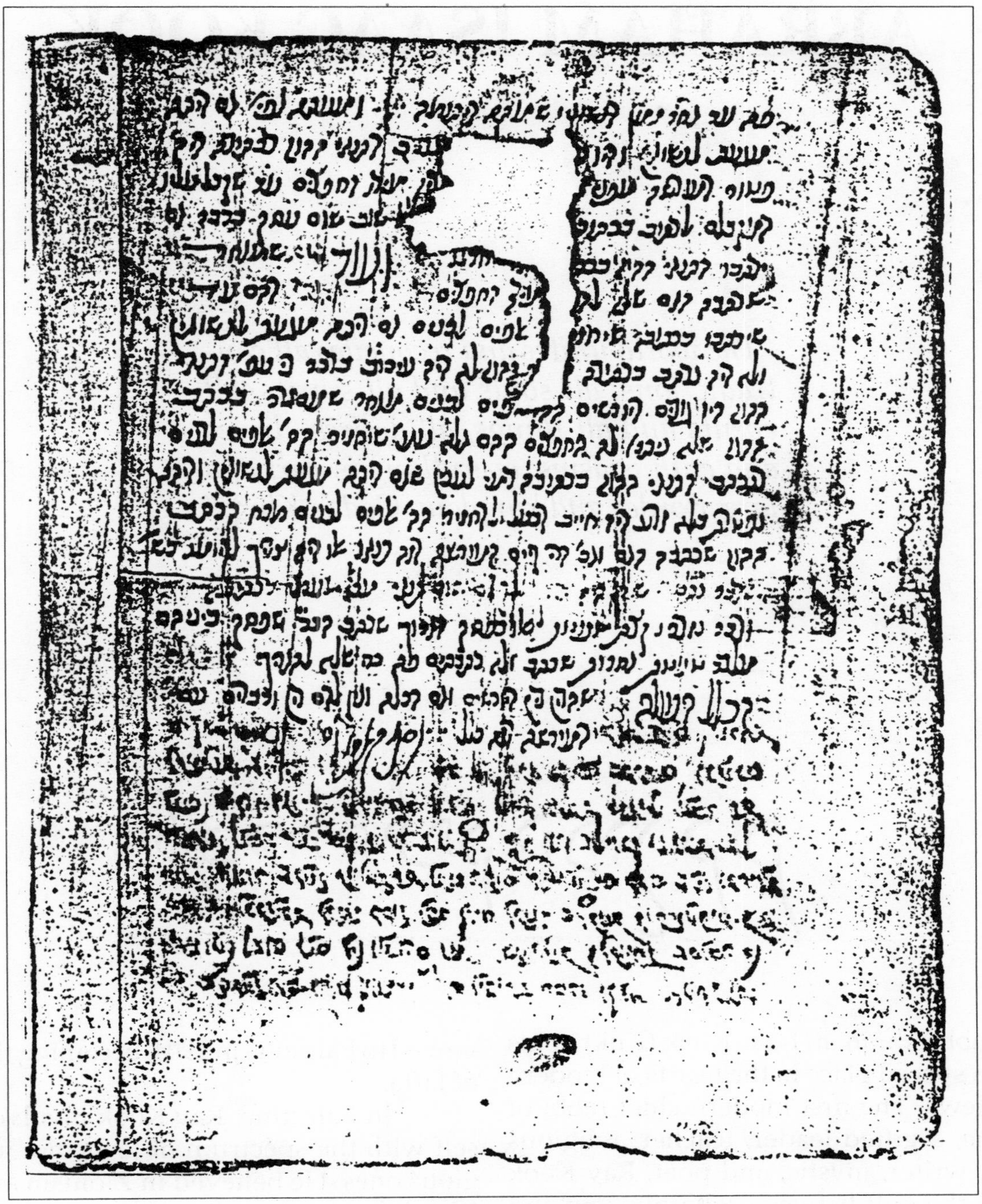

Manuscript with signature of Rabbi Joseph Karo in the body of the text.

ABRAHAM ISAAC KOOK

"The world unites and reconciles all contradictions: all souls and all spirits, all events and all things, all desires, drives and enthusiasms; everything is part of a larger order and kingdom. God is King."

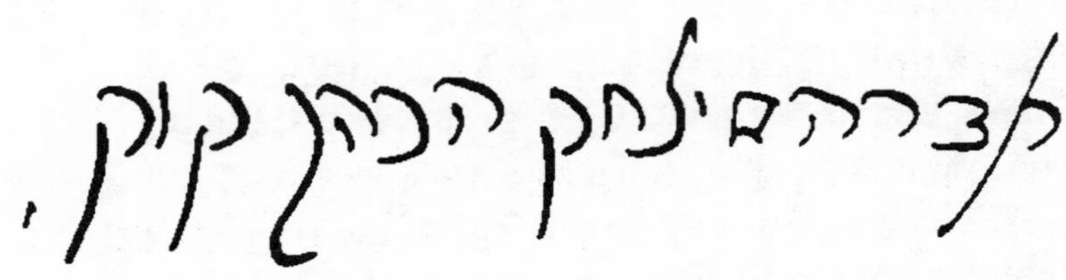

Rabbi Abraham Isaac Kook (Kuk) holds a special place in the hearts of modern Jews. The first modern chief rabbi of Palestine, a gifted leader, teacher, religious thinker, writer, mystic, and poet, Rav Kook bridged the gulf between religious Jew and Zionist believer.

Born in 1865 in the Latvian *shtetl* of Greiva, Rav Kook was recognized as a child prodigy. He studied in the famous Volozhin *yeshivah* and, after receiving rabbinic ordination, took several posts as rabbi in Latvia and Lithuania. A fervent believer in Zionism, he moved to Palestine in 1904, becoming the rabbi of Jaffa.

In Palestine, Rav Kook involved himself with the spectrum of Jews, not just religious ones. He believed in Zionism and Jewish religious nationalism; he saw Zionism—in strong and heated contrast to the mainstream Orthodox thinkers of his day—as a sacred phenomenon. He believed the Land of Israel to be metaphysically different from the rest of the world, and Jews, with their special gift for holiness, could only fulfill their spiritual destiny by returning to Palestine. Shortcomings

and all, Zionism held its own sacredness and holiness.

In support of his beliefs, in 1914 Rav Kook made a special trip to Europe to participate in an Agudat Yisrael conference to urge Jews to migrate to Palestine. The outbreak of World War I prevented him from returning, and he spent the war years in London, actively supporting Zionist political activity. He was involved in the negotiations that led to the 1917 Balfour Declaration.

Following the war, he returned to Palestine where, in 1919, he was appointed chief rabbi of Jerusalem and also established his own *yeshivah*, Yeshivah Merkaz HaRav. In 1921 Kook was elected by the chief rabbinate as Palestine's first Ashkenazic chief rabbi.

During his lifetime in Palestine and until his death in 1935, Kook worked toward bridging the gulf between the romantic ideal and the reality. For centuries Palestine had been the land of the pious pilgrim and the mystic; the early twentieth century was quickly seeing it become the land of modern young men and women. The drive for Zionism was growing stronger year by year. Kook's goal was to complete the Zionist agenda by adding the religious dimension; he believed the national homeland movement should be essentially religious.

As the outstanding figure of the early religious Zionist movement, Kook was often misunderstood by many around him. The extreme ultrareligious groups refused to recognize his official position and consistently excoriated him. The irreligious simply didn't understand him. Kook's writings and teachings were a combination of the old (Torah and Talmud), the new (nationalism, defense of Zionism), and the mystical.

Kook's writings included poetry, philosophy, and three volumes of Jewish law. But he was most acknowledged for his affectionate love for all Jewish people: religious and nonreligious; Zionist and *chasid*; farm worker and *yeshivah* student. His combination of scholarship, religious Judaism, respect for diverse views, and *ahavat Yisrael*—true love for his fellow Jew—all had a practical and tangible effect in smoothing as much as possible the way for intrareligious secular and religious harmony.

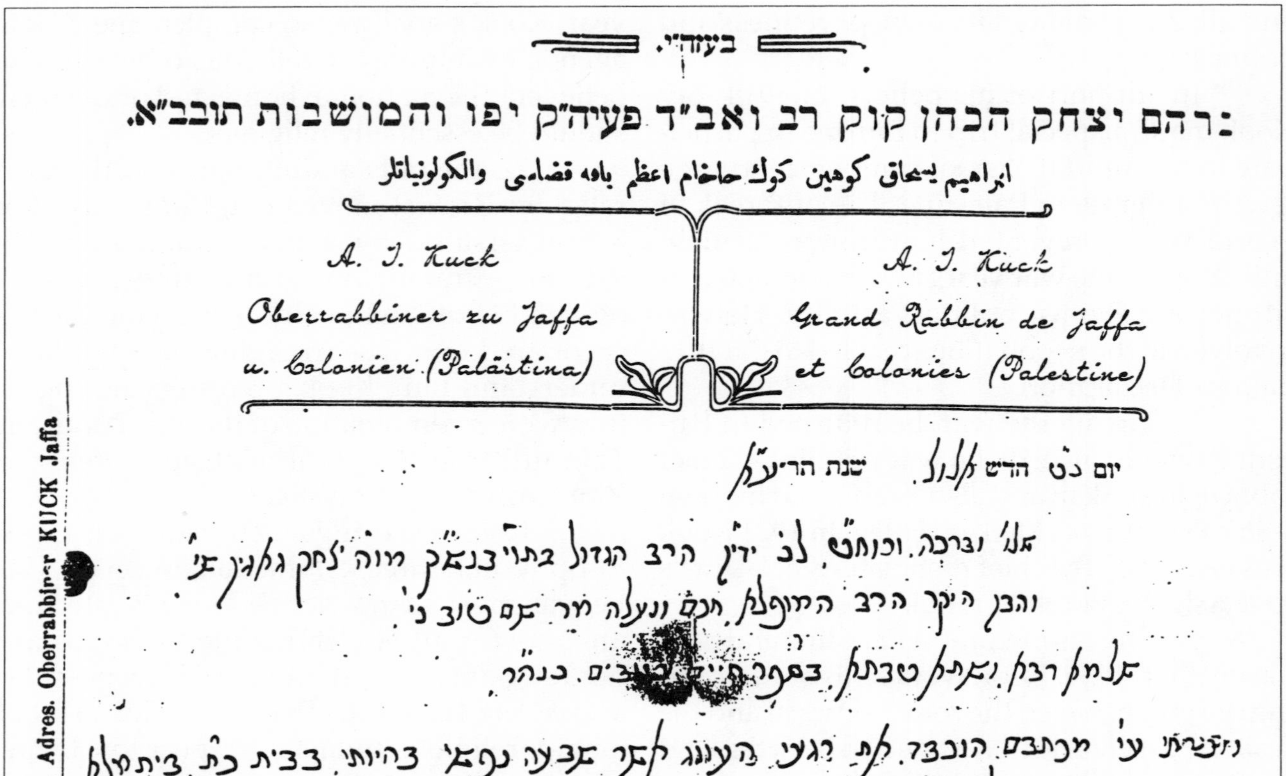

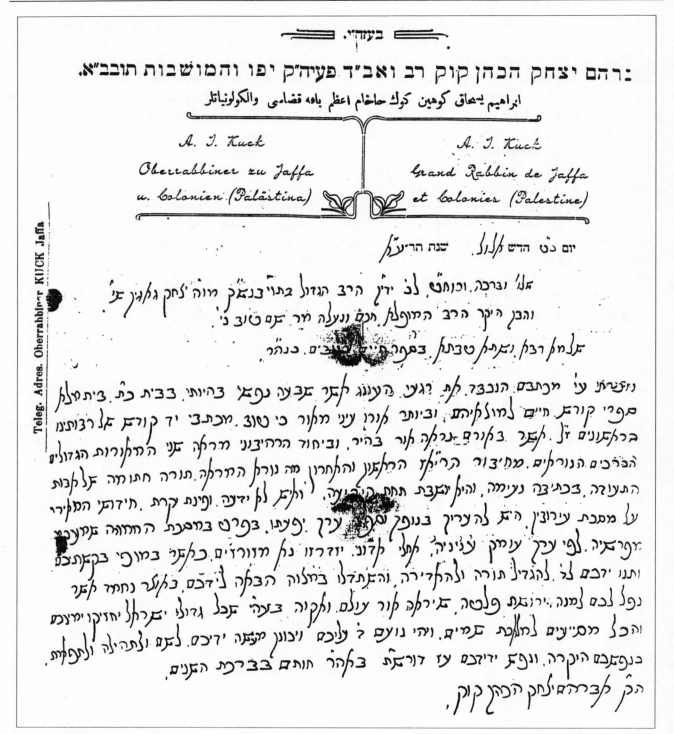

Holograph letter by Rabbi Abraham Isaac Kook, written in Rashi script according to Sephardic custom between rabbis. Rabbi Kook writes to Rabbi Yitzchak Gagine about manuscripts of gedolim, *or distinguished rabbis, which he saw at Rabbi Gagine's home. In part, Rabbi Kook says the manuscripts are a treasure whose light should be brought forth into the world, and Rabbi Kook hopes that they will be published.*

MOSES CHAIM LUZZATTO

"I have written this work not to teach men what they do not know, but to remind them of what they already know and is very evident to them . . . to the extent that they are well known and their truths revealed to all, so is forgetfulness in relation to them extremely prevalent. . . ."
—*Introduction to* Mesillat Yesharim

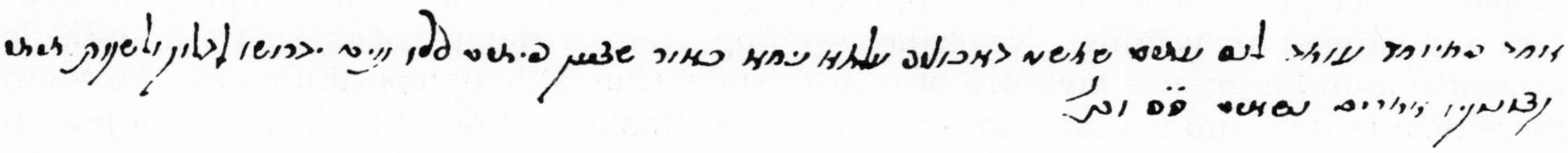

Writing sample.

The mention of Rabbi Moses Chaim Luzzatto (the Ramchal) resounds of mysticism and Jewish ethics. The impact of his life continues strongly to our current day.

Born into one of Italy's most prestigious Jewish families in Padua in 1707 (shortly after the worldwide Jewish disillusionment of the false messiah Shabbtai Zvi), Luzzatto was considered a child prodigy in Jewish learning; he knew Bible, Talmud, *midrash* (biblical exposition), and *halachah* (Jewish law). He was also acknowledged as a master of Italian culture, a linguist, and an expert on the general sciences. But his preoccupation was mysticism and messianic redemption, and it was at the age of 20 that thunder struck.

In 1727, while engaged in the study of Kabbalah (Jewish mysticism), Luzzatto revealed that he had experienced a divine voice, which he believed to be a Maggid, a divine power inclined to reveal celestial secrets to humans. The Maggid, he said, spoke to him frequently and revealed such secrets to him, which Luzzatto recorded. Although most of these writings were lost (a few have survived and been published),

Luzzatto shared these communications with an intimate circle of mystically oriented disciples and colleagues. When information of these "contacts" became widely known, Luzzatto was embroiled in a major controversy regarding his mystical writings and practices. Some rabbis contended that only a perfect scholar and kabbalist might receive such a contact, and Luzzatto, still in his early twenties and unmarried, was considered by some as less than perfect. The bitter and destructive memory of Shabbtai Zvi also played a role in the opposition to Luzzatto. The antagonism to Luzzatto was great and roiling, so much so that in 1730 a formal agreement was reached with his rabbinic opposition: Luzzatto was not to teach Kabbalah outside the Holy Land and he was to surrender his writings.

The controversy did not die, however, and Luzzatto, who had married in 1731 and maintained his side of the agreement, was forced to leave Italy. In 1735 he went to Amsterdam, where he worked as a diamond polisher. There, too, the local rabbis opposed him and banned his writings. Nevertheless, Luzzatto found a greater measure of peace there than in Italy and was able to write, besides his letters, plays, religious poetry, and what would become his masterpiece: *Mesillat Yesharim* ("The Path of the Upright").

If Luzzatto had not engaged in mystical study, if he had not practiced Kabbalah and been involved with messianic concepts, his reputation would still be foremost as the author of *Mesillat Yesharim*, which remains one of the basic texts for the study of ethics. Written in a simple, easy-to-understand rabbinic style, it systematically addresses every problem that stands in the way of ethical and religious perfection. The book enjoyed widespread popularity.

In 1743 Luzzatto moved to *Eretz Yisrael*, living both in Acre and in the city of Safed, famous for its mystics. Four years later, he, his wife, and son died in a plague.

Embattled in life, in death Luzzatto went on to be important in three different trends of Judaism. To the chasidic movement, he was seen as a saintly kabbalist; to the traditional nonchasidic Jew, his *Mesillat Yesharim* was the guidebook to an ethical way of life; and to proponents of the Enlightenment, his writings were an example of a clear, fresh, aesthetic style. Thus, although posthumously, Luzzatto was finally embraced by a variety of Jewish perspectives.

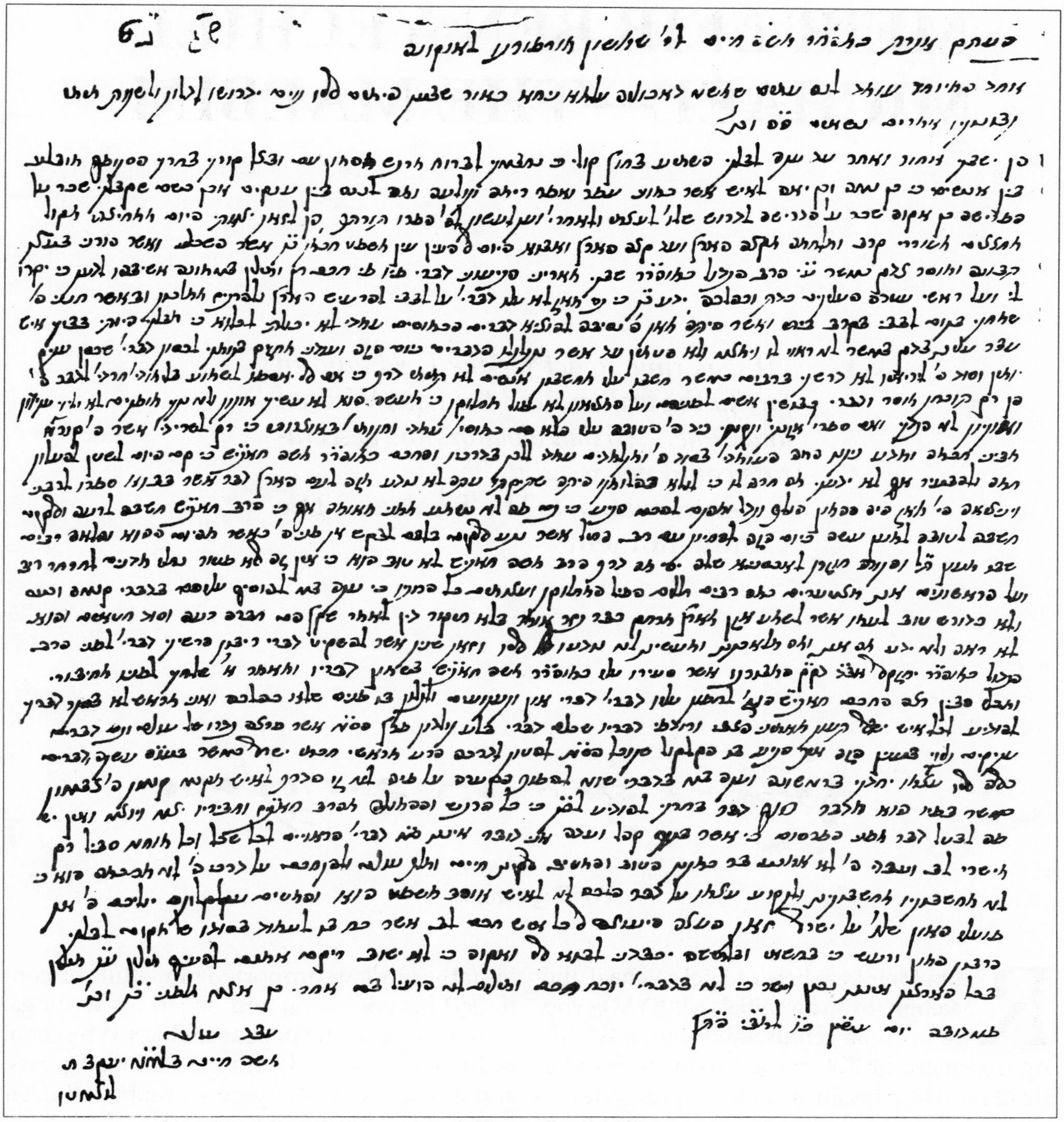

Manuscript dealing with religious topics by Rabbi Moses Chaim Luzzatto. (Photograph by Suzanne Kaufman.)

MEIR LEIB BEN YECHIEL MICHAEL—THE MALBIM

"It was time to act for the Lord, and to fortify the wall around the Law, Written and Oral . . . so that violators and desecrators could not assail it."
—*Introduction to* The Torah and The Commandment

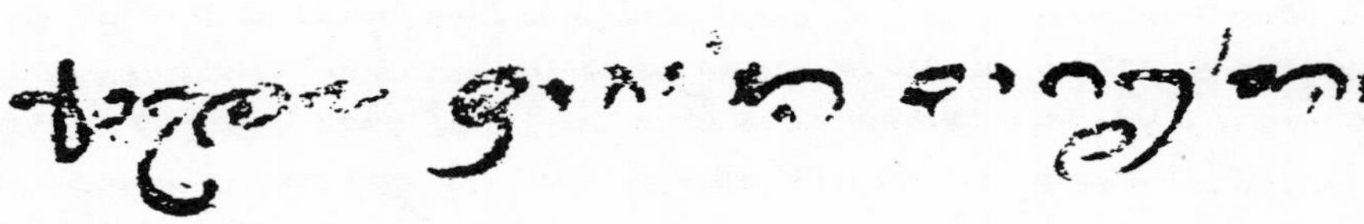

Writing sample.

Rabbi Meir Leib ben Yechiel Michael, the Malbim (from his initials MLBYM), who was a Torah genius, rabbi, and unyielding opponent of Reform Judaism, suffered a life of hardship because of his religious views.

A childhood genius with the reputation of an *ilui*, the Malbim was born in 1809 in Volhynia, Poland. He studied with his father, who died at a young age. Married at the age of 14 but divorced shortly thereafter, the Malbim went to Warsaw and Leczyca to continue his studies. In Leczyca, he married again, and his father-in-law supported him while he continued his education and began his writings. In 1839 he held the post as rabbi of Wreschen, followed by several other rabbinical posts, and in 1858 he was appointed rabbi of Bucharest and chief rabbi of Romania.

The Malbim fought vigorously against Reform Judaism, which he felt would undermine all of traditional Judaism. His uncompromising stance eventually led Jewish assimilationists to report him to government authorities as an enemy of progress. He was

accused of disloyalty and of "impeding social progress" because of his advocacy of maintaining kosher dietary laws. The Malbim was imprisoned and eventually freed only by the intervention of the famed philanthropist Sir Moses Montefiore. The Malbim's appeals to the government were rejected, and in 1864 he was forced to leave Romania. He then became an itinerant preacher, finding himself in continuing conflict and being opposed by assimilationists, supporters of the Enlightenment (*maskilim*), even *chasidim*. He stayed in Königsberg for about four years. He died in Kiev in 1879 while on his way to Kremenchug, Poltava province, where he had been invited to serve as rabbi.

Although unsuccessful in fighting his enemies and the Reform movement, the Malbim achieved widespread popularity for his esteemed commentaries on the Bible. It was his goal to strengthen Orthodoxy in the areas of knowledge of Hebrew, biblical exegesis, and the exposition of the Bible according to its plain meaning. The Malbim enumerated several principles: "(1) In the Torah and the Bible there is no repetition of synonymous phrases; (2) every word has its own specific meaning; (3) there are no redundant or superfluous words; (4) all metaphors are imbued with profound meaning and wisdom, and; (5) the Written and Oral Law are one inseparable expression of God's will."

The Malbim's insights, plus his struggles against those he saw as enemies of Judaism, gave strength to a generation in flux.

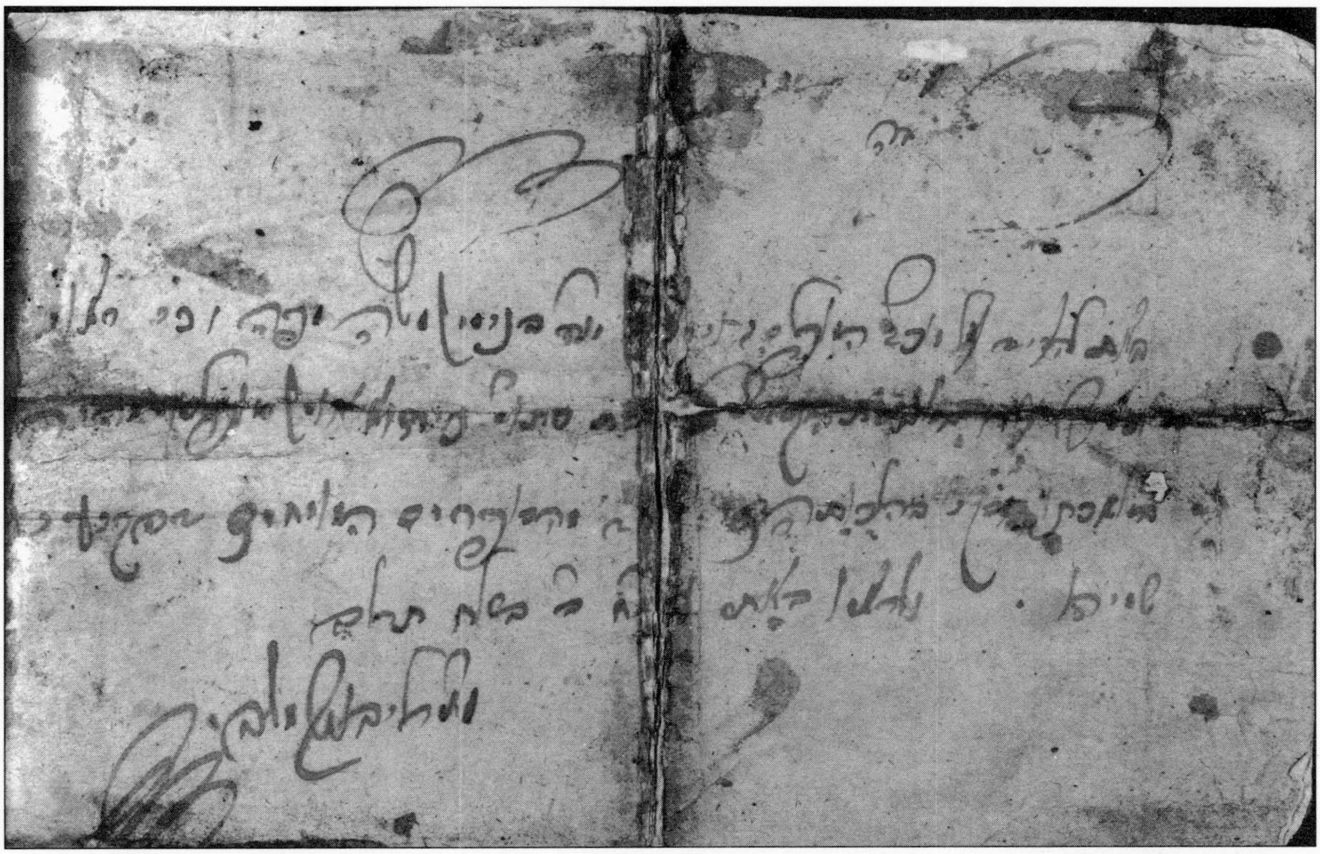

An aged and creased note and signature by the Malbim. (Photograph by Suzanne Kaufman.)

MOSES BEN MAIMON—THE RAMBAM

"From Moses until Moses, there was none like Moses."

—Epitaph

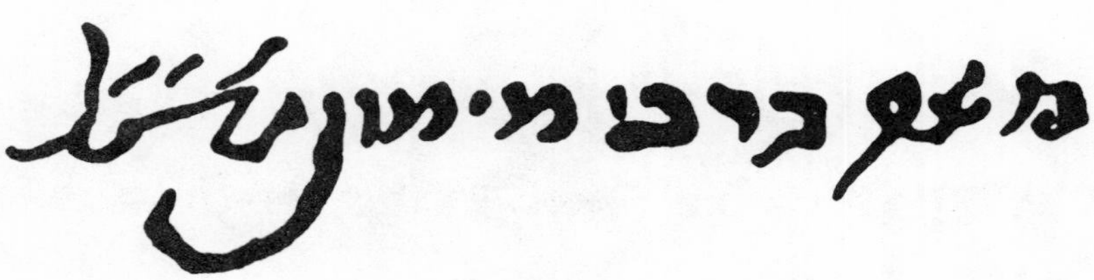

Rabbi Moses ben Maimon, author of *Guide for the Perplexed, The Book of Commandments, Epistle to Yemen*, and the *Mishneh Torah* ("Repetition of the Law"), is universally recognized as the greatest Jewish philosopher of the medieval period. Codifier, halachist, philosopher, and royal physician, Maimonides (Greek for "son of Maimon") holds an unequaled position in Jewish tradition.

The Rambam came from a notable family. (The name *Rambam* is an acronym taken from the Hebrew Rabbi *M*oses *B*en *M*aimon—RMBM, or Rambam.) Born in Cordova, Spain, on March 30, 1135, the Rambam's father, Joseph, was a noted talmudist, mathematician, astronomer, and *dayyan* (rabbinic judge). In his genealogy, the Rambam cites that his grandfather, great-grandfather, and great-great-grandfather were also *dayyanim*. The Rambam lived in Cordova, a city famous for its culture and sophistication, until the age of 13, when the city was overtaken by Islamic conquerors. Mandatory conversion was the rule, and great

numbers of the Jewish community fled, including the Rambam's family.

For nearly ten years, the family wandered through Spain and northern Africa, settling finally in Fez, Morocco, about 1160. During these wanderings, Maimonides had already begun writing. At 16, he had completed a treatise on logical terminology. In Fez, he began his medical education while continuing his talmudic studies. Oppressive Muslim rule prevailed, however, and in 1165 the family left Morocco for the Holy Land, settling in Acre. They stayed in *Eretz Yisrael* approximately six months, touring the country and visiting holy sites, then moved to Cairo, Egypt.

During his first eight years in Cairo, Maimonides had the luxury of writing and being involved with the Jewish community as both a lay and a religious leader. His erudition and integrity brought him to a place of respect, even though he was relatively new to the area. His beloved younger brother David, a successful gem merchant, supported the family. In 1168 David, along with the family fortune and entrusted funds, was lost at sea, which was both an emotional and an economic blow to the Rambam. In a letter dated 1176, the Rambam wrote: *"For nearly a year after I received the sad news, I lay ill on my bed struggling with fever and despair. Eight years have since passed; and still I mourn, and there is no consolation. What can console me? He grew up on my knees; he was my brother, my pupil. He was engaged in business and earned money that I might stay at home and continue my studies. He was learned in the Talmud and in the Bible and an accomplished grammarian. My one joy was to see him."* David's death was a crushing emotional blow.

With his brother's death and the loss of the family's main economic provider, Maimonides, who in accordance with talmudic dictate refused to earn his livelihood from the Torah, began to practice medicine, eventually gaining fame. He rejected a position as physician to a Christian prince and instead accepted the appointment as court physician to the Sultan's vizier. In a letter to his Hebrew translator, Samuel ben Judah ibn Tibbon, Maimonides described the heavy burdens of court physician and community leader:

> My duties to the Sultan are very heavy. I am obliged to visit him every day, early in the morning; and when he or any of his children, or any of the inmates of his harem are indisposed. I dare not quit Cairo, but must stay during the greater part of the day in the palace. It also frequently happens that one or two of the royal officers fall sick, and I must attend to their healing. . . . I do not return home until the afternoon. Then I am almost dying with hunger. I find the waiting rooms filled with people, both Jews and non-Jews, nobles and common people, judges and bailiffs, friends and foes—a mixed multitude, all waiting for my return.
>
> I dismount from my animal, wash my hands, go to my patients and entreat them to bear with me while I partake of some slight refreshment, the only meal I have in twenty-four hours. Then I attend to my patients and write prescriptions and directions for their various ailments. Patients come and go until nightfall. I prescribe for them, lying down, out of sheer fatigue. When night falls, I am so exhausted I can scarcely speak. As a result, no Jew can have a private interview with me except on the Sabbath. On that day, the whole congregation, or at least the majority of the members, come to me after the morning service, when I instruct them as to their proceedings during the whole week. We study together a little until noon, then they leave. Some of them return, and read with me after the Minchah service until the evening prayers. . . .

In addition to his medical responsibilities, by 1177 the Rambam had become the acknowledged leader of the Egyptian Jewish community. His scholarship, leadership, and genius were recognized throughout the Jewish world.

The breadth and depth of the Rambam's writings are unmatched. His works range from medical treatises to religious/philosophical writings to legal jurisprudence to epistles of confidence and fidelity to Judaism, and more.

The Rambam's magnum opus is his eternal *Mishneh Torah*, ("Repetition of the Law"), also known as the *Yad Chazakah* ("The Strong Hand"). A fourteen-volume compendium, it took a decade to write, being completed in c. 1180. The *Encyclopaedia Judaica* notes that the Rambam took upon himself "the task of classifying by subject matter the entire talmudic and posttalmudic halachic literature in a systematic manner never before attempted in the history of Judaism." An introduction to an abridged version comments: "Maimonides condensed all the Jewish lore contained in the Bible, the two Talmuds, the *Midrashim*, and the responsa of the geonic period." The fourteen volumes are:

Book I—Knowledge
Book II—Love of God
Book III—Set Feasts
Book IV—Women
Book V—Holiness
Book VI—Pledging
Book VII—Seeds
Book VIII—Temple Service
Book IX—Sacrifices
Book X—Purity
Book XI—Damages
Book XII—Acquisition
Book XIII—Civil Laws
Book XIV—Judges

To this day, the *Mishneh Torah* is studied, memorized, reviewed, and quoted on a daily basis in *yeshivot* around the world.

Following this decade of intense writings, which for any normal man would be the crowning achievement of a lifetime, in 1190 the Rambam undertook his *Moreh Nevuchim* ("Guide for the Perplexed"). This is considered the most important philosophical work ever produced by a Jew. It was written for the intellectual who was firm in his religious convictions but had studied philosophy and was perplexed by the literal aspects of biblical anthropomorphism and anthropopathism. Another monumental volume of religious, philosophical, and intellectual brilliance, the original Arabic manuscript was completed in c. 1200. It was translated into Hebrew shortly thereafter.

The Rambam died on December 13, 1204, at the age of 69. In Cairo, there was public mourning for three days, by Jews and non-Jews alike. In Jerusalem, there was a public fast and scriptural readings. Worldwide expressions of grief took place. At his own wish, he was buried in Tiberias (Israel), where his grave is visited by thousands annually. "The influence of Maimonides on the future development of Judaism is incalculable," the *Encyclopaedia Judaica* notes. "No spiritual leader of the Jewish people in the posttalmudic period has exercised such an influence both in his own and subsequent generations." It is for this recognition of the Rambam that the epitaph on his tombstone reads *From Moses until Moses, there was none like Moses.*

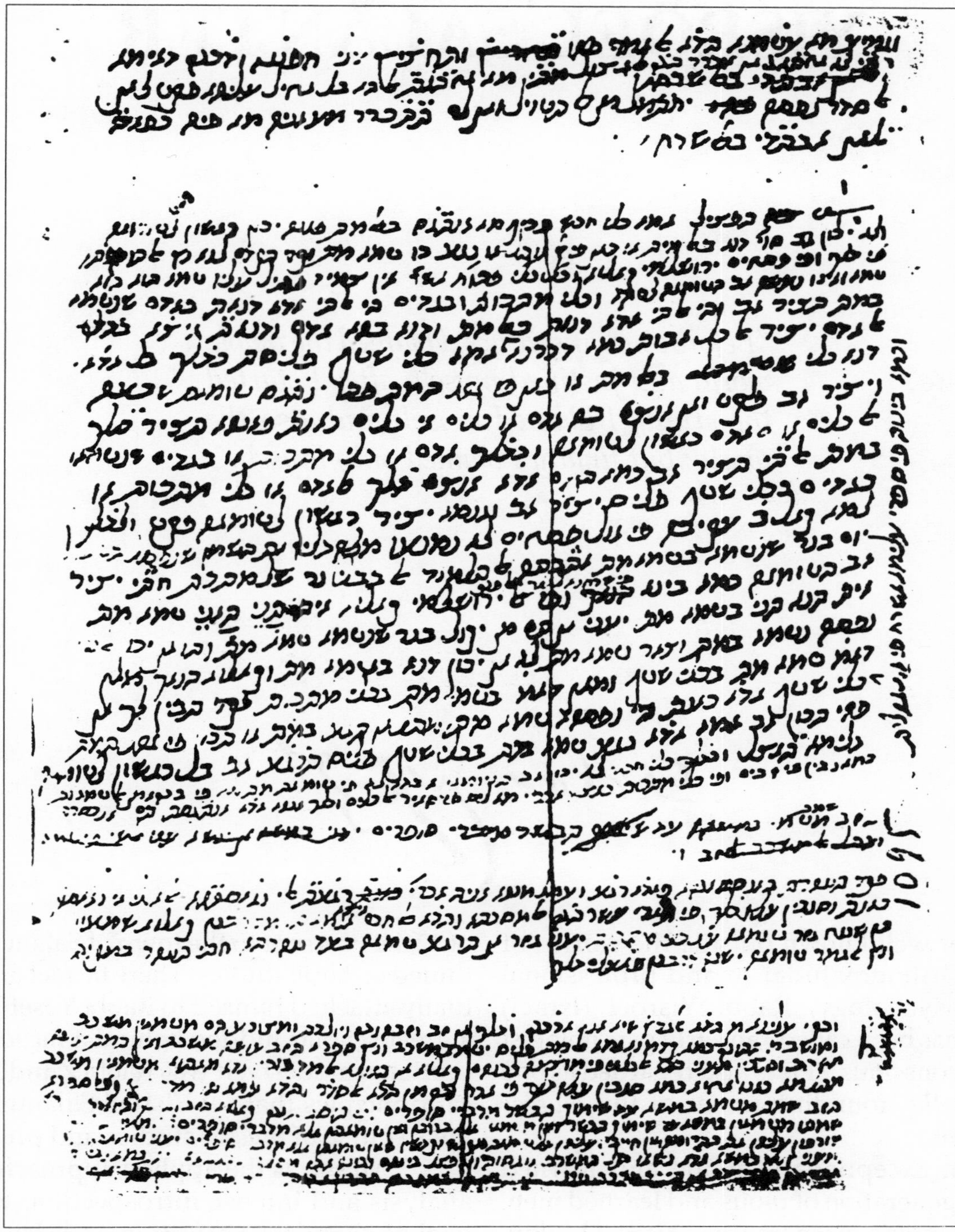

Holograph manuscript by Moses ben Maimon, the Rambam, on the talmudic tractate Tohorot.

YISROEL SALANTER

"Before studying ethics, I blamed the whole world and justified myself; after I started the study, I blamed myself and also the world; but finally I blamed only myself."

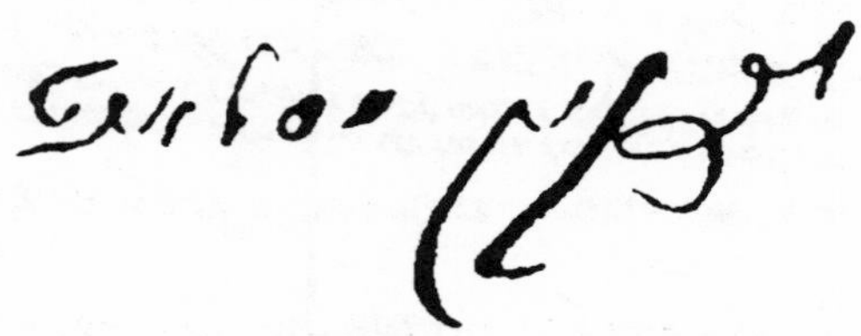

Not well known outside the worlds of Orthodox Judaism and professional psychology, Rabbi Yisroel (Israel) Salanter has been called "an early psychologist of the unconscious." He is also regarded as one of, if not *the,* founding father of the *mussar* movement.

An exceptionally pious and learned man in a generation of pious and learned men, Rabbi Salanter's real name was Yisroel Lipkin. (As was frequently the custom of his century, his surname came from the name of the town in which he spent most of his life: Salant, Lithuania.) He was born in 1810 in Zhagare, Lithuania, where his father was the village rabbi. Lipkin was a child prodigy. At the age of 12, he was sent to the town of Salant for continued *yeshivah* studies. There he met and spiritually attached himself to Rabbi Yosef Zundel, a great scholar hidden behind a facade of exceptional modesty. It was Rabbi Zundel's ethical principles that set Yisroel Salanter on his life's course of *mussar* studies and preaching.

Mussar is the applied approach of self-analysis and intense introspection, with the goal of character perfection and devotion to God. The word *mussar* itself stems from a Hebrew root with meanings of castigation, introspection, reproof, and chastisement, but it is generally translated as ethics. There is a unique set of ethico-religious literature that addresses *mussar* study (notably *The Path of the Upright,*

Duties of the Heart, Ways of the Righteous, The Light of Israel, and several more core texts). In this severe, but not ascetic, discipline, Reb Yisroel Salanter taught and exemplified ethical life.

Salanter was concerned about *K'lal Yisrael*, the collective community of the nation of Israel. He believed that there was no virtue for a man as a solitary individual, but only as a member of society. Knowledge alone was insufficient. One had to have scheduled, fixed studying of ethical texts and understand and overcome selfish urges. He was not preaching socialism. Salanter witnessed the inroads into religious Judaism that the *Haskalah* and general Western European emancipation were making and saw the people falling away from a religious life. For him, an ethical life based on religious underpinnings was the surest way to have people act accordingly in their relationship to both God and their fellowman.

Although appointed head of a *yeshivah* in Vilna, he left that position to open his own school. As his fame, and message, spread, he developed *mussar* study groups. He developed a special study format known as a *bet mussar*—a *mussar* house. His teachings attracted large followings. Salanter was neither a cultist nor an extremist. By virtue of his own integrity, sincerity, personality, leadership, and recognized genius, Rabbi Salanter was a noted presence in Eastern Europe. Salanter was not afraid of new ideas or the *halachah*. This can be seen in his actions in 1848 in Vilna, when desperate measures were called for.

Known as "the Jerusalem of Lithuania" because of its foremost position as the Jewish center outside Palestine, Vilna was also the stronghold of intellectual and rabbinical scholarship. The luster and reputation of the Vilna Gaon was an umbrella to the city. From Vilna came the strongest opposition to the *Haskalah* and, at the time, Chasidism. In 1848, cholera was ravaging Vilna.

Jews and gentiles were terribly afflicted. With health considerations in mind, Reb Yisroel personally tended and oversaw the care of the sick. He suspended Sabbath restrictions, halachically ruling that every kind of work was to be done by Jews and not relegated to gentiles. When Yom Kippur came, Reb Yisroel gave permission to eat and not fast, lest people become weakened. The people, fearful of cholera, were equally fearful of not fasting on the most religious day of the year. On Yom Kippur, Reb Yisroel ascended the *bimah* and, after making the proper blessing, publicly ate in front of the congregation. By virtue of his reputation, the population followed his example.

From 1849 through 1857 Salanter headed a *yeshivah* in Kovno. In 1857 he was struck by a nervous disorder that severely limited and afflicted him the rest of his life. Yet he continued to teach *mussar* and inspired many disciples, who carried his concepts forward. Three schools of *mussar* were developed that took their names from the towns where Salanter's leading disciples established themselves: Navaradock *mussar*, Kelm *mussar*, and Slobodka *mussar*, each with a slightly different orientation.

Following his affliction, Salanter moved to Germany, seeking medical aid and combating Germany's assimilation. He lived there for several years and in Paris for two years, where he continued to teach *mussar*. In 1883 he returned to Königsberg, Prussia, where he died, leaving behind him an unsurpassed legacy of ethical behavior and beyond him the school of Salanterian ethics for future generations.

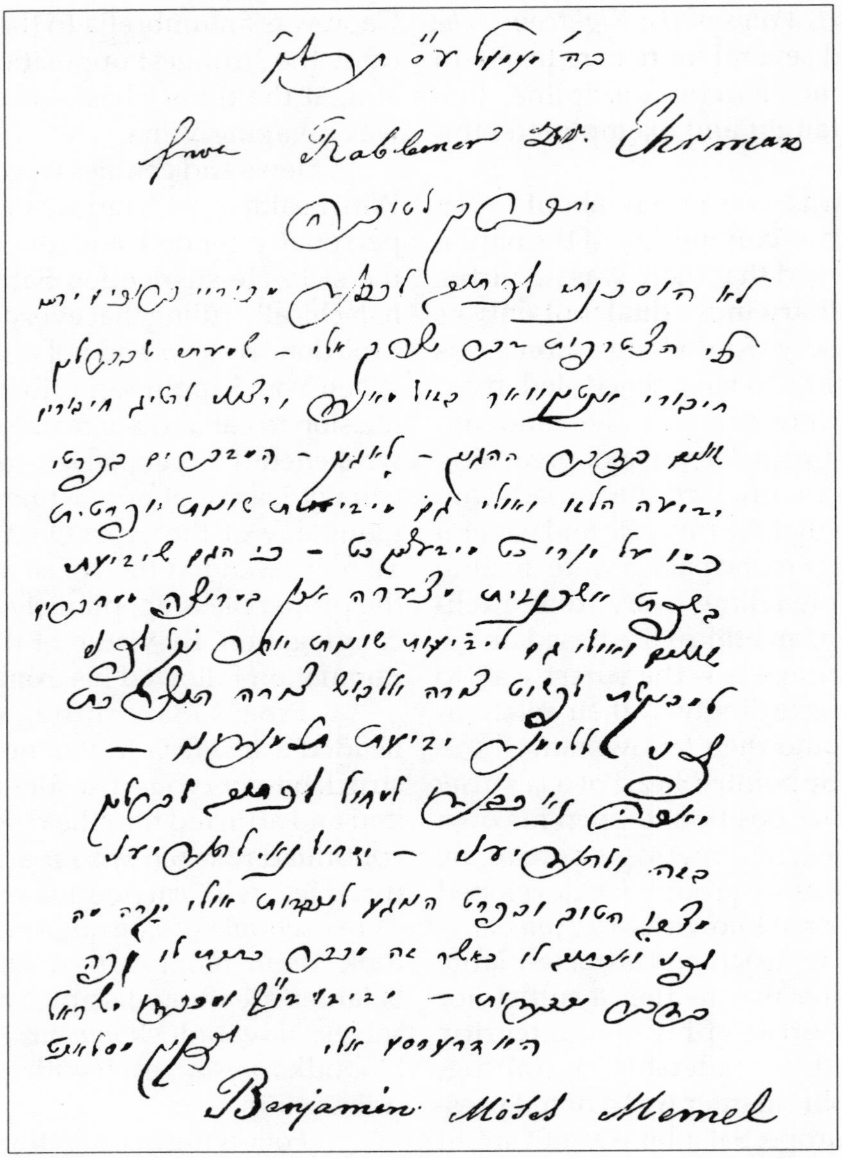
Frau Rabbiner Dr. Ehrmann

Benjamin Moses Memel

Letter by Rabbi Yisroel Salanter. In part he says he would like to obtain some books, but he does not read the s'fas Ashkenaz *(German). He signs his name as "Yisroel of/from [the city] Salant."*

SHNEUR ZALMAN OF LIADI— THE BAAL HATANYA

"Let the mind alway rule over the heart. . . . The source of all virtue is wisdom, reason, knowledge. . . . Virtue arising from Reason is higher than virtue which is not founded on Reason."

—The Tanya, *1796*

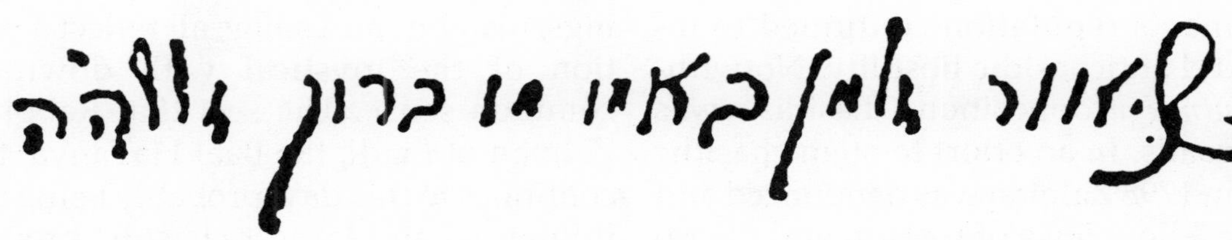

An adherent of the chasidic movement, Rabbi Shneur Zalman was the founder of *Chabad* Chasidism, or Lubavitch *Chasidut*. The name *Chabad* is an acronym for the group's principles: *Chesed* (acts of charity), *Binah* (Understanding), and *Daat* (Knowledge). Lubavitch is the town where the movement first permanently settled.

Shneur Zalman was born in Liozna, Belorussia, on the 18th of *Elul* 1745, according to *Chabad* tradition. By chasidic lore, the 18th of *Elul* is the same birth date as that of the founder of Chasidism, the Baal Shem Tov. By the age of 15, Zalman was both married and already acknowledged as an exceptional Torah scholar. At the age of 20, he went to Dov Baer, the Maggid of Mezhirech, to learn about Chasidism. The Maggid was sufficiently impressed with Zalman's knowledge that he charged him with writing an updated *Shulchan Aruch*, or Code of Jewish Law. Although not a chasidic work, it is a major legal (halachic) treatise and clearly demonstrates Zalman's superior Hebrew writing style, providing lucid ex-

planations and profundity with complexity. Zalman worked on it for many years and although the majority of the manuscript was lost in a fire, approximately one-third was saved and published.

In its infancy, the chasidic movement encountered extreme opposition from traditional Orthodox groups. Harassment, persecution, and excommunication were all methods used to arrest the sect's growth. In 1774 Zalman went to Vilna, the stronghold of the chasidic opposition (*mitnaggdim,* literally "opponents") to meet with Rabbi Elijah ben Solomon (the Vilna Gaon) to reach some type of understanding. The Vilna Gaon, however, absolutely refused to meet with him. Despite this rebuff by the leading sage of the generation, Chasidism continued to appeal to the lay Jew and grew. Shneur Zalman was the teacher and leader of a considerable number of followers.

In 1797 Zalman anonymously published *Likkutei Amarim* ("Collected Sayings"), a compilation and systematic explanation of *Chabad* philosophy and requests for guidance. This became the *Chabad* "bible." In its second printing it was retitled the *Tanya.*

Zalman's reputation continued to increase, as did antichasidic hostility. Notwithstanding *mitnaggid* opposition, Chasidism was making inroads. In an effort to stem chasidic influence, in 1798 Zalman was denounced and accused by fellow Jews of treason and of creating a new religious sect, both forbidden activities under the Russian government. He was arrested, imprisoned, and brought to trial in St. Petersburg. Zalman was acquitted and released, but three years later he was again denounced and arrested. He was released later that year when Alexander I became czar.

Zalman continued to spread and defend *Chasidut* from both *mitnaggdim* and other chasidic sects. The movement's orientation was changing, becoming scholarly and academic and developing its own ways of religious expression. One of Zalman's opponents was Baruch of Medzhibezh, the grandson of the Baal Shem Tov. When the Franco-Russian War broke out, Zalman supported the Russians, fearing that a French victory would be damaging to Judaism. When the French defeated the Russians, Zalman fled with the vanquished Russian armies. He died during this relocation in 1813 and was buried in Hadich, Poltava province.

Zalman was one of the great personalities of his period, a scholar, religious innovator, *posek,* author, mystic, and teacher. In addition, he is credited with composing numerous chasidic melodies for prayer. His writings, insights, and songs all reflect a combination of the mystical with down-to-earth common sense. The sect that Rabbi Shneur Zalman of Liadi, the Baal HaTanya, founded continues to this day, probably being the most influential and largest chasidic group in the world.

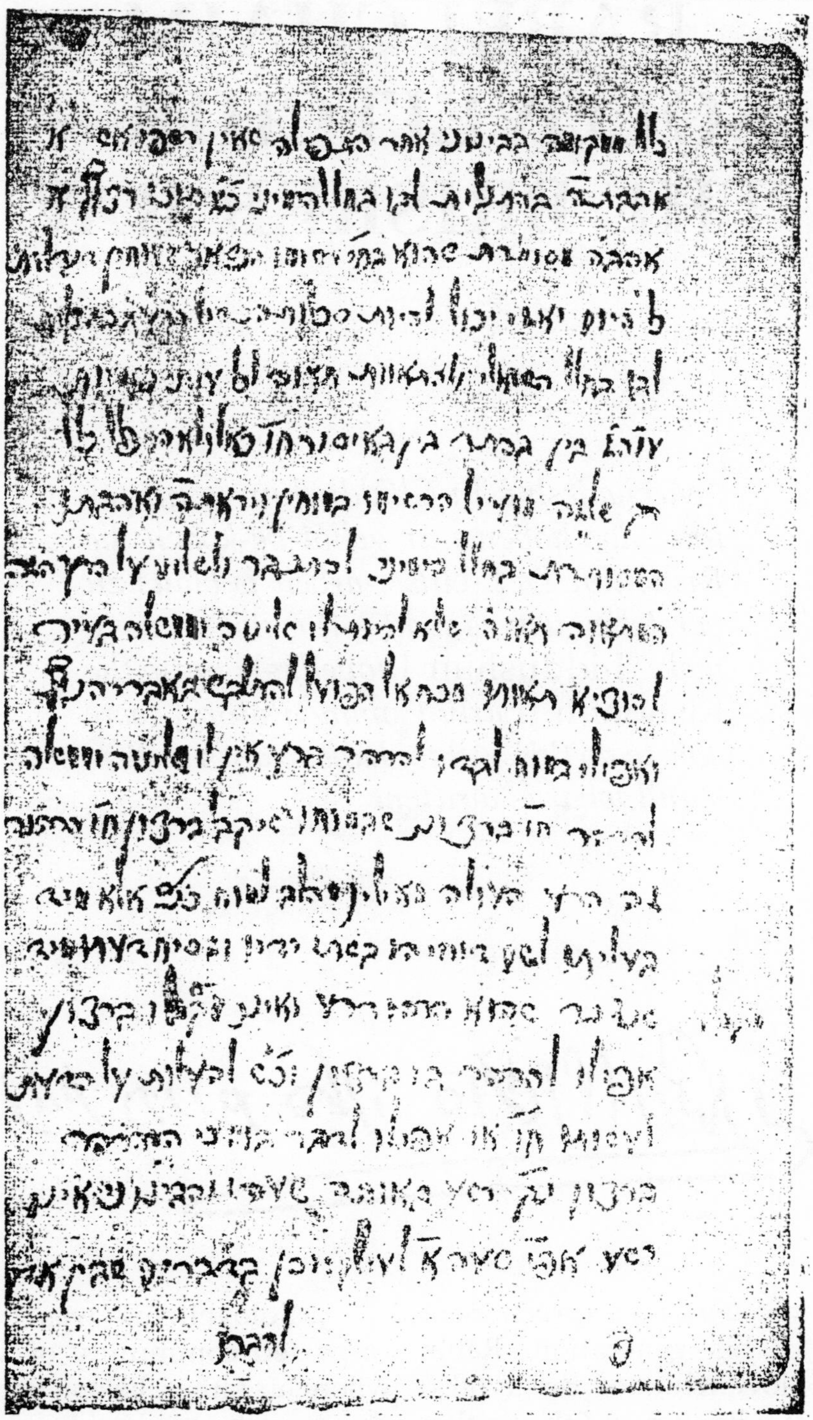

A letter written by Rabbi Shneur Zalman of Liadi.

RABBI CHAIM SOLOVEITCHIK—THE BRISKER RAV

"Mechadesh sein Chiddushim is nit far uns; dos hoben nur gehot be-koach die Rishonim Za'l. Unser arbeit is blaus zu verstehen wos es steht—It is not for us to make hiddushim [*novellas*]*; only the* Rishonim [*Early Commentators*] *were able to do this. All we have to do is understand what is written."*

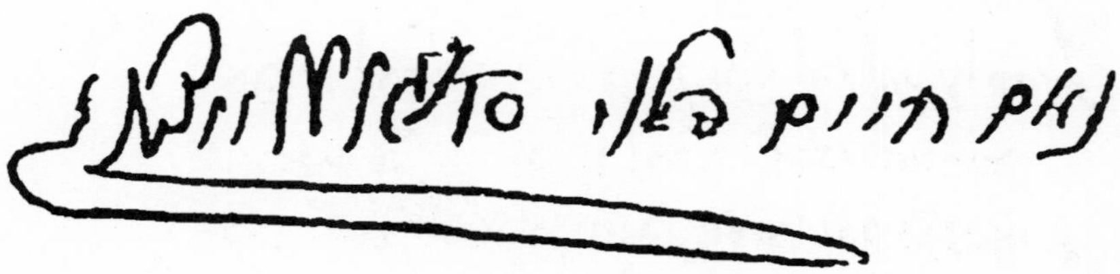

One of the *gedolim ha-dor* (preeminent leaders) of his generation, Rabbi Chaim Soloveitchik of Brisk (also known as Reb Chaim Brisker and the Brisker Rav) introduced a new methodology of Talmud study that gained widespread popularity for its critical, stimulating, and in-depth approach and remains respected and followed to this day.

Soloveitchik was born in the well-respected community of Volozhin in 1853, where his father, Joseph Baer Soloveitchik, an accomplished talmudist in his own right, taught at the *yeshivah* there. He himself studied at the *yeshivah*. At 20, he married one of the daughters of one of the *roshei yeshivah* and by the age of 30 was appointed to a teaching position. As a talmudist, Soloveitchik developed

what came to be known as the *Brisker derech,* or Brisk method of studying Talmud. It involved an insistence on incisive analysis, exact classification and terminology, critical independence, and emphasis on the Rambam's *Mishneh Torah*. To the Jewish world of that time, it was an exciting and intellectual way of learning Torah. Soloveitchik would work with a small circle of from twelve to twenty students for a few years at a time. The students would then return to their respective towns and local *yeshivot*, teaching and spreading Soloveitchik's method. Thus, like the rippling effect of a stone in water, the method progressively spread.

Soloveitchik taught at Volozhin until 1892, when the *yeshivah* was officially closed by the czarist government. He left and went to the town of Brisk (Brest-Litovsk), where his father had been serving as rabbi since 1878. When his father died that same year, Chaim Soloveitchik succeeded him.

Upon assuming his father's position, Soloveitchik immersed himself in both local and international affairs. When the chief rabbinate in Constantinople was threatened by *maskilim*, Soloveitchik defended it. Far from being a small backwater *shtetl*, Brisk was a major town, a crossroads of commerce. Soloveitchik was not only a rabbi's rabbi, but a rabbi of the people as well. He was consulted by both the religious and the nonreligious. His disposition was open, friendly, and approachable. His generosity was legendary, so much so that he personally was frequently in debt. In winter he kept his shed unlocked so that the poor might avail themselves of wood. When the town leaders complained to him that they could not afford the cost of caring for the poor, he replied that he would instruct his wife not to light their own fire: he could not be comfortable while the poor were freezing.

Stringent in his own observances, he was lenient with others, except in public religious practice, where he was uncompromising. Like others of his time, he observed widespread defections from religious Judaism. Yet his own personal integrity and standing were so high that he invariably prevailed against those who sought to introduce changes into the community institutions or *yeshivot*.

Reb Chaim Soloveitchik died in 1918. Three volumes of talmudic novellas, as well as his own novella on the *Mishneh Torah*, have been published. The Brisker Rav left a legacy of genius and a school of Torah learning that is followed to this day.

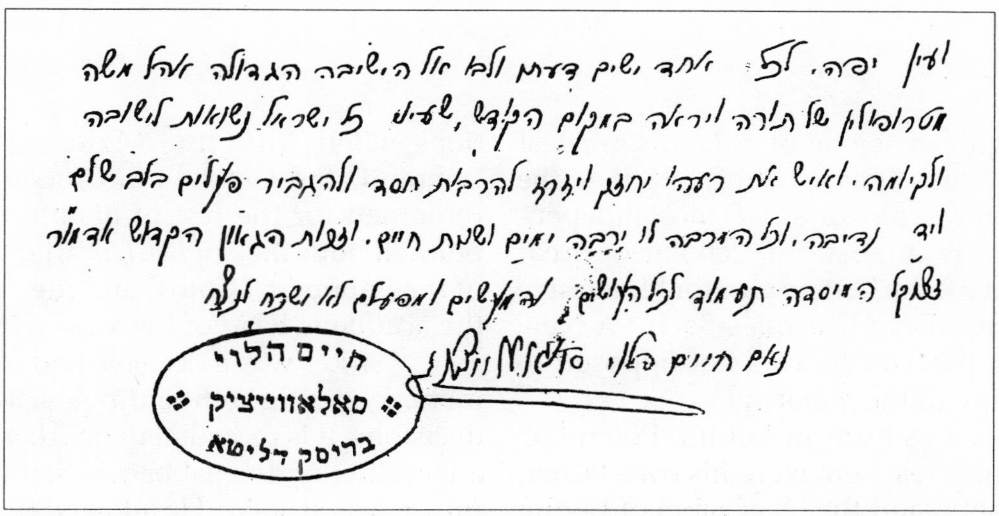

Closing of a letter by Rabbi Chaim Soloveitchik, saying in part that everyone should think of the yeshivah *and its existence.*

JOEL SIRKES—THE BACH

"When he came to Krakow he surrounded himself with important and distinguished students. . . . He didn't teach them once, or twice, but repeatedly, until the text was clear to them (and they could understand and articulate it)."

—*Introduction to* Commentary on the Tur

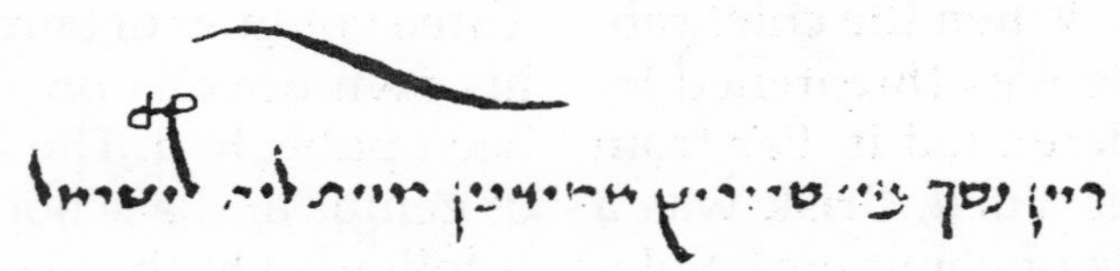

Writing sample.

Recognized as one of Poland's greatest talmudic scholars, Rabbi Joel Sirkes (the Bach) was also one of its most independent and individualistic. A scholar of great wisdom and wealth best known for his incisive commentaries (*Bayit Chadash*—Bach, "A New House") on the *Tur*, he was not opposed to disagreeing with the majority.

Sirkes was born in Lublin, Poland, c. 1561. His early teachers were his own father, himself a rabbi, and the chief rabbi of Lublin at the time, one Rabbi Shlomo. After receiving *s'michah*, (rabbinic ordination), he held positions in Belz, Brisk (Brest-Litovsk), Medziboz, Lubomil, and Cracow. In Cracow, where he remained for the rest of his life, he was appointed both the *Av Bet Din* (the chief justice of the Rabbinical Court) and the *rosh yeshivah*, the academic head of the local *yeshivah*.

Sirkes was a decisive and independent rabbi, rendering both controversial and explicit decisions. It is recorded that Sirkes performed a wedding on the Sabbath when an orphan's future was at stake. He allowed the reading of secular books on the Sabbath, did not oppose the wide-held prohibition of listening to a

woman's singing, and liberalized certain laws for greater enjoyment of the Sabbath. His clear and decisive logic is shown in the following decision:

> Question: A man promised to pay a matchmaker a specific amount if he should succeed in arranging a certain match. The matchmaker put his heart into it and made the match. Now the man recants and says he was only joking and that he owes him only the standard fee. Is the matchmaker entitled to the amount he was promised?
>
> Answer: . . . He must pay the matchmaker the amount he stipulated. The standard fee was instituted only for cases where no fee was agreed upon in advance. This was done in order to avoid quarreling and haggling about the matchmaker's fee. But when the man explicitly agreed to pay a certain amount, it is clear he must pay all that he promised and he cannot say that he meant it only in jest. Besides, it is quite logical. The man knows full well that the matchmaker could arrange the same match with someone else and still receive the standard fee. With that in mind he promised to pay him more, in order that the matchmaker should do his best on his behalf. Therefore, he cannot say now he was only joking. It is the accepted practice in all matters, if you are eager to obtain something, to offer an incentive to a broker to obtain the desired item before someone else gets it. Or if you want a job quickly, you offer the workers a bonus, and you cannot say afterward that you did not really mean it.—Avraham Yaakov Finkel, *The Responsa Anthology*

In another decision, which has meaning even today, the Bach addressed secular music in synagogues:

> Question: Are we permitted to sing in the synagogue melodies that are sung in church?
>
> Answer: I think that only liturgical melodies are forbidden that have been specifically composed for church worship. Since they are strictly religious compositions, they may be likened to a religious statue that is prohibited to be used because it was designed for the purpose of religious worship. . . . But if the melodies were not specifically created for church music, I see no reason to forbid them to be sung in the synagogue.—Avraham Yaakov Finkel, *The Responsa Anthology*

A kabbalist, the Bach developed and raised up a number of leading rabbis, who carried Torah and Judaism forward to the next generation. He was one of the leading rabbis of his time.

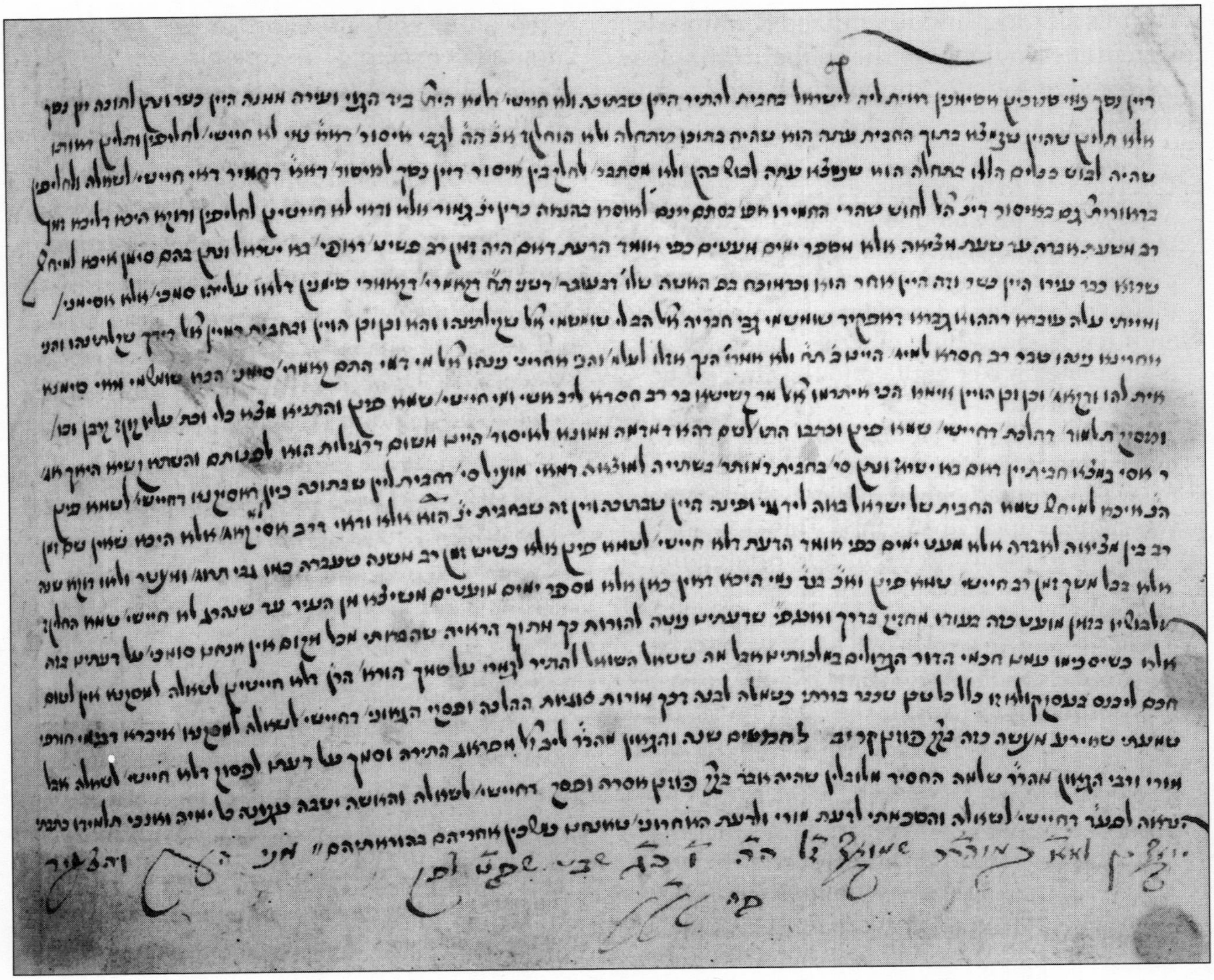

Manuscript with signature of Rabbi Joel Sirkes. (Photograph by Suzanne Kaufman.)

EZEKIEL LANDAU

". . . From my teachers and colleagues I request: do not rely on me, I am not an authority, and especially many of the responsa were written in my childhood, and I am only a scribe. And the reader will understand and remember: and if the words are proper, they will receive them like an offering."

—Introduction to Noda B'Yehuda

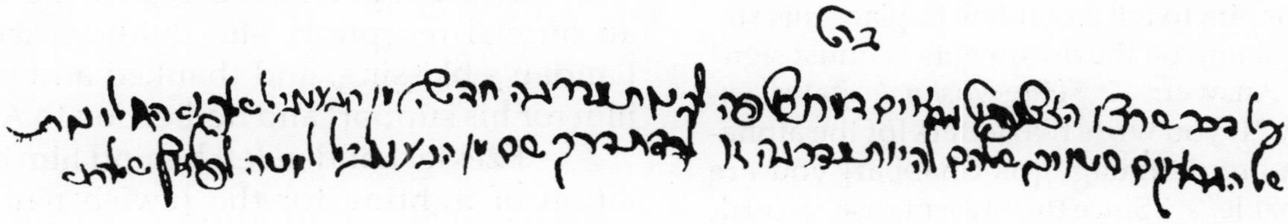

Writing sample.

Ezekiel ben Yehudah Landau was regarded as the prototype of the ideal in a Jew in his period. Halachist, author, and community leader, he was also considered the leading rabbinical figure of his generation.

Landau was born in Opatow, Poland, in 1713, scion of a distinguished family of scholars who traced their lineage to Rashi. A brilliant student who specialized in rabbinic law and Talmud, at 13 he left home to study in Brody, a city acknowledged for its scholarship, and by the age of 20 was appointed one of the city's *dayyanim* (rabbinic judges). By the age of 30 he was appointed chief rabbi of Jampol (Yampol), a position that carried great weight, and at 40 was appointed chief rabbi of Prague and Bohemia. He held the title of chief rabbi of the Austrian Empire.

As chief rabbi of Prague, Landau was teacher, mentor, and judge to the community, and by extension, to the Jewish world. Based on his reputation, the *yeshivah* he founded attracted students from throughout Europe. A traditionalist, although not blind to the world

around him, Landau opposed the messianic movements of his time, notably the infamous Shabbtai Tzvi episode, and was equally critical of the Enlightenment, opposing Moses Mendelssohn's translation of the Pentateuch into German. He was not opposed, however, to secular knowledge in the areas of history, grammar, and natural sciences. As the leading rabbi of his time, he also was looked to for numerous halachic decisions, and he was one of the leading responsa writers of his period. His primary effort was the two-volume *Noda Bi-Yehudah* ("Known in Judah"), first printed in 1766, which contains some 860 responsa. Like many rabbis, he attempted to take lenient approaches to the law when possible, which was not always the case:

> Question: The distinguished Israel asked the following question: Often on Shabbat he had to participate in cabinet meetings in the government administration offices, where he has to sign documents. If he had a facsimile of his signature made into a stamp, would it be permissible for him to tell a non-Jew to place this signature stamp on the documents he must sign?
>
> Answer: . . . The *Mishnah* states expressly "If you write two letters [of the alphabet] in any language [on Shabbat] you are punishable. . . . Since the present case, according to most authorities, is a biblical prohibition, you are not allowed to tell a non-Jew to do it for you, not even in order to prevent a serious loss. Therefore, it is difficult to find a way to sanction this matter.
>
> —Avraham Yaakov Finkel
> *The Responsa Anthology*

Along with his extensive legal opinions, Landau also authored commentaries on the Talmud and *Shulchan Aruch*, as well as a volume of sermons.

In his role as chief rabbi, Landau also acted as liaison to the Austrian government on behalf of the Jewish community. When Prague (then part of Austria) was besieged in the Seven Years' War (1756–1764), Landau mobilized Jewish support for the Austrian position. He instituted a daily prayer to be said on behalf of the government and forbade under penalty of excommunication lending assistance to the enemy. This open and strong support of the government was rewarded with a change in attitude of the Austrian authorities toward their Jewish citizens, from one of doubt to confidence. When Queen Maria Theresa of Austria visited Prague at the end of the war, at an official reception, she publicly accepted Landau's blessing, and thanked and praised him for his support and dedication to Austria.

Ezekiel Landau left behind him a reputation of fighting for the Jewish name and cause through diplomacy, scholarship, leadership, intellect, and unsurpassed character. Ezekiel Landau died in 1793.

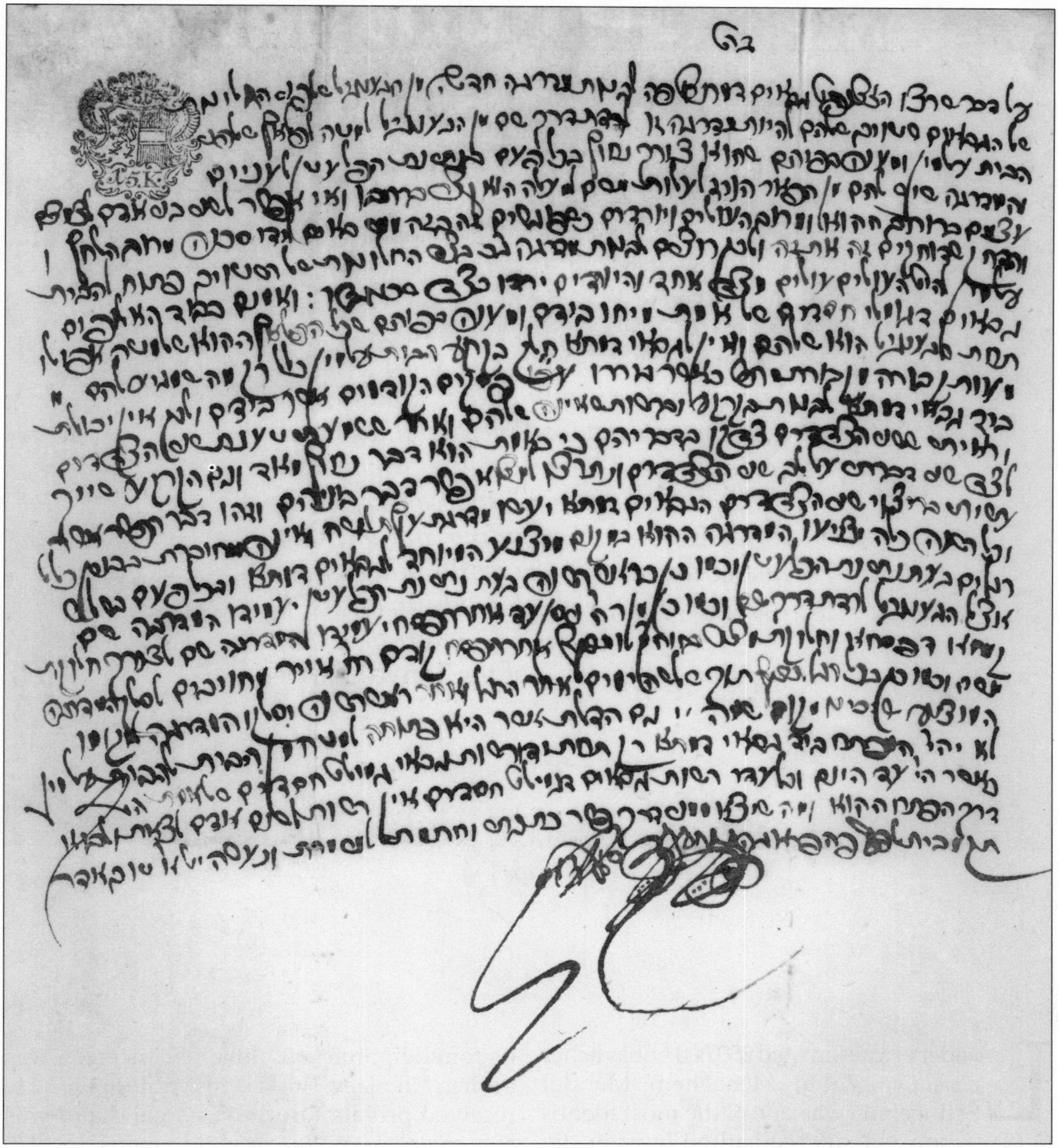

Handwritten letter by Rabbi Ezekiel Landau about the construction of a building, addressing the stairs and windows and the need for accessibility by poor people. (Photograph by Suzanne Kaufman.)

MENACHEM MENDEL SCHNEERSON—THE LUBAVITCHER REBBE

"The Jew is a creature of 'heaven' and 'earth,' of a heavenly Divine Soul, which is truly a part of Godliness, clothed in an earthly vessel constituted of a physical body and animal soul, whose purpose is to realize the transcending and unity of his nature, and of the world in which he lives, within the absolute Unity of God."

—Preface to the original translation of the Tanya, *Part I*

Leader of an estimated 250,000 Lubavitcher *chasidim*, Rabbi Menachem Mendel Schneerson was one of the most identifiable, respected, and consulted Jews in the world. Under him, the chasidic movement specifically, and the Jewish religious revival overall, experienced unprecedented growth.

The seventh rebbe of the Lubavitch (or *Chabad*) *chasidim* and directly descended from its founder, Shneur Zalman, Schneerson was born in Nikolaev, Russia, on April 18, 1902. He received private tutoring as a child and was recognized as an *ilui*, or child genius. In 1929 he married Chaya Mushkah Schneerson, the daughter of the Lubavitch rebbe at that time. Following his marriage, Schneerson did something unprecedented: he attended both the University of Berlin and the Sorbonne in Paris,

where he studied philosophy and received a degree in engineering. He was the first chasidic rebbe to receive a college degree. (He was also fluent in ten languages.)

Schneerson moved to the United States in 1941, following his father-in-law, who had emigrated from Russia upon his release from Soviet prison. For the next nine years, he was actively involved in overseeing educational programs, writing and compiling Jewish legal issues (responsa), and writing on Lubavitch philosophy and talmudic issues.

With the death of his father-in-law in 1950, Schneerson became the Lubavitcher Rebbe. He went on to play an unparalleled role in the awakening of nonobservant Jews to Judaism. His personal scholarship and individual sensitivity were almost lost in his persona as leader of the *Chabad* sect.

Under his direction, *Chabad* Chasidism became one of the highest-profile sects. This was intentionally accomplished through educational, outreach, and proselytizing efforts to assimilated, nonobservant, and secular Jews. The movement's mobile *Mitzvah* Tanks, worldwide television broadcasts of the rebbe's *farbrengen* (town hall community addresses), youths on the street soliciting Jewish males to put on phylacteries, efforts for Soviet Jewry, and public menorah lightings at Chanukah all helped to create a stirring reawakening in Jews who previously were on the periphery of their Jewishness.

The rebbe was also involved in the movement to bring the Messiah. The *Chabad* Lubavitch *chasidim* sponsored newspaper ads, banners, billboards, and bumper stickers, all declaring the desire for and forthcoming approach of the Messiah. Indeed, some of his followers viewed him as the Messiah.

Schneerson established his base of operations in the Crown Heights section of Brooklyn and remained there until his death. For a man with worldwide influence, who led a considerably high percentage of the world's active Jews, he never visited Israel. Yet his influence was both distinctive and considerable.

Menachem Mendel Schneerson died on June 12, 1994, following a severe stroke. Without argument, he proved to be one of the most influential leaders of his generation in bringing Jews back to Judaism.

RABBI MENACHEM M. SCHNEERSON
Lubavitch
770 Eastern Parkway
Brooklyn. N. Y. 11213
493-9250

מנחם מענדל שניאורסאהן
ליובאוויטש

770 איסטערן פארקוויי
ברוקלין, נ. י.

ב"ה, י' ניסן תשמ"ח
ברוקלין, נ.י.

הרה"ג הרה"ח אי"א נו"נ עוסק בצ"צ וכו'
מוה' שמואל שי'

שלום וברכה!

לקראת חג המצות, זמן חירותנו, הבא עלינו ועל כל ישראל לטובה, הנני בזה להביע ברכתי לחג כשר ושמח ולחירות אמתית, חירות מדאגות בגשם ומדאגות ברוח - בכל דבר המעכב עבודת ה' בשמחה ובטוב לבב.

ולהמשיך מחירות ושמחה זו בימי כל השנה כולה.

ובפרט שעבודת השם, כמצווה עלינו בתורתנו תורת חיים, הרי היא בכל עניני האדם ובמשך כל היום וכל הלילה, וכמו שנאמר בכל דרכיך דעהו.

בכבוד ובברכת החג

נ.ב. מכי הניחומים נתקבל בעתו, ות"ח.

Typed Passover greeting on Lubavitch headquarters letterhead signed by Rabbi Menachem Mendel Schneerson.

ISAAC ELCHANAN SPEKTOR

"From my youth until now I have taken upon myself the burden of Torah . . . I am burdened amongst the people with whom I dwell by all manners of questions, even from distant cities, and inquired of regarding both religious and secular matters and therefore I have written succinctly where it might have behooved me to have expounded further . . . thank God the ability to answer questions has not been withheld from me. . . ."

—Introduction to his religious work Baer Yitzchak

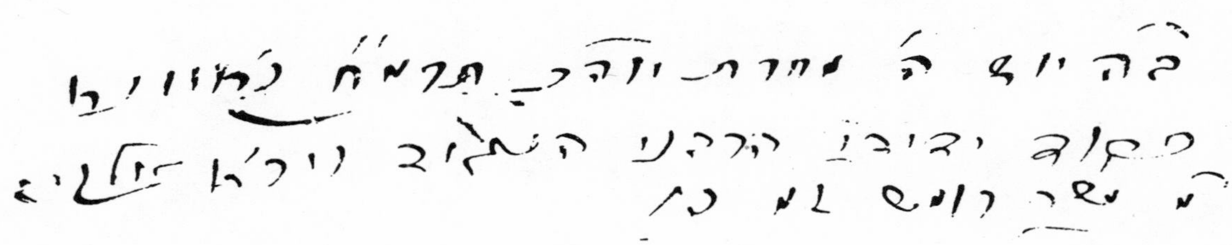

Writing sample.

Namesake of the largest and foremost Orthodox Jewish institution in America, Rabbi Isaac Elchanan Spektor was one of the preeminent rabbis of his generation. A Torah scholar, he was both a leading halachic authority to Eastern European Jewry and an opponent to anti-Semitic governmental authorities.

Born in the Grodno province of Russia in 1817, he served as a rabbi in several small communities until his appointment as rabbi of Kovno. From Kovno (where he officiated until his death in 1896), he worked for Jews far and near. He established a *yeshivah* for training rabbis, maintained a soup kitchen for the needy, lent his name and prestige to the *Hovevei Zion* (Lovers of Zion) movement in Russia, and involved himself in all aspects of Jewish welfare.

A much sought after rabbi, Spektor consistently and persistently fought for Jewish rights in czarist Russia. He was successful in fighting a law requiring a state examination in

Russian from Jewish teachers, and also in defeating a government decree prohibiting Jewish instruction in Jewish elementary schools. He lent his influence to the successful Jewish argument against the ban of kosher slaughtering. He lobbied for kosher food for Jewish soldiers in the Russian army.

With Jewish emigration increasing from Russia at the end of the nineteenth century, Spektor's support of *Hovevei Zion* added great prestige to the movement. Spektor publicly ordained the settling of *Eretz Yisrael* a religious duty. His *psak* (legal religious decision) regarding the question of agricultural labor in the sabbatical (*shemittah*) year, which favored the nominal selling of land to non-Jews, is in force to this day. Spektor also involved himself in the conditions of immigrant Jews in both the United States and Argentina.

A strict traditionalist, Spektor nonetheless exercised lenient decisions in his legal rulings. The questions put forth to him ranged from everyday personal and business problems to those affecting Jews at large. *Agunot*, women whose spouses are presumed dead but their deaths cannot be verified and thus the "widows" require clarification of their marital status (a common problem, for example, during wartime), was one especially thorny problem. Of 158 cases presented to Spektor, he could find only 3 wherein he could not allow the wife to remarry.

Spektor served as rabbi of Kovno until his death in 1896. His passing was marked by worldwide mourning. Spektor's legal decisions and his involvement as a *Guter Yid*—a Jew who fought on behalf of the Jewish good—helped tens of thousands of Jews to overcome seemingly insurmountable religious obstacles. His primary halachic work was *Ein Yitzchak*, a two-volume work published from 1889 to 1895. Many institutions have been named for him, including the Rabbi Isaac Elchanan Theological Seminary of Yeshiva University in New York, America's foremost seminary for the ordination of Orthodox rabbis.

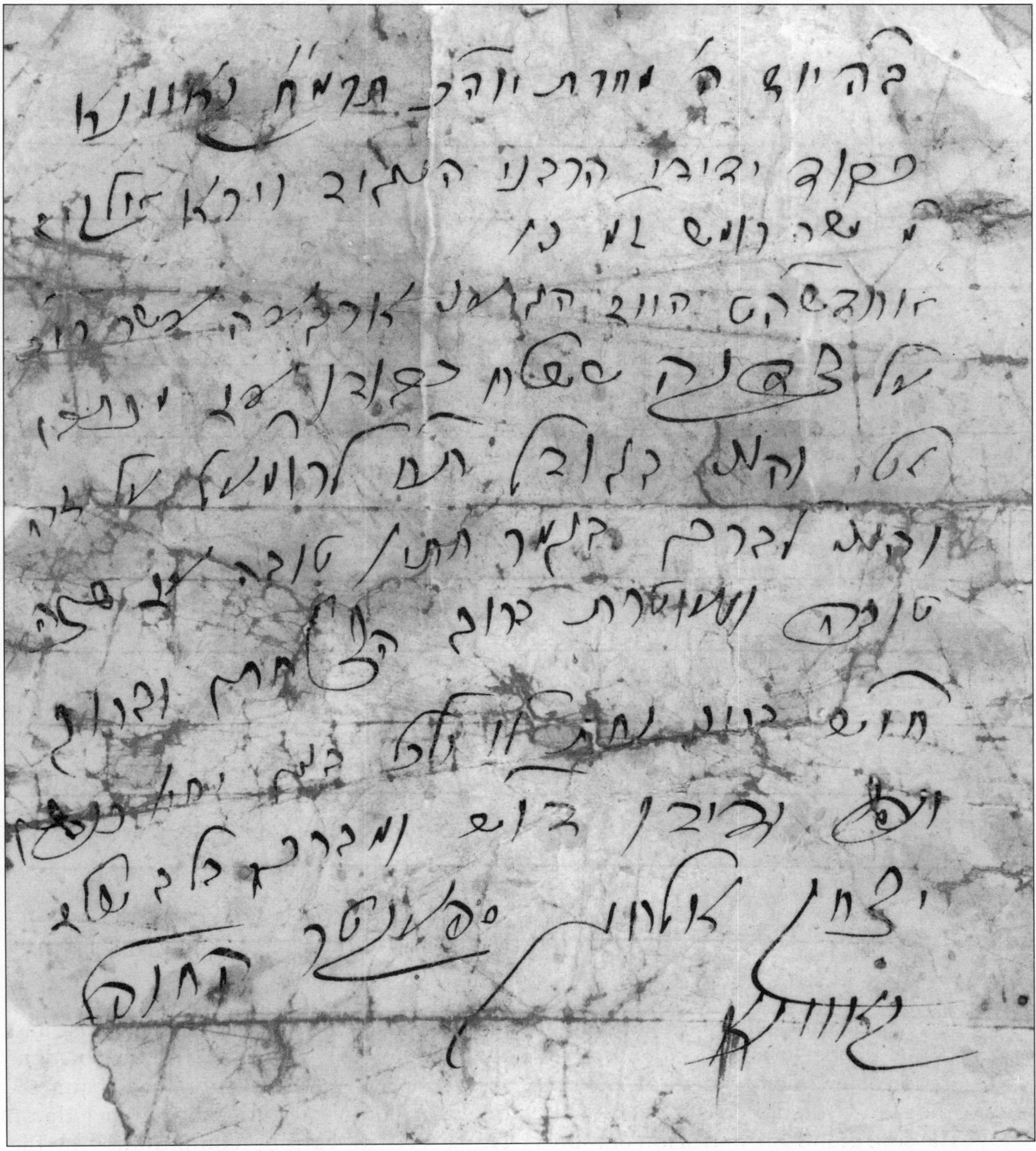

A handwritten thank-you note by Rabbi Spektor about charitable funds. (Photograph by Suzanne Kaufman.)

YOEL TEITELBAUM—THE SATMER REBBE

> *"It is clear beyond any doubt that all the buildings and institutions the misbelievers and atheists have erected and established in our Holy Land will be destroyed by the* Mashiach [*Messiah*]. . . . *God will build holy structures without any infusion of alien culture. . . . We, the few Jews whose eyes are not blinded, must gird ourselves mighty not to get swept along with the popular currents."*
>
> —Divrei Yoel

Writing sample.

Yoel Teitelbaum—the Satmer Rav, or Satmer Rebbe—was the leader of a generation of Jews fiercely dedicated to preserving the ultra-Orthodox chasidic way of life.

The son, grandson, and scion of rabbis (he traced his ancestry to both Rabbi Shmuel Eliezer Eidels [the Maharsha] and Rabbi Moses Isserles [the Rema]), Yoel Teitelbaum was born in Sighet, Hungary, in 1888. Like many of rabbinical lineage, he showed great promise and received his early education from his own father, Rabbi Moshe Teitelbaum. Teitelbaum focused on Talmud, *halachah*, and *mussar* (ethics). He served in various communities in the Carpathians and northern Transylvania and from 1928, the town of Satmer, a stilting of the local name Satu Mare, or Saint Mary.

Known for his heated controversies

with both Zionists and other *chasidim*, Teitelbaum officiated as head of the Satmer *chasidim* in Hungary until 1944 and the Nazi invasion of the area. Through what some deem miraculous fortune, the high-profile leader was one of 1,684 Hungarian Jews on the famous "Kasztner Train," which allowed them passage to Switzerland, safety, and out of Europe. In 1946 he settled in the United States, where he set about reestablishing the religious world Hitler had destroyed.

In the Williamsburg section of New York City and in Israel, he established schools and a complete community. With his outspoken and fiercely religious ways, he attracted both Holocaust survivors and other religious Jews. The Satmer sect is famous for its extreme opposition to the political State of Israel and for any innovation or deviation from traditional Jewish life. Teitelbaum protested the State of Israel with speeches, writings, and demonstrations. He believed that a kosher Jewish state would only be possible with the coming of the Messiah. Teitelbaum ordered his followers who lived in Israel not to take the oath of loyalty to the state, to speak Hebrew as the daily language, to participate in elections, to serve in the military, or to make use of the courts.

For all his open opposition to Israel, the Satmer Rebbe was one of a handful who helped reconstitute the right-wing community that was annihilated in World War II. He oversaw a community that grew, repopulated, and gave direction and strength to a new generation of political and uncompromising, dedicated Jews. An acknowledged and admired scholar and a strong polemicist, the Satmer Rebbe died in New York in 1979.

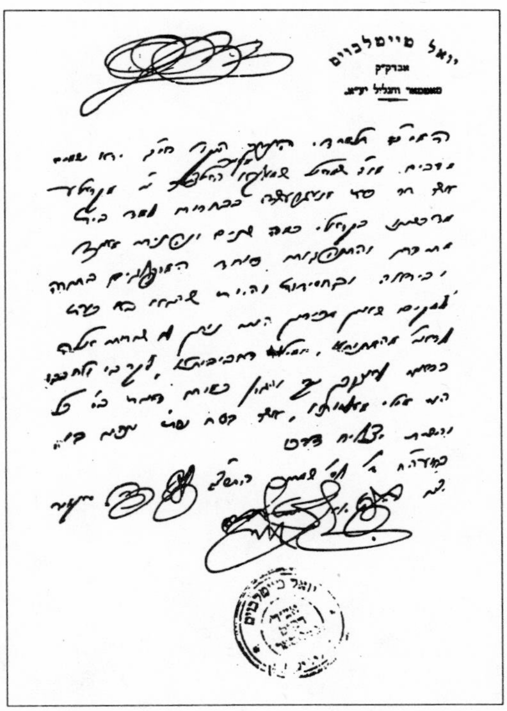

A haskamah, *or letter of endorsement for a book, by Rabbi Yoel Teitelbaum, the Satmer Rebbe.*

II

SCIENTISTS

Science without religion is lame, religion without science is blind.

—Albert Einstein

ALBERT EINSTEIN

"The pursuit of knowledge for its own sake, an almost fanatical love of justice, and a desire for personal independence—these are the features of the Jewish tradition which make me thank my stars that I belong to it."

Albert Einstein's name has come to represent the epitome of intelligence. Einstein forever changed the course of human understanding with his famous and revolutionary theories. In originality, he has been compared to Isaac Newton. A fervent and patriotic Jew, he was also another refugee from German persecution.

Einstein was born March 14, 1879, in Ulm, Germany. As a child, he displayed no signs of gifted intelligence and in fact was often slow at grasping concepts and even slower to speak. Other than a noted early interest in mathematics and music, there was nothing unusual about his academic record. He was educated at the Zurich Polytechnic Institute, receiving his degree at 21, but being unable to obtain a teaching position there, he took an appointment in the patent office at Bern, Switzerland. Since it was not a demanding position, the job left Einstein with the leisure time in which to carry on his own research in physics.

Einstein developed his best-known theories (notably his mass energy equivalence formula, better known as the theory of relativity: $E = mc^2$) between the years 1900 and 1905. In that year he published papers on relativity, the photon theory of light, and the theory of

Brownian motion. He was awarded a Ph.D. that same year from the University of Zurich and four years later became a professor there.

A number of professorships followed, and in 1914 Einstein was appointed to the directorship of the Kaiser Wilhelm Institute for Physics in Berlin. World War I found Einstein at his professional peak, but his personal life had suffered. He had refused to join other intellectuals in the promotion of Germany during the war and had urged an immediate end to the conflict, thus isolating himself from the mainstream of scientists and politicians. In addition, he had divorced his first wife and was separated from his sons.

Fame came to Einstein in 1919, following an expedition by the Royal Society of London. The society, in photographing a solar eclipse, applied Einstein's calculations to determine the exact angle of the deviation of light passing near the sun, thus verifying his general theory of relativity. This created a sensation, and Einstein was offered but refused large amounts of money to write articles, appear in pictures, and endorse commercial products. In 1921 he was awarded the Nobel Prize in physics.

The recognition allowed Einstein to focus on three agendas: (1) continuing his scientific work, (2) supporting pacifism, and (3) furthering the cause of Zionism. He worked for the League of Nations Intellectual Cooperation Organization and publicly spoke out on social issues. Right-wing extremists had already attacked Einstein in speeches and articles, and he knew the anti-Semitism of the national German nature. Not without a wry sense of humor, after the 1919 verification of his theory, Einstein observed: "If my theory of relativity is proven successful, Germany will claim me as a German and France will declare that I am a citizen of the world. Should my theory prove untrue, France will say that I am a German and Germany will declare that I am a Jew."

In 1932, following a brief visit to the United States, and with the Nazis' ascent to power, Einstein resigned his position at the Royal Prussian Academy of Sciences and accepted one at the Institute for Advanced Study at Princeton, New Jersey, where he remained for the rest of his life. He became a U.S. citizen in 1940.

Einstein played a major role in the United States' development of the atom bomb. Following information received by him about the in-progress German uranium project, Einstein wrote to President Franklin Roosevelt about the feasibility and realities of atomic power. In large part because of this letter, the Manhattan Project was created and, through that, the atom bomb.

Throughout his life, Einstein was an ardent Jew. He first met Chaim Weizmann in Prague in 1910, and though the two men were of different scientific disciplines (Weizmann was a chemist) and political leanings (Einstein thought Weizmann a true politico, while Weizmann considered Einstein an impractical idealist) they remained friends. In 1921 Weizmann asked Einstein to join him in a fund-raising tour, seeking money to buy land for Jews in Palestine. Einstein agreed, and the tour was a great success. Einstein visited Palestine and was impressed with what he saw there. He took an active part in Jewish affairs, openly and proudly identified with being Jewish, and was often involved in numerous fund-raising activities. In 1946 he appeared before the Anglo-American Committee of Inquiry on Palestine and gave testimony for the establishment of a Jewish homeland. When the State of Israel was founded, he publicly lauded it as the fulfillment of an ancient dream. Perhaps the highest honor paid to him was upon Chaim Weizmann's death in 1952, when Einstein was asked by David Ben-Gurion to accept the presidency of Israel.

Einstein is remembered for his universally recognized genius, his impact on the science of physics and thus, virtually, the world; his unassuming personality, passion for hu-

manity, generosity of spirit, and pacifist ideals. He wrote both scientific and popular books, including *The Meaning of Relativity*, *On the Method of Theoretical Physics*, *Builders of the Universe*, *Why War?*, *The World As I See It*, and *Out of My Later Years*. A quiet, gentle man, he never forgot that he himself was a refugee, and the reason he was one. When he died on April 18, 1955, he was one of the most respected and embraced men of his generation.

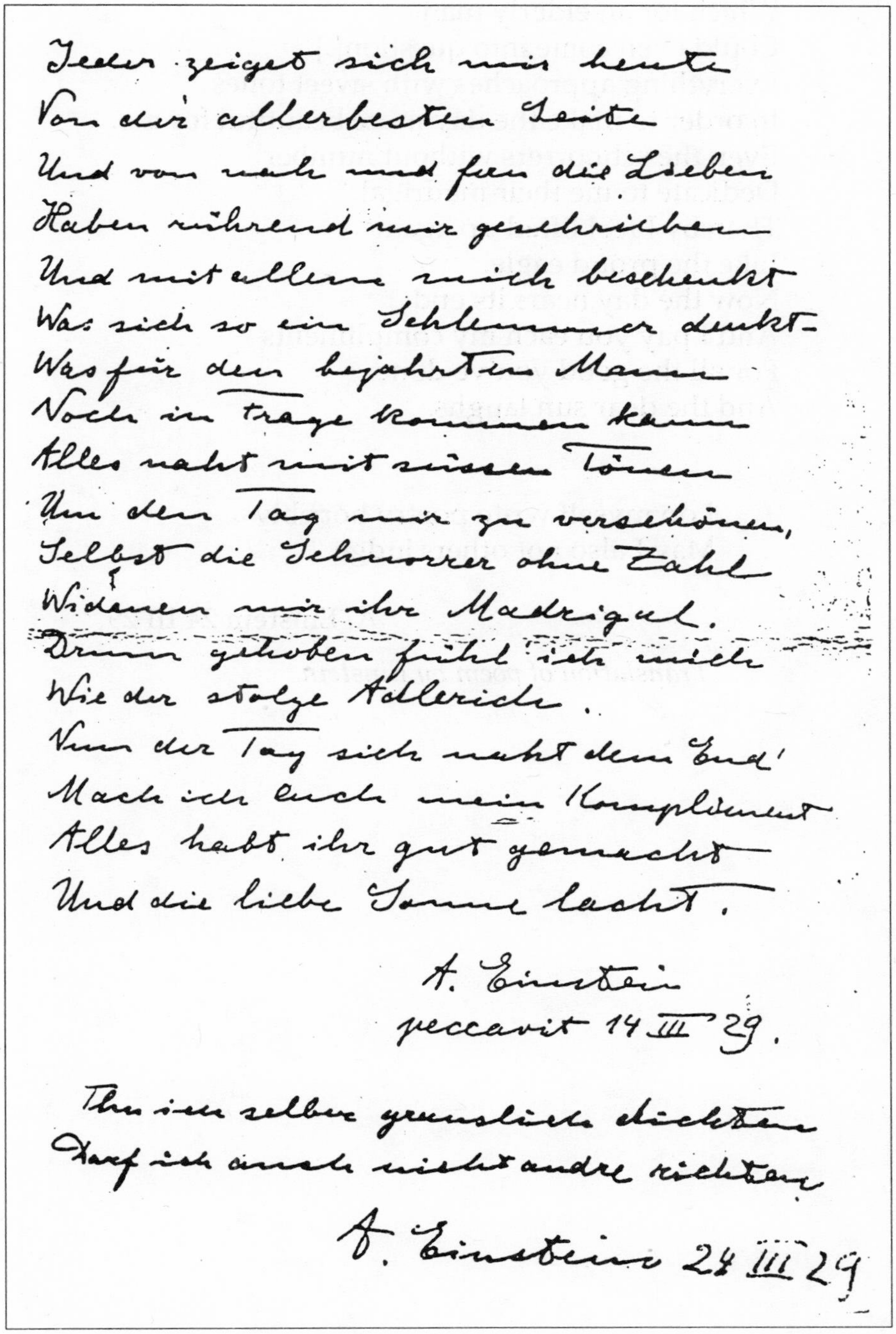

Jeder zeiget sich mir heute
Von der allerbesten Seite
Und von nah und fern die Lieben
Haben rührend mir geschrieben
Und mit allem mich beschenkt
Was sich so ein Schlemmer denkt.
Was für den bejahrten Mann
Noch in Frage kommen kann
Alles naht mit süssen Tönen
Um den Tag mir zu verschönen,
Selbst die Schnorrer ohne Zahl
Widmen mir ihr Madrigal.
Drum gehoben fühl ich mich
Wie der stolze Adlerich.
Nun der Tag sich naht dem End'
Mach ich euch mein Kompliment
Alles habt ihr gut gemacht
Und die liebe Sonne lacht.

A. Einstein
peccavit 14 III 29.

Thu ich selber greulich dichten
Darf ich auch nicht andre richten.

A. Einstein 28 III 29

A handwritten poem by Einstein.

Everyone shows themself to me today
In the very best light
And from near and far the loved ones
Have meantime written me
And they have begifted me with everything
That such a dolt could even think of
Which for an elderly man
Could even come into question[.]
Everything approaches with sweet tones
In order to make the day more beautiful for me.
Even the schnorrers without number
Dedicate to me their madrigal.
Thereby I feel lifted up again
Like the proud eagle.
Now the day nears its end
And I pay you each my compliments
For all the good you've done
And the dear sun laughs.

I do myself write poetry horribly
May I also not others judge.

A. Einstein 24 III 29.

Translation of poem by Einstein.

SIGMUND FREUD

"... It was to my Jewish nature alone that I owed two characteristics that had become indispensable to me in the difficult course of my life. Because I was a Jew, I found myself free of many prejudices which restrict others in the use of their intellect: as a Jew I was prepared to be in opposition and renounce agreement with the compact majority."

Sigmund Freud needs little introduction. As the founder of the discipline of psychoanalysis, he is automatically memorialized.

The son of a merchant and the eldest of seven children, Freud was born in Moravia in 1856. The family moved to Vienna when he was 4 years old. He grew up in an ethnic home, in which he received some religious training and his mother spoke, and knew, only Yiddish. After preliminary and secondary secular education, he attended medical school at the University of Vienna, concentrating on neuroanatomical research. Following graduation, Freud joined the staff of the Vienna General Hospital, where his early medical experiments focused on cocaine as a drug for the alleviation of depression and fatigue. But its effects, including addiction, caused him to abandon this area of research.

At 29, Freud traveled to Paris to study further with the renowned French neurologist Jean-Martin Charcot. While there he observed the application of hypnosis in treating hysterical disorders. This was the turning point that led him to the investigation of hidden psychological factors in abnormal human behavior.

Hypnosis, however, provided only a

temporary state of being, and Freud moved on to develop what would become the foundation of psychoanalysis: free association, in which the patient relaxes and talks about whatever comes to mind. In free association, hints and fragments of unconscious material come out in the patient's conversation. Freud's contribution in this area, as opposed to his predecessors', was to develop a systematic charting of the unconscious.

Freud also gained fame—and ostracism—for his theories involving sex. The id, the superego, the ego, the Oedipus complex, sexual gratification in infancy and childhood, were taboo to the majority of the medical profession. With a core of dedicated students around him, he survived a decade of professional banishment.

Freud's writings and philosophies, which changed over the several decades of his professional life, were extensive. In 1900 he published *The Interpretation of Dreams*, followed by, in 1905, *Three Essays on the Theory of Sex. The Psycho-Pathology of Everyday Life*, *Beyond the Pleasure Principle*, *The Ego and the Id*, *Totem and Taboo*, and *Moses and Monotheism* were all subjects examined by Freud. His career contributions involved three separate but related areas: human development (with a focus on infancy and childhood), personality structure, and techniques for dealing with behavioral disorders (the process of psychoanalysis).

Although not a Zionist or a practicing Jew, Freud was nonetheless well known as being Jewish and had experienced anti-Semitism early in his academic studies. At a time, however, when many Jews were accepting baptism for personal and professional advancement, he was an avowed member of the Jewish community. His wife, Martha Bernays Freud, was the granddaughter of Rabbi Isaac Bernays of Hamburg. Freud himself was active in the Vienna B'nai B'rith Lodge and noted in his autobiography: "My parents were Jews, and I remained a Jew myself." When he was asked once what was Jewish in his teachings, Freud answered, "Not very much, but probably the main thing."

Freud was an inveterate cigar smoker. For the last years of his life, he suffered from prolonged cancer of the jaw and underwent numerous operations, all to no avail. He nonetheless taught and did research until the end. When the Nazis occupied Austria in 1938, Freud's colleagues insisted he leave and helped him get to London. He died there, shortly after the official outbreak of World War II. It has been said that his contributions to the theoretical understanding of mental disturbances and human psychology are without parallel.

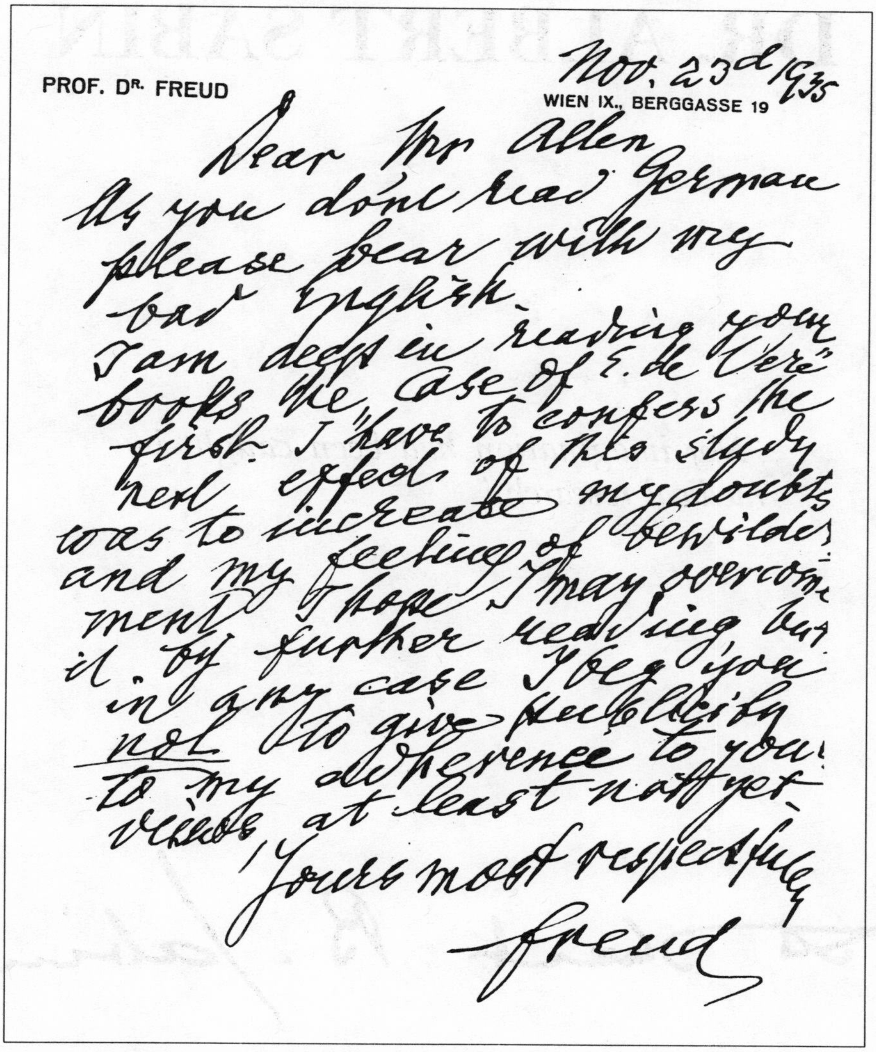

PROF. Dr. FREUD

WIEN IX., BERGGASSE 19

Nov. 23d 1935

Dear Mr Allen

As you don't read German please bear with my bad English. I am deep in reading your books the Case of E. de Vere first. I have to confess the next effect of this study was to increase my doubts and my feeling of bewilderment. I hope I may overcome it by further reading but in any case I beg you not to give publicity to my adherence to your views, at least not yet.

Yours most respectfully

Freud

A letter signed by Freud, dated November 23, 1935.

Dear Mr. Allen,
As you don't read German, please bear with my bad English. I am deep in reading your books, the *Case of E. de Vere* first . . . the next effect of this study was to increase my doubts and my feeling of bewilderment. I hope I may overcome it by further reading. . . . I beg you not to give publicity to my adherence to your views, at least not yet. . . ."

Typed version of Freud's letter to Mr. Percy Allen.

DR. ALBERT SABIN

"My imagination had been caught by medical research."

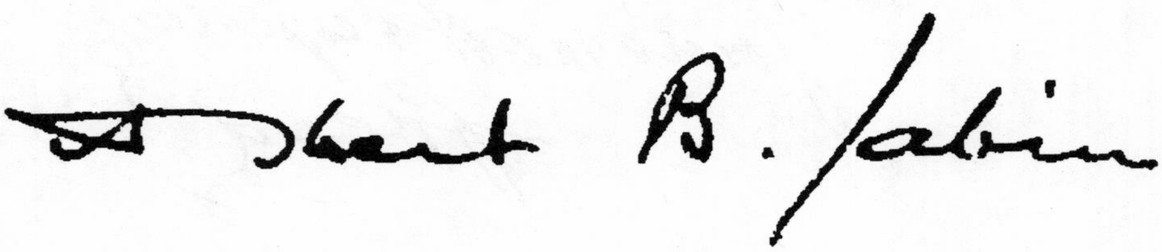

Better known in medical circles than the lay world, Dr. Albert Sabin was a world-famous immunologist, moving in the same circles as his fellow researcher Dr. Jonas Salk.

Born on August 26, 1906, in Bialystok, Poland (then Russia), Sabin's family emigrated to the United States in 1921. Sabin attended New York University, earning his undergraduate degree as well as his M.D. there. As an intern at Bellevue, he did research in isolating virus B, a virus inherent in monkeys and fatal to humans. After his internship, he continued his medical studies in London at the Lister Institute of Preventative Medicine, and in 1935 he joined the staff of the Rockefeller Institute for Medical Research. That was followed by a professorship in pediatrics at the University of Cincinnati College of Medicine, a fellowship at a local children's research hospital, and service in World War II.

Prior to the war, Sabin had begun research on a cure for childhood poliomyelitis. The needs of the military temporarily halted that, but Sabin's knowledge and research in immunology led him to develop a vaccine against dengue fever and Japanese encephalitis in the Pacific theater. Sabin was responsible

for the successful inoculation of more than 65,000 American servicemen. He held the ranks of major and lieutenant colonel.

After the war, he returned to his research in Cincinnati. In 1953 Sabin began testing his vaccine against polio on animals. In 1954 Jonas Salk announced his vaccine and received popular recognition for it. In 1955 Sabin began his testing on humans. Both vaccines were eventually utilized.

Sabin's vaccine involved the more difficult but eventually more beneficial research. While Salk's vaccine was a killed-virus vaccine (a vaccine derived from a dead virus), Sabin's involved a live virus that had been medically deactivated. The benefits of a live-virus over a dead-virus vaccine were several: it was cheaper to manufacture, it could be administered orally, it could be stored for lengthy periods of time, and, most important, it could provide immunity for life. Although his vaccine was nondramatic in America—licensing was delayed until 1961, by which time the Salk vaccine had all but eradicated polio—it was widely used in Russia, where it was administered to more than 90 million people. Overall, his vaccine was considered superior to that developed by Salk.

Sabin published hundreds of academic and medical articles. For his research, he received honors worldwide. He was admitted to prestigious medical societies and received numerous degrees and honors, including the U.S. Medal of Science. In 1970 he moved to Israel, where he became president of the Weizmann Institute of Science. He died in 1993.

מכון ויצמן למדע

THE WEIZMANN INSTITUTE OF SCIENCE

REHOVOT · ISRAEL — רחובות · ישראל

DR. ALBERT B. SABIN
PRESIDENT

ד״ר אלברט ב. סבין
נשיא

May 17, 1970

Mr. Larry Diefenbach
60 North 8 Street
Lewisburg, Pennsylvania 17837

Dear Larry:

Your letter of April 29 addressed to me in Cincinnati reached me in Israel where I am now President of the Weizmann Institute of Science -- one of the foremost scientific research centers in the world.

I hope your interest in Preventive Medicine will continue to grow and that you will ultimately make important contributions to it yourself.

With all good wishes, I am

Sincerely yours,

Albert B. Sabin

Albert B. Sabin

ABS/seo

CABLE ADDRESS: WEIZINST (Israel) :מען למברקים PHONE: 951721 :טלפון

Typed letter signed on Weizmann Institute letterhead by Dr. Albert Sabin.

DR. JONAS E. SALK

"One of man's greatest strivings is to reach into the unknown."

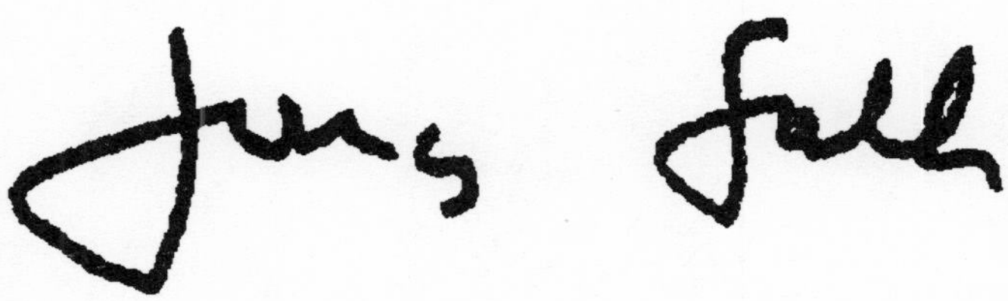

Dr. Jonas Salk has changed forever the nature of disease and its scourge upon mankind. Due to his efforts, crippling polio has effectively been eradicated.

Salk was born October 28, 1914, in New York City, the son of a Russian-born father and an American mother. He attended local schools and universities, receiving his M.D. from the New York University College of Medicine. After a fellowship in epidemiology, he began studies on the nature of the influenza virus, working toward developing a vaccine in commercial quantities. In 1947 he went to the University of Pittsburgh as the director of the Virus Research Laboratory. There, while continuing his influenza studies, he began developing a poliomyelitis serum. The National Foundation for Infantile Paralysis made him director of a three-year project investigating the polio virus.

Finding a vaccine proved difficult. There were three strains of viruses that caused the disease, all of which needed to be neutralized by a vaccine. Building on the research of others (notably the Nobel Prize–winning bacteriologist John Enders, who discovered that

the polio virus could be cultivated using monkey kidney tissue), Salk produced a killed-virus vaccine: a vaccine derived from a dead virus, still having immunization capabilities. He announced its successful experimental use in 1953, one year after a nationwide polio epidemic had struck 50,000 and killed 3,300 children. The National Foundation for Infantile Paralysis began mass vaccinations of school children, and by 1955 the Salk vaccine, as it came to be called, had been proven effective.

Honors and awards were bestowed upon Salk, including the Presidential Citation and the Congressional Medal for Distinguished Achievement. Over the years he accepted several prestigious medical professorships. He was a founder, fellow, and director of the Salk Institute for Biological Studies in La Jolla, California, where he lived. He died in 1995 at the age of 79.

Salk's discoveries and contributions have virtually made his name a household word. Because of the Salk vaccine, childhood poliomyelitis is a conquered disease.

DR. BELA SCHICK

"Children are not simply micro-adults, but have their own specific problems."
—Aphorisms and Facetiae of Bela Schick

For centuries diphtheria was a killer of mass proportions. Striking children usually under the age of 10 in countries with temperate weather, along with measles, smallpox, scarlet fever, and chicken pox, it was still one more disease to be survived. It was an ever-present threat until the efforts of Jewish pediatrician Bela Schick.

A sickly baby himself, Schick was born on July 16, 1877, in Boglar, Hungary. He attended school in Graz, Austria, and was strongly influenced, against the wishes of his father, by his uncle, Dr. Sigismund Telegdi.

Schick received his medical degree from Karl Franz University, following which he joined the medical faculty of the University of Vienna. He stayed there from 1902 to 1918. From the onset of his medical career, Schick was interested in and researched allergies and childhood diseases. In 1913 he successfully announced the third step in conquering diphtheria (the bacteria causing diphtheria and the antitoxin making a vaccine possible had previously been discovered). Known as the Schick test, Schick's procedure was a simple yet conclusive test for susceptibility to the diphtheria virus. Prior to Schick's discovery, there did exist crude serums for immunization purposes, but these yielded such serious side effects that many physicians of the period were

reluctant to use them. Schick's test proved to be a safe and reliable way of eliminating unnecessary and dangerous serum use.

The test made Schick famous at the age of 36, and he was honored for his discovery. In 1923 he came to New York City as guest lecturer at the New York Academy of Medicine. While there he accepted the position of chief pediatrician at Mount Sinai Hospital. He remained at Mount Sinai in that capacity from 1923 to 1942. Schick went on to hold prestigious positions at Columbia University, the Albert Einstein College of Medicine, and Beth-El Hospital in Brooklyn. He was also a founding member of the American Academy of Pediatrics.

Formally retiring at age 65, Schick continued as a consulting physician to a number of hospitals on children's welfare, including neonatal nutrition and feeding. Among the numerous awards, honors, and medals bestowed upon him, Schick received an album of gratitude with the signatures of more than a million children, thanking him for his work on their behalf. He died in New York City on December 6, 1967.

SELMAN WAKSMAN

"I tried my best."

Microbiologist Selman Abraham Waksman not only gave the world medical cures, he gave the English language a new word: *antibiotic*.

Born in the farming community of Priluki, the Ukraine, on July 22, 1888, Waksman grew up in a religious Jewish home. He learned Bible and Talmud from his father and received a primary secular education. Two early events seemed to mold his life: developing a general interest in the earth and watching his sister suffocate from diphtheria at a time when the antitoxin was available in Europe but not in his rural community.

Waksman came to America as an adult in 1910. In 1915 he received a bachelor's degree from Rutgers and in 1918 a Ph.D. from the University of California at Berkeley. After working for several commercial laboratories, he returned to the academic world, where he held two primary positions: as a lecturer in soil microbiology and as a professor of microbiology. For twelve years he headed the division of marine microbiology at the famous Woods Hole Oceanographic Institution in Massachusetts.

In his research over the years with microorganisms, Waksman established two classes: good, which exhibited helpful and beneficial aspects, and bad, which were disease producing and pathogenic. The outbreak of World War II mandated an increased level of medical research to deal with injuries and wounds. Waksman worked with antibacterial substances and coined the word *antibiotic*: "a

substance produced by one organism that kills other microorganisms." In 1943, from the fungus *streptomyces griseus*, Waksman discovered streptomycin, a revolutionary medicine highly effective against a large number of bacteria, particularly those in tuberculosis. He also developed neomycin, which is used topically, and other antibiotics.

Like other groundbreakers, Waksman was lauded with honors and awards, including election to the National Academy of Sciences. He received the Nobel Prize in 1952 for medicine and physiology. The author of several popular and academic books, he died in Hyannis, Massachusetts, on August 16, 1973. Waksman summarized his autobiography, *My Life with the Microbes*, as "the story of the life of an immigrant boy who went from the steppes of the Ukraine to the new world in search of a better education and better opportunities to do what he wanted with his life. . . . I tried my best."

RUTGERS · THE STATE UNIVERSITY

INSTITUTE OF MICROBIOLOGY   October 16, 1963   NEW BRUNSWICK, NEW JERSEY

Dr. Norman W. Drey
15 Vouga Lane
St. Louis 31, Missouri

My dear Dr. Drey:

Your letter addressed to me in Montevideo was forwarded to us here. I greatly appreciate your good wishes. I have recovered quite successfully from the appendix operation and peritoneum infection.

I doubt whether I will be able to undertake very long journeys in the future, although I am planning to go next March to Israel in connection with the Institute of General and Industrial Microbiology that is being planned for the Technion in Haifa.

Mrs. Waksman joins me in sending our kindest regards and best wishes to Mrs. Drey and yourself. Should you have a chance to come to New York in the near future, let us know. Perhaps we could arrange to get together some evening.

Cordially yours,

Selman A. Waksman

Selman A. Waksman
Professor Emeritus

Typed letter signed by Dr. Selman Waksman on letterhead of Rutgers University.

III

SCHOLARS AND PHILOSOPHERS

Learning, learning, learning—that is the secret of Jewish survival.

—Ahad Ha'am

LEO BAECK

"As long as Judaism continues, nobody will be able to say that the soul of man has allowed itself to be subjugated. Its existence through the centuries is by itself proof that conviction cannot be mastered by numbers. The mere fact of Judaism's existence shows that it is impossible to conquer the spirit. Because it has been a minority, Judaism has become a measuring test for the height to which morality has risen upon earth. . . . From Israel's lot men could judge how far they have yet to go until the days of the Messiah."

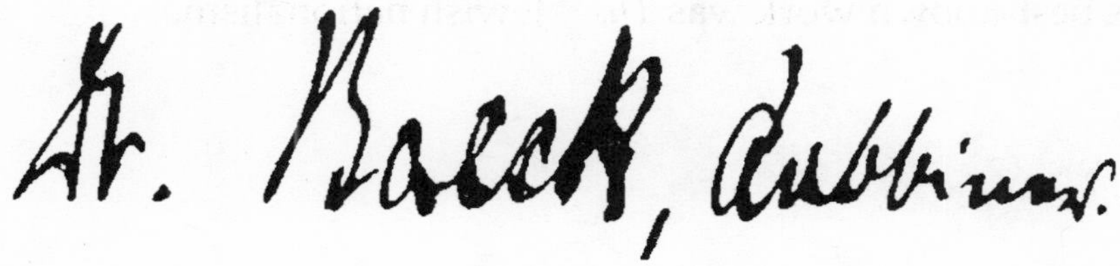

Theologian, national leader, and concentration camp survivor Rabbi Leo Baeck was one of this century's foremost religious figures. To the degree German Jewry survived the Holocaust, a goodly amount of it was due to his courage, leadership, and fidelity to his people.

Son of a rabbi, Baeck was born in Lissa, Prussia (now Leszno, Poland), on May 24, 1873. The name *Baeck* stemmed from the Hebrew *ben kodesh*, a martyr; according to family history, an ancestor in the Baeck family was persecuted and martyred during the Crusades. Baeck's religious and academic background included studies in both Breslau and Berlin, where in 1897 he received his ordination. He held pulpits in several German communities and from 1912 on was a rabbi in Berlin. He served as a chaplain throughout World War I, and in 1922 he became chairman of the national association of German rabbis.

As the Nazis rose to power, Baeck gained national prominence. He predicted that the thousand-year history of German Jewry was coming to an end and in 1933 was appointed chairman of the central committee established to deal with the Nazi government. His courage and leadership were manifestly displayed by his repeated refusal to leave Germany, although he was given the opportunity

on several occasions. He refused foreign appointments as either rabbi or professor, stating that he would remain as long as possible with the last *minyan*.

Baeck was twice arrested by the Gestapo but later released. In 1943 he was deported by the Nazis to Theresienstadt, where he was appointed one of the leaders of the Jewish Council. Baeck was earmarked for deportation to an extermination camp and was saved only through a confusion in names.

After liberation in 1945, Baeck moved to London, where he served as chairman of the World Union of Progressive Judaism and president of the Council of Jews from Germany. In 1948 he moved to the United States. In 1955 the Leo Baeck Institute, a historical and research organization dedicated to researching and documenting Jewish history in German-speaking countries, was founded and named in his honor. Until his death in 1956, he taught at the Hebrew Union College in Cincinnati.

Baeck was a historian of religion and a prolific writer. His best-known work was *The Essence of Judaism*, originally published in 1905 and republished, with a stronger, vastly more assertive tone, in 1936. This was a polemic response to the Protestant theologian Adolf von Harnack's *Essence of Christianity*. Baeck saw the essence of Judaism as morality and distinguished Judaism as a "classic religion," as opposed to Christianity as a "romantic religion." Christianity, Baeck believed, was an "abstract spirit longing for redemption," while Judaism, with its ethical imperatives of man's duties to man, involved the "concrete spirit" seeking earthly improvement: "To be a man means to be a fellowman. The respect we owe to our neighbor is not an isolated commandment but represents rather the whole contents of morality, the quintessence of our duty." Baeck felt that the essence of Judaism was a polarity between the mystery of the Divine and the command of the ethical imperative.

Philosopher, activist, scholar, religious patriot—Rabbi Leo Baeck is revered as a symbol of spiritual resistance, ethical integrity, and Jewish nationalism.

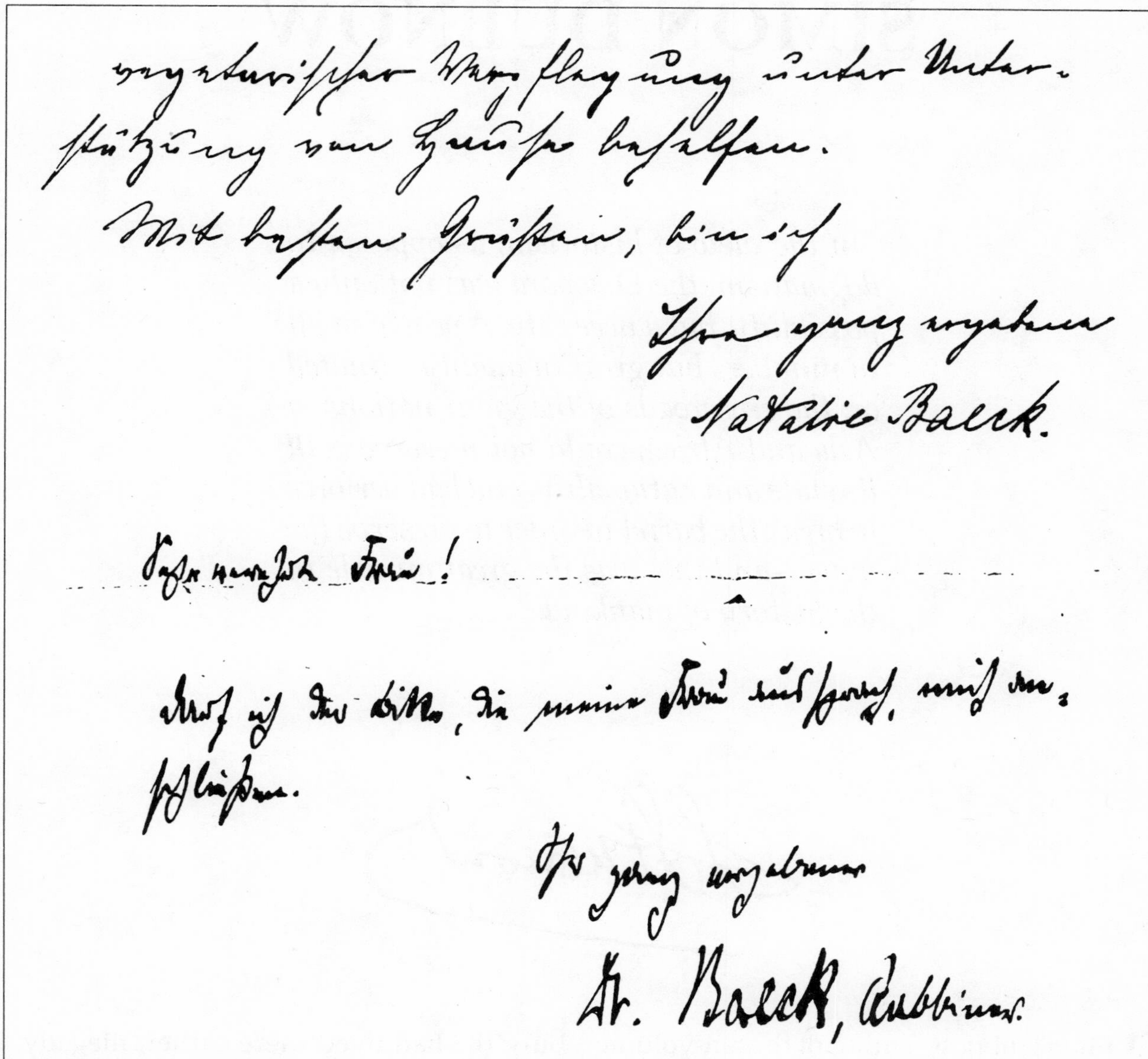
vegetarischer Verpflegung unter Unterstützung von Hause behelfen.

Mit besten Grüßen, bin ich

Ihre ganz ergebene

Natalie Baeck.

Sehr verehrte Frau!

Auch ich der Bitte, die meine Frau ausspricht, mich anschließen.

Ihr ganz ergebener

Dr. Baeck, Rabbiner.

Rabbi Baeck adds a postscript to a note penned by his wife, Natalie, regarding vegetarian meals. This was probably in response to a dinner invitation or for travel arrangements. His addendum is a P.S. to emphasize Mrs. Baeck's wishes.

SIMON DUBNOW

"In the view of historism, as opposed to dogmatism, the Diaspora was not only a possibility, but a necessity. A people small in numbers but great in quality, situated on the crossroads of the giant nations of Asia and Africa, could not preserve both its state and nationality, and had perforce to break the barrel in order to preserve the wine—and this was the great miracle in the history of mankind."

Simon Dubnow, author of the ten-volume *World History of the Jewish People*, is recognized as one of the great Jewish historians of the past hundred years. An ethnic secular nationalist, Dubnow spent his life advocating the recording of Jewish history and its sociological interpretations.

Dubnow was born in Mstislavl, White Russia, in 1860. He received a conventional Jewish education until the age of 11, when he independently became disenchanted with traditional Judaism. He spent his teenage years in Dvinsk, Vilna, and St. Petersburg, seeking secular knowledge. Settling legally in St. Petersburg (he had lived there earlier, illegally, by bribing a clerk for a resident's permit and studying independently at the Imperial Public Library), he divided his time between teaching and journalism. Dubnow taught Jewish history at both the Institute of Jewish Studies and the government-supported Jewish People's University and was a founder and director of the Jewish Historico-Ethnographical Society.

His interpretation of the Jewish people was that they were a continuous "living national organism." This continuum occurred through a historical and ongoing pattern of autonomous Jewish communities wherein he-

gemony occurred: that one community has been more independent, more nationally Jewish creative, and it was that community that was recognized as the Jewish center for a given period. As examples, he proposed Babylonia in the early Middle Ages (taking over the mantle from earlier Palestine), Spain and the Rhineland, and Poland-Lithuania in the 1600s. Dubnow considered Jewish nationality as the highest form of cultural-historical nationhood—a spiritual nation.

Dubnow rejected the martyrdom and literature historiography and introduced the application of the social sciences into the study of Jewish history. He believed that the study of history allowed an understanding of the past, provided for the improvement of the present, and offered a solution for the future of the Jewish people. Dubnow believed, as exampled by the Jews and as was a popular concept of his time, in the "State of Nationalities," which could preserve political empires such as Russia, and Austria-Hungary while satisfying the demands of self-rule for minorities in them. For Jews, he hoped the national religious character would eventually be replaced by a new Jewish secular culture.

Dubnow's ideas (but not his scholarship) placed him in strong opposition to both Zionists and assimilationists. Yet he saw a unique danger to Judaism should the Diaspora countries be emptied of their Jewish populations. Dubnow's extensive writings were well noted for attention to detail. His *History of Hasidism* and *Jewish History: An Essay in the Philosophy of History* reflect this.

In 1922, Dubnow left Russia for Berlin, where he stayed until 1933. With Hitler's rise to power in 1933, rejecting offers to go to America, Switzerland, and Israel, he fled to the Latvian capital city, Riga. There with his wife he continued his work. In July 1941, Riga was captured by the Germans and Dubnow's work was confiscated. On December 8, 1941, while the Jewish community was being rounded up and deported, the 81-year-old historian, sick and febrile, did not move fast enough to satisfy a Nazi guard, and he was murdered.

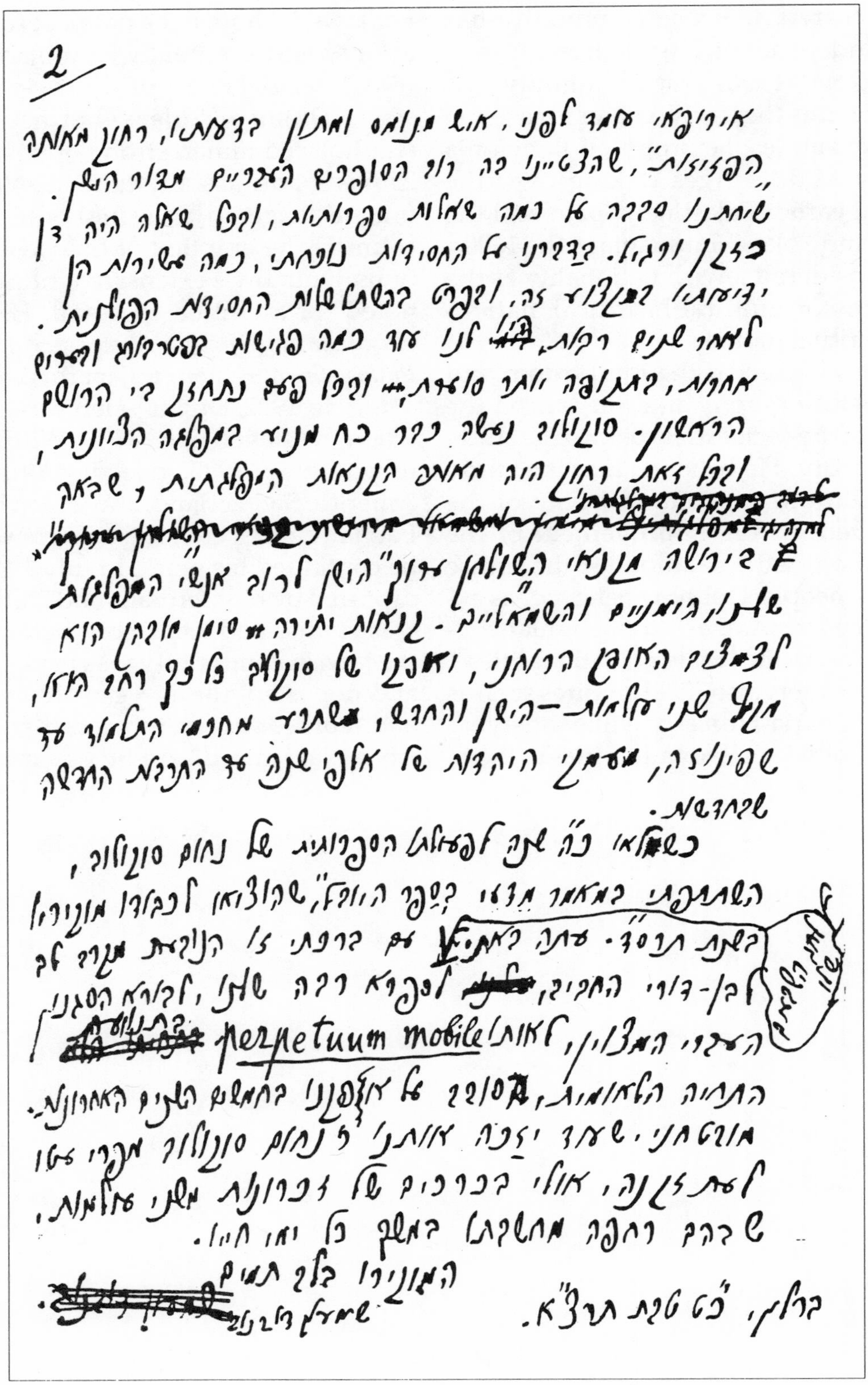
2

אוריגינאלי עומד לפני. אנוש מנומס ומתון בדעותיו, רחוק מאותה
„הפוזות", שהצטיינו בה רוב הסופרים העבריים מדור הישן.
שיחתנו סבבה על כמה שאלות ספרותיות, ובכל שאלה היה דן
בעיון ובהגיון. בדברינו על החסידות נוכחתי, כמה עשירות הן
ידיעותיו בענין זה, ובפרט בראשית תולדות החסידות הפולנית.
לאחר שנים רבות, [illegible] לנו עוד כמה פגישות בפטרבורג ובמדינות
אחרות, [illegible] [illegible], ובכל פעם נתחזק בי הרושם
הראשון. סוקולוב נושא בקרבו כח מניע במפלגה הציונית,
ובכל זאת רחוק הוא מאותה הקנאות המפלגתית, שבאה
[illegible]
בירושה מקנאי „השולחן ערוך" הישן לרוב אנשי המפלגות
שלנו, הימניים והשמאליים. קנאות יתרה [illegible] סימן מובהק הוא
לצמצום האופק הרוחני, ואופקו של סוקולוב כולל רחב מאד,
מקיף שני עולמות — הישן והחדש, [illegible] מחכמי התלמוד עד
שפינוזה, [illegible] היהדות של אלפים שנה עד התרבות החדשה
שנתחדשה.

כשמלאו ס"ה שנה לפעולתו הספרותית של נחום סוקולוב,
השתתפתי במאמר מיוחד בספר היובל, שהוציאו לכבודו מוקיריו
בשנת תרס"ד. עתה כשמלאו [illegible] עם ברכתי לו הנהרות מגיד לב
בן-דורי החביב, לספרא רבה שלנו, לבורא הסגנון
העברי המצוין, לאותו perpetuum mobile בתנועת
התחיה הלאומית, [illegible] על אופקנו בחמשים השנים האחרונות.
[illegible]. שעוד יזכה אותנו ר' נחום סוקולוב מפרי עטו
לעת זקנה, אולי בכרכים של זכרונות משני עולמות,
שבהם רחפה מחשבתו במשך כל ימי חייו.

המוקירו בלב תמים
שמעון דובנוב

ברלין, כ"ט טבת תרצ"א.

Second page of a letter signed in Hebrew by Dubnow.

ABRAHAM GEIGER

"Animated by the breath of complete liberty, constantly more and more imbued with the spirit of science and widening and deepening the view, Judaism of the present will steadily become more and more conscious of its task and strive for its accomplishment . . . to become the religion of mankind. Only that religion which is reconciled with free thought has the justification, but at the same time also, the guarantee of its continuance."

The German theologian Abraham Geiger is considered to have been the most important advocate for religious reform in nineteenth-century Europe. As a most vocal critic of traditional Judaism, his approach was virtually revolutionary; he has been called "a militant reforming theologian and a philologist-historian."

Born in 1810 in Frankfurt, Geiger received both traditional and secular educations. He studied classical and oriental languages at the University of Bonn, from which he received a doctorate (his topic being what Muhammad took from Judaism), and where he became close friends with the Orthodox advocate Samson Raphael Hirsch. In 1831, at the age of 21, he became rabbi of the Jewish community of Weisbaden and immediately began to introduce radical reforms to the prayer service, the prayer book, and the observance of Jewish holidays. He also began publication of the *Wissenschlaftliche Zeitschrift fur Judische Theologie*, a journal dedicated to theological studies and to which leading scholars of the day contributed.

In 1837 Geiger convened the first conference of liberal (Reform) rabbis in Weis-

baden. In 1838 he was invited to become assistant rabbi and a religious judge (*dayyan*) in the community of Breslau, where he remained until 1863. Geiger was a leading personality at the 1846 Reform rabbinical conference held there. In 1863 he accepted the position of rabbi in Frankfurt, and in 1870 he accepted the offer of the same position in Berlin, where he was also the head of the newly established Liberal Rabbinical Seminary (*Hochschule fur die Wissenschaft des Judentums)*. Geiger died in Frankfurt in 1874.

Geiger's approach differed as much as could be from his milieu's traditional Judaism. For example, he introduced a prayer book that omitted any references to angels, resurrection, the chosenness of Jews, the Temple's restoration, the return to Zion, and sacrifices; he introduced sermons in the vernacular (German), the confirmation ceremony, and choral singing; and he rejected the second day of holidays. His personal views were even more stringent. Geiger saw traditional Jewish practices as having lost their validity and lacking aesthetic form, and he defined Judaism as a community of faith but freed from the vestiges of peoplehood, past, ritual law, and dependence on tradition. He wanted to free Judaism from what he saw as its isolation from the rest of the world.

An acknowledged and accepted scholar, Geiger grounded his views in recognized scholarship. His works include *The Original Text and Translations of the Bible in Their Relationship to the Inner Development of Judaism* (1857), *General Introduction to the Science of Judaism* (a series of lectures), *Salomon ibn Gabirol and His Poems* (1867), and *Judaism and Its History* (1864 and 1871). Many of Geiger's reforms were well accepted and his impact is felt to this day.

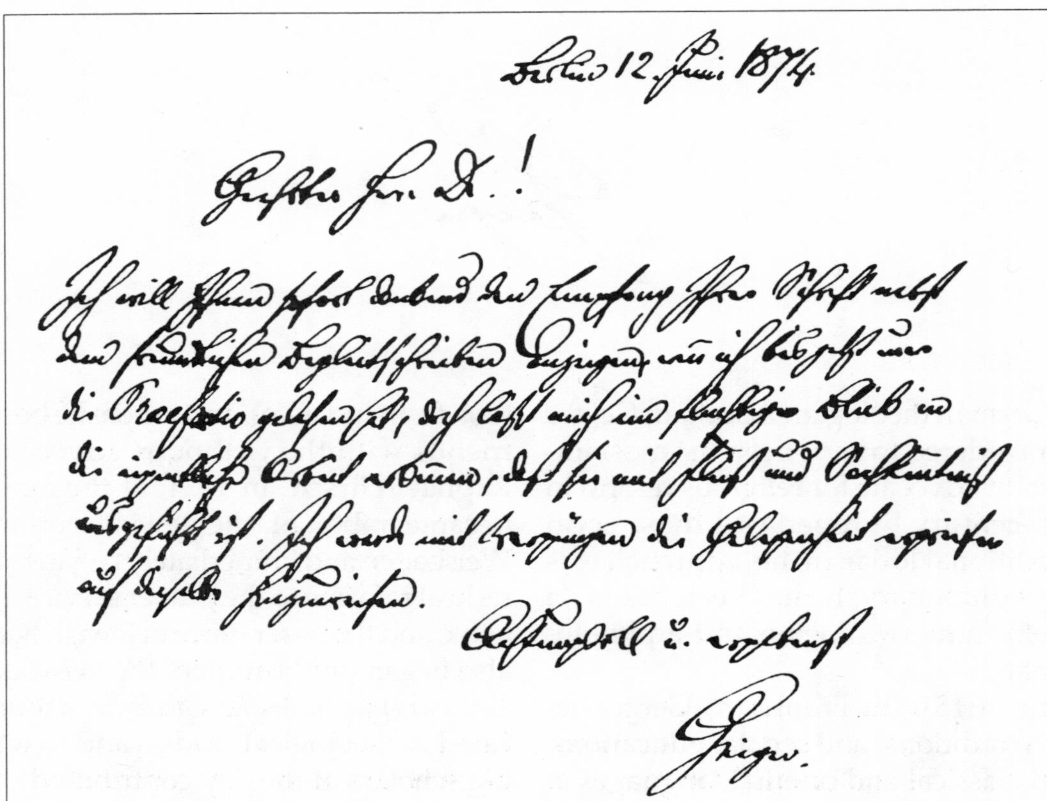
Berlin 12 Juni 1874.

Geehrter Herr Dr.!

Geiger.

Note in German signed by Abraham Geiger.

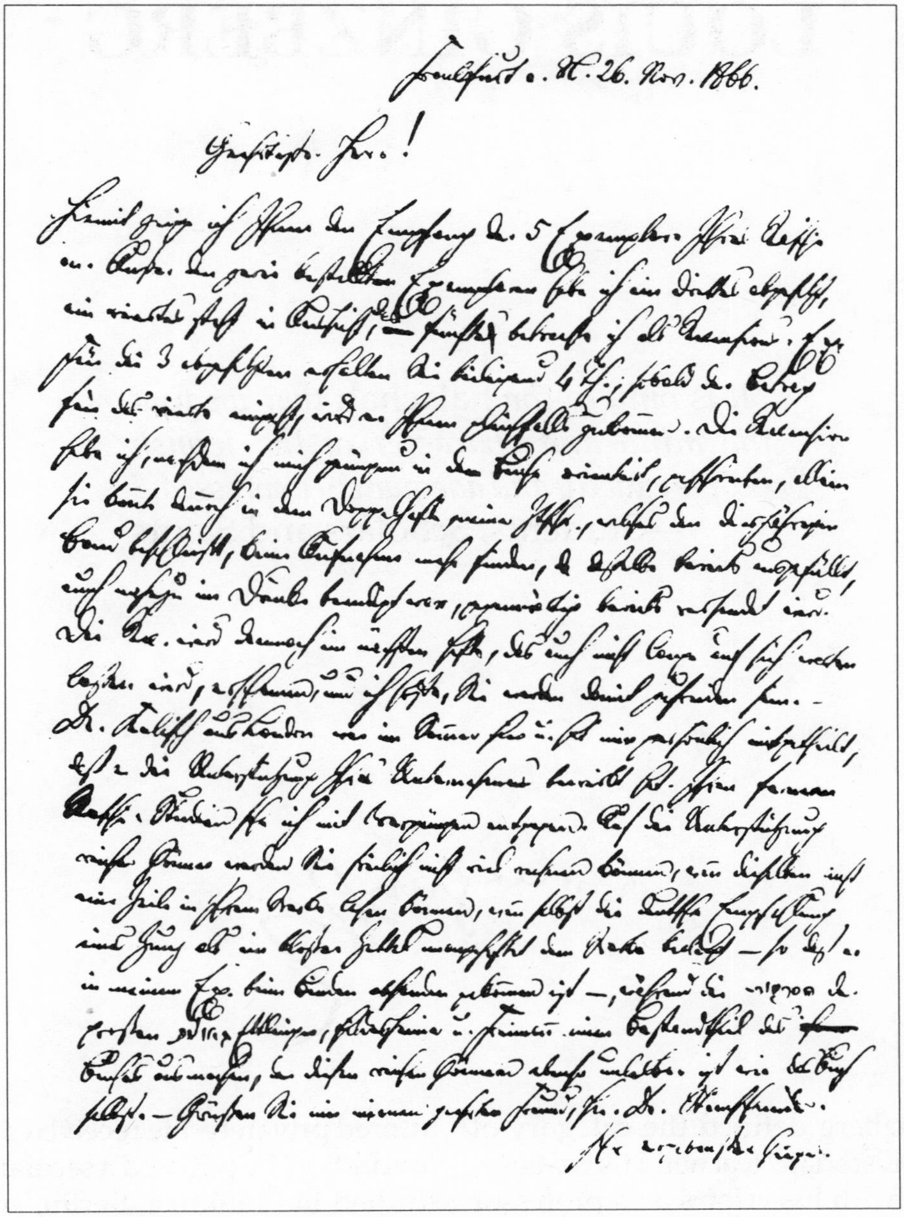

Frankfurt a. M. 26. Nov. 1866.

Geehrtester Herr!

Ihr ergebenster Geiger.

Letter by Geiger.

LOUIS GINZBERG

"It is only in the halachah *that we find the mind and character of the Jewish people exactly and adequately expressed."*
—Students, Scholars and Saints

Louis Ginzberg defined the category of scholar/historian/teacher. His writings, coupled with his efforts as a professor at the Jewish Theological Seminary (JTS) in New York, influenced generations of American Jews and changed the very nature of American Judaism.

Ginzberg was born in Kovno, Lithuania, in 1873, scion of an illustrious Jewish family: his mother was the granddaughter of the brother of the Vilna Gaon (Rabbi Elijah ben Solomon). In terms of education and religious orientation, this marked his future years. Ginzberg attended both the Telz and Slobodka *yeshivot* and was tutored privately. He received *s'michah* in 1894. In addition, he pursued a secular education and studied in Frankfurt, Berlin, and Strasbourg, studying history, philosophy, and oriental languages. He received his doctorate degree in 1898 for his thesis on biblical legends.

In 1899 Ginzberg emigrated to the United States, where eventually he accepted a position with the JTS. His first position at Hebrew Union College, the one for which he had originally come to America, was canceled after school officials discovered that Ginzberg advocated biblical criticism. Before going to the JTS, Ginzberg was the editor of the rabbinic section

of the *Jewish Encyclopedia*, for which he himself wrote an estimated 400 articles.

At JTS, Ginzberg held the position of professor of Talmud for fifty-one years. There he flourished, writing his major works and teaching and influencing two generations of rabbis. (It is estimated that during Ginzberg's tenure—from 1902 to 1951—650 rabbis were ordained, all of whom studied with him.) Working and teaching with Solomon Schechter, Ginzberg virtually helped determine the direction of Conservative Judaism.

In 1920 Ginzberg founded the American Academy of Jewish Research, an organization devoted to stimulating and publishing Jewish studies both in America and abroad. As its president, he was involved in an advisory capacity with the Hebrew University in Jerusalem and its Institute of Jewish Studies. Ginzberg taught there as a visiting professor from 1928 to 1929 and founded its Department of *Halachah*.

A prolific author with an unparalleled memory, Ginzberg researched Cairo *Genizah* fragments and wrote numerous commentaries on rabbinic texts. His writings include *Commentary on the Palestinian Talmud, Geonica, The Significance of the Halachah for Jewish History, Commentaries and Innovation in the Yerushalmi, Petersburg 1789–1950* and *Virginia 1685–1900* (histories of the Jewish communities there), and *Students, Scholars and Saints* (a biography of several great rabbis and leaders). A recurring theme in his writings is that it is not possible to fully understand Jewish history and culture without a solid knowledge of the *halachah*.

Written between 1908 and 1938, the seven-volume *Legends of the Jews* was Ginzberg's major work. This tome is a narrative and historical work of the Jewish people, analyzing Jewish legends and drawing on Bible, Talmud, *Midrash*, rabbinic texts, apocryphal works, Greek and Christian texts, Kabbalah, and other multicultural classics. Written in German, the first two volumes were translated by Henrietta Szold, with whom Ginzberg shared a close friendship. It was republished in an abridged version in 1956.

Ginzberg was elected to the 1905 Seventh Zionist Congress but did not attend, since he did not represent any specific faction. Ginzberg had a lifelong interest in Zionism, but his own efforts and strengths were directed to scholarship and teaching.

On his eightieth birthday, in 1953, the Louis Ginzberg Chair of Talmud was established at the Hebrew University. Ginzberg died that same year. He is remembered in terms of his unexcelled scholarship, his devotion to Talmud, and his leadership as the dean of American scholars.

THE JEWISH THEOLOGICAL SEMINARY OF AMERICA
NORTHEAST CORNER, BROADWAY AND 122ND STREET
NEW YORK CITY

February 12, 1943

Dear Doctor Morgenstern:

It was very kind of you to let me have a reprint of your two articles "Decalogues" and "Demons."

As I am now gradually reaching old age I sometimes become reminiscent. My first acquaintance with higher criticism of the Bible goes back to my school days when I came across Goethe's remark on "A New decalogue." I vividly recollect the great shock I experienced at that time. I am no longer shocked by any theories of higher criticism, as fanciful as they might be.

By the way, the Jews have retained the correct tradition of Lilith as a wind spirit, comp. "Legends of the Jews", V, 87, note 40. On [illegible] comp. ibid, p. 148, note 47.

With kindest regards in which Mrs. Ginzberg joins me,

Very sincerely yours,

Louis Ginzberg

Doctor Julian Morgenstern
Hebrew Union College
Cincinnati, Ohio

Typed letter dated February 12, 1943, on Jewish Theological Seminary letterhead from Louis Ginzberg to Dr. Morgenstern on biblical criticism and the midrashic character Lilith. (*Courtesy of American Jewish Archives, Cincinnati Campus, Hebrew Union College, Jewish Institute of Religion.*)

ABRAHAM JOSHUA HESCHEL

"To pray is to take notice of the wonder, to regain a sense of the mystery that animates all beings, the divine margin in all attainments. Prayer is our humble answer to the inconceivable surprise of living."

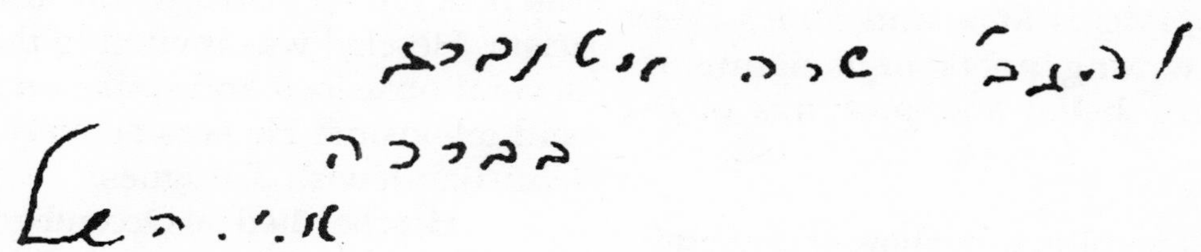

Book inscription by A. J. Heschel.

Abraham Joshua Heschel is considered one of this century's leading theologians. Bridging the gulf between traditional Eastern European learning and piety and modern American philosophies on the rights of the individual, Heschel brought to contemporary Jews a sense of the awe, mystery, and wonder of God and Judaism.

Heschel was born in Warsaw in 1907, scion of a long line of chasidic rabbis . He received an intensive Jewish upbringing combined with chasidic practice. As a child, he was recognized for his maturity, knowledge of classical Jewish texts, and wisdom. Chasidic heritage and position not withstanding, as a teenager he first went to Vilna to pursue secular education and at the age of 20 enrolled at the University of Berlin. He received a doctorate in philosophy in 1933 and also taught at the Academy for Jewish Studies (Hochshule fur die Wissenschaft des Judentums).

In 1937 Buber appointed Heschel as his successor for adult Jewish education in Frankfurt. Heschel was expelled from Germany, however, by the Nazis in late 1938. He returned briefly to Warsaw, then left for London in July

1939, two months before the Nazi invasion of Poland. After a brief stay there, he left for the United States.

Over the next three decades, Heschel taught philosophy and rabbinics at the Hebrew Union College in Cincinnati and, from 1945 until his death, at the Jewish Theological Seminary in New York, where he was a professor of Jewish ethics and mysticism. Along with his philosophical treatises, he wrote on the medieval Jewish philosophies of Saadiah Gaon, Ibn Gabirol, and Maimonides.

Heschel's main efforts have been classified as the study and interpretation of the classical sources of Judaism and the development of an authentic theology based on traditional insights into the problems and questions of the modern Jew. "My major concern is the human condition," he said. "I maintain that the agony of contemporary man is the agony of the spiritually stunted man." Heschel's classical works include *God in Search of Man, Man Is Not Alone, The Sabbath, The Prophets, Who Is Man*, and *Man's Quest for God*. His writing, poetic in its nature, reflects his deep belief and probings of the divine:

> Our greatest problem is not how to continue but how to return. "How can I repay unto the Lord all his bountiful dealings with me?" (Psalm 116:12). When life is an answer, death is a homecoming.
>
> The deepest wisdom man can attain is to know that his destiny is to aid, to serve. . . . this is the meaning of death: the ultimate self-dedication to the divine. Death so understood will not be distorted by the craving for immortality, for this act of giving away is reciprocity on man's part for God's gift of life.
>
> For the pious man it is a privilege to die.
>
> —*Man's Quest for God*

> What we want is not to know Him, but to be known to Him. —*I Asked for Wonder*

> No one is lonely when doing a *mitzvah*, for a *mitzvah* is where God and man meet.
>
> —*Man's Quest for God*

> All of human history described in the Bible may be summarized in one phrase: God is in search of man. —*Man's Quest for God*

Heschel did not confine his efforts to Judaism. In 1965 he marched arm in arm with Dr. Martin Luther King, Jr., in Selma, Alabama, and he participated in rallies protesting American policy in Vietnam. An advocate of ecumenicism, Heschel was invited to the Vatican on several occasions and spoke on Italian radio and television. He was actively involved in Christian-Jewish dialogues.

Heschel died on December 23, 1972. His impact on the two generations he taught has been one of enlightenment, awe, and illumination, and, like other great men of faith, will be felt well beyond this age.

MORDECAI KAPLAN

"From Reform, the capacity to treat Jewish religion as an evolving historical process; from Conservatism, the identification of the Jewish people as a permanent reality; from Orthodoxy, the acceptance of Torah as the Magna Carta of the Jewish religion and as a covenant with the homeland; and from Zionism the concept of Judaism as an all-embracing civilization rooted in the Land of Israel."

Mordecai Kaplan is best remembered as the founder of Reconstructionist Judaism. It was not his original intent.

Mordecai Menachem Kaplan was born in Svencionys (near Vilna), Lithuania, on June 11, 1881, the year that the highly oppressive anti-Semitic "May Laws" were imposed. His family emigrated when he was only 7 to New York City, where his father, Rabbi Israel Kaplan, accepted a position in the New York Rabbinical Court. Kaplan attended both religious and secular schools (including City College of New York and Columbia University). He accepted his first rabbinical position at the age of 22 with the Orthodox congregation Kehilath Jeshurun. However, the rabbinate was not his place, and in 1909 he was appointed dean of the Teacher's Institute at the Conservative Jewish Theological Seminary of America. Rejecting the approaches of Orthodox and Reform Judaism, Kaplan believed that Conservative Judaism needed a new direction. After accepting the role of rabbi, this time with a new synagogue called The Jewish Center, he began to develop and demonstrate his philosophies. Five years later, in 1922, Kaplan founded the Society for the Advancement of Judaism, the embryo of Reconstructionist Judaism.

Kaplan's hopes were for a vibrant,

growing, changing, willing-to-explore Judaism. Among his many innovations were the concepts of worship and leisure activities and the institution of the *bat mitzvah*. Kaplan felt it was essential for the community to feel free to modify rituals as necessary, yet still be within the framework of Jewish commandments and traditions. He saw Israel as a national homeland but believed in the existence of a strong Jewish life outside it, in America as well as in Europe. Kaplan disagreed with the concepts of historical revelation and of God as a "unique, transcendent being," seeing a different, more abstract relationship. Far from being a heretic, however, he understood and pursued the need for the development of Jewish community.

A prolific writer, Kaplan published numerous books, starting with his philosophy of Reconstructionism, *Judaism as a Civilization* (1934). By 1940, the movement had established the Jewish Reconstructionist Foundation, a focal point for the growing offshoot of Judaism. Over the next three decades, Kaplan himself published the magazine *The Reconstructionist*, along with *Judaism in Transition*, *The Future of the American Jew*, *Judaism without Supernaturalism*, *The Purpose and Meaning of Jewish Existence*, *The Religion of Ethical Nationhood*, and several other works, while the foundation published a series of Sabbath and holiday prayer books espousing Reconstructionist philosophy. In 1968 the movement established the Reconstructionist Rabbinical College in Philadelphia, where, from its inception, women were accepted as full students.

Reconstructionism today boasts more than 100 congregations nationwide. On the observance of Kaplan's 100th birthday, the Reconstructionist Foundation issued a statement that, in part, read, "Memories are not enough; Judaism will survive for the next generation only if we give meaning to our experience of it today"—a philosophy that directly mirrored Kaplan's beliefs. Mordecai Kaplan died at the age of 101 on November 8, 1983.

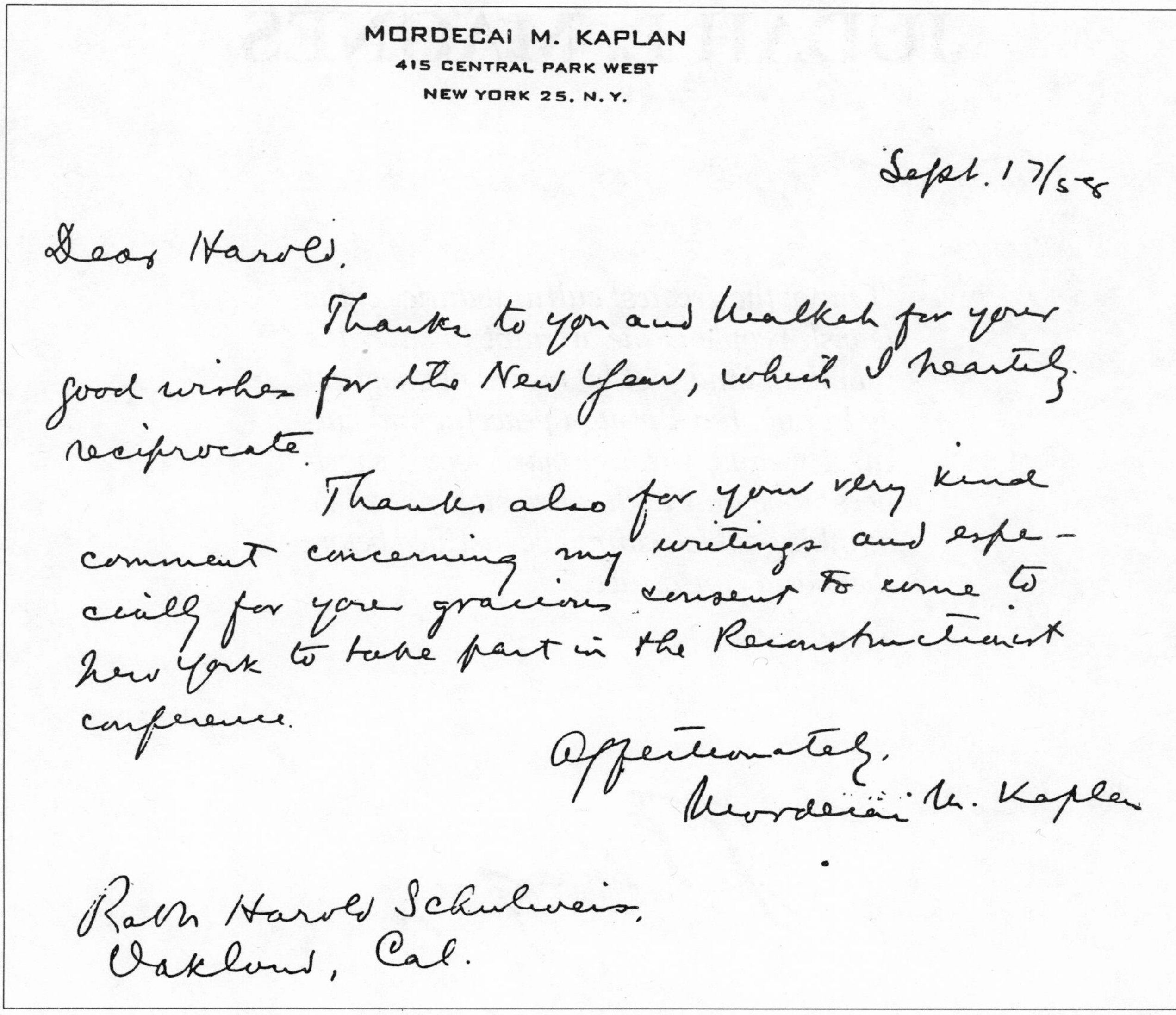

MORDECAI M. KAPLAN
415 CENTRAL PARK WEST
NEW YORK 25, N.Y.

Sept. 17/58

Dear Harold,

Thanks to you and Malkah for your good wishes for the New Year, which I heartily reciprocate.

Thanks also for your very kind comment concerning my writings and especially for your gracious consent to come to New York to take part in the Reconstructionist conference.

Affectionately,
Mordecai M. Kaplan

Rabbi Harold Schulweis,
Oakland, Cal.

Letter from Mordecai Kaplan on personal stationery dated September 17, 1958, to Rabbi Harold Schulweis extending good wishes for a new year and thanking him for attending a Reconstructionist conference.

JUDAH L. MAGNES

"One of the greatest cultural duties of the Jewish people is the attempt to enter the promised land, not by means of conquest as Joshua, but through peaceful and cultural means, through hard work, sacrifices, love and with a decision not to do anything which cannot be justified before the world conscience."

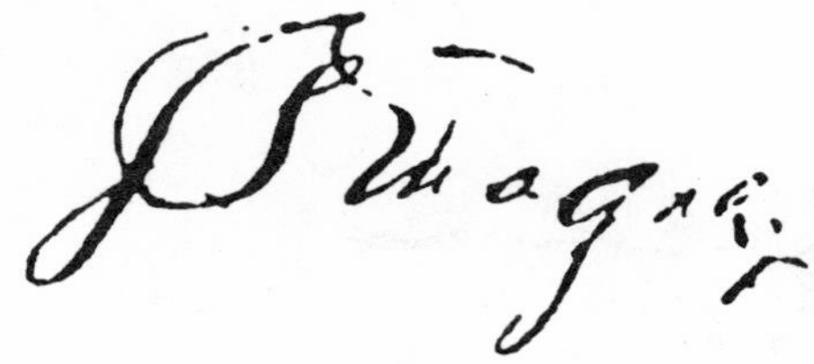

Rabbi Judah L. Magnes, as community leader and founder and first chancellor of the Hebrew University in Jerusalem, was one of the directional forces of Reform Judaism in this century.

The son of Polish and German immigrants, Magnes was born in San Francisco on July 5, 1877. He graduated from the University of Cincinnati in 1898 and was ordained by the Hebrew Union College in 1900. Magnes did postgraduate work in Berlin and in 1902 received his Ph.D. from the University of Heidelberg. He served as librarian at the Hebrew Union College from 1903 to 1904 and in 1904 took his first pulpit.

In 1905 Magnes attended the Zionist Congress in Basel, Switzerland, as a member of the U.S. contingency. Here he met face-to-face with the giants of Eastern European/Russian Judaism and Zionism, and his sympathies for his fellow Jews deepened all the more.

From 1906 to 1910 Magnes was rabbi for New York's prestigious Temple Emanu-El, and in 1908 he also became the president of the Kehillah of New York, a post he held for fourteen years. The Kehillah was an umbrella organization that dealt with issues of Jewish education and religious life. It addressed labor issues and was involved in labor arbitration, while also assisting the police and residents in

immigrant Jewish neighborhoods in combating crime. The Kehillah provided a forum for Jewish public opinion and functioned as an intermediary between "uptown" and "downtown" Jewish factions. Behind it all was Magnes as its leading spokesman, fund-raiser, peacemaker, and philosopher. He was known as a man of conscience who was willing to openly disagree if that were the case.

In 1912 Magnes left the active congregational rabbinate to devote himself to communal work. During World War I, he advocated pacifism, a controversial and generally unpopular stance. He was also active as a founder of the American Jewish Committee, the Joint Distribution Committee, and the New York Board of Jewish Education.

In 1922 Magnes and his family immigrated to Palestine, where he was deeply involved in the establishment and opening of the Hebrew University. Magnes served as its first chancellor from 1923 to 1935 and its first president from 1935 to 1948. He and Chaim Weizmann were granted the university's first honorary degrees.

Magnes's views, one of which was his plan for a binational Jewish-Arab state, differed from those of many mainstream Zionists. One example was his advocacy of the Palestine Jewish population becoming part of an Arab/Near Eastern federation. As a member of several organizations that sought peaceful arrangements between Arabs and Jews, he was a dissenter to the 1937 proposal to partition Palestine. During World War II, while active in rescue efforts of European Jews and directing assistance and relief efforts in the Orient, he also led the opposition to the Biltmore Declaration, a Zionist manifesto demanding a Jewish state. He independently lobbied the U.S. State Department to oppose the official Zionist policy. In 1947 he argued against the United Nations' partition resolution and sought to have President Truman withdraw his support of it.

Magnes died on October 27, 1948, in New York City. Although his pacifism and binational views often put him at opposition to mainstream Zionist leaders, he was acknowledged as a devoted, tireless, driving educator and Zionist spokesman.

PRESIDENT, DR. HARRY [illegible] BALTIMORE
TREASURER, HENR[illegible] JA[illegible]KSON PITTS[illegible]
SECRETARY, J. L. MAGNES. NEW YORK.

CABLE ADDRESS: ZIONISTS.
TELEPHONE CONNECTION.

S' 101a

Federation of American Zionists.

([illegible])

108 SECOND AVENUE.

NEW YORK. Dec. 19, 1907.

Dr. Arthur Ruppin,

Jaffa, Palestine.

Dear Dr. Ruppin:-

Permit me to give expression to my great satisfaction at learning of your definite acceptance of the appointment as head of the Palestine Bureau. I do not wish to write you a long letter at the present time, but wish merely to ask you in what way you and I may be kept in close touch with one another concerning affairs in Palestine. I would very much appreciate an early reply on your part.

Thanking you and with kindest regards, I am,

Yours very truly,

J L Magnes

Secretary.

Typewritten letter signed by Judah Magnes, dated December 19, 1907, on Federation of American Zionists letterhead.

SOLOMON SCHECHTER

"There is something higher than modernity and that is eternity."

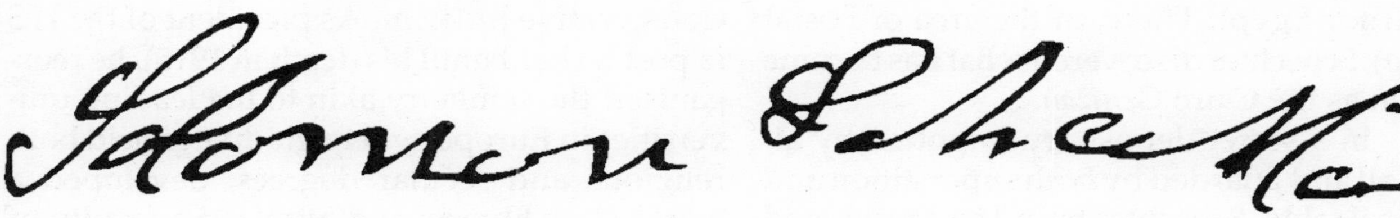

Solomon Schechter is linked with two landmarks in Jewish history: the scholarly retrieval of ancient documents from the Cairo *Genizah* and the founding of Conservative Judaism in America. Schechter was that rare blend of the old and the new, an Eastern European talmudist and a contemporary theologian of the twentieth century.

Schechter was born in 1849 in the village of Foscani, Romania, the son of a *Chabad chasid*. He was named after the Sect's founder, Shneur Zalman of Liadi, and was raised in a traditional chasidic manner. As a child, he ran away to a neighboring village to study at a *yeshivah*. Through his teens and to the age of 25, he studied, under rabbinic masters and independently, and learned at various *yeshivot*. Following his studies at the Rabbinical Seminary of Vienna, he went to the Academy for Jewish Science in Berlin, where he also attended the university there. A whole new world of academics was opened to him, including the scientific method of study. Schechter admired Leopold Zunz and planned to spend his life researching and studying Judaism.

Fate intervened in 1882 when the English scholar Claude Montefiore, grandnephew of Sir Moses Montefiore, asked Schechter to come to England and be his tutor in rabbinic literature. Schechter consented, and the young Montefiore

soon found himself dazzled by the intellect of the newcomer from Eastern Europe. Just as Schechter opened up the world of rabbinic literature for Montefiore, so Montefiore, by bringing Schechter to England, opened up the world for him.

Schechter's brilliance and passion were quickly recognized, and he became a leading figure in Jewish scholarship and traditionalism. In 1890 he was appointed lecturer in talmudics at Cambridge and later rabbinic theology. In 1899 he became professor of Hebrew at University College, London.

It was during this time that Schechter first became involved in history in the making. In 1896 two Englishwomen brought to Schechter fragments of ancient Hebrew manuscripts they had acquired in Egypt. With his encyclopedic knowledge, Schechter recognized them as part of the lost Hebrew Book of Ecclesiasticus, previously known to exist only in Greek translations, and a fragment of the rare Jerusalem Talmud. He was intrigued and soon set off for Egypt. There, in the area of Fostat (Cairo), Schechter discovered what has become known as the Cairo *Genizah*.

In a secret depository forgotten by almost all and guarded by both superstition and the local rabbi, Schechter found and recovered an unbelievable cache of manuscript pages dating as far back as the eighth century. For six weeks he examined the *Genizah*, while documents literally crumbled under his feet. He later wrote, "*For weeks and weeks I had to swallow the dust of centuries, which nearly suffocated and blinded me. I am now under medical treatment. . . . Looking over the mass of fragments in the sifting of which I am occupied, I cannot overcome a sad feeling that I shall hardly be worthy to see all the results which the* Genizah *will add to our knowledge of Jews and Judaism.*" Among the treasures were the previously unknown Hebrew text of Ben Sira (published as The Wisdom of Ben Sira); a holographed and autographed manuscript by Maimonides; ancient Palestinian, Babylonian, and Spanish liturgical poetry; The Covenant of Damascus, a manuscript about the Jews who left Judah and went to Damascus; and other one-of-a-kind historical, theological, and rabbinic documents.

Schechter was able to bring back to Cambridge the majority of the contents of the *Genizah*—more than 100,000 pieces—and there spent years identifying, classifying, and categorizing them. Many eras of little-known Jewish history were filled in. Fifty years later, the discovery of the Dead Sea Scrolls of Qumran validated Schechter's original analyses of what many of the documents were.

After years of examining the Cairo *Genizah*'s contents and teaching and leading the Jewish community at Cambridge, Schechter left England in 1902. At the invitation of American Jewish leaders, he became head of the developing Jewish Theological Seminary (JTS) in New York, the leading institution of Conservative Judaism in the United States. In this role, Schechter was also to become the architect of Conservative Judaism. As president of the JTS (a post he held until his death in 1915), he reorganized the seminary akin to the leading universities in Europe, where graduates held both religious and secular degrees; developed a world-class library; and attracted a faculty of renowned scholars. Schechter steered a course between European Orthodoxy and German Reform, seeking to yoke piety with scholarship and religious flexibility. He established a teachers' seminary and the United Synagogue of America. Under Schechter, the JTS became the core of national revival and Jewish intellectualism and learning.

Schechter was not opposed to flexibility in the doctrines and practice of Judaism. He viewed Judaism as a "living organism" that can evolve from period to period, but evolving on unchangeable teachings. Schechter coined the term "the collective conscience of Catholic Israel," Catholic Israel being his translation of the Hebrew *K'lal Yisrael*, meaning the

Jewish nation as a whole determines choice and change.

A firm believer in Zionism, Schechter attended the 1913 Congress in Vienna. He was elected an honorary president of the Hebrew language and culture. A firm believer in Zionism himself (his twin brother lived in a *kibbutz* in Palestine), Schechter was an academic and scholar but not a pioneer. Having met Ahad Ha'am, Schechter believed in Ha'am's cultural Zionism. But his own tasks were education and scholarship.

Schechter died in New York City, on November 19, 1915. He brought to the Jewish people a wealth of scholarship, discovery, and leadership. American Judaism would not be what it is today had it not been for Solomon Schechter.

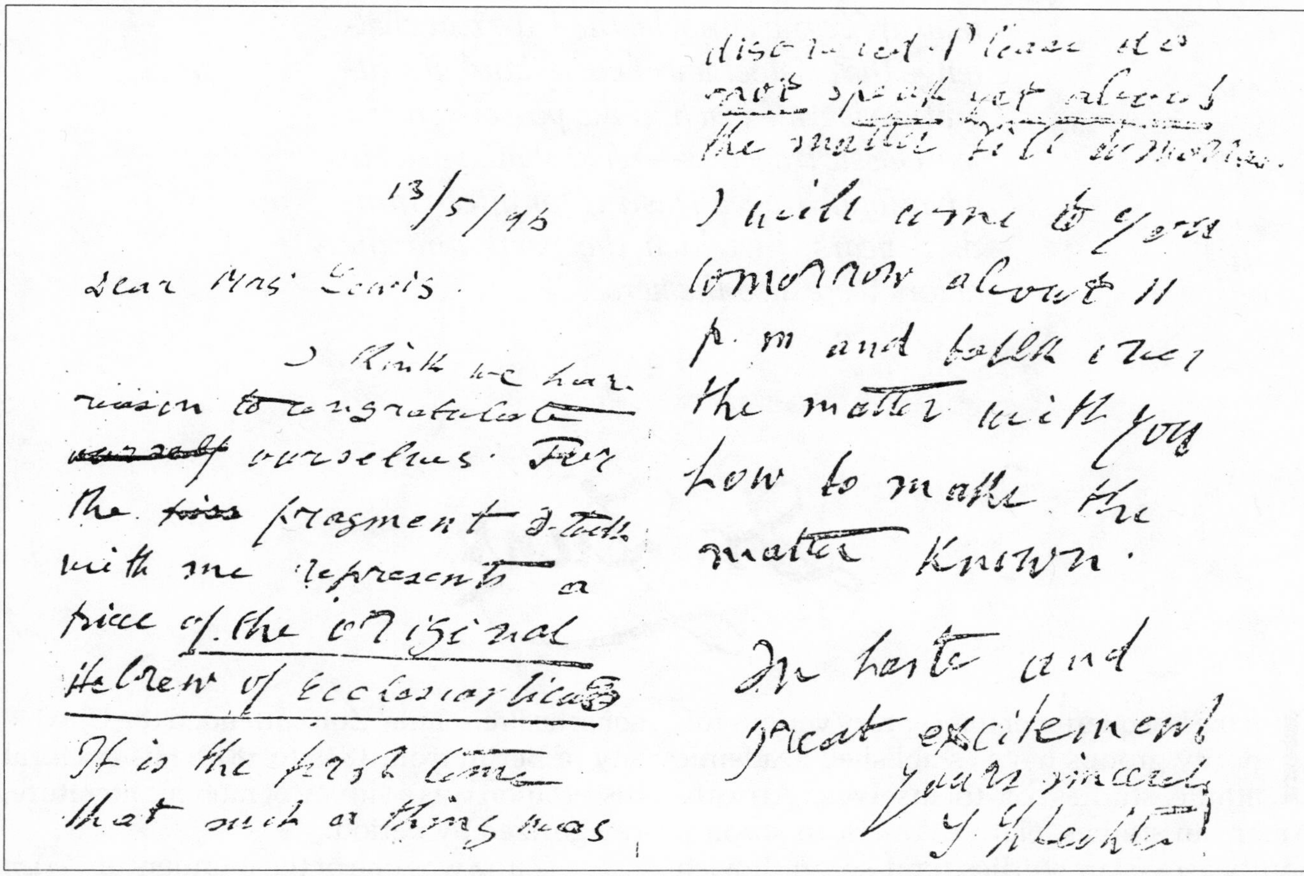

13/5/96

Dear Mrs Lewis.

I think we have reason to congratulate ~~myself~~ ourselves. For the ~~first~~ fragment I took with me represents a piece of the original Hebrew of Ecclesiasticus. It is the first time that such a thing was discovered. Please do not speak yet about the matter till tomorrow. I will come to you tomorrow about 11 p.m and talk over the matter with you how to make the matter known.

In haste and great excitement

Yours sincerely

S. Schechter

May 13, 1896, note signed by Solomon Schechter discussing the finding of a fragment of the original Hebrew of Ecclesiasticus.

LEOPOLD ZUNZ

"If there are ranks in suffering, Israel takes precedence of all the nations; if the duration of sorrow and the patience with which they are borne ennoble, the Jews can challenge the aristocracy of every land; if a literature is called rich in the possession of a few classic tragedies—what shall we say to a National Tragedy lasting for fifteen hundred years, in which the poets and the actors were also the heroes?"

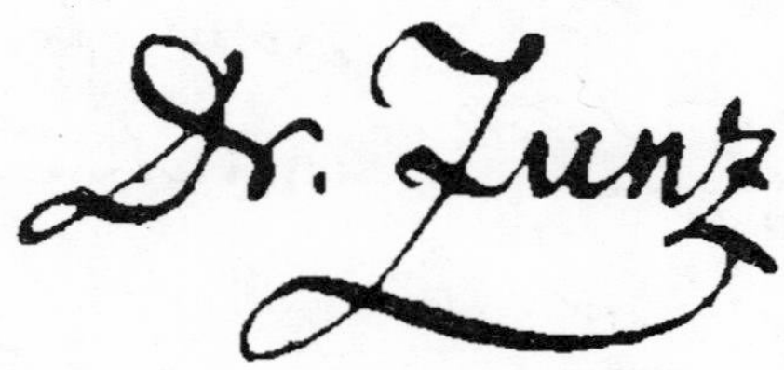

In the last quarter of this century various minority groups have established academic ethnic studies of themselves: African-American studies, Native American studies, Southeast Asian studies, and so on. Jewish studies is also a curriculum. But Jewish studies was first academically addressed by Dr. Leopold Zunz in the nineteenth century.

Born in Detmold, Germany, in 1794, Zunz was one of the pioneers of scientific Jewish studies. As a child, he showed early independence and secretly studied Hebrew grammar. His strong scholasticism brought him to the local high school. Following graduation he worked as an assistant teacher at the Samsonsche Freischule. Zunz attended the University of Berlin from 1815 to 1819. His doctoral dissertation was a survey of rabbinic literature, categorized by period.

Zunz was one of the founders of *Verien fuer Cultur und Wissenscahft der Juden*, the Society for Jewish Culture and Science, in 1819. The society, a response to anti-Jewish riots, proposed to investigate the nature of Judaism by contemporary scientific methods. The purpose of this was to bring out the universal value of Jewish culture and fight stereotypes of Jews as being inferior. Zunz's focus was on Jewish literature and history.

It was inappropriate to restrict and

separate Jewish literature from general culture, Zunz argued. Jewish literature supplemented general culture, and there was a mutual influence of each upon the other. Jewish literature dealt not only with law but with natural sciences, the humanities, and the whole array of the human experience. Zunz's scope of Jewish literature began with the Torah and continued through the Enlightenment and religious reformers.

Beginning in 1820 Zunz delivered sermons at various synagogues and institutions. In 1832 he wrote "Sermons of the Jews," which was a defense against a royal Prussian decree that forbade Jews from preaching in the vernacular. This essay presented historical evidence that Jews had indeed preached in the dozens of vernaculars they spoke wherever they lived. In 1834 Zunz gave a series of public lectures on the Psalms and served as a preacher to a private Jewish religious association in Prague. In 1836 he was commissioned by the Berlin Jewish community to write a treatise on Jewish names. This was in response to a royal decree banning the use of German first names by Jews; Zunz's study showed that Jews had always used foreign names.

In 1840 Zunz was appointed as director of the Berlin Jewish Teachers' Seminary, a position he held for ten years, after which the community granted him a lifelong stipend. For the remainder of his life, until his death in 1886, Zunz continued to write and preach. The contributions he made showed that Jewish literature and history are an integral part of the human story. His application and development of scientific methods found an answer to the problems of previously traditional Jewish religious life and learning to modern Western knowledge and understanding of the Jew.

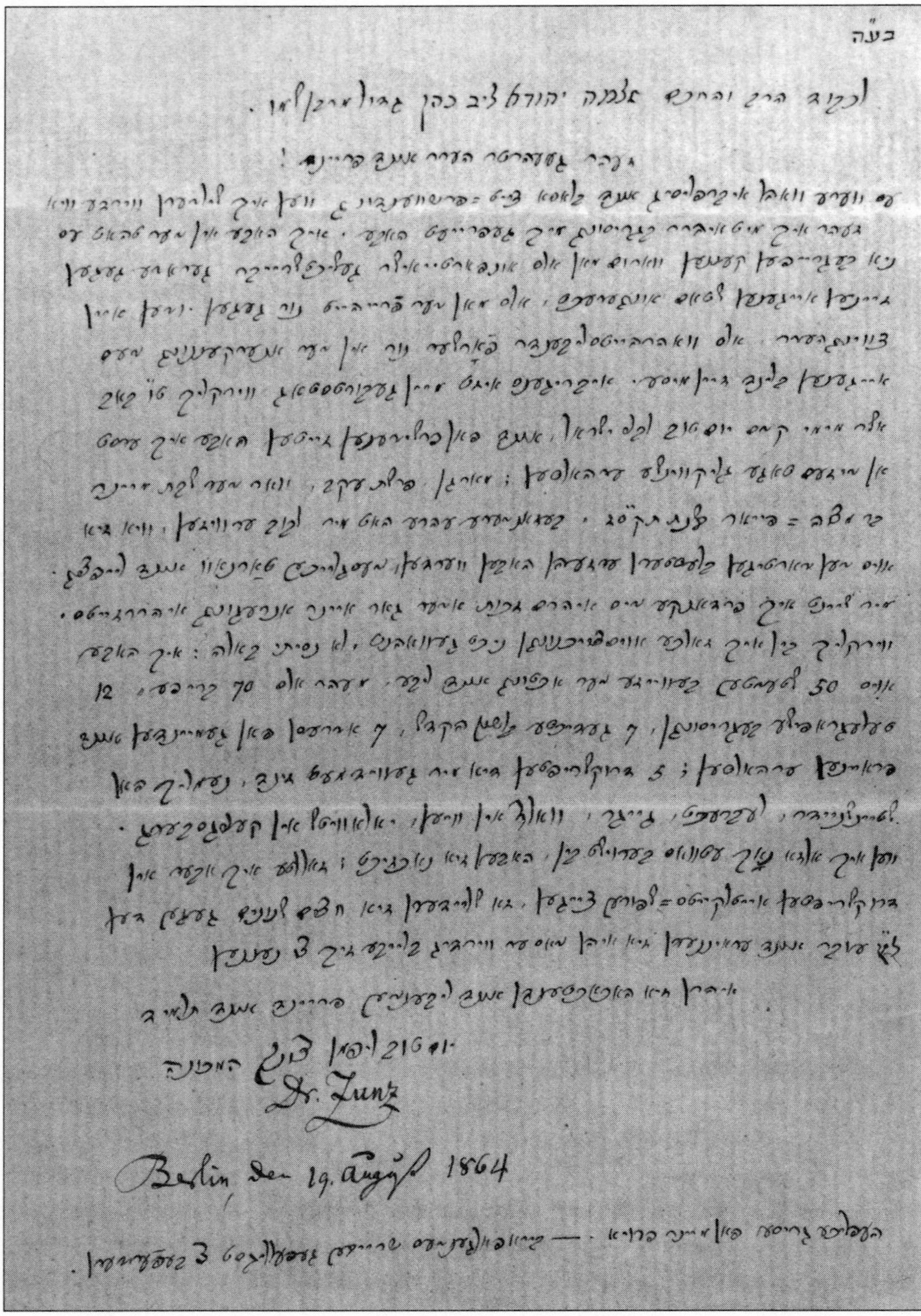

בעה

Dr. Zunz

Berlin, den 19. August 1864

Letter signed by Zunz. (Photograph by Suzanne Kaufman.)

IV

ZIONISTS

When Lord James Arthur Balfour asked Chaim Weizmann why he was against the Uganda Plan, the younger man, with some effrontery, asked Balfour whether, if he were offered Paris, he would abandon London. "No, but London is the capital of my country." Weizmann replied, "Jerusalem was the capital of our country when London was a marsh."

DAVID BEN-GURION

"I'm living in a house and I know I built it. I work in a workshop which was constructed by me. I speak a language which I developed. And I know I shape my life according to my desires by my own ability. I feel I am safe. I can defend myself. I am not afraid. This is the greatest happiness a man can feel—that he could be a partner with the Lord in creation. This is the real happiness of man—creative life, conquest of nature, and a great purpose."

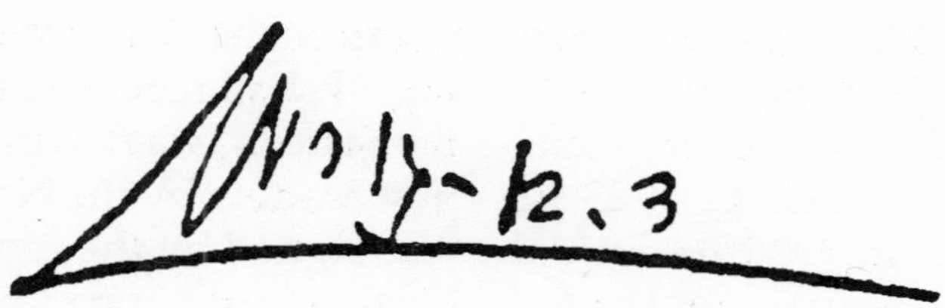

Visionary and realist, pioneer, patriot, and prime minister, the name David Ben-Gurion and the political State of Israel are inseparable. David Ben-Gurion was one of the creators of the State of Israel for forty years before its statehood, at the birth of its statehood, and for almost twenty years after its creation.

Born David Gryn (Green) in 1886 in Plonsk, Russia, he received from his father, Avigdor, a love for and belief in Zionism. Even as a boy he showed political leanings and organized the Ezra Society to encourage the study of Hebrew and Zionist ideology. At the age of 18, he was a founder of the Zionist Socialist Party—*Poale Zion* (Workers of Zion)—in Poland. In 1906, at the age of 20, he immigrated to Palestine, where he became an agricultural worker and watchman.

It was during these years that his political beliefs were translated into an actual physical love of labor. "The settlement of the land is the only true Zionism," he maintained. He continued his political work and was one of the founders of *Poale Zion* in Palestine. The party's agenda emphasized the need for Jewish labor and defense, the revival of Hebrew as the national language, and the creation of a just, equal, and progressive state. In 1910 Gryn moved to Jerusalem, working as an editor,

political writer, and speaker, and hebraized his name as Ben-Gurion, "Son of a Lion Cub."

In 1913 Ben-Gurion went to Turkey to study law at the Ottoman University. His studies were cut short, however, with the advent of World War I and his expulsion from Palestine for "subversive Zionist activities." He then went to New York, where he wrote, did Zionist political campaigning, and advocated the establishment of a Jewish Legion within the British army for the purpose of liberating Palestine from the Turks. In 1917 he married fellow *Poale Zion* member and nurse Paula Munweis. When a Jewish Legion was formed, he returned to Palestine in a British army uniform in June 1918.

Through the 1920s and 1930s, Ben-Gurion expanded his political roles in a variety of undertakings and established himself as one of the foremost Jewish leaders, always pressing the concept of a united workers' movement to prepare for the not-too-distant years of mass immigration and settlement of a liberated Jewish state. In 1920 he was a charter founder of Histadrut, the General Federation of Trade Unions, and served as its secretary general from 1921 to 1935. In 1923 he visited the Soviet Union. In 1930 he united Histadrut with the new Mapai, or United Workers Party, the dominant political party from 1930 to 1977. In 1935 he became the chairman of the Jewish Agency, the international arm of the World Zionist Organization. He held that position until 1948.

Along with Chaim Weizmann and Moshe Sharett, Ben-Gurion played a leading role in the establishment of the State of Israel. At the May 1939 Round Table Conference in London, the British government issued the Palestine White Paper, limiting Jewish immigration to Palestine and effectively banning the sale of land to Jews there. When World War II erupted four months later, Ben-Gurion declared, "We shall fight the white paper as though there was no war, and we shall fight the Nazis as though there was no white paper." During the war years, he was involved in political and diplomatic efforts in New York, London, and Washington. When World War II ended, the butchered remnant of European Jewry looked to their Jewish brothers in Palestine for help. And the Jews in Palestine were determined to create a sovereign Jewish state.

In 1946 Ben-Gurion assumed leadership of the Jewish Agency's defense portfolio and began preparing the *Haganah* for fighting a War of Independence. When the actual war broke out in December 1947, Ben-Gurion headed the defense efforts, organized the raising of financial support and acquiring arms, and prepared actual operations plans. Ben-Gurion also had to deal with, and incorporate, opposing but fellow Jews in semiautonomous military units. His successful accomplishment of this paved the way for the future Israeli army. On May 14, 1948, despite strong international political pressure, Ben-Gurion announced the Declaration of Independence, saying, "I shall read you the Foundation Scroll of the State of Israel, which has been approved in first reading by the National Council." After it was signed by the representatives there, Ben-Gurion further proclaimed, "The State of Israel has arisen. This session is closed."

Ben-Gurion was appointed both prime minister and minister of defense of the provisional government. War broke out immediately with the adjacent Arab states, and under his leadership Israel waged its first successful war on four separate fronts. In 1949, after the first elections were held, Ben-Gurion was officially elected prime minister. As in the British system, the prime minister of Israel is the actual chief of state; the presidency carries considerably less authority. Also in 1949, Ben-Gurion declared Jerusalem the capital of Israel. He formed a coalition government, setting the pattern for future governments, when no one party obtained a

majority vote. He was again elected prime minister in 1951.

Over the next fourteen years, both in and out of office, he continued to lead the emerging nation, focusing on strengthening the military, developing civilian control over the armed forces, and working internationally to gain support for Israel's struggle to remain independent. Ben-Gurion personally influenced the very character of Israel. He emphasized the need to gather to Israel all Jewish exiles worldwide, introduced free education, clarified the need for military service, and placed much emphasis on science and research in the development of the country.

His first retirement was in 1953, after almost fifty years in politics. He and his wife joined the *kibbutz* Sde Boker in the Negev, where Ben-Gurion expected to spend the remainder of his life reading, studying, writing letters, essays, and articles, and working on his biography. However, history had other plans for him, and with the 1956 war with Egypt looming, he was called out of retirement to take over the positions of prime minister and minister of defense. Under his leadership, Israel's second national war was fought successfully. Ben-Gurion negotiated terms of peace with Great Britain, France, the Soviet Union, and the United States, including shipping rights through the Suez Canal.

Ben-Gurion again retired from office but was in and out of government. In 1963, at age 77, he officially retired to Sde Boker. There he received a steady stream of visitors, from writers to world politicians to students.

In 1968, his wife, Paula, died. She had been his greatest supporter and his most devoted and dedicated helper. Ben-Gurion died five years later at the age of 87. He was buried beside her in a simple grave at Sde Boker.

Ben-Gurion—Zionist, farmer, politician, diplomat, orator—helped to shape the State of Israel. His wife summarized him when she said: "Anyone can be prime minister of Israel, but there is only one man who can be Ben-Gurion."

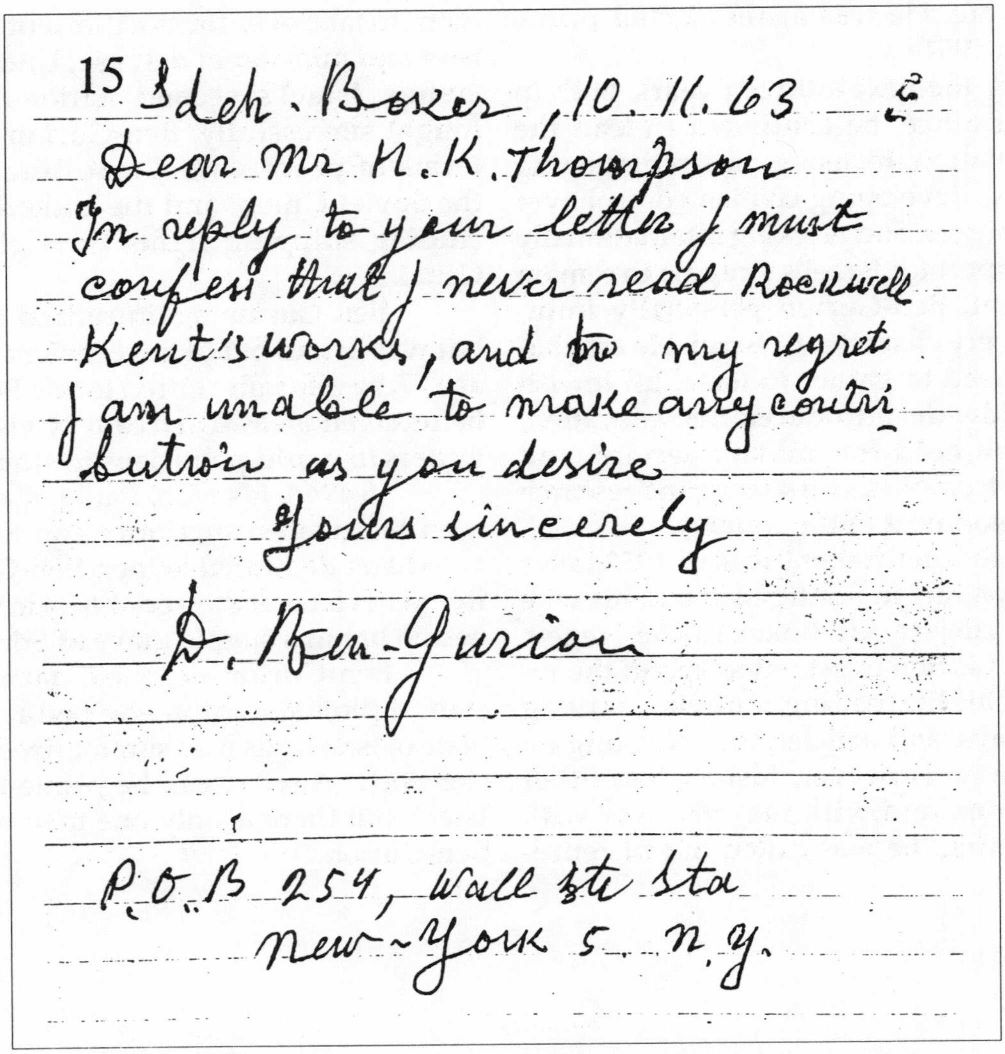
15 Sdeh. Boker, 10.11.63

Dear Mr H.K. Thompson

In reply to your letter I must
confess that I never read Rockwell
Kent's works, and to my regret
I am unable to make any contri
bution as you desire

Yours sincerely

D. Ben-Gurion

P.O.B 254, Wall Str Sta
New-York 5 N.Y.

David Ben-Gurion autographed letter in English.

YITZCHAK BEN-TZVI

> *"At that moment [while giving a speech] I asked myself, 'Why am I here and not in Jerusalem? Why are all of us here and not there?' By the time I had finished my speech, I reached a decision. My place was in the Land of Israel. I had to go there and dedicate my life to its rebuilding at the earliest possible moment."*
>
> —*Reflections on a 1905 speech*

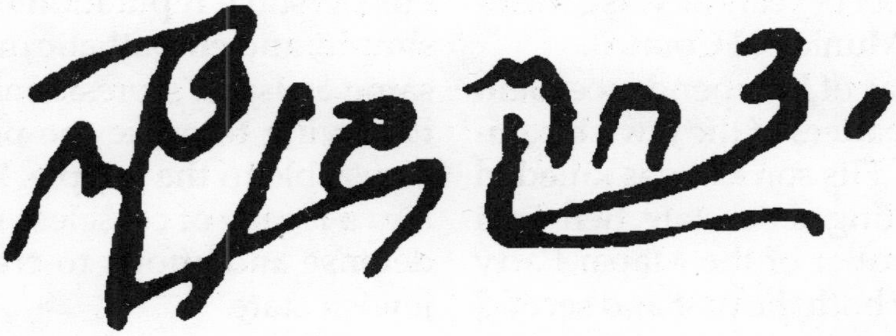

The second president of the State of Israel, Yitzchak Ben-Tzvi was not only a political leader, Zionist, founder of and leader of Zionist socialism but a scholar and diplomat as well. He was as conversant with firearms and fighting for the Jewish cause as he was diplomatically working for it.

Born in Poltava, the Ukraine, in 1884, Ben-Tzvi had a traditional Jewish upbringing. He also experienced Russian anti-Semitism. Ben-Tzvi attended both the traditional *cheder* as well as a Russian *gymnazium*. He entered the University of Kiev, but his studies were interrupted by political turmoil and then pogroms. He became active in Jewish self-defense and helped found the *Poale Zion* Socialist Party. In June 1906, his family's home was searched by Russian police. Ben-Tzvi escaped, but his family was imprisoned; his father served sixteen years of a lifetime exile in Siberia before moving to Palestine. Ben-Tzvi emigrated to Palestine in 1907. He immersed himself in Zionist activities, helping found the Palestine chapter of *Poale Zion* (Labor Zionist Party), and in 1909

he was a founder of the famous *Ha-Shomer*, (The Watchman), the forerunner of Jewish self-defense in the country.

Like his friend and fellow student David Ben-Gurion, Ben-Tzvi studied law in Turkey until the outbreak of World War I. Expelled from Palestine by the Turkish government, he and Ben-Gurion went to America, working for several years in Socialist Zionist fields among American Jews. In 1917, the two joined the Jewish Legion of the British army and returned to Palestine as soldiers in 1918. Ben-Tzvi became a member of the *Haganah* as well as representing the *yishuv*, the Jewish community at-large in Palestine, in negotiations with the British.

From the founding of the *Vaad Leummi* in 1920, Ben-Tzvi held a succession of positions, from a founding member to its presidency. Two of his key involvements during this time (1920–1945) were the Histadrut Trade Union Federation and welfare and development of Jerusalem. For a number of years he was a member of the Jerusalem Municipal Council.

During the War of Independence, Ben-Tzvi was one of the leaders of the Jewish community in Jerusalem. His son Eli was killed in battle. With the founding of the state, Ben-Tzvi was elected as a member of the Mapai Party and was a member of both the first and second Knessets. When President Chaim Weizmann died, Ben-Tzvi was elected to serve as Israel's second president. He was reelected again in 1957 and 1962, the only Israeli leader to ever serve as president three times.

Not content to be exclusively a politician, Ben-Tzvi pursued the scholarly interest of his youth and was a prolific author and ethnologist. He published scholarly works on a number of sects in Palestine and Israel, including the Karaites, Shabbateans, Samaritans, Jewish communities in Asia and Africa, and wrote on numerous other topics as well. He was a recognized authority on the ancient populations of Israel and its antiquities and traditions. He was the head of the Institute for the Study of Oriental Jewish Communities in the Middle East, which he founded in 1948 and which eventually was renamed after him as the Ben-Tzvi Institute.

Ben-Tzvi died on April 23, 1963, shortly after election for the third time as president. His personal reputation was that of a modest, simple, and empathetic individual; he was the same as Israel's president, being well known for trying to make the position of president accessible to the people. Ben-Tzvi left behind him a legacy of ceaseless work for Jewish self-defense and efforts to create an independent Jewish state.

MENACHEM BEGIN

"My generation, dear Ron, swore on the Altar of God that whoever proclaims the intent of destroying the Jewish state or the Jewish people, or both, seals his fate."
—*Letter to Ronald Reagan*

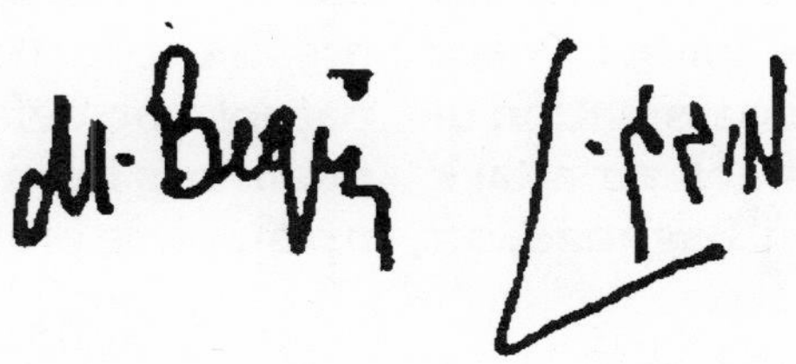

Israeli prime minister, Holocaust survivor, military and political hawk, and Nobel Peace Prize winner, Menachem Begin came to symbolize the "fighting Jew," a term he himself coined and what came to be a mind-set in Israeli politics: *"The fighting Jew loves books, loves liberty, and hates war. But he is prepared to fight for liberty."*

Begin was born in Brest-Litovsk, Poland, on August 16, 1913. Politically active, he was a leader in Vladimir Jabotinksy's Revisionist Zionism and commanded the Betar movement. Begin was trained as a lawyer at the University of Warsaw, but with the outbreak of World War II, he escaped the Nazi invasion and fled to Russian-occupied Vilna. There he was arrested and sentenced to eight years in a Soviet labor camp. (His parents were murdered by the Nazis.) Being a Polish citizen, he was released from the camp at the end of 1941. He arrived in Palestine in 1942 as part of the Polish army forces.

In Palestine, the militant Begin was appointed commander of the national military organization *Irgun Tzvai Leumi*, better known as the Irgun. The Irgun was considered a radical, sometimes renegade, unit of the Jewish self-defense establishment. Its purpose was armed resistance against British rule in Palestine, and while its methods and actions were

sometimes criticized, it worked effectively in hurrying eventual Jewish independence from the British. At one time, the British offered a reward of 10,000 pounds for Begin's arrest.

When the State of Israel was established in 1948, Begin founded the *Herut* (Freedom) Party. For more than twenty years he was the main political opposition leader. A right-wing party, *Herut* advocated the annexation of all historical borders of Israel. In 1965 it joined political forces with portions of the Liberal Party bloc to found the Gahal bloc, with Begin as one of its representatives. At the time *Herut* was the second-largest party in the Knesset. Begin served as a minister without portfolio in the government from 1967 to 1969.

From 1977 to 1983 Begin served as prime minister. These six years witnessed several unprecedented events. First was the negotiation of the Camp David Accords of 1979, an Israeli-Egyptian peace treaty in which U.S. President Jimmy Carter served as intercessor. For this, both Begin and Egyptian President Anwar Sadat later shared the Nobel Peace Prize. (This led, in part, to the assassination of Sadat.) Second was the 1981 Israeli air attack on an Iraqi nuclear reactor near Baghdad, an act that proved favorable for Israel, the whole Middle East balance of power, and later U.S. involvement in the 1991 Gulf War. And third was the heavy settlement of the occupied Left Bank by Jewish militants.

Begin retired from office in 1983, following heavy criticism of questionable Israeli military deployment in Lebanon. His remaining years were spent in self-imposed seclusion, and he died on March 9, 1992. Throughout his life, Begin was an uncompromising hard-liner: as a member of the Irgun, he argued with and even fought against Ben-Gurion and the *Haganah;* in 1952 he led the *Herut's* protest campaign against a reparations agreement with West Germany; his Gahal bloc withdrew from the government when the majority agreed to a U.S. initiative for peace talks with the Arabs. Yet he is best known for his negotiated peace with Egypt. It was said that Begin had moved the entire country to the right. And yet it was under him that an Egyptian head of state was received in Jerusalem with full diplomatic honors and courtesies. An unrelenting Zionist, patriot, and defender of Jewish lives and rights, Begin has been called "the hawk who picked up an olive branch."

MOSHE DAYAN

"I set out to be a farmer—and I think I made quite a good farmer. Yet I have spent most of my adult life as a soldier, under arms."

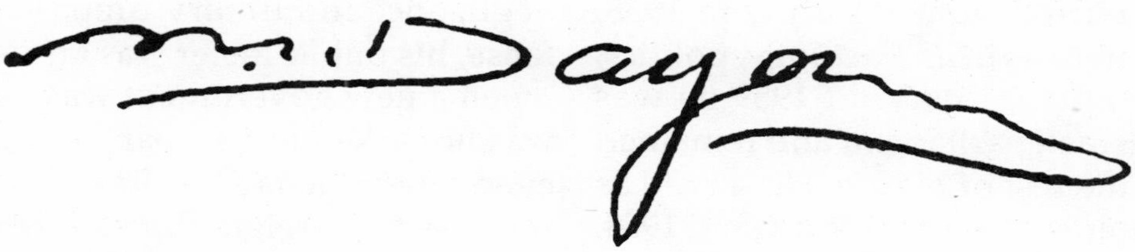

With his war-inflicted black eyepatch, Moshe Dayan, probably more than any other Israeli fighting man, represented to the world the military Jew of the modern Israeli state. A multifaceted, enigmatic, and controversial figure, Dayan was Israel's legendary war hero.

Dayan, a *sabra*, was born on May 4, 1915, on the northern Galilee *kibbutz* of Degania. His Russian parents had separately immigrated to Palestine, where they met and married. Dayan attended school and a teachers' seminary and settled in Nahalal as a farmer. War, however, was his destiny. At the age of 12, he was involved in defending his settlement against Arab marauders. He joined the *Haganah* at an early age, and by 1939 he had the distinction of being sentenced to jail by British authorities for illegal possession of arms. Released from jail in 1941 to help the British evict the Vichy regime from Syria and Lebanon, Dayan served along with other Palestinian Jews as a scout. While on a routine mission, he was shot at by a sniper. The round shattered his binoculars, and Dayan was permanently blinded in his left eye. The black eyepatch he wore became his symbol.

During the War of Independence, Dayan was recognized as a daring and fearless

leader. Of his own disregard for himself in battle, Dayan remarked, "When I see shells exploding around me I am able to remain calm. When I hear bullets whistling, I have no reaction." He commanded the 89th Battalion, capturing strategic positions and fighting in the Negev. In September 1948, he was appointed commander of Israeli forces in Jerusalem and was involved in secret peace talks with Jordan. His rise in the military has been called meteoric, and by 1952 he was the Israeli chief of operations. In November 1953, he was appointed Israel's military chief of staff, a position he held for five years.

Dayan was a professional soldier, with country coming first. He oversaw the establishment of specialized units, including strike forces and paratroopers, advocated retaliation against Arab attacks, oversaw the rearmament of the armed forces, and basically reorganized the army. As chief of staff during the 1956 Egyptian-Suez campaign, he led an assault that captured all of the Sinai in 100 hours.

Dayan retired from the army in 1958, pursuing his interests in archaeology, politics, and, of course, the military. In 1959 he was elected to the Israeli parliament and remained a member for the rest of his life. He served as Ben-Gurion's minister of agriculture until 1964. In 1966 Dayan made a well-publicized trip to Vietnam, going on patrols with U.S. troops, observing both American tactics and weaponry.

The historic 1967 Six-Day War saw Dayan "drafted" as defense minister. With the lightning success of the war, Dayan was seen as one of its heroes, providing decisive leadership. His leadership, however, went far beyond military prowess and extended to diplomacy. As a symbolic act, for instance, Dayan had the barbed wire and concrete barriers dividing the Jewish and Arab quarters of Jerusalem torn down. In place since 1948, these barriers were more than a physical division, and their removal immediately opened up and unified the city. Always sympathetic toward the Arabs, Dayan developed liberal occupation policies and kept certain border locations open for commerce and trade purposes. He also allowed Arabs from the occupied areas to work in Israel. Dayan stayed in government service and was a major figure in Golda Meir's government. He was active in a number of diplomatic negotiations involving Egypt and the Suez Canal.

Dayan was heavily criticized, however, for Israeli losses in the 1973 war. Dayan had warned that war with Egypt was imminent, but he did not demand full Israeli tactical alertness. When the Yom Kippur War broke out and Israel sustained heavy casualties, the public blamed him. Even though he was later cleared by a formal blue ribbon panel of any negligence in military preparations and defense, his public luster was tarnished. In 1974, when a new government was elected, Dayan was not asked to be a part of it. In 1977, however, when Menachem Begin asked Dayan to serve as his foreign minister, he immediately accepted. Dayan was involved and credited with resolving sensitive negotiations with the Camp David Peace Accords. He left Begin's cabinet in 1979 after disagreements with Begin on certain Palestinian policies and withdrew from politics. He died on October 16, 1981, of a heart attack.

Intelligent, courageous, self-confident, and bold, Moshe Dayan developed the Israeli Defense Forces into one of the premier military organizations in the world.

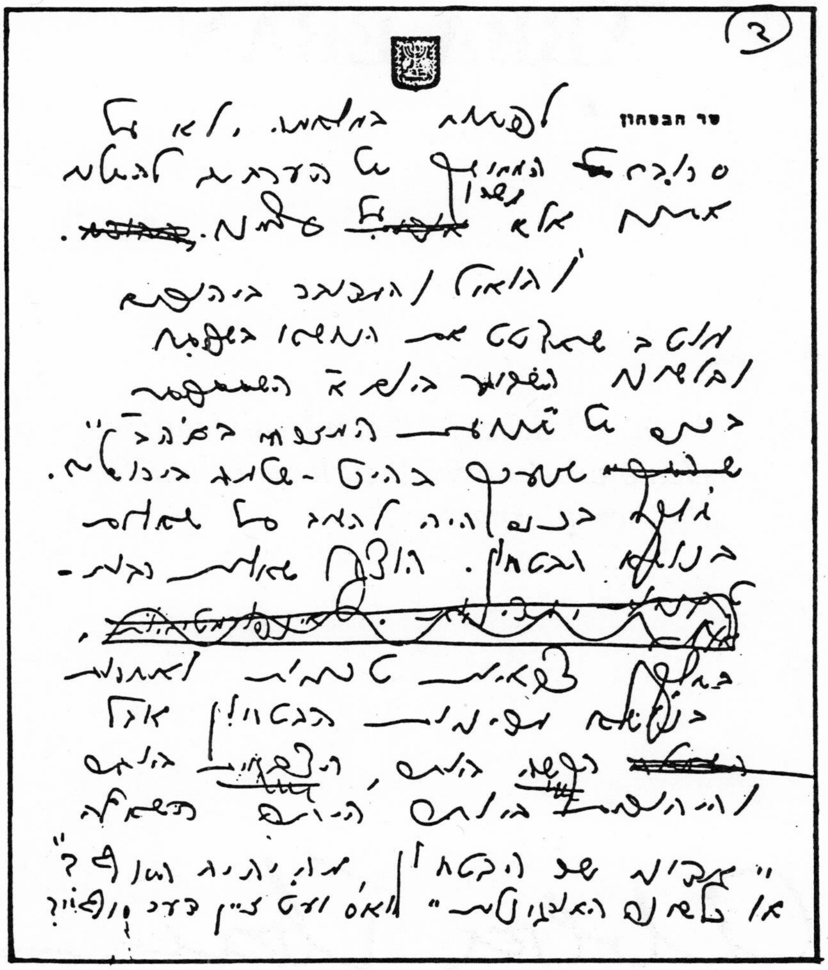
שר הבטחון

Part of a handwritten speech on military letterhead by Moshe Dayan.

ABBA EBAN

"History teaches us that men and nations behave wisely once they have exhausted all other alternatives."

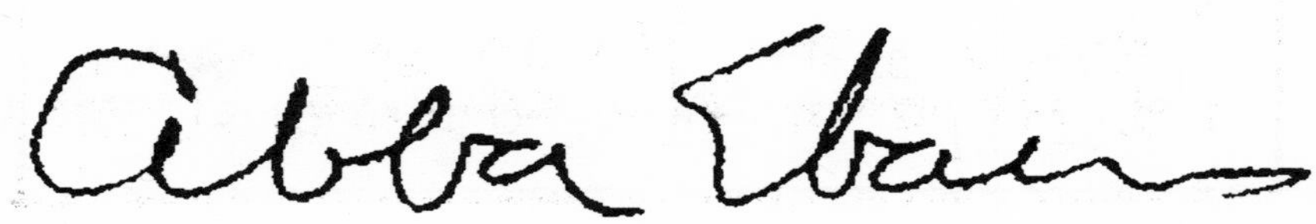

One of the most distinguished and eloquent representatives of Israel is Abba Eban.

Born in Cape Town, South Africa, in 1915, Eban, whose birth name was Aubrey Even, was brought up in England. He studied oriental languages and classics at Cambridge University, and from 1938 to 1940 he was a lecturer and research fellow in Arabic. During World War II, he held the rank of major in the British army and served in Cairo on the staff of the British minister of state. As an intelligence officer in Jerusalem, he trained Jewish volunteers for resistance in anticipation of a German invasion. Following the war he moved to Jerusalem. From 1946 to 1948 he served as a political information officer in London for the Jewish Agency. When Israel declared its independence, Eban served as its first representative and later ambassador to the United Nations. From 1950 to 1959 he served as both the chief delegate to the UN and the Israeli ambassador to Washington, D.C.

Upon his return to Israel in 1959 and for the next decade, Eban served in a number of positions: a member of the Knesset representing the Mapai Party, minister of education and culture, deputy to Prime Minister Levi Eshkol, president of the Weizmann Institute at Rehovot and foreign minister. Eban has served

Israel both at home and abroad as its eloquent spokesman. He has also been a visiting professor in political science and Middle East history at Columbia University.

For the past decade Eban has been more involved in teaching history than in making it. Through his writing, television broadcasts, and recordings, he has spread the ancient and modern histories of Israel: its cultures, conquests, religious and political philosophies. With his cultured and mellifluous English accent and respected political standing, Abba Eban remains the diplomatic symbol of the modern State of Israel and its senior statesman-at-large.

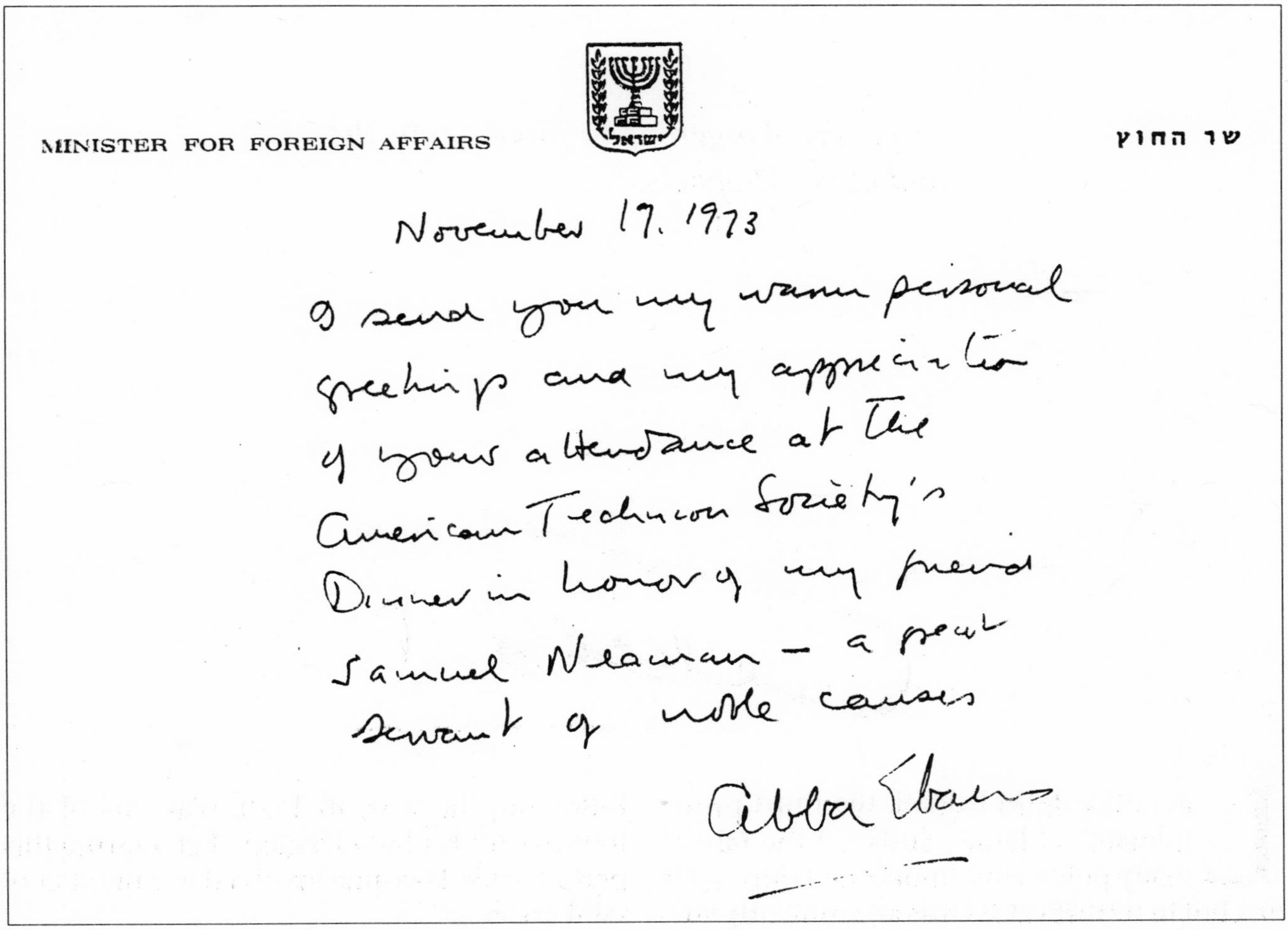

MINISTER FOR FOREIGN AFFAIRS

ישראל

שר החוץ

November 17. 1973

I send you my warm personal greetings and my appreciation of your attendance at the American Technion Society's Dinner in honor of my friend Samuel Neaman — a great servant of noble causes

Abba Eban

Handwritten note in English by Abba Eban dated "Nov. 17, 1973," on Minister for Foreign Affairs letterhead thanking the unnamed recipient for attending an American Technion Society dinner in honor of Samuel Neaman.

LEVI ESHKOL

"It is very dangerous to prophesy in the land of the Prophets."

Levi (Shkolnik) Eshkol, the third prime minister of Israel, suffered the fate of many politicians: underrated during his life, but in retrospect seen as an eminently successful leader.

Eshkol was born in 1895 into a well-to-do chasidic family in Oratova, the province of Kiev (Ukraine). He received a traditional *cheder* education and was privately tutored. At the age of 16, he entered the Hebrew high school in Vilna, where he joined the Ze'irei Zion movement. In 1914 he immigrated to Palestine, becoming an agricultural worker. He served during World War I in the Jewish Legion and following the war, in 1920, was one of the founders of Kibbutz Degania Bet. During this period Eshkol became involved in a number of vital areas.

At the *kibbutz*, Eshkol initially labored in the fields, but he later became its treasurer and worked toward obtaining funding. He also became involved with the Histradut (the Labor Federation) for arms acquisition (he was arrested for several weeks by the Viennese police for "illegal" purchases), and developed an expertise in an area essential to a developing agricultural economy in an arid region: water resources. He was one of the founders,

and for fourteen years the director, of the Mekorot Water Company, raising the annual water supply from an initial several hundred thousand gallons to more than 20 billion. Eshkol's interests ranged from finances to Jewish self-defense forces to agriculture to politics.

Eshkol ascended to one of the leading positions in the powerful Mapai Party and was its treasurer from 1942 to 1945. From 1944 to 1948 he was the powerful secretary of the Tel Aviv Workers' Council. During the War of Independence, he was deputy defense minister under David Ben-Gurion. Because of his financial experience as treasurer for the *Haganah,* he served as minister of finance from 1952 to 1963, a period when Israel experienced the absorption of close to a million immigrants. In 1952 he was also elected to the Knesset. During the bitterly divisive Lavon Affair (a covert Israeli intelligence mission in Egypt that went awry, resulting in the executions of two Israelis and the imprisonment of several others), Eshkol displayed the political skills for which he became famous. He developed a reputation as a man who got things done through negotiation and conciliation.

Eshkol was appointed prime minister in June 1963, following Ben-Gurion's resignation. He also took over the ministry of defense cabinet position and was responsible for overseeing Israel's military readiness. In his role as prime minister, Eshkol promoted moderation, deterrence, conciliation, close relations with the United States, and economic ties with Europe. His strengths as a negotiator and abilities to keep even political opponents friendly were seen by his critics, however, as hesitancy and uncertainty.

During the Six-Day War of 1967 Eshkol turned over the ministry of defense responsibilities to Moshe Dayan. In 1968 he visited with President Lyndon Johnson at his Texas ranch and through these talks was able to reinforce U.S. support for Israel. Eshkol was successful not only in getting President Johnson to agree to maintain a balance of arms in the Middle East, but in gaining a promise of American military aid, including Skyhawk planes and Phantom jet fighters.

Eshkol died on February 26, 1969, following a heart attack. A patriot, he both exalted and suffered in the political arena. His multifaceted skills saw Israel through some of its harshest times, and his contributions strengthened the country immeasurably.

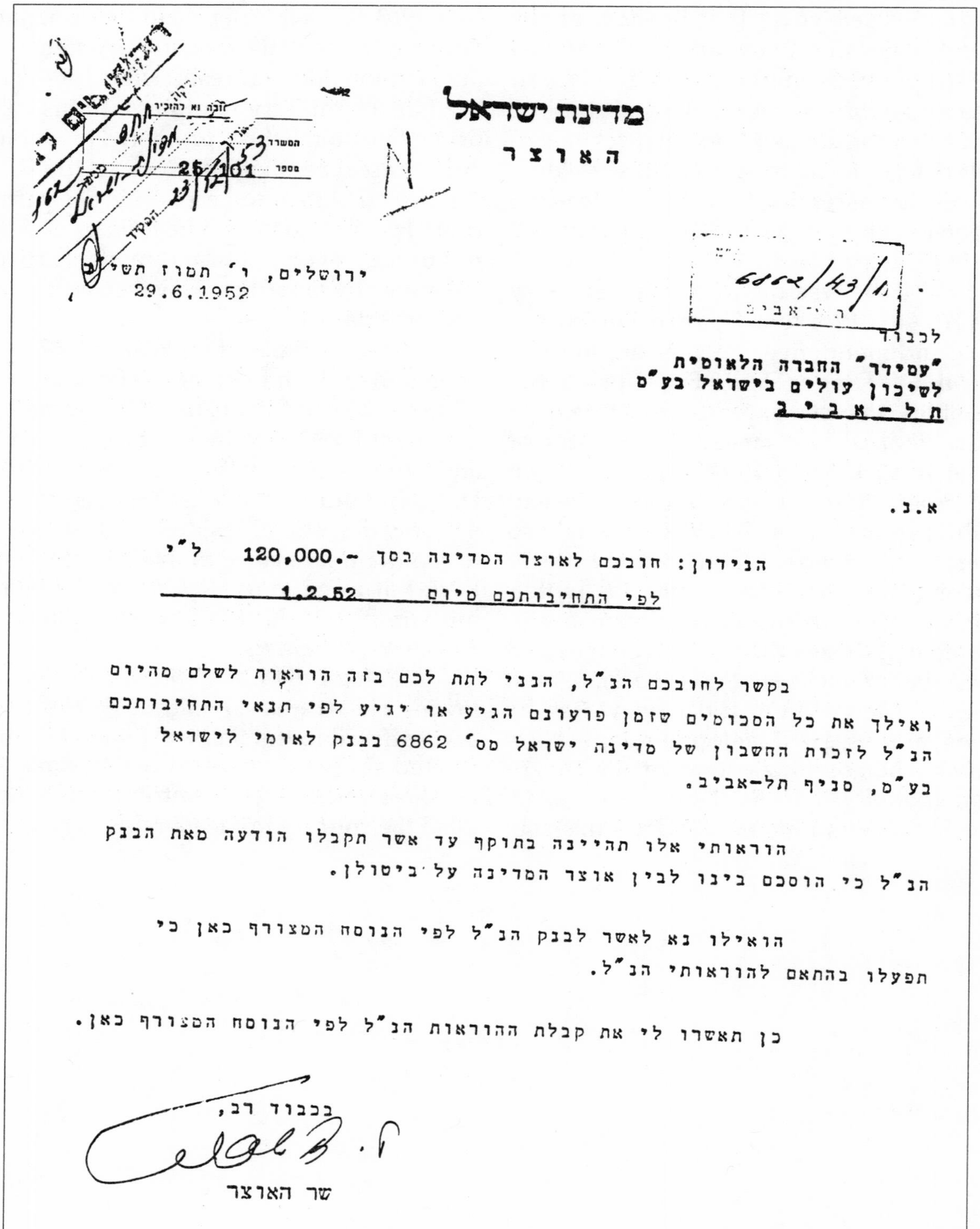

מדינת ישראל

האוצר

ירושלים, ו' תמוז תשי"ב
29.6.1952

לכבוד
"עמידר" החברה הלאומית
לשיכון עולים בישראל בע"מ
תל-אביב

א.נ.

הנידון: חובכם לאוצר המדינה בסך -.120,000 ל"י
לפי התחיבותכם מיום 1.2.52

בקשר לחובכם הנ"ל, הנני לתת לכם בזה הוראות לשלם מהיום ואילך את כל הסכומים שזמן פרעונם הגיע או יגיע לפי תנאי התחיבותכם הנ"ל לזכות החשבון של מדינה ישראל מס' 6862 בבנק לאומי לישראל בע"מ, סניף תל-אביב.

הוראותי אלו תהיינה בתוקף עד אשר תקבלו הודעה מאת הבנק הנ"ל כי הוסכם בינו לבין אוצר המדינה על ביטולן.

הואילו נא לאשר לבנק הנ"ל לפי הנוסח המצורף כאן כי תפעלו בהתאם להוראותי הנ"ל.

כן תאשרו לי את קבלת ההוראות הנ"ל לפי הנוסח המצורף כאן.

בכבוד רב,
ל. אשכול
שר האוצר

Typed letter on Treasury Department, State of Israel letterhead signed by Levi Eshkol. The letter advises the recipient, an organization, that it owes the government 120,000 lira. Signed by Eshkol as minister of finance.

THEODOR HERZL

"If you will it, it is no myth."

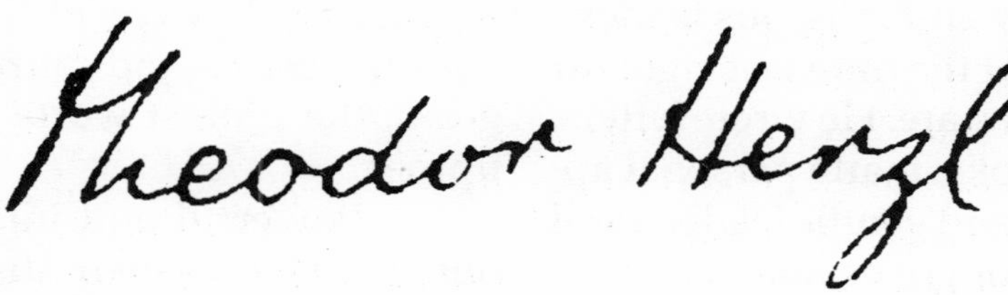

Theodor Herzl, founder of political Zionism and visionary of the contemporary State of Israel, was a lawyer by training, a journalist by practice, a Zionist by deed, and a legend by right.

Herzl was born on May 2, 1860, in Budapest, Hungary, into a nonreligious Jewish family. He received a cursory Hebrew education and attended the University of Vienna, earning a law degree there in 1884. He subsequently practiced in Vienna and Salzburg. Realizing he could never rise to a position as judge as a result of the anti-Semitism of the time, he left law and began writing.

Over the next five years, Herzl wrote several plays, establishing a name for himself. One play, *Tabarin*, was produced in New York. He was soon approached to have his other plays produced and to write for several newspapers. In 1889 he married Julie Naschauer, whom he knew as a student in Vienna, and they settled in Vienna.

The year 1894, with the storm surrounding the Dreyfus affair, proved to be a turning point in his life. Herzl himself acknowledged this. *"The Dreyfus trial,"* he wrote, *"made me a Zionist."* Herzl, the trained journalist, noted the reaction of the French masses. "Down with the

Jews," not "Down with Dreyfus" was what the crowds shouted, and Herzl recognized that if such fervent anti-Semitism could take root in a liberal country like France, Jews had no hope for equality in any country except their own.

Beginning in 1895 Herzl undertook an unrelenting campaign that would, in time, lead both to the firm planting of the imperative for a Jewish state and to Herzl's own death. He also started writing a Zionist diary and his masterpiece, *Der Judenstaat* ("The Jewish State"). When *Der Judenstaat* was published in February 1896, Herzl was immediately thrust into the limelight and encouraged by enthusiastic supporters.

Herzl knew that the only way a Jewish state could come into being was with the blessing of the world powers. With the help of his many new supporters, he embarked upon plans to meet with the Russian czar, the German kaiser, and the Turkish sultan. Herzl, however, was to meet resistance not only from these world powers but also from the majority of world Jewry's lay and religious leaders, who did not believe that the time was right for an independent Jewish state. He wrote letters, articles, essays and books, made personal appearances with Jewish and gentile leaders, and knocked on the doors of governments.

Herzl helped to organize the First Zionist Congress in Basel, Switzerland, in August 1897. At this meeting the constitution for the Zionist Congress was established, its organizational structure was laid out, the journal *Die Welt* ("The World") was started, and the financial arm of the congress was set up. On top of all that, the World Zionist Organization (WZO) was founded and the Basle Plan was drawn. Herzl recorded in his journal: *"At Basle I created the Jewish State. If I were to say this out loud everybody would laugh at me. In five years, perhaps, but certainly in fifty everybody will agree."*

In 1898, following the Second Zionist Congress, Herzl made his sole trip to Palestine. In London the following year the Jewish Colonial Trust—the financial arm of the WZO—was incorporated. Between the years 1898 and 1901 Herzl solicited and had audiences with the German kaiser and the Turkish sultan and wrote to the Russian czar, all with negative results. In his meeting with Sultan Abdul Hamid II, Herzl offered to pay the Turkish national debt in exchange for a declaration of support for Jewish settlement in Palestine. The sultan refused the offer but honored Herzl with a Turkish decoration.

In January 1902, the sultan of Turkey offered Herzl a compromise: he would grant a charter for settlement, but not in Palestine. Mesopotamia or Syria was to be considered. Herzl rejected this offer, but the die was cast for future alternate plans. The British colonial secretary than advanced the offer of El Arish in Africa for Jewish settlement. Herzl sent emissaries to investigate the proposed site, but the British changed their minds and offered an area in Uganda instead. When Herzl expressed an inclination at the Sixth Zionist Congress in August 1903 to accept the offer, particularly after the brutal and murderous Kishinev pogrom, the Zionist world was thrown into an uproar.

Powerful and intense conflicts broke out over Herzl's mere suggestion of considering the Uganda Plan. To Herzl, it was not to be a permanent home, just an interim one. Nonetheless, equally dedicated Zionists, such as Chaim Weizmann, forcibly opposed the plan, and splinter Zionist factions developed. Herzl promised to completely abandon its consideration.

By this time Herzl was physically weakened. He had traveled around the world, fought with Jewish groups, and petitioned openly anti-Semitic governments, all in an effort to gain for the Jews what all other nationalities had. He was exhausted. Three years before, on May 2, 1901, Herzl had written in his diary, *"It will soon be six years since I began this movement, which has made me old, tired, and poor."*

He was not at home when his father died in 1902 and felt neglectful of not having been there. He spent long months away from his family. His burning passion was consuming him. He had already been diagnosed with heart problems.

Early 1904 found Herzl in Italy, meeting with the Italian and Vatican governments. His disappointment continued when Italy, like other major powers, first appeared interested, then declined support. Herzl returned to Vienna. His health in jeopardy, he continued unabatedly writing letters and articles and receiving visitors. In June he left for a summer retreat in the mountains, where, on July 3, 1904, his heart gave out. He was only 44 years old.

Many generations dreamed, prayed, wept, and died for a Jewish state, for a sanctuary for the Jewish people. Herzl virtually willed it. It has been written that "more than any other one man, Theodor Herzl changed the course of modern Jewish history."

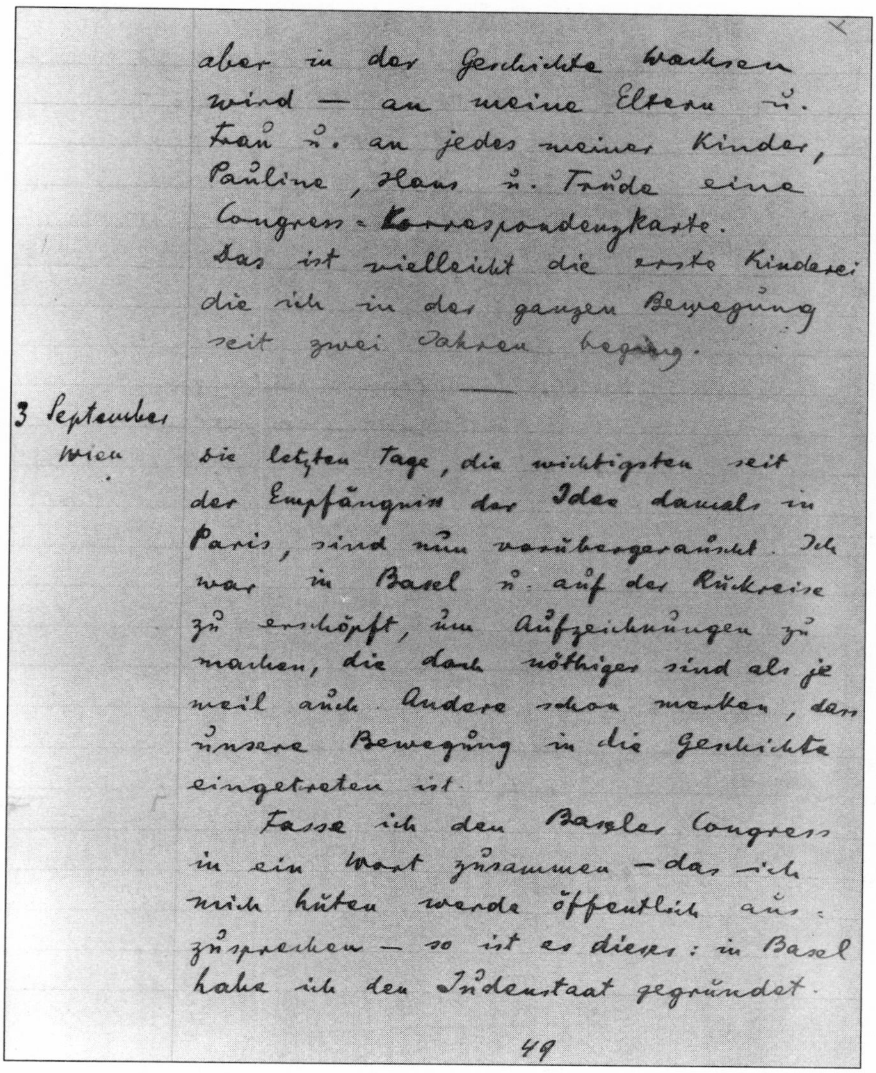

aber in der Geschichte wachsen
wird — an meine Eltern u.
Frau u. an jedes meiner Kinder,
Pauline, Hans u. Trude eine
Congress-Korrespondenzkarte.
Das ist vielleicht die erste Kinderei
die ich in der ganzen Bewegung
seit zwei Jahren beging.

—

3 September
Wien.

Die letzten Tage, die wichtigsten seit
der Empfängniss der Idee damals in
Paris, sind nun vorübergerauscht. Ich
war in Basel u. auf der Rückreise
zu erschöpft, um Aufzeichnungen zu
machen, die doch nöthiger sind als je
weil auch Andere schon merken, dass
unsere Bewegung in die Geschichte
eingetreten ist.

Fasse ich den Basler Congress
in ein Wort zusammen — das ich
mich hüten werde öffentlich aus-
zusprechen — so ist es dieses: in Basel
habe ich den Judenstaat gegründet.

49

Handwritten entry by Theodor Herzl dated September 3, 1897, Vienna, where he states that he founded the Jewish State.

3 September, Vienna. The last few days, the most important ones since the inception of the idea at that time in Paris, have passed now. I was in Basel and on my return trip I was too exhausted to make notes, which indeed are more necessary than ever for others who are starting to realize that our movement has entered history. If I were to condense the Basel Congress into one phrase—which I would be reticent to utter in public—it is this: "In Basel I have founded the Jewish State."

Translation of September 3 entry.

VLADIMIR JABOTINSKY

"The first aim of Zionism is the creation of a Jewish majority on both sides of the Jordan River."

Writing sample.

Vladimir (Ze'ev) Jabotinsky was that rare firebrand of the complete Zionist: leader, political patriot, writer, orator, and military man. He fought all his life to advance the Jewish cause, from his roles as political party founder and military officer to orator and journalist.

Born in Odessa, Russia, in 1880, Jabotinsky received both Jewish and secular educations. He mastered Hebrew at a young age, and during his youth he displayed an inclination to literature and journalism. Following high school, he studied law while working as a foreign correspondent for Odessa newspapers in Rome and Bern.

Jabotinsky returned to Russia in 1901 and began dual careers as a writer and Zionist. He was a forceful, charismatic personality and had strong oratorical and literary skills. Jabotinsky advocated, as did others of the period, that Jews educate themselves in their culture, heritage, and values and take pride in nationalism. During World War I, he covered the conflict for a Moscow newspaper. In 1915 he was in Egypt, where large numbers of Jews, including Joseph Trumpeldor, had been expelled by the Turks, who then ruled Palestine. Jabotinsky campaigned for a Jewish military unit to fight for the liberation of Palestine under the auspices of the British. The concept

was initially rebuffed, but later the 38th Royal Fusiliers Battalion was formed, in which Jabotinsky served as an officer and fought in Palestine. After the war, Jabotinsky remained in Palestine. He was active in local politics and commanded the Jerusalem defense forces during the Arab riots of 1920. For this, Jabotinsky was arrested, tried, and sentenced to fifteen years at hard labor.

Released after a few weeks, Jabotinsky went to England, participating in the 1920 Zionist Conference. He was one of the founders of Keren Hayesod, the fund-raising branch of the World Zionist Organization. In 1921 he was elected to the Zionist Executive and continued his Zionist activities in both England and Palestine. In Berlin, in 1923, Jabotinsky founded the Revisionist movement within Zionism.

Jabotinsky's policies were active and immediate, unlike the mainstream Zionism of that time. Jabotinsky rejected official Zionist leadership concepts of gradual immigration to Palestine; instead, he advocated unlimited, unrestricted mass immigration. He also pushed for the creation of a Jewish fighting force for any potentiality. Most distinctive of all was Jabotinsky's stance that a Jewish state should be established "on both sides of the Jordan." His Revisionist brand of Zionism called for political action: "Ninety percent of Zionism may consist of tangible settlement work, and only ten percent of politics; but those ten percent are the precondition of success." He disagreed with other Zionists (notably the dominant Labor movement in Palestine) who believed in communal enterprises, arguing instead that private enterprise was more effective. Jabotinsky's activities and policies caused a considerable rift between him and the official Jewish leadership in Palestine. Britain, in fact, barred him from living in Palestine. The conflict was such that, in 1934, Jabotinsky and David Ben-Gurion reached a formal agreement to relieve the increasing tensions between them. Nonetheless, in 1935 Jabotinsky quit the World Zionist Organization in protest, accusing the leaders of ineptitude and deserting Herzl's political visions. He then founded his own party, the New Zionist Organization, with one of its major focuses being the mass immigration of Jews, illegally if necessary, to Palestine. During the intense Arab riots of 1936 to 1939, Jabotinsky strongly promoted his immigration concepts and, in conjunction with other activist groups, led violent retaliation against the Arab population.

With the outbreak of World War II, Jabotinsky again urged the establishment of a Jewish army to fight with the Allies against the Nazis. In February 1940 he came to the United States, seeking support from Jews and non-Jews alike. While visiting a political Jewish summer camp in August 1940, he suffered a heart attack and died. In his will, Jabotinsky wrote: "My remains will be transferred [to *Eretz Yisrael*] only on the instructions of a Jewish government." In 1964, the State of Israel reinterred Jabotinsky and his wife on Mount Herzl.

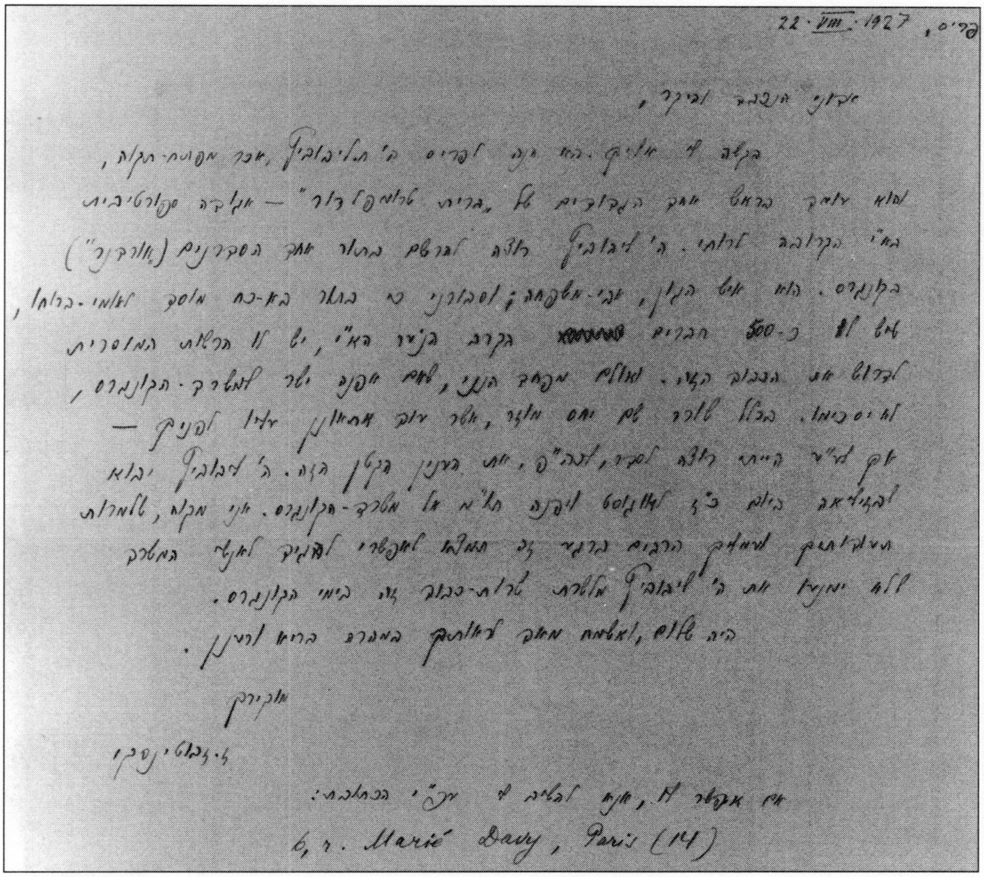

פריס, 22·VIII·1927

אדוני החבר היקר,

היה שלום, ואשמח מאד לראותך במהרה בריא ורענן.

מוקירך

ו. ז'בוטינסקי

6, r. Marié Davy, Paris (14)

Autographed Hebrew letter by Vladimir Jabotinsky.

GOLDA MEIR

"Above all, this country is our own. Nobody has to get up in the morning and worry what his neighbors think of him. Being a Jew is no problem here."

Like fellow pioneer and prime minister David Ben-Gurion, Golda Meir was and remains a symbol of Israel. The grandmotherly-in-appearance Meir was indeed a grandmother for Israel: nurturing, supportive, loving, and protective.

Meir was the product of, and was formed by, Jewish oppression. Born Golda Maibovitch in Kiev in 1898 and raised in Pinsk, her overriding memories were of severe poverty, hunger, and fear. In her autobiography, she recalled the terror of her family and the other Jewish townspeople right before a pogrom. In 1906 her family immigrated to Milwaukee, following her father, who had come three years earlier.

Meir attended public schools and a vocational teachers' training school and later taught adult education courses. As a teenager, she became attracted to the Socialist Zionist (*Poale Zion*) movement. Fluent in English and Yiddish, she was recognized as a skilled orator. In 1921 she and her husband, Morris Myerson, immigrated to Palestine. One of the conditions of her marrying him was that he agree to immigrate.

Meir's early years in Palestine were marked by hard work, poverty, and personal

difficulties. Her first three years were spent on *Kibbutz* Merhavia, where she became involved with the Women's Workers Council and the Histadrut (the Trade Union Federation). In 1924 she and her husband moved to Jerusalem for his health. Their finances were such that Meir took in laundry to pay kindergarten fees for her two children. In 1928 she separated from her husband. Meanwhile she became increasingly active in politics, and soon was executive of the Women's Workers Council.

In 1930 Meir was one of the founders of the Mapai Party and was already known throughout Palestine as a major political figure. She was invited in 1934 to join the executive committee of the Histadrut and rose rapidly in the Labor movement. She was recognized for having a keen mind and strong organizational skills.

The 1940s saw Meir involved in a variety of activities, particularly in dealing with the British mandatory government. With the 1946 arrest of Moshe Shertok, Meir was chosen to be the acting head of the Political Department of the Jewish Agency, and thus the principal political representative for the Jews of Palestine. She negotiated with the British government during its final months of rule and conducted secret talks with King Abdullah of Jordan. When the War of Independence broke out in May 1948, she was sent to the United States with the desperate mission to raise both political support from the U.S. government and funds from American Jewry. Being familiar with the United States, she had complete credibility with both American-born and immigrant Jews. Meir raised the incredible sum of $50 million, prompting Ben-Gurion to say upon her return: "Someday, when the history of our people will be written, it will be said that there was a Jewish woman who raised the money which made the state possible."

With the establishment of the state, Meir was appointed Israel's first minister to Moscow. Her eight-month presence in Moscow sparked enormous long-suppressed Jewish identity and public expression. Upon her return to Israel, she was elected a member of the Knesset, a post she was to hold for twenty-five years. She was also appointed to Ben-Gurion's cabinet as the minister of housing and labor. As minister, she initiated large-scale infrastructure improvement, housing and road-building programs in particular, and advocated a policy of unrestricted Jewish immigration. In 1956 she became foreign minister. In the capacity of Israel's chief international spokesperson, Meir initiated strong foreign relations with emerging and third-world nations in Africa, sending both financial aid and Israel's own version of the Peace Corps. She was very visible on the international political scene, always promoting and advancing Israel's interests and its moral position and defending it from accusation and criticism. Possessing a sharp wit, she was well known for making her points: "We intend to remain alive. Our neighbors want to see us dead. This is not a question that leaves much room for compromise."

In 1965 Meir retired from the position of foreign minister and became the secretary-general of the Mapai Party. With the 1967 Six-Day War, she was active in trying to quell friction between Israeli political parties. At the same time, she was trying to ease out of politics. However, upon the death of Levi Eshkol in February 1969, she was appointed Israel's fourth prime minister. As prime minister, Meir's foreign policies centered on the principles of Israel as a center for the united Jewish people and peace through any means. She worked actively and positively with the American political establishment in keeping Israel in a favorable light. With the 1973 Yom Kippur War, however, Meir suffered serious political setbacks, both within Israel and abroad. Unusually high casualties for the Israelis brought heavy at-home criticism, while foreign powers, although admiring Israel for its self-defense, criticized its offensive actions.

Meir recognized that Israel, while winning militarily, had lost politically. She resigned her position in 1974 and turned her attention to writing her memoirs, being a grandmother, and acting as Israel's senior statesman-at-large. She died four years later, in 1978.

Through Meir's efforts Israel changed from a closed, British-ruled Palestine to a free, inviting, self-ruling state. Among a score of Jews in this century, she has represented the Jewish people, and the nation of Israel, to the world. Golda Meir was particularly indispensable in her role as spokesperson for Israel in some exceedingly critical times. Her life could be summed up in her own words: "We only want that which is given to all peoples of the world, to be masters of our own fate, not of others, and in cooperation and friendship with others."

DR. MAX NORDAU

"If you are insane, we are insane together. Count on me!"
—*Nordau to Theodor Herzl*

A psychiatrist by training, a philosopher and writer by nature, Max Nordau was the cofounder of the World Zionist Organization and confidant of Theodor Herzl. He was also one of the seven authors of the Basel Program, the original basic statement of Zionism.

Nordau was born Simon Maximilian Sudfeld in Budapest in 1849. He received a traditional religious education and was a religious Jew, although later he became a Darwinist. His first poem was published at age 14, and at 16 he was a theater critic. While a student he wrote for several Budapest newspapers, and in 1873 he legally changed his name to his pseudonym, Max Nordau. In 1875 he received his medical degree from the University of Pest, and in 1880 he settled in Paris, where he both practiced as a psychiatrist and wrote as a social critic and thinker.

A prolific writer, Nordau was a severe critic of contemporary society and the arts. He wrote a number of controversial and reactionary books, including *The Conventional Lies of Our Civilization* (1883) and *Degeneracy* (1892), an attack on the "superstitions" of nationalism, religion, and racism. While the former brought him initial fame, the latter brought him world-

wide prominence. Published in a number of countries and a number of languages, his books were likewise banned.

Nordau's involvement with Zionism began after he treated Herzl as a patient. The two first met while both were on the staff of the French paper *Neue Freie Presse* as German-language correspondents. Together they witnessed the Dreyfus affair and the increasing public anti-Semitism. When a friend suggested to Herzl that he see a psychiatrist because of his political beliefs and mental condition, which the friend believed verged on insanity, Herzl saw Nordau. Upon hearing Herzl's concerns and expression of Zionism and a Jewish homeland, Nordau enthusiastically agreed with Herzl: *"If you are insane, we are insane together. Count on me!"*

At the First Zionist Congress in 1897, Nordau presented the Basel Program, the official agenda of the Zionist Organization. Nordau served as vice-president of the first six Zionist congresses, as president for the next four. His addresses to the congresses were considered classics in Zionist literature. Nordau accurately surveyed the world Jewish condition, assessing not only the plight of the Eastern European Jew but also the plight of the assimilated Western European Jew. At the Congress of 1911, Nordau predicted the destruction of the six million Russian and Eastern European Jews, if current political trends continued.

Nordau was a stalwart of political Zionism, versus cultural Zionism, which the thinker and writer Ahad Ha'am advocated, or practical Zionism, which claimed Chaim Weizmann. Although Nordau staunchly supported Herzl, he was not Herzl's second, nor was he in his shadow. Nordau had achieved his own fame long before Herzl. Nonetheless, he believed in Herzl, as Herzl did in Nordau. When Herzl advocated the Uganda Plan, a controversial alternative establishing Uganda as a temporary Zionist home, Nordau supported Herzl, even though he himself did not like the plan. (*"The first condition a community should set, if it aspires to be a nation,"* Nordau wrote, *"is to own the land whereon it lives, and supply its own needs."*) Nonetheless, Nordau coined the term *nachtasyl* ("night asylum," or temporary shelter) to emphasize the transient nature of the idea. Together, Herzl and Nordau strengthened the revolutionary platform of political Zionism. When Herzl died in 1904, Nordau was offered the presidency of the Zionist Organization, which he refused; he preferred to remain outside the official political hierarchy. After 1911 he stopped attending the Zionist congresses, partially as a protest of the way the organization was moving.

Nordau spent World War I in exile in Spain. He favored Vladimir Jabotinsky's idea of a Jewish Legion and supported the 1917 Balfour Declaration. His idea of having half a million Jews settle in Palestine immediately, followed by 600,000 more every year for ten years, was not taken seriously. In 1921 Nordau retired from active Zionist work. He died two years later in Paris. In his will he stipulated that he should be buried in Palestine; in 1926, he was reburied in Tel Aviv.

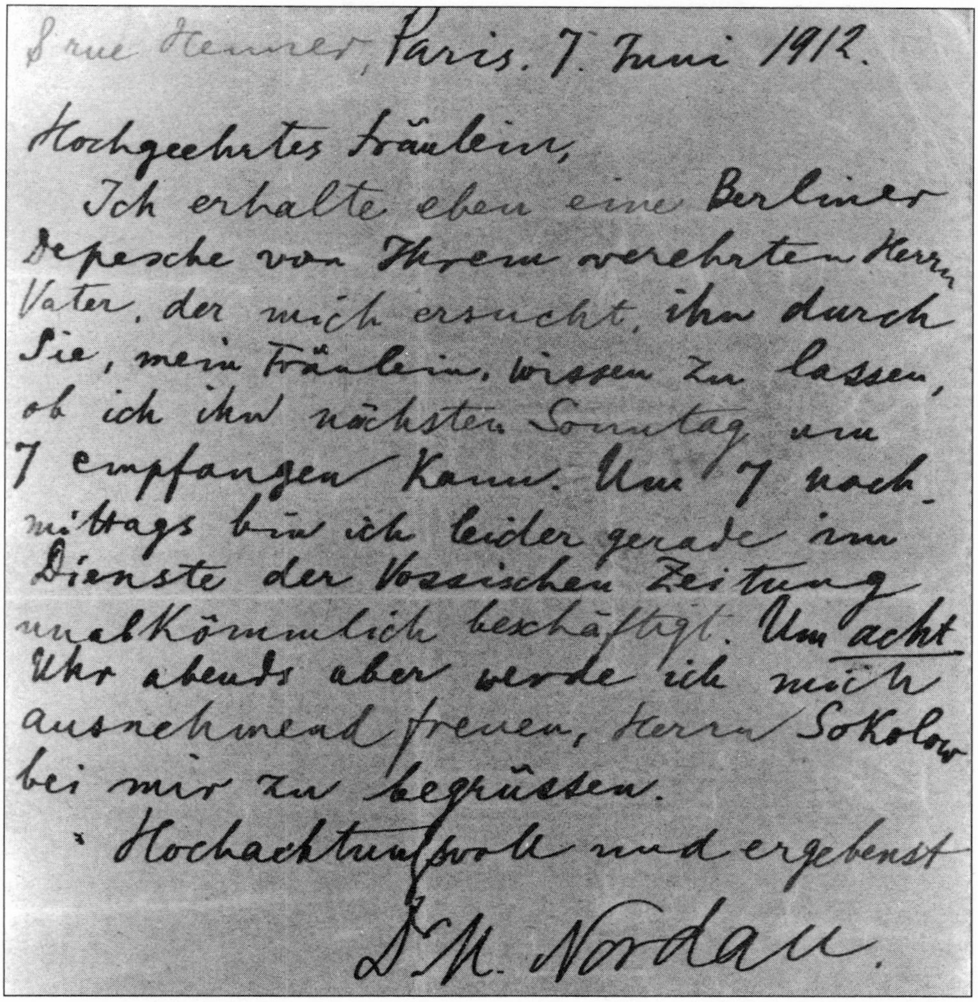

8 rue Henner, Paris. 7. Juni 1912.

Hochgeehrtes Fräulein,

Ich erhalte eben eine Berliner Depesche von Ihrem verehrten Herrn Vater, der mich ersucht, ihn durch Sie, mein Fräulein, wissen zu lassen, ob ich ihn nächsten Sonntag um 7 empfangen kann. Um 7 nachmittags bin ich leider gerade im Dienste der Vossischen Zeitung unabkömmlich beschäftigt. Um acht Uhr abends aber werde ich mich ausnehmend freuen, Herrn Sokolow bei mir zu begrüssen.

Hochachtungsvoll und ergebenst

Dr M. Nordau.

Note in German from Dr. Max Nordau to an unnamed woman saying he's unavailable at a certain time for an appointment but will be available afterward.

MOSHE SHERTOK

". . . Quiet, reserved, careful as against impulsive and impetuous, his speeches explanatory as against the declaratory . . . his Capital C meaning Caution."

—Partial self-definition

Moshe Shertok, the first foreign minister and the second prime minister of the State of Israel, was another multifaceted, multitalented founder of the modern Jewish state.

The son of a fervent Zionist, Shertok (who later changed his name to Sharett) was born in 1894 in Kherson, Ukraine. At the age of 12, his father, who had previously immigrated to Israel but returned to Russia, resettled the whole family in the Palestine Arab village of Ayn Siniya, where the young Shertok learned Arabic as well as growing up in a Hebrew-speaking home. His father was a founder of Tel Aviv, and Shertok was a graduate of the first class of the Herzliyah High School in Tel Aviv. Following graduation, he went to Constantinople to study law, but like other Jewish students, he left at the outbreak of World War I. Shertok volunteered for military service and with his fluency in seven languages served as an officer and an interpreter.

Following the war, Shertok studied at the London School of Economics and returned to Palestine in 1923. There he was appointed one of the editors of the Trade Union Federations newspaper, *Davar*.

In 1931, Shertok joined the political de-

partment of the Jewish Agency, a move that led to career politics. He was appointed its head following the assassination of the previous director, Chaim Arlosoroff. In this role, which he held until 1948, Shertok was in charge of foreign policy for the complete Jewish community in Palestine. He was responsible for day-to-day contacts with the governing British authorities, the preparation and presentation of the Jewish cause overall to British authorities, and general public relations and information. Shertok was noted for his moderate and cautious stance, following the Chaim Weizmann approach (as opposed to a more aggressive David Ben-Gurion perspective). Based on his push, the Jewish Supernumerary Police were established during the Arab Riots of 1936 to 1939, and he was instrumental in the creation of the Jewish Brigade (the only independent national Jewish organization in the British army). No puppet, however, of the British, Shertok was one of a number of Jewish national leaders arrested on "Black Saturday" (June 29, 1946) and imprisoned. He was held for four months.

Shertok headed the thrust that led to the November 29, 1947, United Nations Partition resolution giving the State of Israel international national status and legitimacy.

With the founding of the State of Israel on May 15, 1948, Shertok, who then changed his name to Sharett, became Israel's first foreign minister. He held this position through 1956. Sharett focused his energies on negotiating reparations agreements with the Germans, establishing trade with Asia, securing international recognition for the new Jewish state, and trying to develop intra-Israeli political coalitions. In 1954, Sharett succeeded David Ben-Gurion as prime minister while keeping his foreign ministry portfolio. He held the premiership for two years, when Ben-Gurion again succeeded him.

For the last five years of his life, Sharett held the position of chairman of the Jewish Agency. He died in Jerusalem in 1965, leaving behind him a legacy of having developed the methods and mechanics of Zionist and Israeli diplomacy. Sharett was also considered one of Israel's most cultured leaders, being not only a polished diplomat, politican, and linguist but also a writer and orator. He translated poetry into Hebrew and demonstrated a deep appreciation for music. A modest man despite his high profile and many accomplishments, he requested that no streets or settlements be named after him.

HENRIETTA SZOLD

"I have not lived one life, but several, each one bearing its own character and insignia."

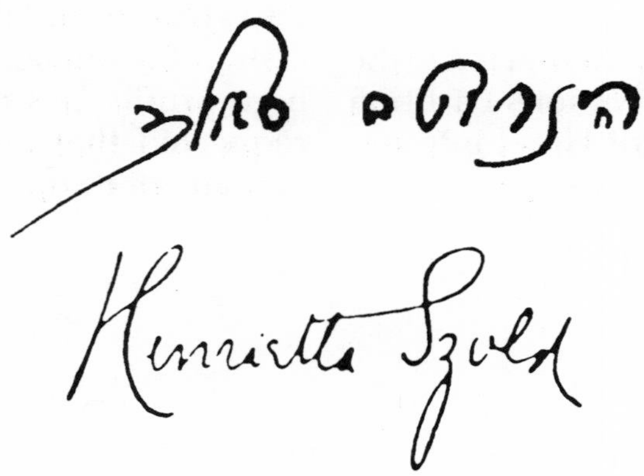

Henrietta Szold's life has been called a phenomenon. Teacher, school administrator, writer, editor, translator, Zionist organizer, medical administrator, fund-raiser—each phase of her many careers was a commitment with depth, impact, and permanency. A Zionist of the first order and a national patriot with the ardor of biblical zealots, Henrietta Szold fought for the Jewish cause throughout her life.

The daughter of a Hungarian rabbi, Henrietta Szold was born in Baltimore in 1860, shortly after her family's arrival in America. She was the oldest of eight daughters, and Rabbi Szold gave her a traditional education normally reserved for a son. In addition to German, the Szold household language, her father taught her French and Hebrew, along with Bible and Jewish history. After graduating from high school, she embarked on two of

her many careers: she became a writer and the Baltimore correspondent for the *New York Jewish Messenger* under the pen name "Sulamith," as well as a teacher of French, German, botany, and mathematics. During these years she also became active in a number of social and civic groups.

Her Zionist commitment was aroused by the influx of Russian Jews following the 1881 czarist May Laws. Szold suggested what has been called "an experiment in practical education," a night school for immigrants. For five years, from 1888 to 1893, she headed such a school in Baltimore. This period also marked the beginning of her experience with fund-raising—she was responsible for funding, staffing, and leasing space for classrooms. The school proved a vital success in the Americanization of immigrants. By 1898, when the school was taken over publicly by the city of Baltimore, Szold was a committed Zionist. To Szold, Zionism was "an ideal that can be embraced by all, no matter what their attitude may be to other Jewish questions."

At age 33 Szold's life took a new turn. With her knowledge of German, English, and Hebrew, plus her own impressive education (she audited classes at the then fledgling Jewish Theological Seminary in New York), she became the paid secretary for the editorial board of the Jewish Publication Society of America. She worked there for twenty-three years. Over the years she helped to build JPS as a publisher of prestige and scholarship, while she herself became its main editor and translator.

While there, Szold also became closely associated with Dr. Louis Ginzberg, who wrote the classic *Legends of the Jews*. Between her work and a nonmutual emotional involvement with Ginzberg, Szold took ill. A several-month hiatus took place, which led her to the next phase of her life.

In 1909 Szold and her mother made their first journey to Palestine. There she witnessed the beauty of the land, the problems of the country, and the misery of the Jews. She was motivated to better the lot of the Jews and Zionism. Upon her return to the States, she became active in Zionist circles, leaving her scholarship behind and becoming secretary for the Federation of American Zionists. At the time she was fifty years old.

The next two years saw speeches and campaigning for Jewish institutions and enterprises in Palestine. On February 24, 1912, thirty-eight women chartered themselves as the Hadassah Chapter of Daughters of Zion. In 1914, at the group's first convention, the name was changed to Hadassah (the Hebrew name of Queen Esther) and Henrietta Szold was elected its first president. In 1916 a group of Zionist supporters led by Judge Julian Mack provided Szold with a lifetime stipend. This stipend freed her from the worry of financial support and allowed her to work full time for Zionist causes. By 1916 Hadassah membership had grown to more than 4,000.

Following the turmoil of World War I, Szold left the United States for Palestine in February 1920 for a two-year assignment: overseeing the American Zionist Medical Unit. One result of this assignment was her remaining in Palestine. She never returned to a permanent home in the United States but made only necessary trips back. Upon her arrival in Palestine, she was greeted by a mutiny: the overall situation was such that forty-five doctors resigned and seventeen nurses went on strike. Szold brought the situation under control and began organizing the establishment of dispensaries, welfare stations, and laboratories throughout the country. To a backward populace, Szold brought twentieth-century medical care, including home instruction in preventive medicine. Arab and Jew were treated alike. In 1934, at the age of 74, Szold was a keynote speaker in Jerusalem at the cornerstone laying for the now world-famous Hadassah Hospital.

By this time, Szold had entered yet an-

other phase of her life. Seven years earlier, she had been elected by the World Zionist Organization as one of the three governors of Zionist affairs. Holding the portfolio of minister of health and education, she charged herself with the responsibility of social work for all of Palestine. She focused on youth. Especially notable were her rehabilitation efforts aimed at juvenile delinquency and the establishment of vocational schools.

At age 73, Szold became director of Youth Aliyah. She made several trips to Germany in the 1930s and saw clearly the ascent of the Nazis. Many German Jews were fleeing Germany and coming to Palestine. Szold made it her personal campaign to save children. She took charge of those children who were without parents and saw to their welfare. By 1935, 1,000 German-Jewish children were settled in various communities: children who knew only one culture, one language, one way of life and were being transported to a strange land with a different culture and a different language. She took urban children from one of the world's foremost technical societies and put them into agricultural settings. She became more famous, and beloved, for personally meeting each boat that brought children to Palestine and for sitting with the children on the buses as they were delivered to their new homes. A grandmotherly figure, it was her personal charisma that made Youth Aliyah a success. By 1948, an estimated 30,000 children were being cared for under Szold's program.

Henrietta Szold died at the age of 84, active up until her last year, when illness confined her to a hospital bed. She died in February 1945. At her funeral, *Kaddish*—the prayer usually recited by a son of the deceased—was said for her by 15-year-old Simon Kresz. No blood relation to Szold, he was one of the rescued Polish-Jewish children saved from the Nazi death machine through Szold's efforts. Years before Szold had written, "*Deep down in my heart I have always held that I should have had children, many children.*" Kresz was representative of "her" children—those she rescued.

Henrietta Szold was convinced that, for the Jews to survive, they must have their own homeland. Throughout her life, she knew the future of the Jew was "If not Zionism, then nothing!"

כ׳ באדר״א תרנ״ן

85111/8264 29 בפברואר 1940

№ 1145 17 3367
26. MAR. 1940

אל מחלקת הכספים

מאת הלשכה לעלית הנוער.

הננו להודיעכם, כי מנינו את הגברת אילזה ביקרד לפקידה קבועה במשרדנו, כמזכירה לעניני גרמנית, וקבענו את סוגה כסוג ב׳. גברת ביקרד תחל בעבודתה הקבועה ביום 1 במרס ש״ז. בהתחשב בעובדה, כי היא עובדת במשרדנו זה שנים ומחודש ינואר 1939 לא הפסיקה את עבודתה הפסקה כלשהי, החלטנו לאשר לה הוספת ותק של שנה אחת. קבענו, אפוא, את משכורתה החדשית לסכום 11.400 לא״י.

הינריטה סאלד

שלח/ר

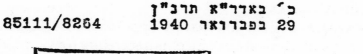

Typed letter signed by Henrietta Szold in Hebrew.

To: the Finance Dept., 20 Adar A', 5700
From: Youth Aliyah Dept., February 29, 1940

We wish to inform you that we appointed Mrs. Elsa Pikard as an official constant clerk at our office, as a secretary for German affairs. We fixed her level as 'B' (professional rank). Mrs. Pikard entered her new position on March 1, 1940. Due to the fact that she is working with us for many years, and since January 1939 did not get any vacation—we decided to credit her with one additional year of seniority. Therefore, we have fixed her salary to 11 Palestine Pounds & 400 Mils per month.

Henrietta Szold

Translation of letter.

JOSEPH TRUMPELDOR

"Never mind; it is good to die for our country." ("Ein davar; tov lamut be'ad artzenu.")

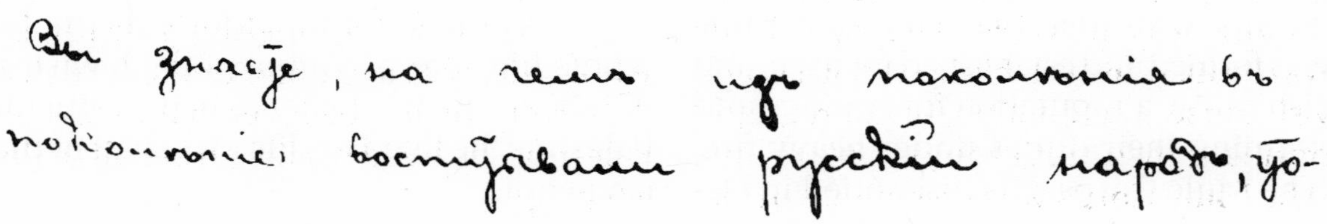

Writing sample.

A Zionist patriot who gave his life for his people, Joseph Trumpeldor will always be remembered as a symbol of Jewish courage and pioneering spirit.

Born in 1880 in Pyatigorsk, Northern Caucasus, Russia, Trumpeldor was educated in Jewish religious schools before attending a Russian municipal school. Prior to his being conscripted into the czar's army in 1902, he studied dentistry (having been denied admission to the *gymnazium* because he was a Jew). Upon conscription, he fought with distinction in the Russo-Japanese War; he was subsequently wounded and his left arm was amputated. Although eligible for discharge, he asked to be returned to the front. After the fall of Port Arthur, he was taken to a Japanese detention camp as a prisoner of war but was returned to Russia in 1906. He was awarded a number of major decorations and, rare for a Jew, commissioned as an officer.

Trumpeldor then turned to the study of law. During this period, he formulated a plan with several associates to immigrate to Palestine. Trumpeldor had been influenced by Tolstoy's ideas of collective communes; his

own idea for the settlement of *Eretz Yisrael* was of a network and economy of agricultural communes. In 1912 he and six friends emigrated, setting out for Degania, the first *kibbutz* established in Palestine.

With the outbreak of World War I in 1914, Turkey became allied with Germany, and all Jews in Palestine holding foreign citizenship were offered three choices: renounce their own citizenships and become Turkish citizens, be imprisoned, or be deported. Trumpeldor chose to leave and was deported to Egypt.

In Egypt, Trumpeldor met Vladimir Jabotinsky, a Zionist-oriented Jewish correspondent for a Moscow newspaper. Together they developed the idea of having a Jewish unit within the British army to assist in fighting the Turks. With a hundred volunteers, they approached the British, who would only allow them to assist as support troops: as mule handlers. Highly insulted, Jabotinsky completely rejected the British offer, but Trumpeldor accepted, feeling it was important to fight the Turks in any way possible. The`Zion Mule Corps was formed and established for itself, and the Jewish cause, a reputation for courage and for performing their duties under heavy fire.

The Mule Corps was disbanded in December 1915, and the British at that time still refused to have a Jewish unit. With the revolution of 1917, Trumpeldor went to Russia to seek the support of the new government there. When that mission failed, he began developing Jewish self-defense units and organized groups of young Zionists of Russia with the purpose of bringing them to Palestine. Trumpeldor returned to Palestine in 1919. Following World War I, elements of the European powers struggled for dominance in the Middle East. France, in particular, was engaged in skirmishes with the Arabs. On March 1, groups of Arabs in the Upper Galilee attacked the Jewish community of Tel Chai, ostensibly looking for French troops. A battle broke out. During the fighting, Trumpeldor was wounded three times, including in the stomach, but refused to be evacuated. In the evening, as he was being removed for medical treatment with other casualties, he died. His reputed last words were: "Never mind. It is good to die for our country."

Not just Trumpeldor's death, but his whole life, was a symbol of the Jewish cause. A "never say die" believer in the settlement of Palestine, he lived his life on behalf of the Jewish people.

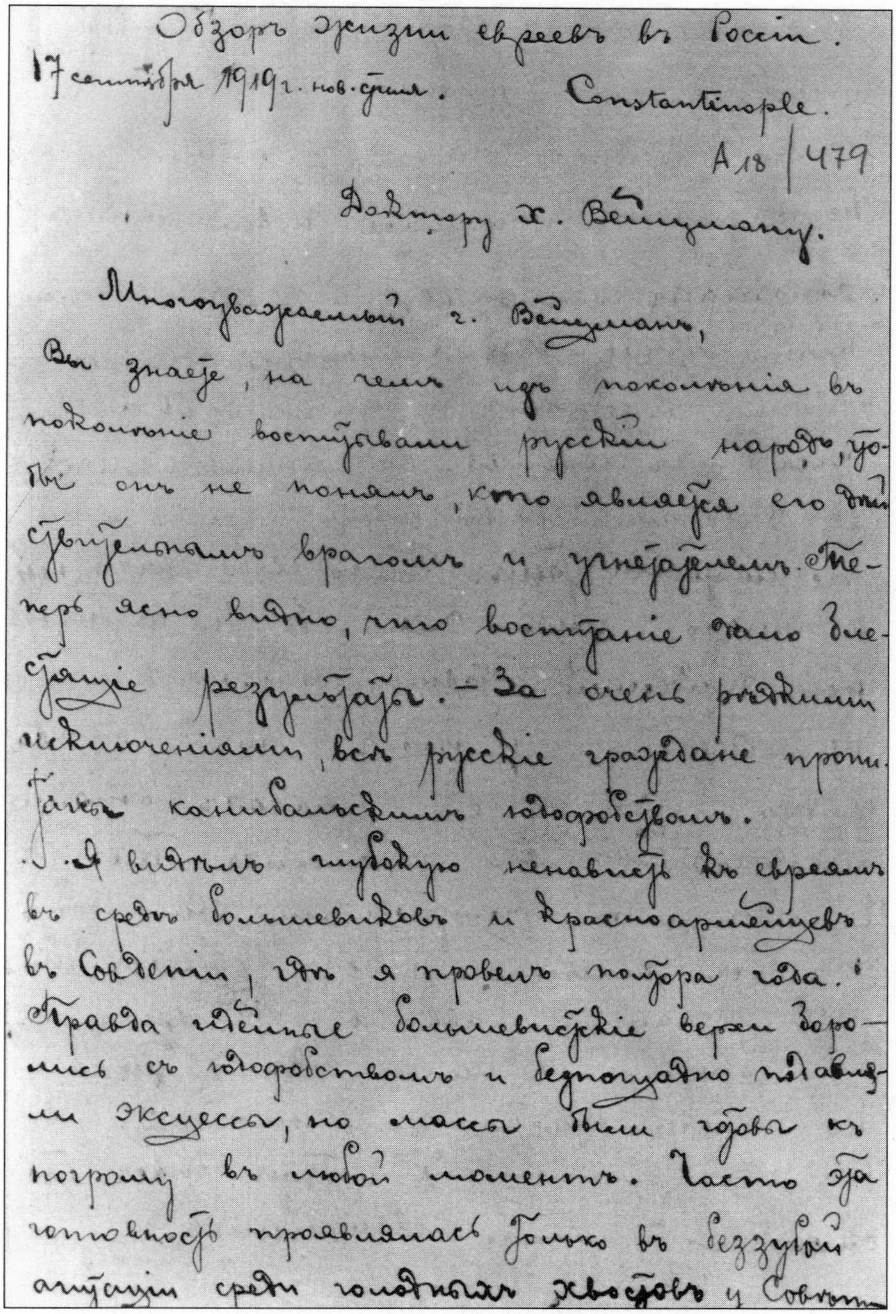

Обзоръ жизни евреевъ въ Россіи.

17 сентября 1919 г. нов. стиля. Constantinople.

A 18 | 479

Доктору Х. Вейцману.

Многоуважаемый г. Вейцманъ,

Вы знаете, на чемъ изъ поколѣнія въ поколѣніе воспитывали русскій народъ, чтобы онъ не понялъ, кто является его дѣйствительнымъ врагомъ и угнетателемъ. Теперь ясно видно, что воспитаніе дало блестящіе результаты. — За очень рѣдкими исключеніями, всѣ русскіе граждане пропитаны каннибальскимъ юдофобствомъ.

Я видѣлъ глубокую ненависть къ евреямъ въ средѣ большевиковъ и красноармейцевъ въ Совдепіи, гдѣ я провелъ полтора года. Правда центральные большевистскіе верхи боролись съ юдофобствомъ и безпощадно подавляли эксцессы, но массы были готовы къ погрому въ любой моментъ. Часто эта готовность проявлялась только въ беззубой агитаціи среди голодныхъ хвостовъ у Совнар-

Letter in Russian by Joseph Trumpeldor.

MENACHEM USSISHKIN

"Our task today is harder than Moses'; he had only to deliver Israel from one Egypt, we must deliver it from many."

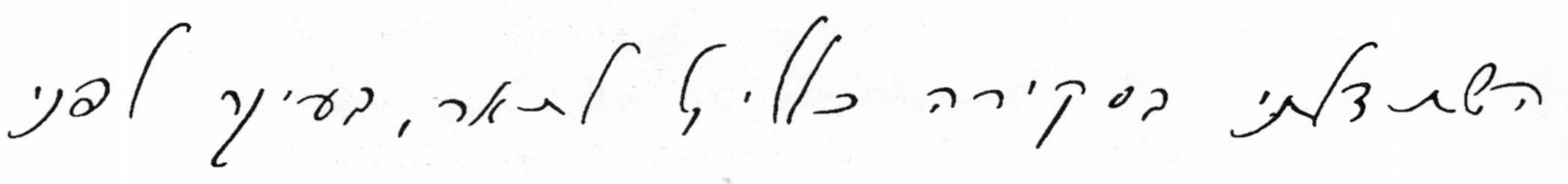

Writing sample.

Forceful, dedicated, and focused, Abraham Menachem Mendel Ussishkin was another of the transitional generation who made the State of Israel a reality. Although he died a few years prior to statehood, his efforts were instrumental in its founding.

Born into a chasidic family in the town of Dubrovno, in the Russian province of Mogilev, Ussishkin received a thoroughly traditional Jewish education. In 1871, when he was 8, his family moved to Moscow, where he also received a secular education. Ussishkin early on studied Hebrew as a contemporary language and also read the works of Enlightenment (*Haskalah*) writers.

The widespread and vicious pogroms of 1881 led Ussishkin to an early belief in Zionism. He joined a Moscow Zionist group and, when admitted in 1882 to the Technological Institute in Moscow, founded a Jewish students' society. Throughout the 1880s Ussishkin was deeply involved in Zionist organizations. As one of the founders of the Moscow student Zionist group *Bene Zion*, in 1887 he was elected to go to a major Zionist convention in Druzkeniki, where he was recognized as an upcoming and promising young Zionist leader.

In 1889 Ussishkin joined Ahad Ha'am's *Bene Moshe* group. Like others, he was deeply impressed and swayed by Ha'am's perspectives

of cultural Zionism. Ussishkin was a staunch advocate of Hebrew and believed deeply in the agricultural settlement of Palestine. These beliefs were strengthened by his first visit in 1891 to Palestine. Upon his return from there to Russia, he became a leading Russian Zionist in advocating mass immigration. In 1896 he met Theodor Herzl and Dr. Max Nordau, and although he disagreed with their views of political Zionism, he accepted Herzl's offer to help organize the First Zionist Congress, at which he was elected Hebrew secretary.

Ussishkin was deeply involved in the Zionist Congress for the rest of his life. At the second congress, he was elected to the general council, on which he served for the rest of his life. At the third, he was elected to head the Yekinteroslav Russian district for all Zionist activities. This area included all of southern Russia and the Caucasus. Under his leadership, his district became one of the leading areas involved with Russian Zionism. Throughout this period, Ussishkin also gave specific attention to the dissemination of Hebrew literature and periodicals.

Ussishkin returned to Palestine in 1903 for the express purpose of purchasing land that would be parceled out to Zionist settlers. He organized a conference in Zicharon Yaakov to discuss the organization of the Jewish community throughout the land of Palestine. Although short-lived, the conference did result in the founding of the Hebrew Teachers' Association.

Returning to Russia in September 1903, Ussishkin was greeted with the news that the Zionist Congress had passed a resolution calling for the consideration of Uganda as an alternate homeland for the Jews. Strong supporter of Herzl that he was, Ussishkin nonetheless broke ranks with Herzl and the congress on this issue and strongly opposed any such plan. In reaction, he founded the Zionists for Zion group (*Ziyyonei Zion*), chairing a conference in Vilna in 1905. This group demanded that Herzl abandon the Uganda Plan. In 1904 Ussishkin published "Our Program," a five-point plan for practical Zionism: political action, land acquisition, emigration, settlement, and educational and organizational work among the Jews. "Our Program" addressed the establishment of an independent political, cultural, and economic state. It also discussed the creation of a Jewish labor brigade. Under Ussishkin's direction, the *Ziyyonei Zion* was successful in having the Seventh Zionist Congress reject the Uganda suggestion.

With the announcement of the Balfour Declaration in 1917, Ussishkin organized a mass demonstration in Odessa to celebrate it. Two hundred thousand people, both Jews and non-Jews, attended. In 1919 Ussishkin, at the invitation of Chaim Weizmann and Nachum Sokolow, attended the Paris Peace Conference. There, as a representative of the Jewish people, he addressed the delegates in Hebrew, the first time this had ever been done at an international conference. In that same year, he settled in Palestine and was appointed the head of the Zionist Commission. This agency led the fight of the Jewish community in Palestine to establish a national homeland. In 1923 Ussishkin was chosen to lead the Jewish National Fund, the agency responsible for acquiring land. In this role, he was responsible for raising funds worldwide in order to purchase large tracts of land to be owned by the Jewish people. He held this position until his death and helped to increase land holdings from approximately 5,500 acres to more than 140,000. Ever active in education, Ussishkin was also intimately involved in the founding of the Hebrew University. He was elected to both the board of trustees and the university's executive committee.

Ussishkin died in Palestine in 1943; he was active in Zionist affairs until his death. For more than sixty years, he had participated in every major Zionist national event that took place, leaving his own impression on them. Although he did not live to see it, Ussishkin was truly one of the developers of Israel.

השתדלתי בסקירה כללית לבאר, בעיקר לפני ה

הצעיר של עובדינו, את המומנטים האופייניים המאחדים את

שני היובלות לחג אחד - ואותם הפכו בה והפכו בה, כי הכל

בה. ידעו הדור היהודי והציונים שבכל העולם, כי בכבד

לנצח את הגלים הזדונים, אשר סביב שתו עלינו מן

ומאת, דרושים: אמונה, סבלנות, קרבנות עצומים,

וראש וראשונה הכרה מוחלטת ברגלינו. - אך

הכרע יהיה לנו - הארץ גאולתנו. עם ישראל

יגאל את ארץ ישראל וארץ ישראל

תגאל את עם ישראל. -

מ. אוסישקין

Letter by Menachem Ussishkin.

CHAIM WEIZMANN

"Independence is never given to a people; it has to be earned; and having been earned, it has to be defended."

Dr. Chaim Weizmann will be remembered forever as the first president of an independent Jewish state.

One of fifteen children, Chaim Weizmann was born in the village of Motol, Pinsk region of Russia, on November 27, 1874. He received a religious and secular education and seemed destined to be a Jewish leader. As a child, he recognized the endemic anti-Semitism and, at the age of 11, expressed his feelings in a letter preserved at the Weizmann Archives in Rehovot, Israel: "*Why should we look to the Kings of Europe for compassion that they should take pity upon us and give us a resting place? In vain. All have decided: The Jews must die, but England will nevertheless have mercy upon us. In conclusion to Zion! Jews to Zion let us go.*"

Finishing his secondary education in Pinsk, Weizmann chose not to apply to Russian universities—where Jewish quotas were strictly maintained—but instead went to Germany, where he studied chemistry and biochemistry at Darmstadt and Berlin. In 1898 he was awarded a doctorate in chemistry from Fribourg University in Switzerland. In 1901 Weizmann became an assistant lecturer at Geneva University and embarked on a career as a scientist. As a chemical researcher, Weiz-

mann was eventually to take out over 100 patents. He would later credit his research of chemical reactions affected by bacteria as assisting him in his Zionist efforts with the British government.

It was in Berlin that Weizmann first began associating with other intense young Zionists, including Theodor Herzl, who had just published his revolutionary concept of Zionism. Weizmann also came under the influence of Ahad Ha'am, whose Zionism stressed cultural and spiritual identity. In 1898 he was a delegate to the Second Zionist Congress.

The years from 1900 through World War I saw Weizmann develop as a leading scientist and Zionist personality. In 1901 he was the leader of a group of Zionists known as the Democratic Faction, whose aim was to further Ahad Ha'am's concepts of cultural, social, and educational institutions. Weizmann advocated the establishment of a Jewish university, complete with scientific and cultural/spiritual endeavors. While both sought the same goal, Weizmann and Herzl believed in different methods of achieving it. In 1907, at the Eighth Zionist Congress, Weizmann, by now a major Zionist figure, coined the phrase "synthetic Zionism." This was to be a merger of political and practical Zionism: politics to win Jewish nationhood and settlement of Palestine coupled with cultural action. In the same year he also made his first visit to Palestine.

During World War I Weizmann was active in both the British war effort and Zionism. He achieved a certain degree of prominence for his scientific contributions to the Allied war effort and as head of the British Admiralty Laboratory worked on a chemical process to manufacture acetone, a vital component in the production of explosives. His work brought Weizmann in contact with such key political figures as Winston Churchill, Lord Arthur Balfour, and Lloyd George. He was thus able to advocate the Zionist cause in political circles and enlist powerful support.

Primarily through Weizmann's efforts, the historic Balfour Declaration was issued on November 2, 1917. This was a historic breakthrough in modern Jewish history: for the first time in two millennia, a world power had agreed to help create a Jewish homeland. As an official act of foreign policy, the British government declared its sympathy for "Jewish Zionist aspiration." In part, the Balfour Declaration (named for and signed by England's foreign secretary, Lord Arthur James Balfour) stated: "His Majesty's Government view with favour the establishment in Palestine of a national home for the Jewish people, and will use their best endeavors to facilitate the achievement of this object."

In 1918 Turkey, which had ruled Palestine, was conquered by the British. With Palestine under English rule, and with a statement of sympathy such as the Balfour Declaration, Weizmann went to Palestine to head the Zionist Commission to coordinate activities with the British military authorities. Although the British had stated their support for a homeland, it was by no means a fait accompli; there was still a major national Arab population with which to deal. Weizmann conferred with Emir Feisal of Transjordan, the leader of Arab nationalism, reaching an agreement with him for peaceful Arab-Jewish coexistence. In the same year, he also laid the cornerstone in Jerusalem for the Hebrew University, of which he would later serve as president.

In 1919 Weizmann appeared at the Paris Peace Conference, soliciting world endorsement of a national Jewish homeland. His status as an established scientist proved useful; Weizmann was treated as both a Jewish and international head of state. He was given audiences, treated with high-ranking political deference, and received as though he were already a head of state. In 1920 Weizmann was elected president of the World Zionist Organization (WZO).

Throughout the 1920s and 1930s, Weiz-

mann was at the center of all mainstream Zionist activities. He traveled extensively, as both a fund-raiser and a political persona. In 1929 he presided over the founding of the Jewish Agency, an umbrella organization for both Zionists and non-Zionists; it also was the representative group for the WZO. Weizmann served as president of the WZO from 1920 to 1931, and again from 1931 to 1946. In addition, he worked to create the Daniel Sieff Institute (later renamed the Weizmann Institute of Science) in Rehovot, the premier Jewish scientific institute. These years were not all sweet success, however. Weizmann came under heavy criticism from various Jewish factions, especially in 1929 following Arab riots against Jews in Palestine. His close ties with the British government were also criticized, particularly when England limited immigration to Palestine. Both in 1929 and 1939, when British policy limited Jewish immigration and self-destiny, Weizmann found himself in conflict with the British government.

With the advent of World War II, Weizmann offered the British government the aid and support of the Jewish population in Palestine. Likewise, he offered scientific assistance. However, his status among the British was not what it was in World War I, and his offers were rebuffed. Even when his oldest son, Michael, was killed in action with the Royal Air Force over the English Channel, there was little sympathy toward Weizmann. Although he received strong support from Winston Churchill, he was given little other reason for hope. He spent a great part of 1941 and 1942 in the United States, building support among American Jews and politicians. He was one of the founders of the Biltmore Plan, a program that would establish an independent Jewish commonwealth upon the end of World War II. But the world's problems were overwhelming and there was little active movement toward a Jewish homeland, even with the horrors of the Holocaust.

In 1946 Weizmann suffered serious political and personal problems. Politically, Jewish support was moving toward other leaders within the Zionist movement, while international relations between England and world Jewry were rapidly disintegrating—not even Weizmann's former relations with Britain could reverse the direction. As Great Britain more and more rejected Jewish requests—particularly a request to have 100,000 European survivors come to Palestine—Weizmann found his influence lessening and Jewish political leadership was passing to others. Equally as depressing, Weizmann's health was failing; glaucoma was leading him to blindness. He was 71.

Weizmann, however, was not finished with politics; nor were the Jewish people finished with him. He was still recognized as the preeminent elder statesman of Zionism. He was active in lobbying the United Nations for a partition decision, and he persuaded President Truman to support it, including the Negev for Palestine in the plan. When Israel declared its independence on May 14, 1948, Weizmann, who was in New York pressing for support for the Jews, was chosen as president of the provisional government. Because of Weizmann's contacts with Truman, the United States, in a bold diplomatic step, immediately recognized the new political state. In a personal visit to Washington and President Truman a few days later, while the streets of Washington were lined with American and Israeli flags, Weizmann thanked Truman for his support and secured from him a pledge of American financial support of $100 million. In February 1949, Weizmann was elected first president of the State of Israel. His presidency of Israel was best reflected by David Ben-Gurion's statement: "I doubt whether the presidency is necessary to Dr. Weizmann, but the presidency of Dr. Weizmann is a moral necessity for the State of Israel."

Weizmann died on November 9, 1952.

His last few years were racked by severe declining health. For virtually his entire life, he had fought and lobbied on behalf of the Jewish people. Weizmann, unlike other Zionist leaders, did live to see world Jewry change from the times of czars and pogroms and worldwide dispersion to the establishment of a homeland for Jews.

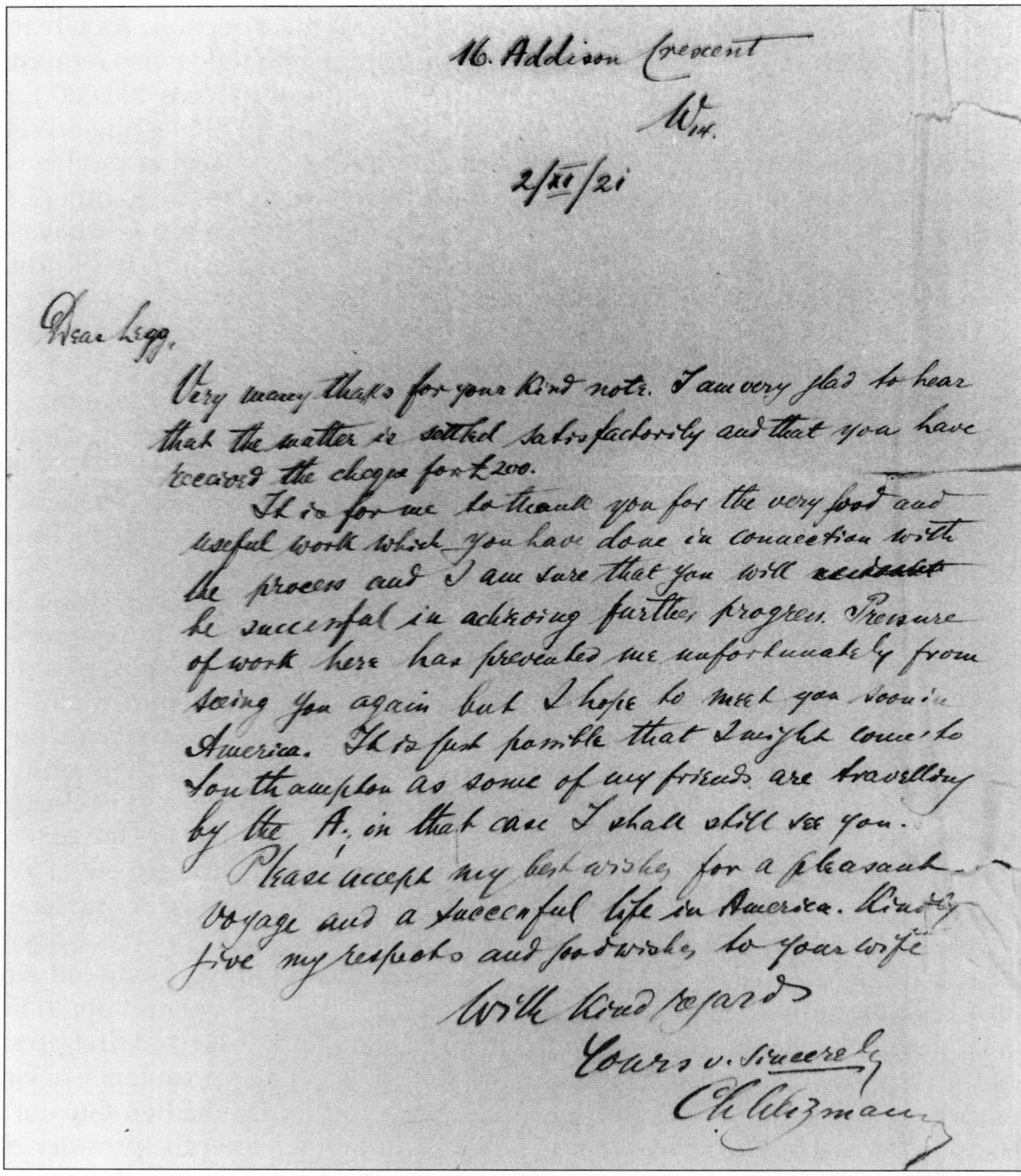

16. Addison Crescent
W14.
2/XI/21

Dear Legg,

Very many thanks for your kind note. I am very glad to hear that the matter is settled satisfactorily and that you have received the cheque for £200.

It is for me to thank you for the very good and useful work which you have done in connection with the process and I am sure that you will be successful in achieving further progress. Pressure of work here has prevented me unfortunately from seeing you again but I hope to meet you soon in America. It is just possible that I might come to Southampton as some of my friends are travelling by the A., in that case I shall still see you.

Please accept my best wishes for a pleasant voyage and a successful life in America. Kindly give my respects and good wishes to your wife

With kind regards
Yours v. sincerely
Ch Weizmann

Letter in English signed by Chaim Weizmann to a Mr. Legg, apologizing for not seeing him personally due to work constraints and wishing Legg a successful life in America, where Weizmann hopes to meet him again.

V

LITERARY FIGURES

The three aims of writers ought to be: to teach our people good taste and understanding; to bring the daily life of their world and their actions into the sphere of literature in order to make the public fonder of the latter; to instruct and prove beneficial.

—Mendele Moicher Seforim

S. Y. AGNON

"QUIET. AGNON IS WRITING."
—Sign placed by Jerusalem mayor Teddy Kollek near Agnon's home

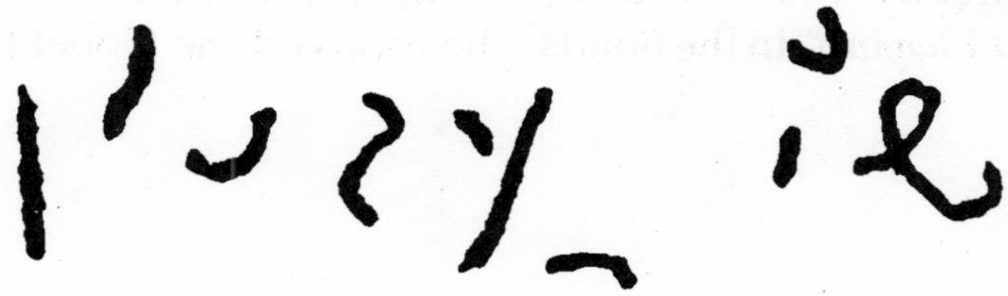

S. Y. Agnon was the first Hebrew writer to receive the Nobel Prize for literature. One of the foremost writers in modern Hebrew fiction, a product of roiling times, his works reflect the experiences, insights, doubts, depression, and soul of a troubled people.

Born in Buczacz, Galicia, in 1888, Agnon was raised in a bicultural household. His father taught him talmudic legends, while his mother recited German stories. Agnon had private tutors for both Talmud and German and read chasidic literature, as well as secular Hebrew and Yiddish writings. During his teenage years he published over seventy pieces in Hebrew and Yiddish. But after leaving his birthplace, he never wrote in Yiddish again.

In 1908 Agnon settled in Palestine, where he felt complete anomie. The Russian-Jewish population there held him in contempt for being a *Galitzianer* (Galician Jew), and the new settlers, whose prize ethic was manual labor, were a different breed from Agnon. In emigrating, Agnon severed himself from both his religion and his family. He was no longer religious, yet he could not connect with the modernity of the new breed of pioneers. Although at the center of the Hebrew revival, he felt himself to not be a part of it.

In this same year Agnon published the story "*Agunot*" ("Abandoned Wives"), from which his pen name derived. (His family surname was Czaczkos.) *Agunot*, the plural for *agunah*, means abandoned, deserted, forsaken. That was clearly what Agnon was experiencing.

Agnon returned to Germany in 1912, and through 1924 he found a comfortable life after his four disconcerting, alienated years in Palestine. He associated with Zionist officials and Jewish scholars, deepened his own knowledge and understanding of Judaism, read extensively in German and French literature, wrote, found financial stability, and his works began to be translated into German from Hebrew. He became well known among German Jews and enjoyed a satisfying, successful, and financially rewarding life.

During this period he also began collecting rare Hebrew books and manuscripts. Catastrophe struck in 1924 when fire broke out in his home, destroying not only his home and collection but also his personal manuscripts, notably a long book already announced for publication, *Be-tzeror Ha-Chayim* ("In the Bonds of Life"). By this time, fortunately, he was well established and had already published three collections of stories.

In 1924 Agnon returned to Palestine, settling in Jerusalem. His personal library and manuscript collection were again destroyed by fire, this time in 1929 as a result of the Arab riots. Many books and rare manuscripts dealing with the history of Jewish settlements in Palestine were lost. In his novel *A Guest for the Night*, Agnon parallels the symbolism of these two fires in his life with the destruction of the Holy Temple in Jerusalem, and compares his time in Germany with the Jewish exile.

Agnon's writings blend the milieu of the *shtetl* with the modern life that was emerging. His works reflect the pious lives and lifestyle of his childhood surroundings and the developing inroads of modernism and Western civilization. In them he addresses contemporary spiritual concerns, the disintegration of traditional Jewish life, the loss of faith, and the absence of identity. Agnon won the coveted Israel Prize in 1954 and again in 1958. In 1966 he received the Nobel Prize. He died in 1970.

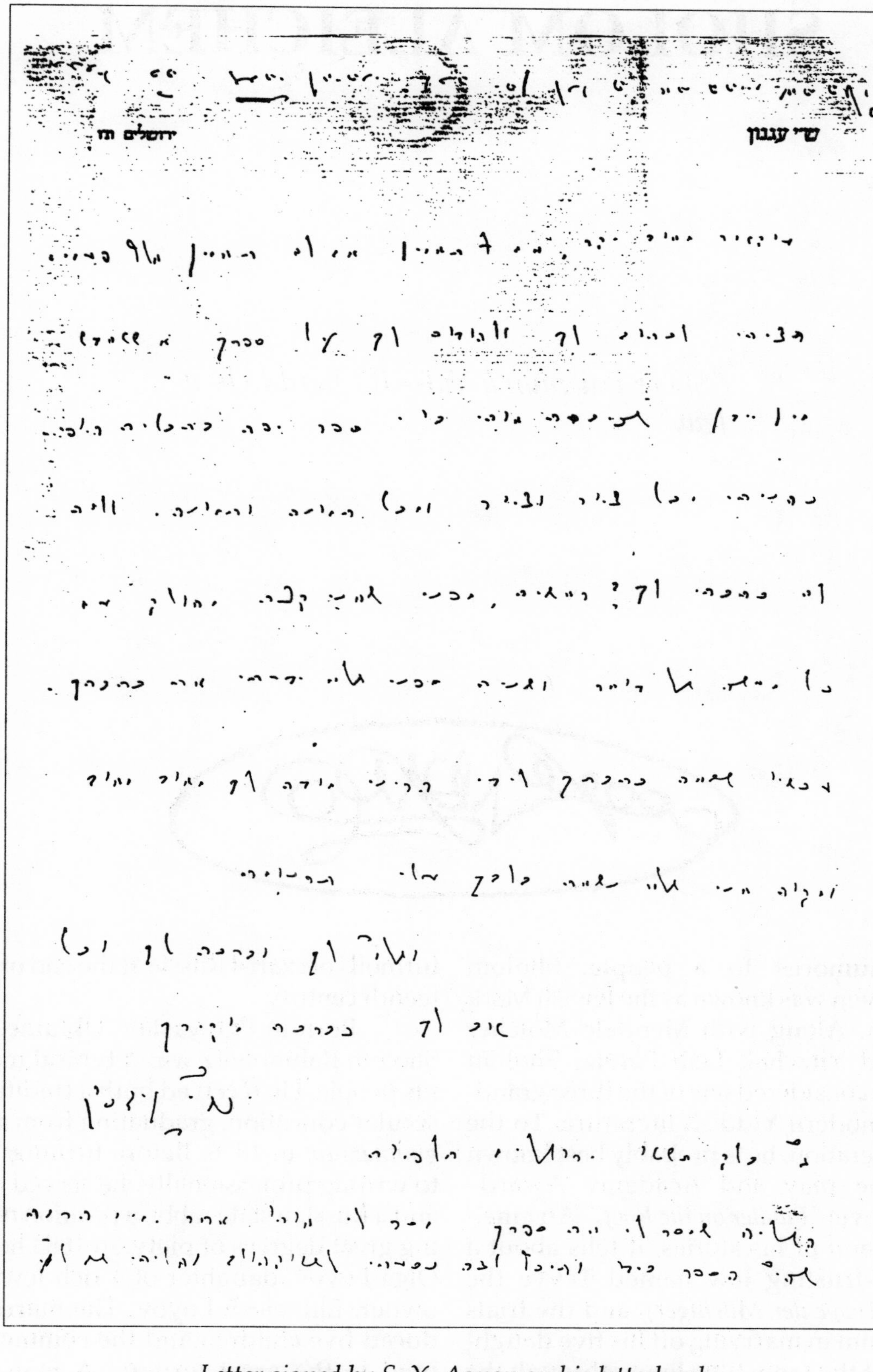

Letter signed by S. Y. Agnon on his letterhead.

SHOLOM ALEICHEM

"Shver tzu zayn a Yid—It's hard to be a Jew."

Folk humorist to a people, Sholom Aleichem was known as the Jewish Mark Twain. Along with Mendele Moicher S'forim and Yitzchak Leib Peretz, Sholom Aleichem is considered one of the three grandfathers of modern Yiddish literature. To the current generation, he is probably best known through the play and Academy Award–winning movie *"Fiddler on the Roof."* An amalgam of several of his stories, it tells about a plain, God-trusting Jew named Tevye the Milkman (*Tevye der Milchiger*), and the trials that befall him in marrying off his five daughters while at the same time living through the turmoils of czarist Russia at the end of the nineteenth century.

Born in Pereyaslav, Ukraine, in 1859, Sholom Rabinowitz was a typical member of his people. He received both a traditional and secular education, graduating from a Russian *gymnazium* in 1876. Before turning his hand to writing professionally, he served as a tutor and a Russian state rabbi, a position not requiring great degrees of piety. In 1883 he married Olga Loyov, daughter of a rich Jewish landowner, Elimelech Loyov. The marriage produced five children and the comment attributed to the great writer: "A man enters a

wedding canopy living, and comes out a corpse."

He first began writing in 1879, with his real output beginning in 1883. Over the next decade, he wrote numerous essay, articles, and stories, including five novels. In 1888 he founded a Yiddish literary annual, *Di Yiddishe Folksbibliotek* ("The Popular Jewish Library"), a mechanism meant to raise the stature of writing in Yiddish. Successful in concept, it was limited economically.

The 1890s saw the creation of two of his greatest characters: Tevye the Milkman and Menachem Mendel (a character not yet well known to the English-only public). Sholom Aleichem's appeal lies in his understanding of and complete identification with the common man. His pen name alone—Sholom Aleichem—remains the daily greeting among Jews the world over and reflects his commonality, his everyman identity: peace unto you. His writings touched upon and mirrored the pain and suffering and struggles of the Jews of the Russian Pale. Through characters like Tevye, Menachem Mendel, and the orphan Mottel, he touched the main nerve of virtually millions of Jews struggling for economic, religious, ethnic, and emotional survival. His humor was the humor of the people, the heartaches, the wrenchings, the need to emote:

> When I finish talking she falls on my neck and begins to weep. "Goodbye, Father," she cries. "Goodbye! God alone knows when we shall see each other again." Well, that was too much for me. I remembered this Hodel when she was still a baby and I carried her in my arms, I carried her in my arms. . . . Forgive me, Reb Sholom Aleichem, for acting like an old woman. If you only knew what a daughter she is. If you could only see the letters she writes. Oh, what a daughter. . . .
>
> And now, let's talk about more cheerful things. Tell me, what news is there about the cholera in Odessa?

Following the pogroms in 1905, Sholom Aleichem resolved to come to America. Like many writers, he was unsuccessful in financial dealings and was constantly plagued by money problems. America held out the hope of financial security, and while he did come to America, the hope was not fulfilled. From 1906 until the end of his life, he traveled extensively from America to Russia and Europe, giving highly popular public readings and seeking financial security. The traveling and financial worries took a cumulative toll on his health, resulting in tuberculosis and a generally decreased state of well-being. Financial success was partially achieved in 1909, when his fiftieth birthday was celebrated throughout the Jewish world and a committee of fellow authors established an endowment for him for his royalties from his various publishers.

World War I found Sholom Aleichem in Germany, and only with great difficulty and over several months was he, a Russian citizen, able to get his family to Denmark. He returned to the United States, which had only bitter memories for him. In 1915 he was shocked by the news of his son Misha's death. Between emotional and physical ills, Sholom Aleichem weakened and on May 13, 1916, after being ill for only a few weeks, he died. His funeral cortege in New York was escorted by hundreds of thousands. The introductory remarks of his will reflect the love he had for his fellow Jews:

> Wherever I may die, let me be buried not among the rich and famous, but among plain Jewish people, the workers, the common folk, so that my tombstone may honor the simple graves around me, and the simple graves honor mine, even as the plain people honored their folk writer in his lifetime.

SHOLOM ASCH

"We were worms in our physical creation; we have become human in our hunger for divinity."

Yiddish playwright, novelist, and dramatist Sholom Asch was one of a handful of Eastern European writers who helped present Jewish life and literature to international audiences.

Asch was born in the city of Kutno, Poland, in 1880, the son of scholarly parents. He received a traditional Jewish education, but at 17 he discovered the Psalms in Moses Mendelssohn's transliterated German. Asch taught himself German and went on to read many of the classics. His parents were concerned about Asch's straying from the traditional Jewish world and sent him to relatives in a Polish village, where Asch experienced for the first time peasant village life. He became a Torah teacher for children. A few years later, before he turned 20, he moved to Wloclawek, where he earned his way as a professional letter writer for the illiterate.

Asch was directed on his literary path by the Yiddish luminary I. L. Peretz, to whom Asch showed his first works. Asch's early writing revealed Russian, Polish, Hebrew, Yiddish, and German influences. Peretz advised him to concentrate on Yiddish. By 1903 Asch had published one Yiddish and two Hebrew books, along with a number of short stories and articles.

In 1904 his first play, *With the Stream,* won Asch considerable recognition. This play was followed by others that were performed on German, Russian, and Polish stages. As his writing developed, Asch shifted his literary focus from *shtetl* life to the larger Jewish world. He had traveled to Palestine in 1908 and the United States in 1910. During World War I, Asch moved to the United States, returning to Europe and living in France afterward. Throughout, his style deepened, mellowed, and matured as he wrote of Jewish life, conditions, and history.

Asch authored numerous works, with wide-ranging topics, among them *Kiddush Ha-Shem* (about the Chmielnitzki massacres of 1648), *The Way to One's Self* (dealing with worldwide Jewish problems), and *The Song of the Valley* (about Palestine and Jewish settlers). One of his most controversial works was the trilogy *The Nazarene, The Apostle,* and *Mary,* all dealing with the beginnings of Christianity. Critics saw elements of Christian missionaryism in them. As a result, Asch was semiostracized, and he voluntarily withdrew from Jewish social life. He continued writing, however.

Asch died in 1957. The *Encyclopaedia Judaica* describes him as "deeply attached to the legacy of the Jewish past, which he enshrined in novels and dramas of aesthetic beauty and moral grandeur; he connected the Yiddish world to the mainstream of American and European culture, becoming the first Yiddish writer to enjoy a truly international vogue."

CHAIM NACHMAN BIALIK

"Hebrew is our very flesh and blood, and each encounter with it is a fixture of our soul."

Chaim Nachman Bialik was the foremost poet, essayist, and writer of his generation. His name is as familiar to Jews as Carl Sandburg's, Henry Wadsworth Longfellow's, Edna St. Vincent Millay's, and Walt Whitman's are to other Americans.

Bialik was born in the Ukrainian village of Radi (near Zhitomir) in 1873. His experiences in youth were mixed. Until the age of 7, when his father died, he had a happy childhood. But upon his father's death, his mother sent him to live with her own father, a well-to-do but stern Orthodox traditionalist. For nine years Bialik lived with his grandfather, being schooled in the local synagogue and by tutors, but also learning by himself. His youthful, expanding zest for life was stifled by the circumstances around him. When he left at age 16 to study in the famed Volozhin *yeshivah*, he hoped to find a way to blend the horizons of the *Haskalah* with Orthodoxy. While at Volozhin, he joined a secret *yeshivah* group—*Netzach Yisrael*—which sought to combine Jewish nationalism and enlightenment with traditionalism. At this time, along with his talmudic studies (in which he was acknowledged as a good student), Bialik read Russian poetry, European literature, and the essays of

Ahad Ha'am, and began writing Hebrew prose and poetry.

Bialik left the *yeshivah* in 1891. He spent the next ten years moving from Zhitomir, Korostyshev, and Sosnowiec, having married and joined his father-in-law's timber business. During this time he wrote poems and essays expressing his despair of the timid and apathetic, and confidence in the nascent Jewish revivalist movement. In 1900 he moved to Odessa, where he entered into the literary and Zionist life of the city, joining ranks with such notables as Ahad Ha'am, Simon Dubnow, and Mendele Mocher Seforim. Jewish life was undergoing tremendous change, and Bialik, who had experienced both traditional and enlightened lifestyles, could express the despair and hopes of all Jews.

The year 1903 saw the infamous Kishinev pogroms, which produced worldwide shock waves. In response, Bialik wrote his famous poems *On the Slaughter* and *In the City of Slaughter*. The former calls for heaven to either exercise justice or destroy the world. The latter expressed indignation at the victims' pusillanimous submission and the absence of justice.

Except for a one-year absence to Warsaw, Bialik lived in Odessa until 1921. His output was prolific in all areas, save for a period right before World War I when he stopped writing. With the help and intervention of Maxim Gorki, Bialik left Odessa and lived for three years in Berlin, after which he settled in Palestine. He was a noted figure and was seen as the poet of Jewish nationalism. As such, he was frequently sent abroad as a representative of Zionism. At the height of his fame, Bialik died in 1934 of a heart attack.

Bialik's greatness lay in his expression of the universal Jew, whether religionist or nationalist. He embodied the despair and disillusionment of what was and should have been, and the joy and promise of what could and would some day be. His mastery of Hebrew was considered so superb that he was compared to Yehuda Ha-Levi. His literary career is considered a watershed in modern Hebrew literature. Just as Herzl created a new kind of Jew, so Bialik created a completely new Jewish literature.

PALESTINE FRIENDS OF THE
HEBREW UNIVERSITY IN JERUSALEM
JERUSALEM

אגודת שוחרי
האוניברסיטה העברית בירושלים
ירושלים

Jerusalem
P.O.B. 917

24.7.1933

ירושלים
ת. ד. 917

כב'
ד"ר שלום פרייברגר
אוסיעק, יוגוסלביה.

א.נ.

אגודת שוחרי האוניברסיטה העברית בא"י החליטה לקרוא בשעת כנוס הקונגרס בפראג לפגישה של באי-כח אגודות שוחרי האוניברסיטה העברית בכל הארצות ועסקני-צבור המתענינים באוניברסיטה העברית בירושלים ובהתפתחותה.

בפגישה זאת ידונו על הדרכים שבהם צריכה לפעול העמולה המיועדת לקרב את רעיון האוניברסיטה העברית ללב העם. אין צורך להרבות בדברים בכדי לנמק את חשיבות הפגישה הזאת של אנשים אשר רעיון האוניברסיטה העברית קרוב ללבם. המאורעות האחרונים הראו לכל העם היהודי מה גדול הצורך לשכלל את האוניברסיטה שלנו במדה כזאת שתוכל לשרת את כל צרכי האומה, חוקריה ומלומדיה בכל ענפי העבודה והתרבות העברית והאנושית. דעת הקהל היהודית מוכנת לפעולה למען האוניברסיטה; צריך רק למצוא את הדרכים לפעולה זאת ועל הנושא הזה תדון פגישתנו. אנו מקווים שכב' יסכים להשתתף בה. אי-אפשר כעת לקבוע בדיוק את הזמן של הפגישה. דבר זה תלוי במהלך הקונגרס. אנו מבקשים להתקשר עם ד"ר ברגמן בפראג (כתובתו: (Beth Haam, Dlouha 41, Praha

ויחד עם זה נבקש להודיע לנו ע"י טלגרמה (על-פי הכתובה: (Justice Frumkin, Jerusalem את הסכמת כב' להשתתף בפגישה זאת.

בתקוה שכב' יקבל את הזמנתנו הננו חותמים בכל הכבוד

ח.נ. ביאליק השופט גד פרומקין

Letter from Chaim Nachman Bialik signed "Ch. N. Bialik" in Hebrew.

To the leader of the Yugoslav Jewish community, Dr. Sholom Frieberger, Bialik announces a meeting of the "Palestine Friends of the Hebrew University to discuss ways of generating good publicity and feeling for the University from Jews everywhere. There is no need to tell you . . . how important the University is today, especially since the advent of the Nazis. We have to improve our University to serve the needs of all the nation's scholars and researchers in all fields and disciplines, both Jews and non-Jews. . . . This will be the subject of the next meeting. . . ."

English translation of letter.

ABRAHAM CAHAN

"Foreigners ourselves, and mostly unable to write English, we had Americanized the system of providing clothes for the American woman of moderate or humble means. . . . Indeed, the Russian Jew had made the average American girl a tailor-made girl."

—The Rise of David Levinsky

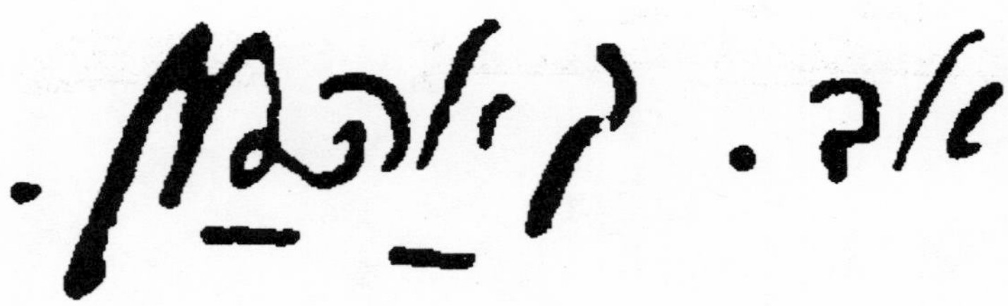

Abraham Cahan has been called "the single most influential personality in the total cultural life of well over two million Jewish immigrants and their families." Cahan himself was one of the people for whom he wrote.

Born in Vilna, Lithuania, on July 7, 1860, Cahan attended the Teacher's Institute in Vilna and taught at a government school. His original plans of preparing for the rabbinate were derailed when he met left-wing student politicos who introduced and won him over to radical socialism. Following antigovernment political activities, Cahan had to flee Lithuania and came to the United States in 1882.

Arriving penniless, Cahan became one of the legions of workers who began life in America in the cigar factories. Within several months, two factors came into play that would change his life: he learned English and he met Morris Hillquist, a leading figure in the socialist movement. Cahan quit his job and with Hillquist founded the *New York Arbeiter Zeitung* ("Workers' Newspaper"), a Yiddish daily propounding socialist philosophy and ideas, as well as offering suggestions for improving working conditions in the country. At the same time, Cahan edited the newspapers *Naye Zeit* ("New Times") and *Zukunft* ("Future").

In 1896 Cahan published his first novel, *Yekl: A Tale of the New York Ghetto*. A critical success, *Yekl* was hailed for its portrayal of the lives of Cahan's fellow immigrants. In 1897 Cahan helped found the *Jewish Daily Forward*, which is still published. However, he soon disassociated himself from radical socialism and quit the paper. For the next five years, he wrote feature articles, in-depth portraits of the immigrant experience, and literary criticism for New York English language newspapers.

Cahan rejoined the *Jewish Daily Forward* in 1902. As editor-in-chief (a position he held for the next half century), he modified the format of the paper. Cahan wrote on customs and manners, politics, economics, theater, the arts, working conditions, and so on—the scope of American life. The column *A Bintel Brief* ("A Bundle of Letters"), a combination of "Dear Abby," "Miss Manners," and "Dr. Brothers," was especially popular. At its peak in the 1920s, the *Forward* boasted a circulation in excess of 200,000.

Cahan went on to become a powerful voice for labor, especially in the fighting for the abolition of the sweatshop. His fictitious yet highly autobiographical *Rise of David Levinsky* (1917) was acclaimed as the best immigrant novel ever written and is still in print today. Among his other books is the five-volume *Bleter Fun Mein Leben* ("Pages from My Life"), first published in 1931.

Cahan died on August 31, 1951. His writings and politics guided, informed, and molded countless numbers of refugee Jews, all strangers in a strange land.

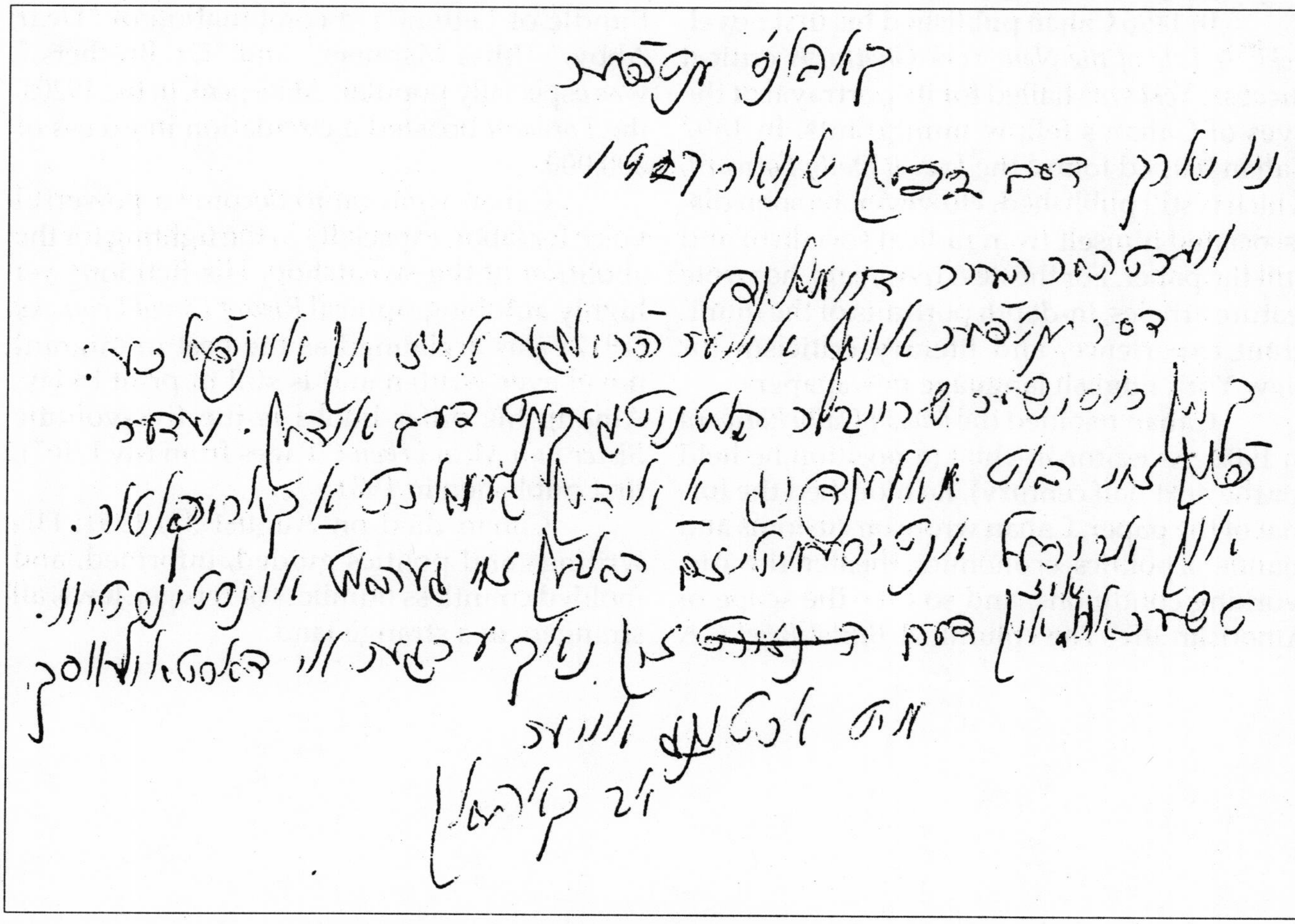

Handwritten note in Yiddish signed by Abe Cahan.

AHAD HA'AM

"Learning—learning—learning: that is the secret of Jewish survival."

One of the most influential Zionist thinkers and essayists in the late 1900s was Asher Hirsch Ginsberg, better known by his pen name Ahad Ha'am ("One of the People"). Ha'am advocated cultural Zionism, with an emphasis on Jewish culture, over the political Zionism of Theodor Herzl.

Ahad Ha'am was born into a chasidic family in Skvira (Kiev province), Russia, in 1856. He received an intense traditional background, studying Talmud and philosophy and being particularly influenced by Maimonides' *Guide for the Perplexed*. Independently, he also studied languages (German, French, English, and Latin) and became familiar with *Haskalah* literature. From his chasidic background, Ha'am developed a rationalist approach to life.

In 1884 Ha'am settled in Odessa, a city known for its Hebrew literature and Zionist politics. He gravitated to the Zionist *Hovevei Zion* movement and through it met leading Hebrew authors of the day. Although a member of the group, he disagreed with its philosophy. He believed not in the immediate settlement of Palestine but in the promotion of educational work as the forerunner of later dedicated, physical toil in rebuilding the ancient national Jewish homeland. In 1889 he published his first important piece, *Lo Zeh HaDerech* ("This Is Not the Way") under the

pseudonym Ahad Ha'am. In the essay, Ha'am questioned the preparedness of the people and worried that a rash move to Palestine might fail and thus cause irreparable national psychological damage. The piece thrust him into the public spotlight.

Ha'am subsequently became the spiritual leader of *Bnai Moshe*, a semisecret, elite group of *Hovevei Zion* who for eight years worked to open Hebrew libraries and pave the way for elementary schools where the language would be Hebrew.

In 1891 and 1893 Ha'am visited Palestine. His visits supported his earlier beliefs and upon his return each time, Ha'am reiterated his stance that immigration must be preceded by Jewish education. In 1896 he became editor of *Ha-Shiloach*, the most important journal of Zionistic and Hebrew literature in Eastern Europe.

Ha'am disagreed with Theodor Herzl and Dr. Max Nordau. He was concerned that a national home should not be solely a refuge but an answer to the question of Jewish emancipation for Europe, Russia, and the ghetto mentality. Ha'am questioned the estrangement that assimilated Jews like Herzl had from Jewish values and culture. Cultural education was vital to prepare the people against assimilation and cultural sterility.

Ha'am's writings were laden with a sense of responsibility. His style has been called lucid, pragmatic, and "chiseled." He espoused not only Jewish philosophy and culture but Jewish literature as well. By unceasingly promoting Hebrew literature, he sought to forward the Jewish mind as well as the spirit. In 1903 Ha'am retired from the editorship of *Ha-Shiloach* and went into the private sector. In 1907 he moved to London, where, over the next fifteen years, he remained active in communal affairs. He was particularly involved in persuading the British government to issue the Balfour Declaration.

Ha'am moved to Palestine in 1922. There he continued his writing and had great influence on those around him. Chaim Nachman Bialik referred to Ha'am as the most important person in his life. Ha'am saw himself not so much as a writer but as a thinker. In Palestine, he completed his four-volume set of essays—*Al Parashat Derachim* ("At the Crossroads")—which he had begun in 1895. He died in 1927. His advocacy of cultural Zionism was to play a huge role in the development of the people's sense of identity.

EMMA LAZARUS

"Give me your tired, your poor,
Your huddled masses yearning to breathe free.
The wretched refuse of your teeming shore,
Send these, the homeless, the tempest-tost to me,
I lift my lamp beside the Golden Door."

The above are undoubtedly some of the most famous words in the world. Generations of Americans, newly arrived or born here, have seen, heard, read, and memorized them. Inscribed on the base of the Statue of Liberty, those words remain the dream and greeting of America to oppressed people everywhere. And they were written by the American Jewish poet Emma Lazarus.

Born in New York City on July 22, 1849, Lazarus came from a well-to-do family and received a private education. Her gift for poetry displayed itself early, and at 17 her first book (*Poems and Translations*) was published. It received public praise from Ralph Waldo Emerson, with whom she began an extended and personal correspondence. Her first published poem dealing with a Jewish subject was included in her second book and was entitled "In the Jewish Synagogue at Newport."

Writing and publishing over the next decade, it was not until the late 1870s when Lazarus began to feel herself a closer part of the overall Jewish community. The second wave of Jewish European refugees were streaming into America. With her writings and her monies, Lazarus took up the defense of Judaism and the immigrant persecuted Jews. She was extremely involved in relief and rehabilitation work. Lazarus was deeply affected by what she

saw, later writing: "*I am all Israel's now. Till this cloud pass—I have no thought, no passion, no desire, save for my own people.*" In 1882, she published *Songs of a Semite*, a collection of her essays on behalf of the Jewish cause.

Lazarus wrote "*The New Colossus*" in 1883. American writers, including Mark Twain, Walt Whitman, and Henry Wadsworth Longfellow were solicited to submit manuscripts for possible inscription on the base of the Statue of Liberty. Hers was selected, defining America and the statue forever.

Emma Lazarus died four years later, on November 19, 1887, at the age of 38.

MENDELE MOICHER SEFORIM

"In my eyes the three aims of the writers ought to be: to teach our people good taste and understanding; to bring the daily life of their world and their actions into the sphere of literature in order to make the public fonder of the latter; to instruct and prove beneficial."

—Wedded to the Muse

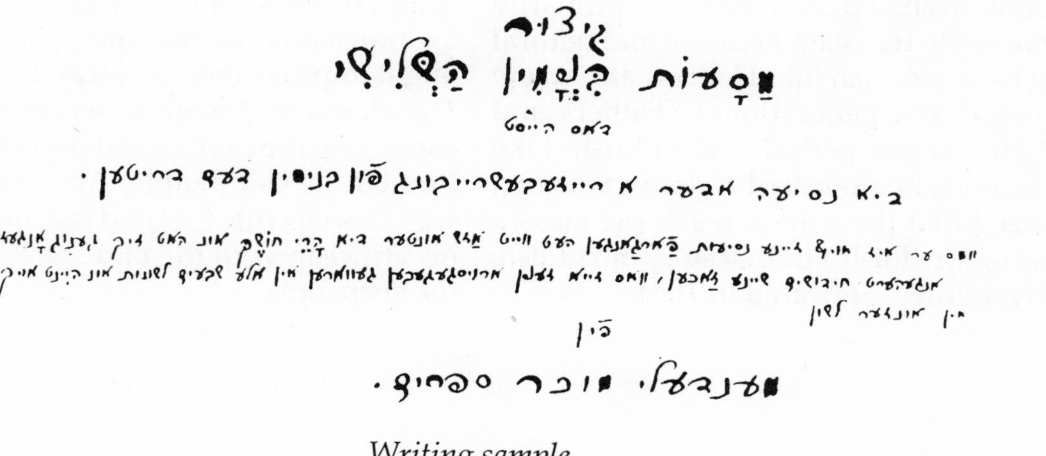

Writing sample.

The Jewish life of nineteenth-century Russia was in flux: The Enlightenment was challenging Jewish tradition, the czarist government was becoming increasingly oppressive, Zionism was growing stronger, and the Jewish population was expanding. And there to document it was the pioneer Hebrew and Yiddish writer Shalom Jacob Abramovitz, better known by his pen name Mendele Moicher Seforim, "Mendele, the Bookseller."

Abramovitz was born in the village of Kapulye (Minsk province), White Russia, in 1835. He received the mandatory *cheder* edu-

cation of Jewish children and is said to have memorized most of the Bible by the age of 9. After the death of his father when he was 14, he attended various *yeshivot* in a number of villages, acquiring both a deep knowledge of Talmud and a deep impression of village people and community life. When his mother remarried in 1853, he returned home and began to write.

With his background, Abramovitz obtained a position as a teacher in a Jewish school, as had his brother. In 1857, in a letter to his brother, who had earlier written complaining of the difficulties of teaching, Abramovitz wrote on the principles of modern education. When, through a friend, this found its way into print, Abramovitz was recognized both for his clear style of Hebrew and for his clear approach to successful teaching.

In 1858 Abramovitz moved to the city of Berdichev, where he was married and, because his father-in-law was a wealthy man, was afforded the opportunity to continue writing. In this, his first period, he wrote primarily in Hebrew. He translated science and natural history from German into Hebrew and wrote his satirical and generational "Fathers and Sons." His second period was Yiddish. Like many writers, he preferred Hebrew but soon recognized that the way to reach the masses was through Yiddish. His first story in Yiddish, "The Hypocrite," appeared in 1864.

A social critic, it was in Yiddish that Abramovitz wrote his famous *Fishke the Lame*, *The Nag*, *The Meat Tax*, and *The Travels and Adventures of Benjamin III*. Because of the openly critical nature of *The Meat Tax*, in which Abramovitz attacked and castigated Berdichev for its recessive and exploitive meat tax on the poor, in 1871 he was forced to leave the city, and moved to Zhitomir.

With a wife and five children, Abramovitz soon found that his literary earnings were not enough to cover his expenses. A stipend from a baronial admirer assisted him. Later he became principal of a Jewish school in Odessa. There he translated into Hebrew a number of his earlier works. He died in 1917.

Abramovitz was the first to write about the common man in Yiddish, recording the voices of a people in their own language. His pen name, Mendele the Bookseller, is a character in his book *The Heavenly and Earthly Academies*. Mendele is an itinerant publisher of wills, vignettes, confessions, autobiographies, stories received from various sources intended for translation so that the people as a whole might improve their social and moral bearing. The character Mendele serves as a conduit, conveying the praises and the criticisms of the Russian Jewish people. Abramovitz himself was a social critic first and last, but he softened his criticism with the bittersweet love he had for his people.

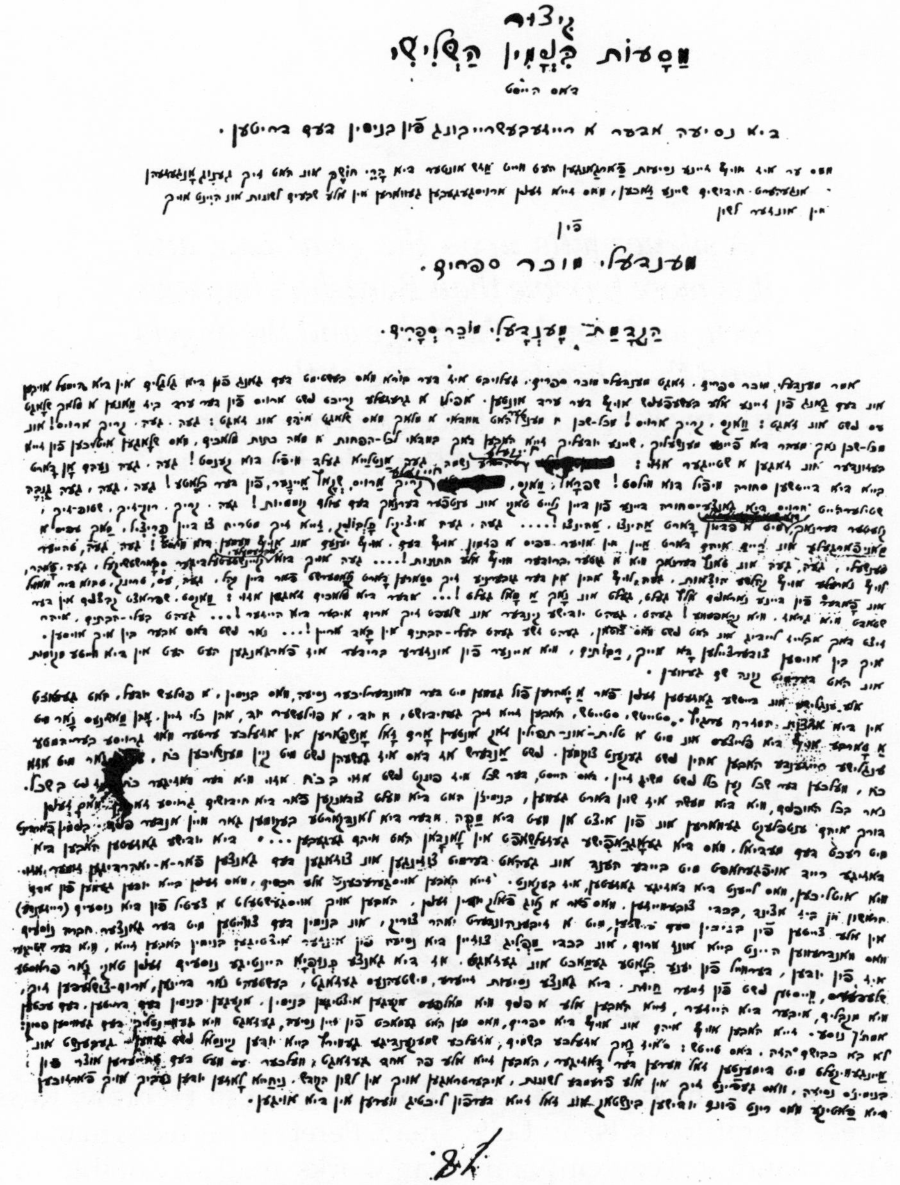

אָריגינעלער כתב־יד אין ראובן ברײנין אַרכיוו,
יידישע פאַלקס ביבליאָטעק, מאָנטרעאָל.

אַרויסגעגעבן צו דער 49-טער יערלעכער פאַרזאַמלונג
פון דער יידישער פאַלקס-ביבליאָטעק,
געווידמעט דעם 100-יאָריקן יובל פון מענדעלע מוכר ספרים.

Original handwritten manuscript of Mendele Moicher Seforim. (*Courtesy of the Reuben Brennen Archives, Jewish Folk Library, Montreal.*)

ISAAC LEIB PERETZ

"A silence falls upon the great hall, and it is more terrible than Bontsha's has ever been, and slowly the judge and the angels bend their heads in shame at this unending meekness they have created on earth."
—"Bontsha the Silent"

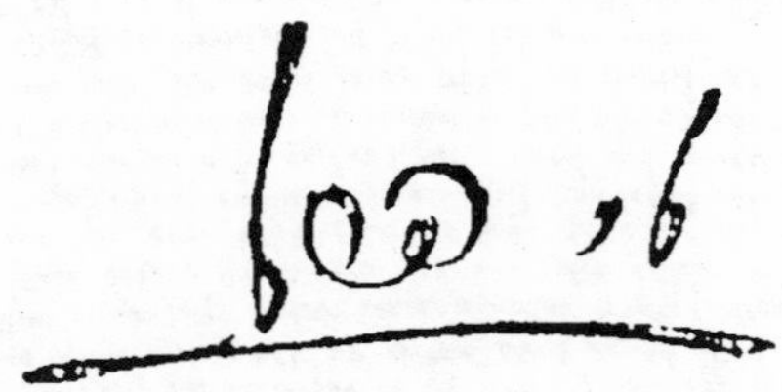

One of the masters of modern Yiddish and Hebrew literature is Isaac Leib Peretz. Like a handful of contemporaries, he was a product of late-nineteenth-century Eastern Europe and was born with an ability to relate the human condition in a way very few could.

Peretz was born in Zamosc, Poland, into a traditional family. His father, a prosperous merchant, was open to liberal ideas, but his more staunchly religious mother prevented him from having a widespread secular education. Tutored in Hebrew, Russian, and German, Peretz in his teens managed to read secular works made available to him from the library of an enlightened Jew. At 18, he was married in an arranged match that was to prove unhappy and unsuccessful. By the time he divorced six years later, he had a son and multiple financial problems.

Peretz went to Warsaw to study law, passed the necessary examinations, and became a successful lawyer. He returned to Zamosc and remarried in 1878. Having previ-

ously written and published in Polish, in 1875 he returned to his native languages and published in both Yiddish and Hebrew. But it was not until 1886, upon his reacquainting himself with Warsaw's literary circle, that Peretz began to write again.

In 1888, following a false accusation to the government that he was a socialist, Peretz lost his license to practice law. In desperate financial straits, he began writing full time in Yiddish. In 1890 he joined a group financed by a Jewish philanthropist that was surveying Jewish life in numerous small towns and villages. Peretz went along as a surveyor and observer of backwater Jewish life. Upon the team's return to Warsaw, Peretz, again unemployed, involved himself in social and cultural activities. In 1891 he obtained a position with the Jewish civic community, which he was to keep for the rest of his life. With full-time employment, he turned back to writing for and of the Jewish people in Eastern Europe.

Peretz's writings concern two main audiences: the everyday folk and *chasidim*. The everyday people were in a world of turmoil, depression, degeneracy (from persecution), apathy, and poverty. Of the *chasidim*, whom Peretz once held in contempt, he later wrote positive, rewarding, enriching stories. Peretz's sensitivity and compassion reflected the lives of the poor, the simple, the ignorant, the faithful. Writing of social hypocrisy, Peretz tried to expose Jews to their own shortcomings, while opening larger vistas of truth. Like his peers, he wrote in Yiddish, reaching the masses; Hebrew was not the everyday language. Yiddish, though held in disregard by the intelligentsia, was. Peretz believed that where four million people spoke a language, there was a literature, no matter if the language was Yiddish. As Peretz's popularity grew, he translated his Yiddish works into Hebrew and his Hebrew works into Yiddish. He was influential among Jewish intellectuals and writers.

Peretz wrote consistently until his death, attracting a circle of younger and older writers. He died in 1915. It was estimated that more than 100,000 people attended his funeral.

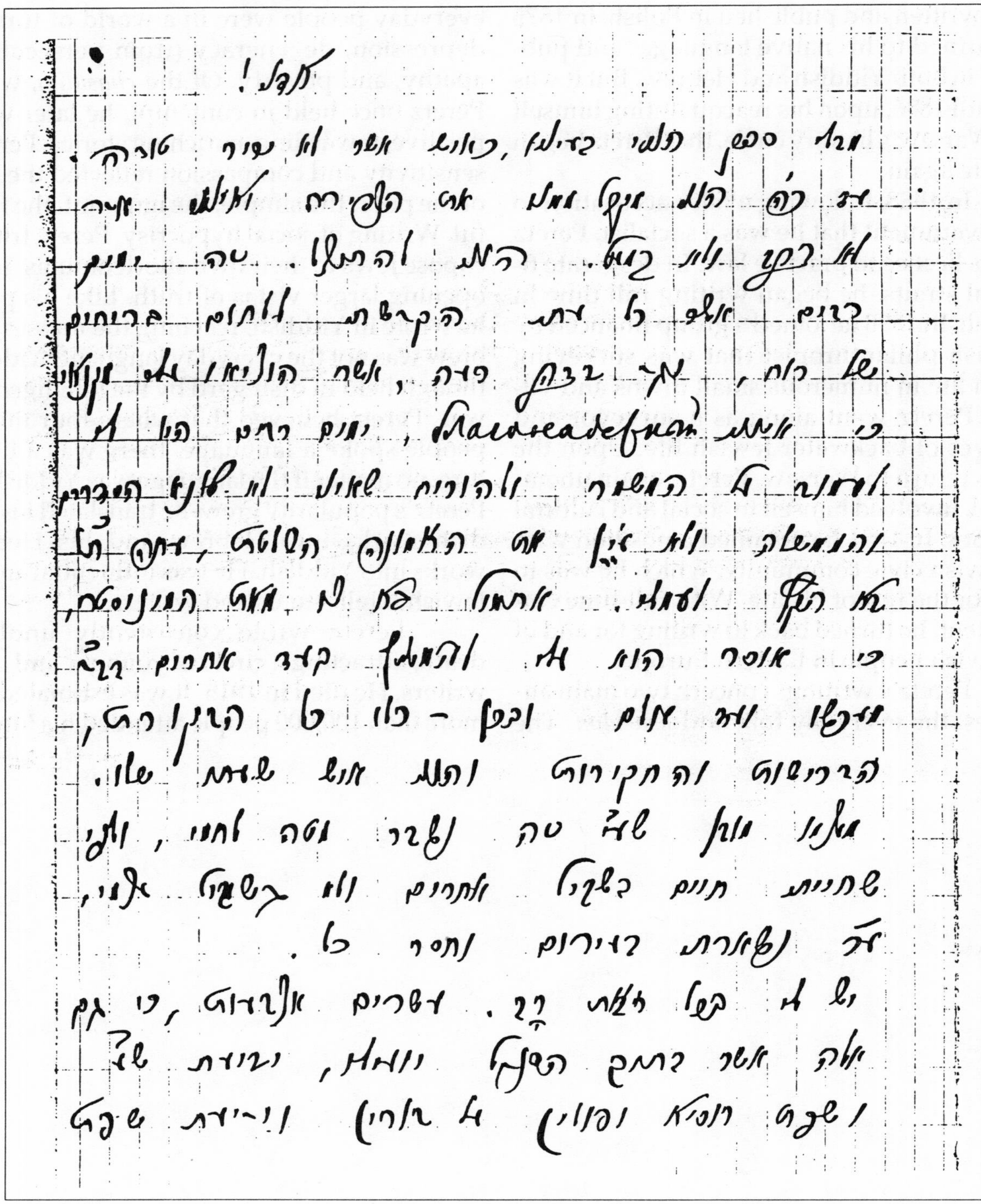

Two-page handwritten letter by I. L. Peretz.

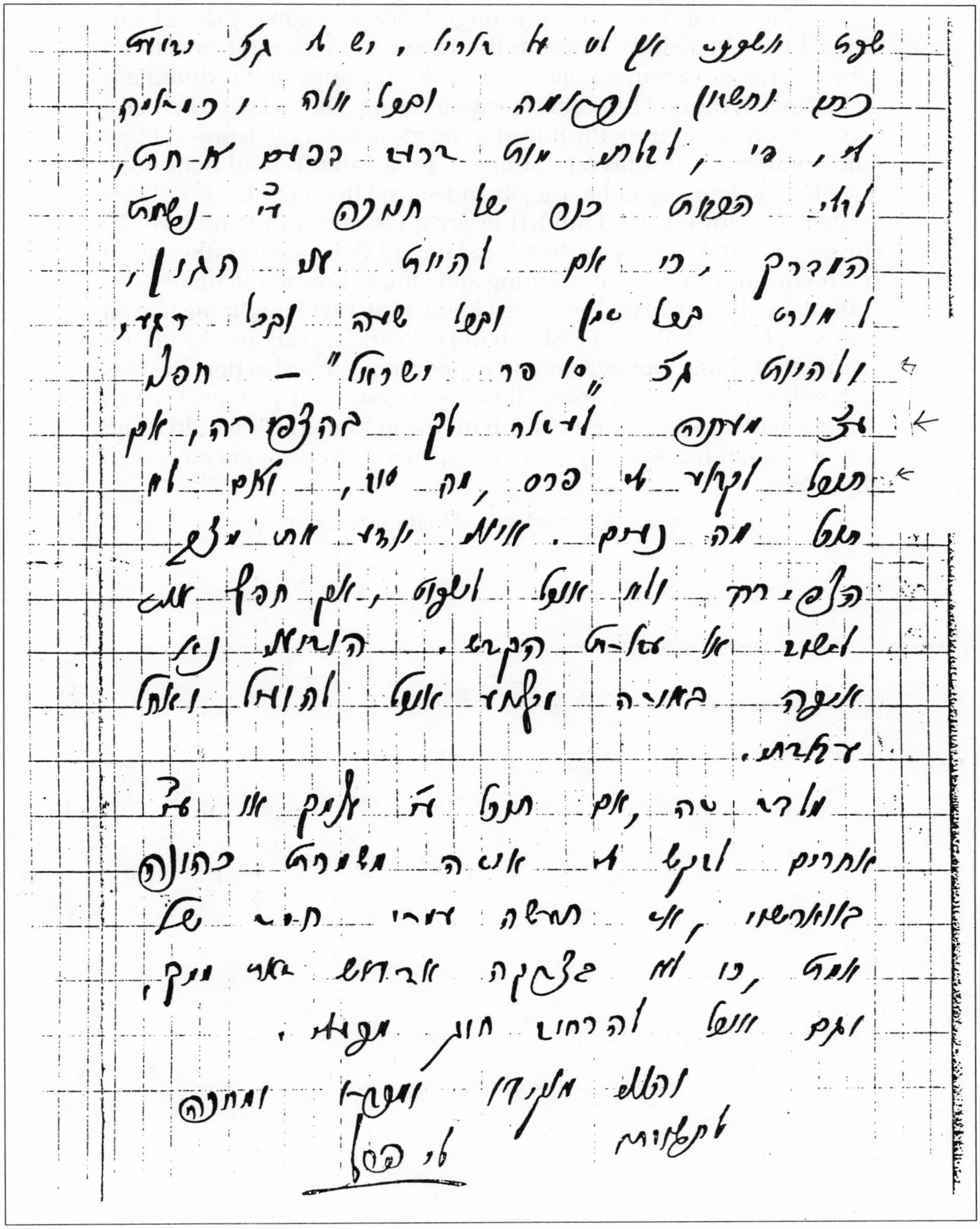

Please forgive me for my long silence, as for many days I was forced to fight against "hand-mills of wind" in order to prove that I am not the government enemy and do not oppose the dominant belief. Now, the end has come to my suffering. Yesterday I received a special command from the minister, no more law practicing—but no more suffering and investigations. I am a calm/restful man now. Obviously, I no longer have a job and since I lived my life for others rather than for myself, I am left in great poverty. But I still have 20 fingers . . . and I know perfect Russian and Polish, and rather good German. I have a fine handwriting and I know how to calculate . . . so I think I will not starve. But since I know now that I might die like all of us . . . I would like to assist you in HaTzfira. If you can pay for my work, that is fine, but even if you cannot pay—it is also fine. Besides a possible job in your paper, I'll be most grateful if you, or through others, will arrange a kind of a job for me in Warsaw. It would be an act of real kindness from you. Waiting for your reply, very sincerely, L. Peretz.

Translation of letter to Nachum Sokolow.

ISAAC BASHEVIS SINGER

"I am not ashamed to admit that I belong to those who fantasize that literature is capable of bringing new horizons and new perspectives—philosophical, religious, aesthetical, and even social. . . . In their despair a number of those who no longer have confidence in the leadership of our society look up to the writer, the master of words. They hope against hope that the man of talent and sensitivity can perhaps rescue civilization. Maybe there is a spark of the prophet in the artist after all."

—*Nobel Prize lecture, 1978*

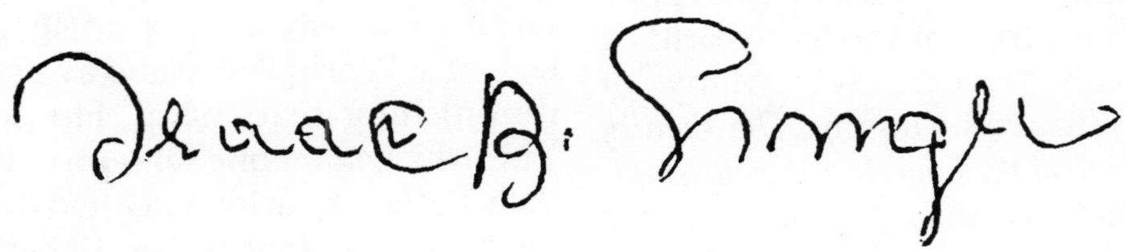

One of the great Jewish writers of the twentieth century was Isaac Bashevis Singer. Writing only in Yiddish, although he lived in America for over fifty years, Singer brought forth in his stories universal themes on the human condition.

Singer was born July 14, 1904, in Radzymin, Poland. His father was a rabbinical judge, one who made legal decisions based on Jewish law. Raised in the Jewish quarter of Warsaw, where his family moved when he was 4, Singer grew up and was educated in the very heart of Polish Jewry. He received a traditional Jewish education and studied for several years at a rabbinic seminary.

Following the lead of his older brother and noted writer in his own right, I. J. Singer, Bashevis Singer began writing in the 1920s as a journalist, first in Hebrew and later in Yiddish. His early stories appeared in several Warsaw Yiddish journals and newspapers. For three years he was coeditor of *Globus*, a Jewish publication, until he left Poland and came to the United States in 1935.

Residing in New York, Singer began to write for the *Jewish Daily Forward*, one of the

foremost Yiddish dailies. His stories and books were serialized. His first book, *Satan in Goray*, was published in 1935. Well known to the Yiddish reader, he was considered by many the inheritor of Sholom Aleichem's mantle. It was not until the 1950s that his work became noticed in the English press. He was awarded the National Book Award twice (1970 and 1974), and his stories appeared routinely in *The New Yorker* and other prestigious magazines. In 1978 he received the Nobel Prize for literature. The inscription on his award read in part: "The Nobel Prize for Literature to ISAAC BASHEVIS SINGER, for his impassioned narrative art which, with roots in a Polish-Jewish cultural tradition, brings universal human conditions to life."

Singer's books range in time from primitive Poland to modern man. He explored Holocaust neuroses, modern man's psychoses, and the supernatural: "His pages are filled with people broken by the Holocaust, the devil in various disguises, agonizing rabbis, brutish peasants, fumbling lovers and failed writers, set against the backdrop of the lost world of Eastern European Jewish life." Many of Singer's novels are well known: *The Family Moskat* (1950), *Gimpel the Fool* (1957), *The Magician of Lublin* (1960), *The Slave* (1962), *The Manor* (1967), *The Estate* (1969), and others. Prodigious, he also wrote numerous children's books, including *Mazel and Shlimazel, Or the Milk of a Lioness, When Shlemiel Went to Warsaw, Zlateh the Goat*, and *Yentl the Yeshiva Bocher*. Singer was always proud of his children's writings, and he explained to the Nobel Prize banquet why he wrote for children:

> There are five hundred reasons why I began to write for children, but to save time I will mention only ten of them.
>
> Number 1. Children read books, not reviews. They don't give a hoot about the critics.
>
> Number 2. Children don't read to find their identity.
>
> Number 3. They don't read to free themselves of guilt, to quench their thirst for rebellion, or to get rid of alienation.
>
> Number 4. They have no use for psychology.
>
> Number 5. They detest sociology.
>
> Number 6. They don't try to understand Kafka, or *Finnegan's Wake*.
>
> Number 7. They still believe in God, the family, angels, devils, witches, goblins, logic, clarity, punctuation, and other such obsolete stuff.
>
> Number 8. They love interesting stories, not commentary, guides, or footnotes.
>
> Number 9. When a book is boring, they yawn openly, without any shame or fear of authority.
>
> Number 10. They don't expect their beloved writer to redeem humanity. Young as they are, they know that is not in his power. Only the adults have such childish illusions.

Singer was often questioned about his writing exclusively in Yiddish, a language attacked in World War II and available to an ever-diminishing readership. He denied being a Yiddishist, someone who proselytizes for Yiddish. Rather, he acknowledged that Yiddish was his language, that he wrote better in Yiddish than in English or Hebrew or Polish: *"For me, Yiddish is my language. There are people in Albania and they speak Albanian. Do they care that only a milion people speak Albanian? They don't mind. They are among their own people; it's their language—and it's the same with me and Yiddish."*

Singer died in New York City on July 24, 1991. His works have been translated into more than fifteen languages, including German, Dutch, and Japanese. Singer's writings enlivened the inner world of European Jewish humanity with a sensitivity that continues to find universal appeal.

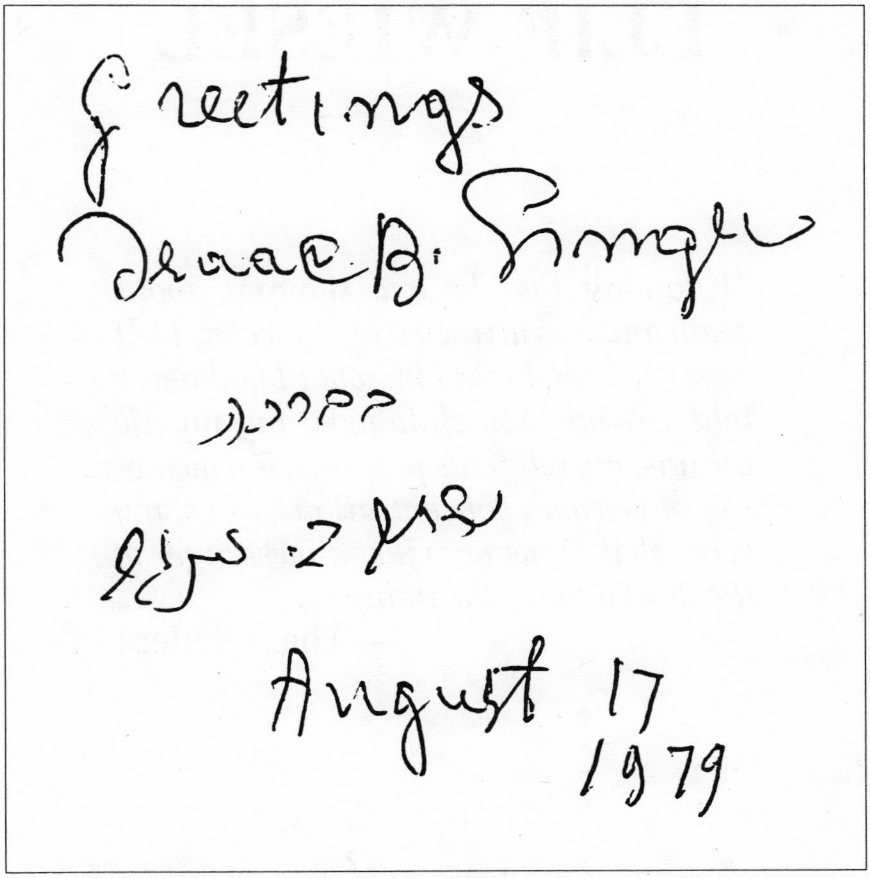

Salutation in English and Hebrew by Isaac Bashevis Singer.

ELIE WIESEL

"Knowing that he had thought about death and was attracted by its secret, I felt closer to him. I told him what I had never told anyone. My childhood, my mystic dreams, my religious passions, my memories of German concentration camps, my belief that I was now just a messenger of the dead among the living. . . ."

—The Accident

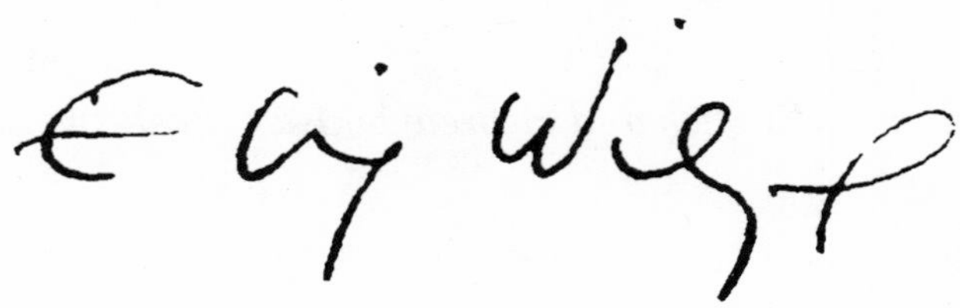

The philosopher, writer, novelist, peace activist, concentration camp survivor, and Nobel Prize winner Elie Wiesel is the quintessential witness to the Holocaust and the dark side of the human condition. He has been lauded as one of this era's most important writers and described as "a voice that is humanist and universal even as it is Jewish-minded and special. . . ." He has been called "a modern Job" and "the conscience of the Holocaust."

Wiesel was born in 1928 in the small village of Sighet, Transylvania, an area ruled at the time by Romania but Hungarian-speaking. From a religious family, he received a traditional talmudic education, studying with chasidic rabbis in the village. In 1944 all of Sighet's Jewish inhabitants were deported to concentration camps. Along with other relatives, Wiesel's mother, father, and younger sister were murdered. (Two other sisters survived.) Following liberation, Wiesel was sent to France to be a ward of a French Jewish children's agency.

From 1948 to 1951 Wiesel studied at the Sorbonne, taught Hebrew and Bible, worked as a correspondent for the Israeli newspaper *Yediot Achronot*, and spent a year sojourning through India seeking mystical and religious insights. In 1956 he went to New York, and in

1963 he became a U.S. citizen. Over the past years, in conjunction with his Holocaust writings, Wiesel has been at the forefront of social activism and has supported causes from Soviet Jewry to world peace to refugee conditions in Cambodia and Thailand. In 1978 he was named chairman of the U.S. Holocaust Memorial Council and is currently a professor of humanities at Boston University.

Although he has written books about chasidic masters and biographies of various individuals, Wiesel's writings are almost overwhelmingly about the Holocaust. He seeks to understand what happened, how it happened, and what the consequences of such wholesale murder are. He examines the Holocaust both as an individual and as a member of a group slaughtered for no comprehensible reason. Although much of his writing is fiction, it is clearly drawn from his own experiences as a teenager and his life after the camps. He has sought, and fought, to bear witness—for himself and for those were murdered—to what really did happen.

Wiesel's writings are a combination of prose, poetry, wonderings, wanderings, and reflections. They have been described as "dark" and many are clearly troubling. One reason for the acceptance of his work is the universality of his themes. Murder and genocide are understood whether the victims are Jews, Muslims, Bosnians, Somalians, Rwandans, or Laotians. Wiesel's memories as a survivor mirror every survivor's experience.

In his first book, *Night*, Wiesel commented on his loss of faith:

> Never shall I forget that night, the first night in camp, which has turned my life into one long night, seven times cursed and seven times sealed. Never shall I forget that smoke. Never shall I forget the little faces of the children, whose bodies I saw turned into wreaths of smoke beneath a silent blue sky. Never shall I forget those flames which consumed my Faith forever. Never shall I forget that nocturnal silence which deprived me, for all eternity, of the desire to live. Never shall I forget those moments which murdered my God and my soul and turned my dreams to dust. Never shall I forget these things, even if I am condemned to live as long as God Himself. Never.

One critic has said that Elie Wiesel's writings are "so charged, so subtle, superb, so dangerously lucid, that his memory becomes our reality." Wiesel's presence has probably best been described by the inscription on the Congressional Gold Medal that was awarded to him. It states simply: AUTHOR, TEACHER, WITNESS.

Boston University

University Professors
745 Commonwealth Avenue
Boston, Massachusetts 02215
617/353-4566

Elie Wiesel, *Andrew W. Mellon Professor in the Humanities*

5 · 18 · 92

Dear Mr. Bullard —

Thanks for your letter —

Racism is growing. So is antisemitism. Both must be eradicated. How? I believe in education —

Elie Wiesel

Letter discussing racism and anti-Semitism signed by Elie Wiesel on Boston University letterhead stationery.

VI

AMERICANS

I am a Jew who is an American. I was a Jew before I was an American. I have been an American all my life, 64 years, but I've been a Jew for 4,000 years.

—Stephen S. Wise

BERNARD BARUCH

"RECIPE FOR ACHIEVEMENT: Take the obvious, add a cupful of brains, a generous pinch of imagination, a bucketful of courage and daring, stir well, and bring to a boil."

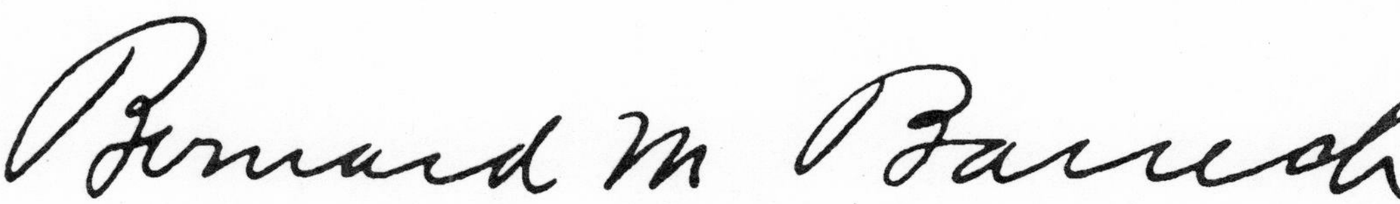

An advisor to presidents from Woodrow Wilson to John F. Kennedy, Bernard Mannes Baruch inspired public confidence and represented keen financial acumen.

Baruch was born in Camden, South Carolina, on August 19, 1870, the son of an immigrant German physician and an American-born mother. The family later moved to New York City, where Bernard attended City College. Following graduation, he worked as an office boy on Wall Street, then America's financial capital. In 1890 he began investing in the stock market, and within ten years, he had become a multimillionaire.

With his financial security taken care of, Baruch's interests turned to politics. In 1912 he contributed heavily to Woodrow Wilson's candidacy and with Wilson's election, Baruch became an adviser to the president. By 1915 Baruch was a leading Democratic advocate for a militarily and industrially strong United States, anticipating America's involvement in the war raging in Europe. With America's entry into the war in 1917, Baruch became chairman of the War Industries Board, which was responsible for mobilizing national resources. In November 1919 Baruch accompanied President Wilson to Paris for the peace conference and played an instrumental part in developing the economic aspects of the treaty.

In the years between World Wars I and II, Baruch became an unofficial economic ad-

viser to the president, an unofficial commentator on public events, and an overall colorful character. He was famous for giving advice and interviews from a park bench in New York's Central Park, where he even received mail. His advice was frequently sought from high political officials, both domestically and abroad. He was a good friend of Winston Churchill. On the home front, he remained active in national Democratic affairs. He advised Franklin Roosevelt to prepare for World War II and was the chairman of the Rubber Survey Committee, an adviser to the national war mobilization director, and a member of the committee dealing with postwar adjustment problems. He also authored the first official U.S. policy proposal on the control of atomic energy and in 1946 was appointed a member of the American delegation to the United Nations Atomic Energy Commission. He authored two books about his own life and in 1964 donated his papers to Princeton University as a nucleus for the collection of the Center for Studies in Twentieth-Century American Statecraft and Public Policy.

Baruch considered himself an American first and a Jew second. He intermarried and his children were raised in his wife's religion (Episcopalian). He vacillated on the idea of Israel as a national Jewish state and supported Uganda as an alternate site. That notwithstanding, he contributed funds for the assistance of Jewish refugees and supported Zionism during the UN's debates on the subject in 1947.

Baruch's strong public service to his country, backed by astute financial policies, made him one of a handful of important governmental experts and citizens-at-large. His role as an unofficial adviser to eight presidents secured his position as one of America's elder statesmen. He died in New York City on June 20, 1965.

JUDAH PHILIP BENJAMIN

". . . the Mephistopheles of the Southern Confederacy."

—James G. Blaine

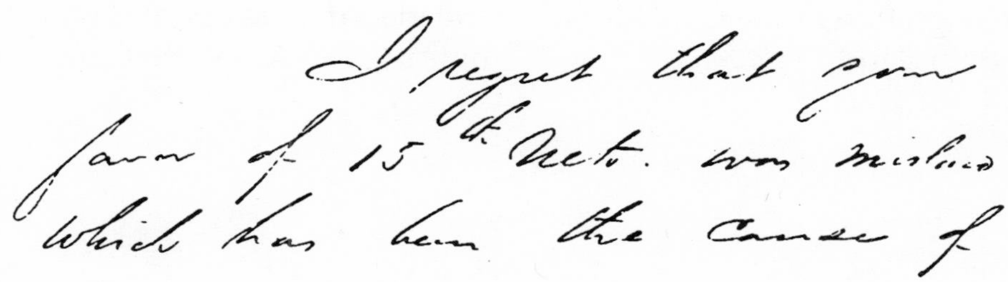

Writing sample.

Attorney, statesman, and plantation owner, Judah P. Benjamin has been referred to as "undoubtedly the most prominent nineteenth-century American Jew."

Born in St. Thomas, the Virgin Islands, on August 6, 1811, Benjamin was a British citizen and subject by birth. His family moved to Charleston, South Carolina, where he spent his boyhood, was raised, and early on began displaying the intellect for which he was later renowned. He attended Yale University for two years but left without attaining a degree. He returned to the South, where he studied law in the traditional fashion of the time—by clerking under an already bar-admitted attorney. In 1832 he was admitted to the Louisiana bar.

Over the next fifteen years, Benjamin became one of the state's leading attorneys. In 1834 he published a compilation of Louisiana law, and later published a major work on contracts that was to remain a standard text. In 1849 he was admitted to practice before the

U.S. Supreme Court and in 1853 declined a nomination to the court as a justice.

Benjamin was elected as a Whig to the U.S. Senate from Louisiana in 1852 and served until Louisiana's secession from the Union in 1861. One of the South's earliest and leading secessionists, he made major, impressive speeches on the legal basis for slavery. While in the Senate, he became friends with the senator from Mississippi, Jefferson Davis. In March 1861, President Jefferson Davis of the Confederate States of America appointed Benjamin attorney general of the Confederacy. Subsequently, he would also be appointed its secretary of war and secretary of state.

Throughout the war, and particularly as the Confederacy suffered increasing setbacks and defeats, Benjamin came under anti-Semitic attacks. He was referred to as "Judas Iscariot Benjamin" and "the Jew whom the President retained as his counsel." Benjamin, however, maintained the responsibilities of his various offices and continually worked in diplomatic circles to seek recognition of the Confederacy from France and England.

Following the surrender of the Confederacy, Benjamin, like several other Confederate politicos and senior military men, went into exile. From Florida, he escaped to Nassau and from there to England, where his life began anew.

Benjamin reestablished himself in England as an attorney. He rose to unprecedented personal heights, gaining both recognition and wealth and becoming one of England's leading legal minds. He received the appointment of Queen's Counsel, drew high fees, enjoyed a thriving practice, and published several volumes on English law. At his retirement, he was toasted by both the Lord Chancellor and the Lord Chief Justice as "the only man who has held conspicuous leadership at the bar of two countries."

Following his retirement in 1882 due to poor health, Benjamin spent his final years with his family, from whom he had long been separated. He died in Paris on May 6, 1884. Although not a committed or ethnic Jew, Benjamin was still identified as one and was considered a key figure in the American Confederacy.

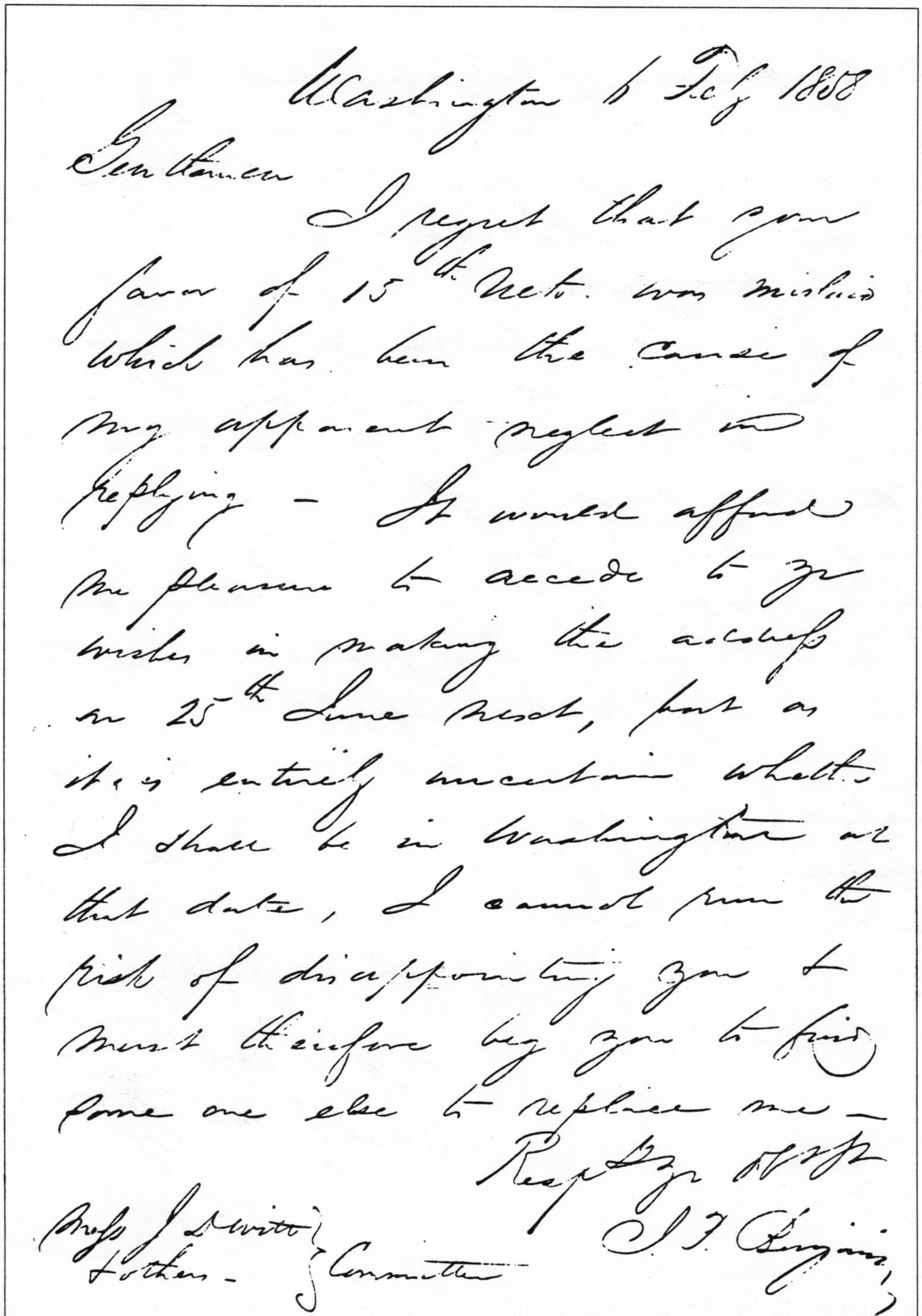

Washington 6 Feby 1858

Gentlemen

I regret that your favor of 15th Octo. was mislaid which has been the cause of my apparent neglect in replying — It would afford me pleasure to accede to yr wishes in making the address on 25th June next, but as it is entirely uncertain whether I shall be in Washington at that date, I cannot run the risk of disappointing you & must therefore beg you to find some one else to replace me —

Respy Yr obt svt

J. P. Benjamin

Profs J. Dewitt & others — } Committee

Letter signed by Judah Benjamin apologizing for answering late, and regretting that he won't be available for an engagement.

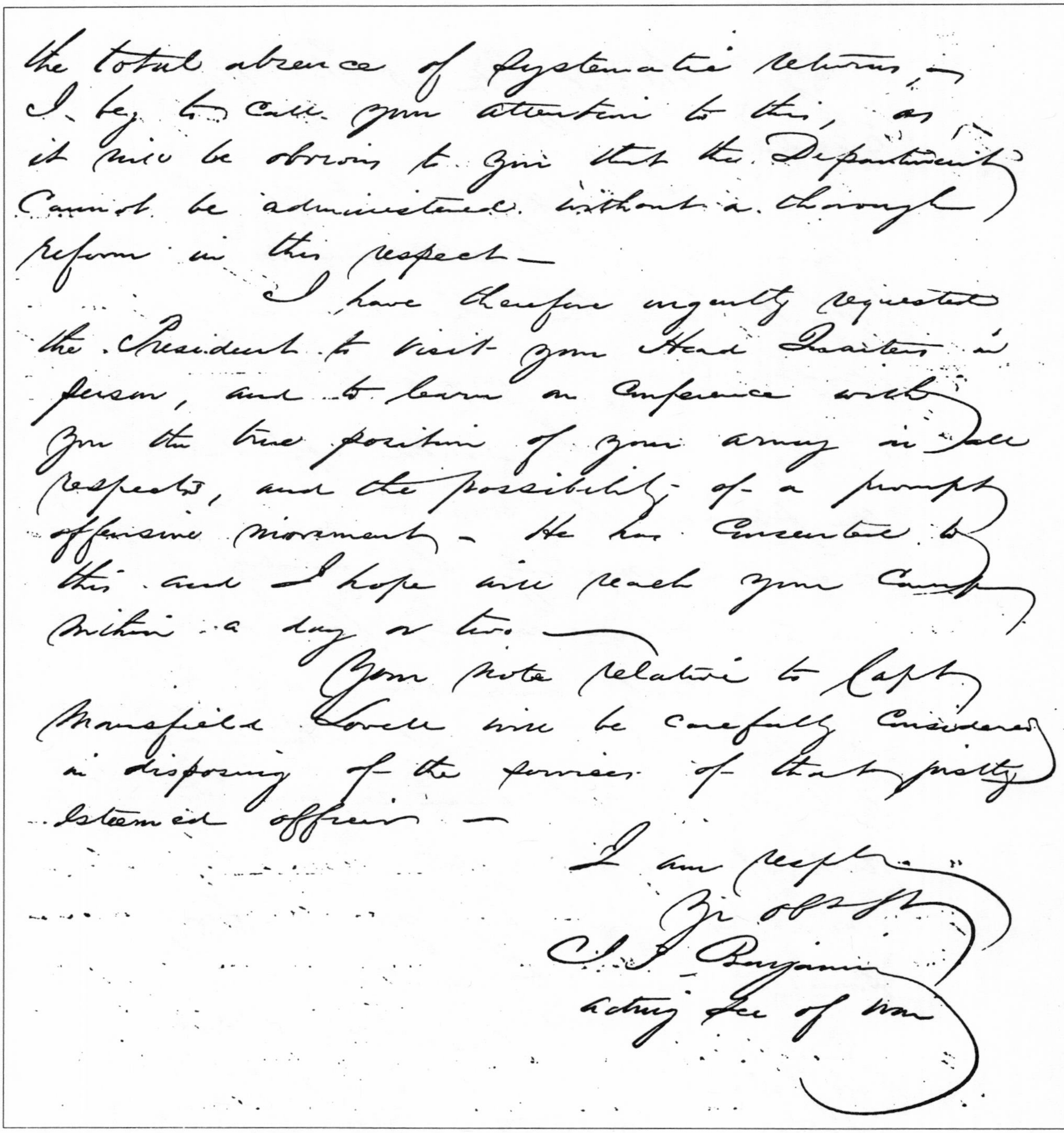

the total absence of systematic returns,— I beg to call your attention to this, as it will be obvious to you that the Department cannot be administered without a thorough reform in this respect—

I have therefore urgently requested the President to visit your Head Quarters in person, and to learn in conference with you the true position of your army in all respects, and the possibility of a prompt offensive movement— He has consented to this and I hope will reach your Camp within a day or two—

Your note relative to Capt Mansfield Lovell will be carefully considered in disposing of the services of that justly esteemed officer—

I am respy
Yr obt st
J. P. Benjamin
acting Sec of War

Handwritten letter by Judah Benjamin as Confederate acting secretary of war, in part addressing military situations and a possible offensive movement by select Confederate troops.

LOUIS D. BRANDEIS

"The twentieth century ideals of America have been the ideals of the Jew for more than twenty centuries."

Louis Dembitz Brandeis holds an important place in the annals of American Judaism and American law: he was the first Jew appointed to the U.S. Supreme Court.

Brandeis was born in Louisville, Kentucky, on November 13, 1856, to parents who had emigrated from Prague. He attended schools in Louisville and Dresden, Germany, after which he attended Harvard Law School. Graduating at the head of his class in 1877, he developed a name for himself as an outstanding and brilliant law student. Underneath the law practice he established in Boston was Brandeis's drive to understand all the forces affecting the creation of law. His liberalism—for which he would become famous—caused him to focus on social and economic issues. Taking cases without fees, he was an early "consumer's advocate" and was seen as a defender of unions. He soon became recognized as "the people's attorney." Representative of this was Brandeis's work in developing the life insurance system in Massachusetts in 1907. This followed two years of scandals in which many leading financiers associated with the Equitable Life Assurance Society of New York were ousted. Life insurance was for the rich only, or, as it operated, only the rich benefited. Going beyond the basic legal requirements, Brandeis developed a plan that made life in-

surance possible for and within reach of the common workingman.

His approach was later termed the Brandeis brief. When preparing legal briefs, he not only incorporated the required persuasive and supportive legal arguments but also brought to bear economic, sociological, and statistical data and historical background, thus bringing into the law nonlegal factors that nonetheless aided in its development.

By 1914 Brandeis had become one of America's best-known attorneys. In that year he wrote *Other People's Money and How the Bankers Use It*; the book showed how the investment bankers controlled industry. Because of his progressive ideas, the established financial community disliked and feared Brandeis. When Woodrow Wilson became president, Brandeis was considered a shoo-in for a cabinet position, but he wasn't chosen.

His 1916 nomination to the Supreme Court was opposed by special interest groups and anti-Semites, but they were unable to block his confirmation. Once on the bench, Brandeis, a committed liberal, displayed his advocacy for social and economic egalitarianism.

Brandeis's identity with Judaism came through his personal beliefs in liberalism and his legal duties, combined with Judaism's severe emphasis on justice. This was in accordance with the Reform Judaism of the time, which focused on ethical values and the belief that Judaism had a universal mission. Brandeis's personal belief aligned with this sense of Reform Judaism. His first concentrated involvement with large numbers of Jews came in 1910, when he arbitrated the garment workers' strike in New York and received his first views of the intense moral convictions of the Jewish masses. Incrementally, he became involved in Jewish causes.

In 1914, with the title of chairman of the Provisional Committee for General Zionist Affairs, Brandeis was charged with the leadership of U.S. Zionism. Like others, he found himself in the position of having to defend himself against accusations of dual loyalty. In response, Brandeis advocated cultural pluralism. Brandeis's friendship with President Wilson helped to ensure Wilson's support of the Balfour Declaration. After World War I, Brandeis was named honorary president of the World Zionist Organization.

In this position, however, a severe rift developed between Brandeis and American Zionists and Dr. Chaim Weizmann and European Zionists. The rift, dealing with financial and political handlings, became so severe that Brandeis and his followers withdrew from the Zionist movement. Brandeis continued to support the Zionist cause and established the Palestine Economic Corporation, which encouraged investment in Palestine. He remained committed to Zionism all his life, and at his death he left ample amounts for it in his will.

Brandeis's vision of fairness and equality, along with his legal decisions and position, greatly enhanced American Jewish posture. His legacy among American Jews and in American law is profound.

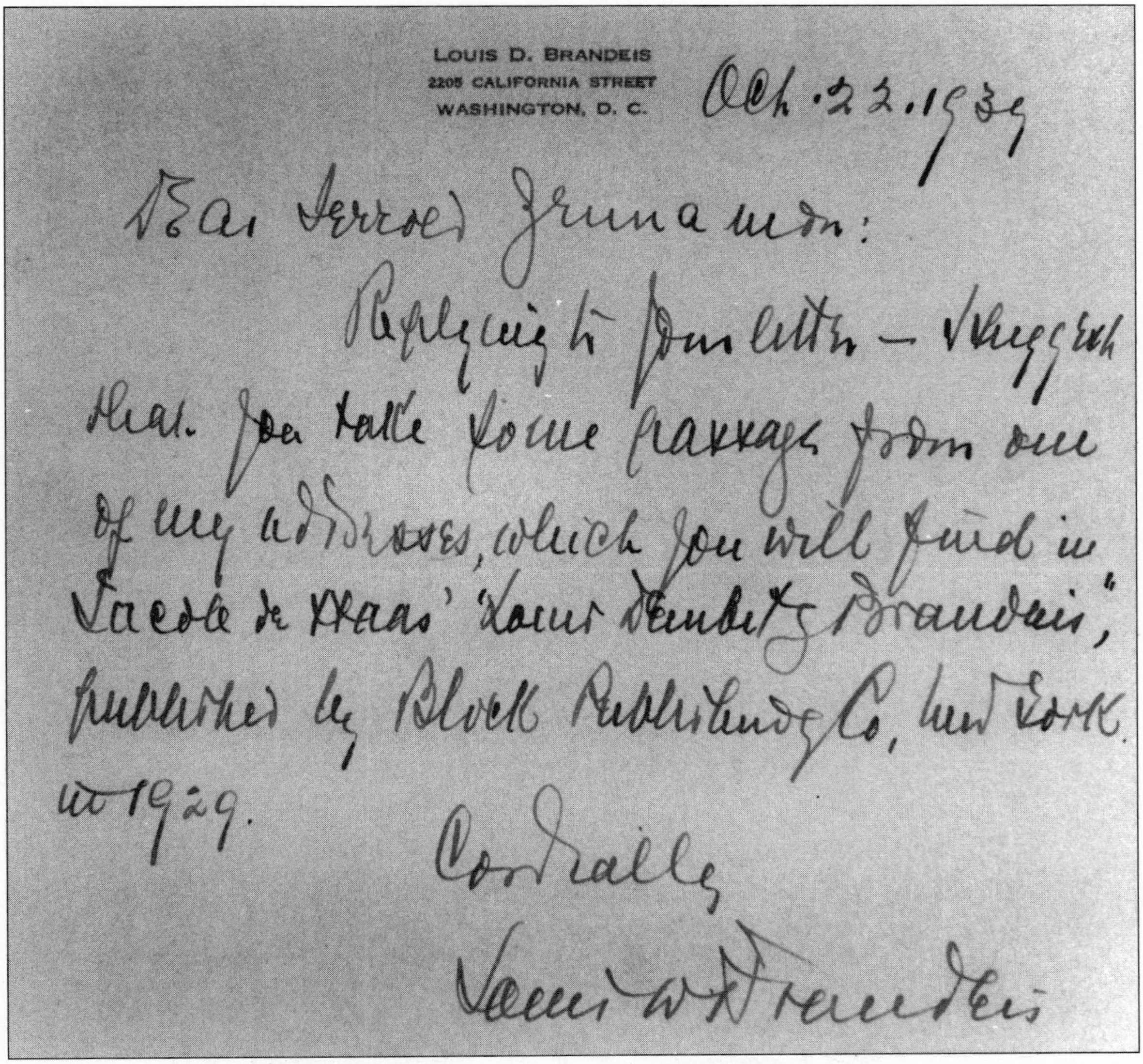

LOUIS D. BRANDEIS
2205 CALIFORNIA STREET
WASHINGTON, D. C.

Oct. 22. 1939

Dear Jerrold [illegible]:

Replying to your letter — I suggest that you take some passage from one of my addresses, which you will find in Jacob de Haas' "Louis Dembitz Brandeis", published by Bloch Publishing Co, New York in 1929.

Cordially,

Louis D. Brandeis

Note discussing locating a passage from one of his addresses, signed by Louis Brandeis on personal stationery.

BENJAMIN CARDOZO

"Not the origin, but the goal, is the main thing. There can be no wisdom in the choice of a path unless we know where it will lead."

Benjamin Cardozo, a descendant of prominent Sephardic Jews who came to America before the Revolution, has been ranked as one of the ten foremost judges in U.S. judicial history.

The son of a New York State Supreme Court justice, Benjamin Nathan Cardozo was born in New York City on May 24, 1870. He attended under- and postgraduate schools at Columbia, including its law school. He was admitted to the New York bar in 1891.

Unknown to the public at large, but well known and respected among his legal peers, Cardozo was considered a lawyer's lawyer. At the age of 33, he published *Jurisdiction of the Court of Appeals of the State of New York*, which is still considered the authoritative work on the subject. In 1913 he was elected an associate justice of the New York Supreme Court, where he served for the next fourteen years. In 1927 he was appointed its chief justice.

Over the years, Cardozo displayed his skills, intellect, and sense of justice for the rights of people as individuals. His decisions

are said to demonstrate an evolutionary application of legal principles; he felt that a judge had to look beyond the legal authorities to meet the needs of those seeking justice. In cases like *MacPherson* v. *Buick Motor Company* (1916) and *Ultramares Corporation* v. *Touche* (1931), Cardozo advocated the rights of consumers and the responsibilities of corporations.

In 1932 Cardozo was nominated to the U.S. Supreme Court. Opposition was swift and strong: among other arguments, some opposed the nomination of another Jew to the court. His appointment, however, was confirmed and he took his seat.

In his six years on the bench, Cardozo's contributions included strong support for New Deal programs (such as social security and old-age pensions), establishment of the foundation for a broad interpretation of federal powers, clarification of the due process clause of the Fourteenth Amendment, and reassertion of the division of authority between state and federal government. Cardozo's strength was in blending legal rule with social need.

Cardozo was an active member of the Spanish and Portuguese Synagogue in New York. He lived with his older sister Nel, who had raised him after their parents' deaths while he was still young, and he never married. He maintained an active interest in Jewish education and was involved in the Jewish Educational Association. Believing firmly in Americanism, Cardozo remained distant from Zionism. But although he was not a Zionist, the events in Europe in the 1930s caused him to appreciate the value of Palestine as a refuge for his people.

Cardozo died on July 9, 1938, at the age of 68. Considered one of the most respected men of his time, he was eulogized in part by Chief Justice Charles Evans Hughes, who said, "No judge ever came to this court more fully equipped by learning, acumen, dialectical skill, and disinterested purpose."

State of New York,
Court of Appeals.

Benjamin N. Cardozo
Associate Judge

NOV 5 1925

36 West 44th Street
New York City
November 4, 1925.

My dear Mr. Nordlinger:

I have read with care and with lively interest your article "Law and Arbitration."

I think it is admirably done. One would have difficulty in finding a better presentation of the contest between litigation and its competitors. I am altogether in sympathy with your thesis and with the general tone and tenor of your remedies.

When you pass to specific reforms, I confess to greater doubt. For example, I should feel a good deal of hesitation as to Nos. 2, 5, and 8. I should need to think carefully before adopting some of the others. Changes so important should not rest on first impressions.

The Commonwealth Fund has a law reform committee of which I am a member. Under its guidance, a sub-committee, of which Prof. Morgan is Chairman, has investigated the subject of reforms in the law of evidence. I am not a member of the sub-committee, but I have seen the preliminary draft of its work, and I hope the report may soon be ready. I think it will be very helpful to those who wish to simplify this department of the law.

I thank you again for sending me your article, and congratulate you upon the production of so fine and thoughtful a piece of work.

Very sincerely yours,

Benjamin N Cardozo

H. H. Nordlinger, Esq.,
67 Wall Street,
New York City.

Typed letter on New York State Court of Appeals letterhead signed by Benjamin Cardozo.

FELIX FRANKFURTER

"One who belongs to the most vilified and persecuted minority in history is not likely to be insensible to the freedoms guaranteed by our Constitution."

—*Flag Salute Cases*,
319 US 624, 646(1943)

Supreme Court justice, Harvard law professor, founding member of the American Civil Liberties Union, legal adviser to the National Association for the Advancement of Colored People, and immigrant son to America—Felix Frankfurter was a distinguished American Jew who made an indelible mark on the very fabric of this country.

Frankfurter was born in Vienna on November 15, 1882. He came to America at the age of 12 and settled with his parents on New York's Lower East Side. He graduated from the City College of New York with honors and from Harvard Law School with highest honors. Following a brief stint in private practice, Frankfurter accepted an offer from Henry Stimson, then U.S. attorney for New York, to be an assistant U.S. attorney. He held this position until Stimson was appointed secretary of war by President Franklin Roosevelt.

In 1914 Frankfurter accepted an appointment as a law professor at Harvard University. He taught there for twenty-five years, focusing on administrative law and process. From the early positions he took, Frankfurter developed a reputation as both a leading liberal and a radical. During World War I, he was legal adviser on industrial problems to the secretary of war, secretary to and later counsel of the President's Mediation Commission, and

chairman of the War Labor Policies Board. In these positions, Frankfurter was brought to the forefront of the era's labor struggles, generally ruling in favor of unions. His liberal reputation was later strengthened by his cofounding of the ACLU, his work with the NAACP, and his advocacy for a new trial for Sacco and Vanzetti.

During World War I, Frankfurter also became actively involved in Zionist affairs through his relationship with Louis Brandeis. This eventually led to Frankfurter's attending the 1919 peace conference along with the Zionist delegation. There he met with both T. E. Lawrence and the Emir Feisal, head of the Arab delegation. Although he later withdrew from formal participation in the Zionist movement, he always maintained his interest in the development of a Jewish national homeland.

In 1932 Frankfurter declined President Roosevelt's offer of Office of the Solicitor General but did accept, in 1939, the president's appointment to the Supreme Court. In the twenty-three years he sat on the bench, Frankfurter developed a second reputation far different from his first: Frankfurter gave greater importance to federal and state legislative action than to individual rights. He rejected claims of absolutism in areas such as free speech, assembly, and religious belief, subordinating them to the legitimate concerns of society as expressed through government.

Frankfurter retired from the Supreme Court in 1962, when a stroke forced him to relinquish his responsibilities. In 1963 President John F. Kennedy awarded him the Medal of Freedom. Frankfurter died February 22, 1965.

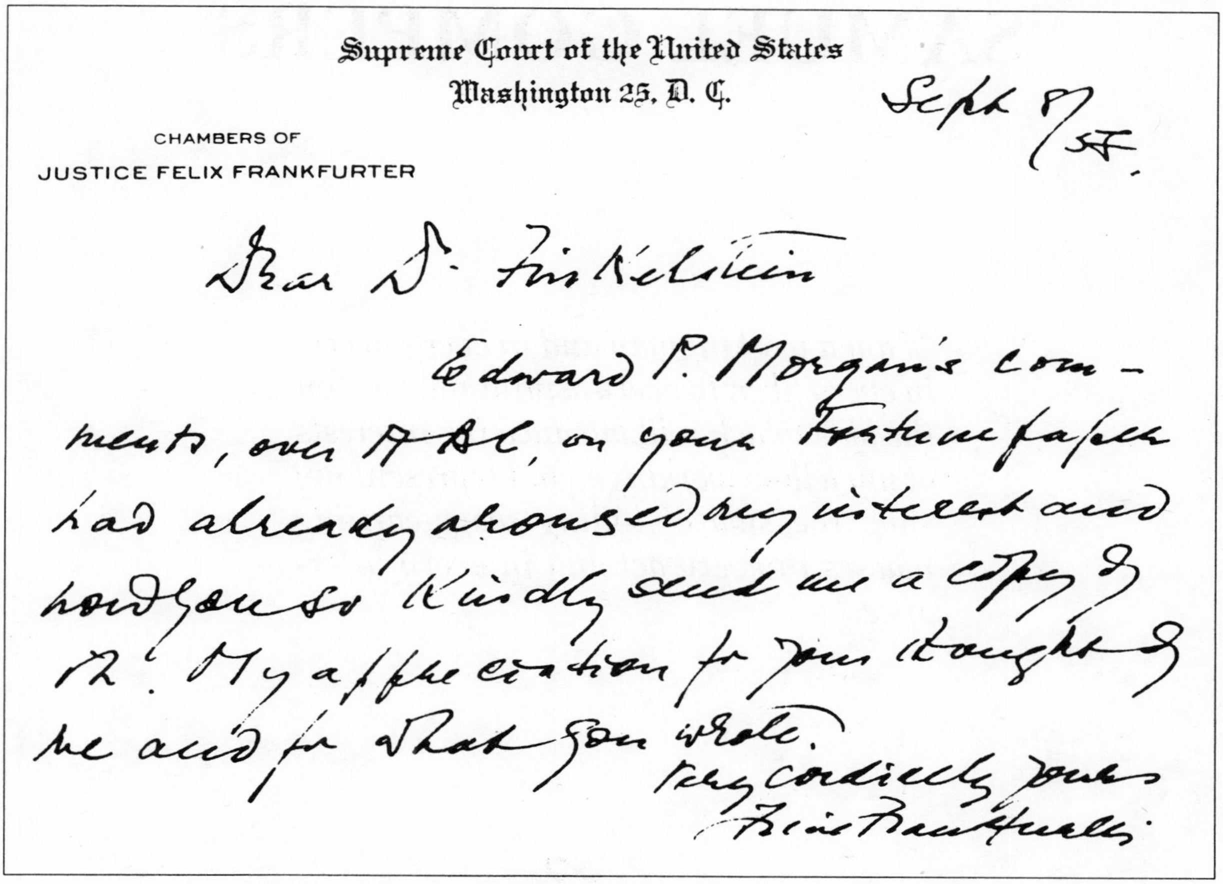

Supreme Court of the United States
Washington 25, D. C.

CHAMBERS OF
JUSTICE FELIX FRANKFURTER

Sept 8/57.

Dear Dr. Finkelstein

Edward P. Morgan's comments, over ABC, on your Fortune paper had already aroused my interest and now you so kindly send me a copy of it. My appreciation for your thought of me and for what you wrote.

Very cordially yours
Felix Frankfurter

Handwritten note signed by Felix Frankfurter on U.S. Supreme Court stationery.

SAMUEL GOMPERS

"I am a workingman and in every nerve, in every fiber, in every aspiration, I am on the side which will advance the interests of my fellow workingmen. I represent my side, the side of toiling wage-earning masses in every act and in every utterance."

Samuel Gompers is best remembered for his role as president of the American Federation of Labor. Through his advocacy, he helped to change the nature of the American labor system.

Gompers was born into a working-class family in London on January 27, 1850. His formal education ended at age 10, when he was apprenticed as both a shoemaker and a cigar maker. His family moved to the Lower East Side of New York in 1863, and there he followed his father as a cigar maker. In 1872 he joined the local branch of the Cigar Makers' National Union, and in 1877 he reorganized the union by introducing increased dues, sickness and death benefits, strike and pension funds, and considerable control of the locals by national officers. In 1881, countering the Knights of Labor, Gompers helped found the Federation of Organized Trades and Labor Unions of the United States and Canada. This was reorganized as the American Federation of Labor in 1886. With the exception of one year, Gompers was its president until his death. He later served on the Council of National Defense during World War I and accompanied Presi-

dent Wilson to the Versailles Peace Conference as an adviser on international labor relations.

Gompers despised socialism and rejected industrial unionism and political action. He advocated the power of collective bargaining as a direct economic tool in dealing with employers. He firmly established the system of negotiations and written contracts, a baseline that still prevails in current U.S. management–labor relations. Gompers held that labor had to be independent of intellectuals, politicians, and nonlabor sources. The workers' welfare could be addressed through capitalism provided it could guarantee an adequate standard of living for the workingman. Despite his own background, he advocated limiting immigration, thus protecting the American worker.

From his simple immigrant beginnings, Gompers became a powerful and decisive influence, universally acknowledged as the spokesman of the American labor movement. "The labor of a human being," he wrote, "is not a commodity . . . of commerce." He died on July 13, 1924, in San Antonio, Texas. His two-volume autobiography, *Seventy Years of Life and Labor*, was published in 1925.

AMERICAN FEDERATION OF LABOR

Executive Council.
President, Samuel Gompers.
Secretary, Frank Morrison.
Treasurer, Daniel J. Tobin,
222 E. Michigan St., Indianapolis, Ind.

First Vice-President, James Duncan,
25 School Street, Quincy, Mass.
Second Vice-President, Jos. F. Valentine,
Commercial Tribune Bldg., Cincinnati, Ohio.
Third Vice-President, Frank Duffy,
Carpenters' Bldg., Indianapolis, Ind.
Fourth Vice-President, William Green,
1103-8 Merchants Bank Bldg., Indianapolis, Ind.

Fifth Vice-President, W. D. Mahon,
260 East High Street, Detroit, Mich.
Sixth Vice-President, T. A. Rickert,
175 West Washington St., Chicago, Ill.
Seventh Vice-President, Jacob Fischer,
222 East Michigan Street, Indianapolis, Ind.
Eighth Vice-President, Matthew Woll,
6111 Bishop Street, Chicago, Ill.

LFL.

A. F. OF L. BUILDING

LONG DISTANCE TELEPHONE MAIN 3871-2-3-4-5-6
CABLE ADDRESS, AFEL.

Washington, D.C. October 14, 1921.

Prof. V. Y. Russell,
1109 Hasbrook Street,
Kansas City, Kansas.

My dear Sir:-

Replying to your letter of October sixth which is just received. I am very happy to comply with your request by sending to you under separate cover one of my pictures bearing my autograph.

Enclosed you will please find list of pamphlets published by this office. If you can make use of any of these in your work as teacher of history, I shall be glad to send them to you ~~but~~, of course, this does not include the A. F. of L. History Encyclopedia and Ready Reference Book, the AMERICAN FEDERATIONIST, or the printed proceedings of annual conventions of the A. F. of L.

Hoping to hear from you further, I am,

Very truly yours,

Saml Gompers

President,
American Federation of Labor.

Enclosure

Typed letter signed by Samuel Gompers on American Federation of Labor stationery.

URIAH P. LEVY

"I beg to make the most solemn appeal . . . in the presence of this court . . . whoever may be the party arraigned, be he Jew or Gentile, Christian or pagan, shall he not have the justice done to him which forms the essential principle of the best maxim in all their code, 'do unto others as ye would have them do unto you.'"

—Defense statement made by Levy at his third court-martial

American naval officer and patriot Uriah P. Levy helped to establish the American navy and confront institutionalized anti-Semitism.

Levy was born April 22, 1792, in Philadelphia. He ran away to sea at the age of 10, becoming a cabin boy. By the age of 20, he was a sailing master of a ship of which he was part owner. He applied for a commission with the navy and was granted one. When the War of 1812 broke out, Levy was given a lieutenancy and put in charge of a captured British vessel. The vessel was eventually recaptured by the British, and Levy was taken as a prisoner of war. He was detained until a prisoner exchange took place when the war ended.

After the war, Levy was involved in a constant struggle to achieve a place of standing in the U.S. Navy. A Jew and a visionary, Levy fought two lifelong battles: one against the anti-Semitism of the naval establishment, the other against corporal punishment in the

naval service. Common at the time was the brutal and standard practice of flogging men with a cat-o'-nine-tails to enforce discipline. Author of *A Manual of Informal Rules and Regulations for Men-of-War*, Levy was one of but a small handful of naval officers who openly advocated, against the common philosophy of the time, having flogging abolished. In 1850 a bill sponsored by U.S. Senator John Hale was passed eliminating flogging.

A controversial and confrontational figure, Levy suffered for his professional opinions, for not having been commissioned directly from midshipman, and for his religion. He was court-martialed six times, expelled from the service twice (and reinstated), and involved in one duel in which he was forced to kill his opponent. The court-martial proceedings established that his career had been obstructed because he was a Jew. Levy fought against these injustices and prejudices and in 1857, two years after having been dropped from the official captains' list, was reinstated. In 1859 Levy was given a command and by 1860 was serving as commodore of the U.S. fleet in the Mediterranean. His battle against institutionalized military anti-Semitism played an instrumental part in opening the door for other Jewish officers.

A great admirer of Thomas Jefferson, Levy, during his years of inactive naval service, had acquired Jefferson's neglected and dilapidated Monticello. At considerable personal expense he refurbished it, with Monticello eventually becoming a summer home for one of his nephews, Congressman Jefferson M. Levy. Uriah Levy's mother is buried on its grounds.

When the Civil War broke out, Levy was 68 years old and retired from the military. He nonetheless offered his personal fortune to Abraham Lincoln for the Union's defense needs. Levy died in New York City on March 22, 1862. A member of Congregation Shearith Israel, he was buried in its Cypress Hill Cemetery in Brooklyn. In his will, he left Monticello to the United States with the intent of its becoming a public monument.

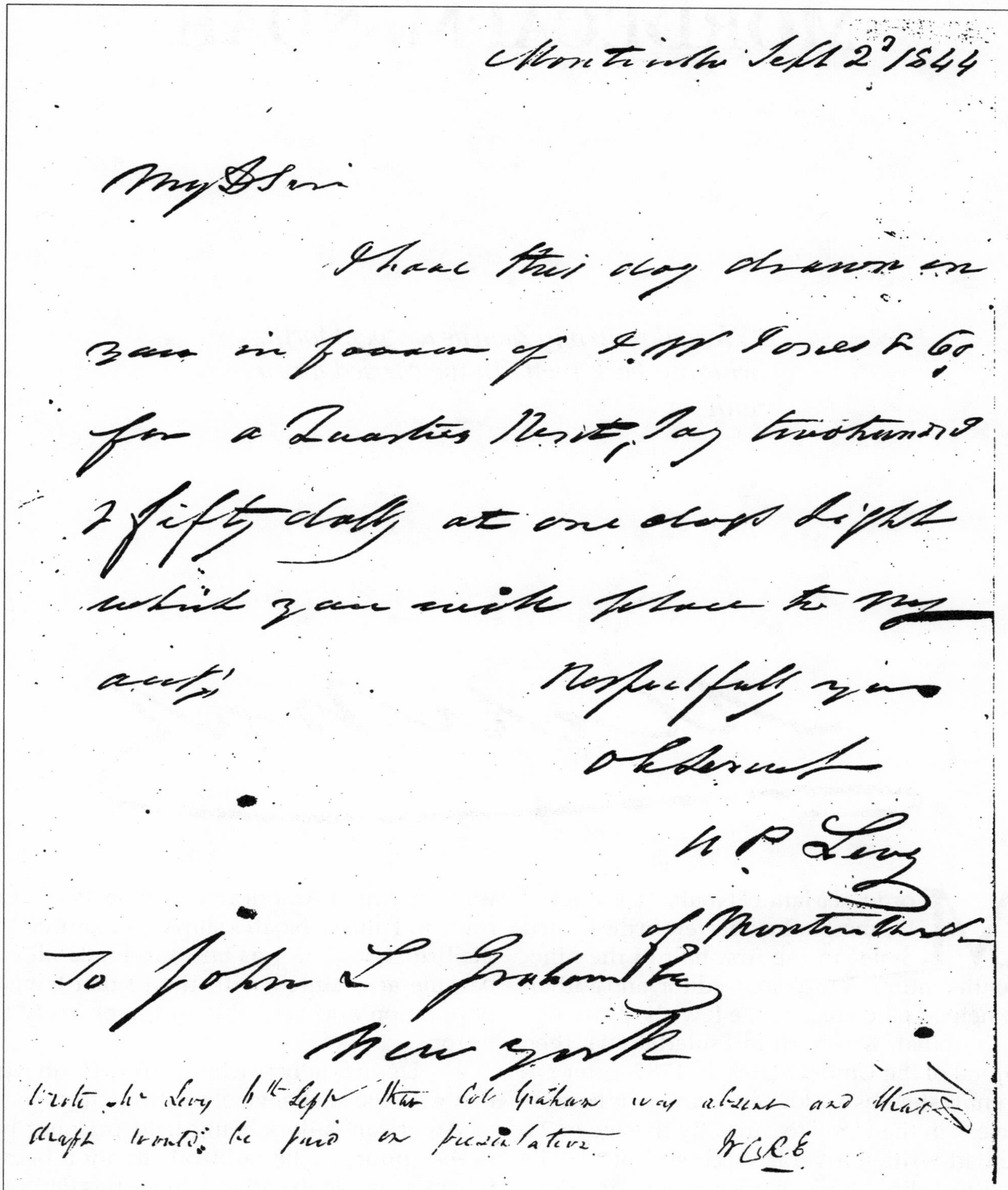
Monticello Sept 2d 1844

My Dr Sir

I have this day drawn on you in favour of J. W. Jones & Co. for a Quarter's Rent, say two hundred & fifty dolls at one days sight which you will place to my acct.

Respectfully yours
obt Servt
U P Levy
of Monticello

To John L Graham Esq
New York

Wrote Mr Levy 6th Sept that Col Graham was absent and that draft would be paid on presentation. W.C.R.E.

Letter signed by Uriah P. Levy dated September 2, 1844, to a Mr. John Graham of New York.

MORDECAI M. NOAH

"We will return to Zion as we went forth, bringing back the faith we carried away with us."

Mordecai Manuel Noah is considered the most influential Jew in the United States in the first half of the nineteenth century. A diplomat, editor, and author, he helped give voice to the Jewish cause.

Noah was born in Philadelphia, then capital of the United States, in 1785. After apprenticeships as a gilder and carver, he became a clerk in the U.S. Treasury. By the age of 24, he had written several successful plays. His political-diplomatic career began in 1808, when he backed James Madison for the presidency. A war hawk, he supported U.S. involvement in the War of 1812, and in 1813 he was appointed American consul in Tunis. En route to Tunisia, Noah's ship was captured by the British and he was taken to England. He became acquainted with the British Jewish population and was able to travel freely in Europe.

Upon finally reaching Tunis, Noah was met with the challenge of securing the release of American sailors being held prisoner by Berber pirates. The political situation being what it was, Noah had to achieve this without any apparent official U.S. government involvement. Ransoming the prisoners using his own funds, Noah successfully obtained their re-

lease. When he requested reimbursement from the federal government, the State Department not only refused his request but also revoked his appointment. Upon Noah's return to the United States, he contested the State Department's refusal and eventually was paid.

Noah left federal service and in 1817 became the editor of the *New York National Advocate,* and later its editor. In 1822 he became high sheriff of New York County and in 1824 was elected grand sachem (the head position) of Tammany Society. He also served as surveyor of the port of New York.

In 1825, in what was an early concept of modern Zionism, Noah purchased a large tract of land on Grand Island in the Niagara River (near Buffalo, New York) with the purpose of establishing a temporary Jewish state as a haven—called Ararat—in the United States, until the Jews could return to Zion. The project failed, but Noah turned even more strongly toward Palestine as a national Jewish home.

Noah remained active in politics, supporting a variety of causes—the Texas revolt against Mexico in 1836 and the founding of the Native American Party—and in 1841 became a judge in the Court of Sessions. As the best-known American Jew of his time, he addressed numerous Jewish groups and advocated the Jewish cause. Noah died in 1851.

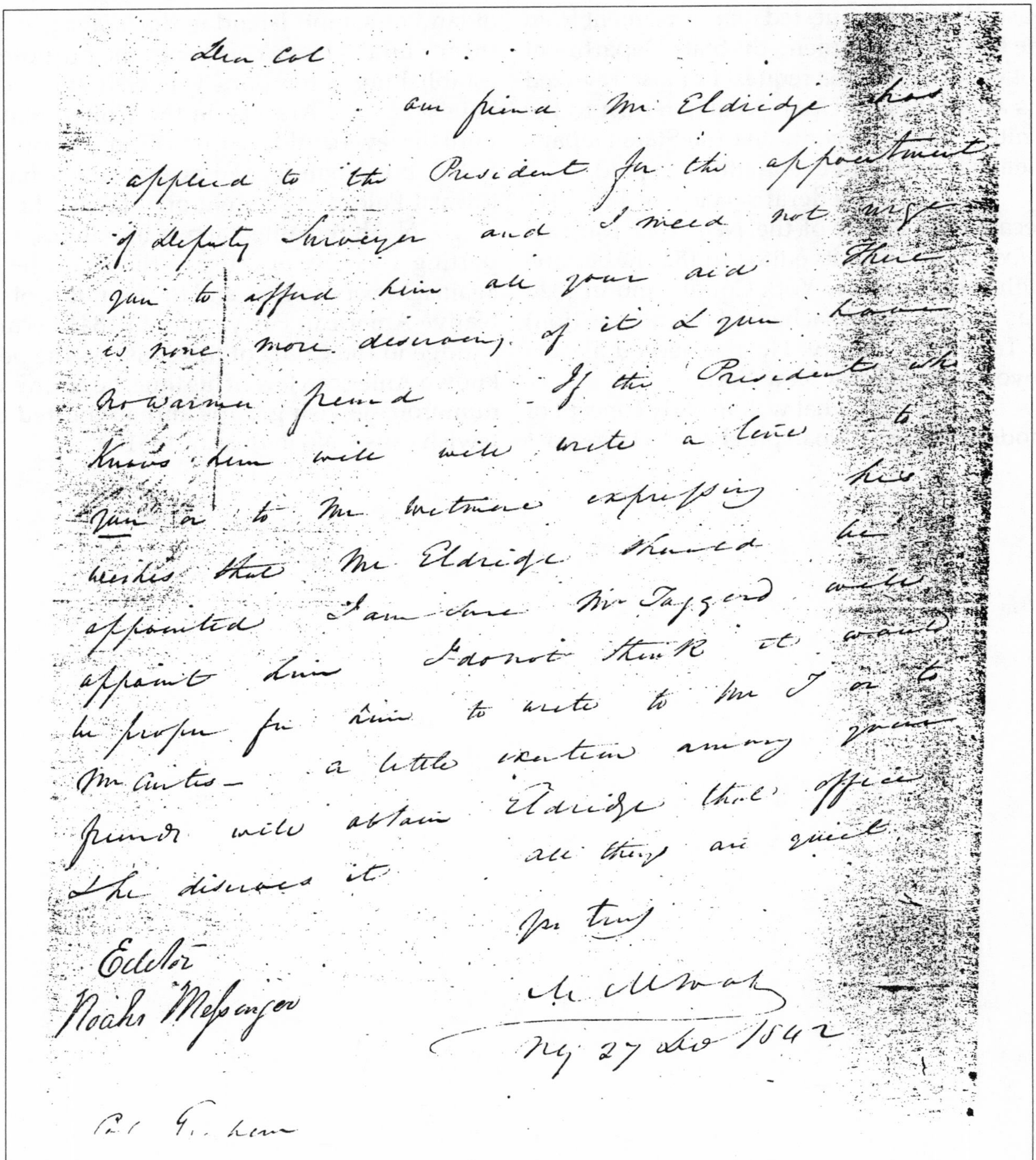

Dear Col

am informed Mr Eldridge has applied to the President for the appointment of Deputy Surveyor and I need not urge you to afford him all your aid. There is none more deserving of it & you have no warmer friend. If the President who knows him will write a letter to you or to Mr Wetmore expressing his wishes that Mr Eldridge should be appointed I am sure Mr Taggard would appoint him. I do not think it would be proper for him to write to Mr T or to Mr Curtis — a little exertion among your friends will obtain Eldridge that office. He deserves it. All things are quiet.

Yrs truly

M M Noah

NY 27 Dec 1842

Editor
Noahs Messenger

Col Graham

Handwritten letter by Mordecai Manuel Noah to a Colonel Graham, dated December 27, 1842. (Courtesy of the Henry E. Huntington Library and Art Gallery.)

HAYM SALOMON

". . . the patriotic devotion of Haym Salomon to the cause of American independence cannot, in their judgment, be questioned. . . . The committee are induced to consider Haym Salomon as one of the truest and most efficient friends of the country in a very critical period of its history. . . . He seems to have trusted implicitly to the national honor. . . ."

—Committee Reports,
29th United States Congress

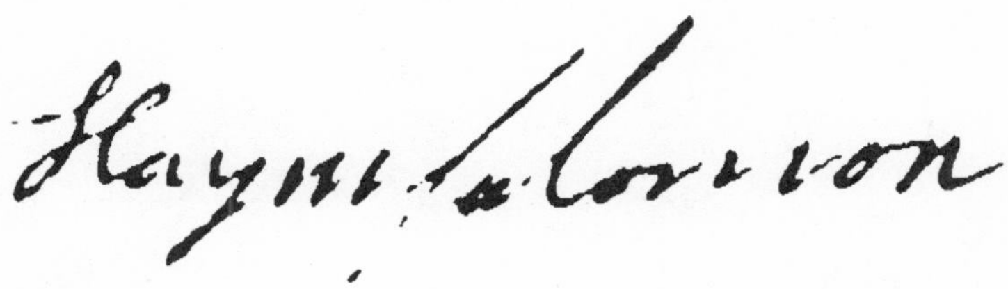

Haym (a misspelling of Chaim) Salomon is best remembered as the Jewish financier, banker, and patriot of the American Revolution. A man of many talents and unique capabilities, he is favorably remembered in U.S. history.

Born in Leszno, Poland, in 1740, Salomon was university educated in Europe and traveled extensively throughout Europe before immigrating to the American colonies in 1772. Financially astute and gifted in languages (he spoke Polish, French, Italian, Dutch, Russian, German, and English), Salomon initially worked as a provisioner to nascent American forces in the Lake George area of New York. In the summer of 1776 he was suspected of being an American spy and imprisoned by the British. His gift of languages brought him to the attention of a Russian general who had him released and who then utilized his services at a commissary serving Hessian officers working with the British.

Why Salomon was so sympathetic toward the American cause is unknown, but like so many other European immigrants, it was probably the aspects of liberty that most attracted him. While in his commissary post, Salomon induced some Hessians to defect to the American forces. At the same time, using his own funds, he helped American and French

prisoners to escape. When Salomon's activities became known, he was sentenced to death. Fleeing the New York area for Philadelphia, he left behind his wife, Rachel, and his month-old son. His personal property was confiscated by the British.

In Philadelphia, Salomon started over financially, developing himself into a bond broker for both the Americans and the French. In 1779 he negotiated a loan of $400,000 for General George Washington's army. In addition to lending funds to the new American government and the Second Continental Congress, he financed individuals, among whom was James Madison, who wrote of Salomon: "The kindness of our little friend on Front Street . . . is a fund which will preserve me from extremities, but I never resort to it without great mortification as he obstinately rejects all recompense."

Salomon was also a noted philanthropist and advocate of Jewish life in America. In 1782 he donated one-fourth of the needed funds to build the Mikveh Israel synagogue in Philadelphia. He vigorously fought against the religious oath public servants were required to take. For all his success as a bond merchant, when he died at the age of 45 on January 6, 1785, he was personally bankrupt; he had invested his own funds heavily in Continental stocks and bonds but had suffered severely in the recession of 1783. His canceled checks showed over $500,000 in funds written to the federal government. His newspaper obituary referred to him as "an eminent broker of this city [Philadelphia] . . . remarkable for his skill and integrity in his profession, and for his generous and human deportment." When the United States celebrated its bicentennial in 1976, a special stamp with his likeness was issued. He was the only Jew of the Revolutionary War period to be so honored.

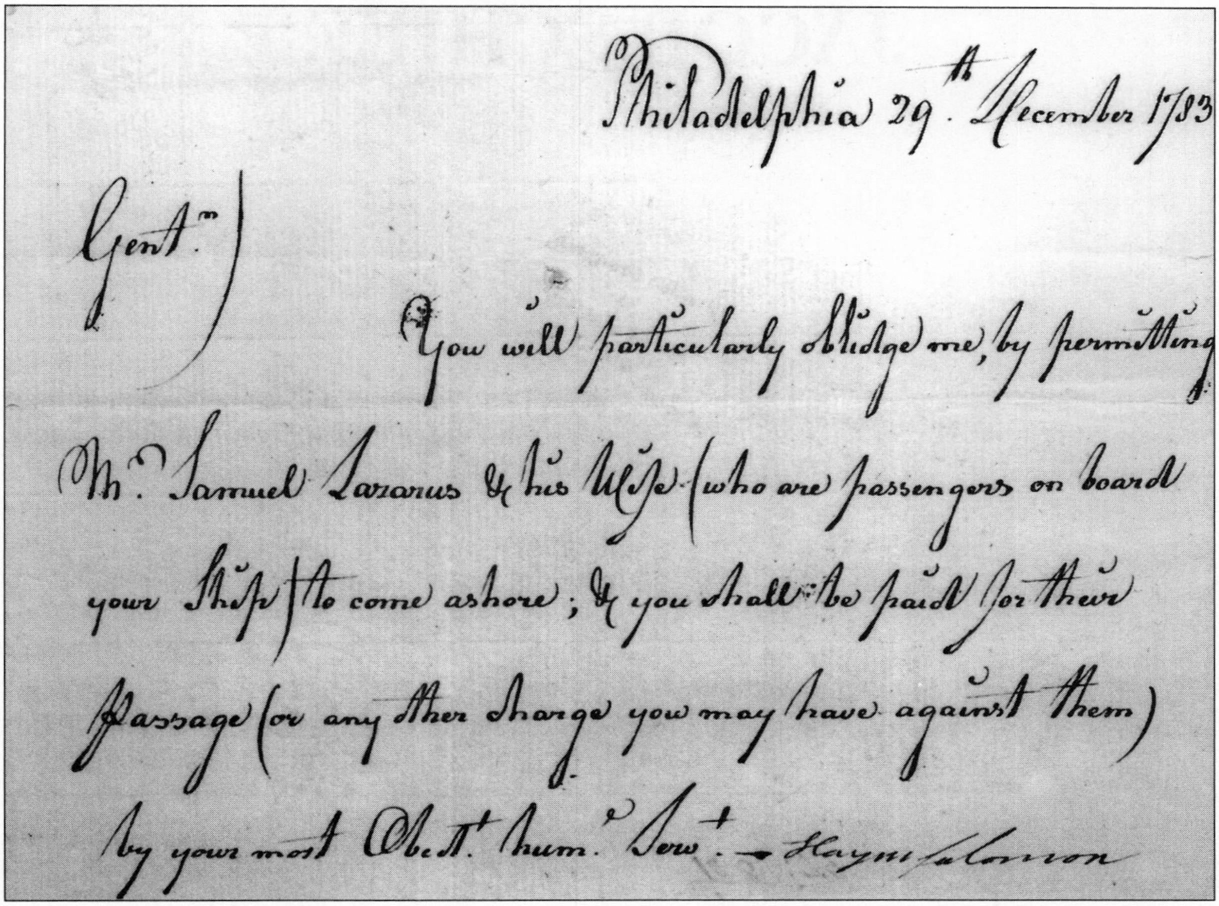

Philadelphia 29th December 1783

Gentn.)

You will particularly obledge me, by permitting Mr. Samuel Lazarus & his Wife (who are passengers on board your Ship) to come ashore; & you shall be paid for their passage (or any other charge you may have against them) by your most Obedt. humn. Servt. — Haym Salomon

Note signed by Haym Salomon requesting that passengers on board a vessel be allowed to come ashore. (Photograph by Suzanne Kaufman.)

JACOB SCHIFF

"Charity outweighs all other religious commandments."
—*Talmud* Baba Batra

One of the major American financiers of the late nineteenth and early twentieth century, Jacob Schiff is best known for his philanthropic efforts on the part of both Jewish and non-Jewish institutions worldwide.

Jacob Henry Schiff was born in 1847 in Frankfurt, Germany, into a distinguished Jewish family whose ancestors included rabbis, bankers, and scholars and who traced their roots to the fourteenth century. He received a strong secular and religious education, his Jewish training being under the guidance of Rabbi Samson Raphael Hirsch. At the age of 16, Schiff joined his father, Moses, in the Frankfurt stock exchange; two years later, he left for America to pursue a career in finance. He became a partner in the New York brokerage firm of Budge, Schiff and Co., but after marrying the daughter of Thomas Loeb, the namesake partner in Kuhn, Loeb, and Co., in 1875, he joined that firm. By 1885 he was appointed head of the company.

Schiff's firm was one of the most influential private investment banking institutions in America. Its specialty was railroads—the backbone of industrialized society—and the firm soon established itself as a key figure in the consolidation and development of railroads in America. Schiff's collaboration with E. H. Harriman of the Illinois Central Railroad led to the accumulation of the single greatest railroad fortune in the world.

Schiff was also involved in international financing. In this arena, he helped to arrange an incredible $200 million loan to the Japanese against czarist Russia in the 1904–1905 Russo-Japanese War. Schiff was strongly opposed to the Russian government for its anti-Semitic policies and labeled it "the enemy of mankind." He exercised his influence in dissuading others from loaning money to Russia. When Japan proved victorious, Schiff was officially invited to the Japanese Imperial Palace for dinner, the first foreigner ever so honored.

The range of Schiff's philanthropic involvements was unending. Raised Orthodox, he affiliated with New York's prominent Reform Temple Emanu-El, but he retained many of his Orthodox ways, including daily morning prayers. His philanthropy included major contributions to the establishment of the Jewish Theological Seminary (JTS), to New York's Yeshivath Rabbi Isaac Elchanan (later Yeshiva College and University), and to Hebrew Union College (HUC). He supported the teachers' institutes at both JTS and HUC and provided assistance to the Bureau of Jewish Education, the New York Kehillah, the Uptown Talmud Torah, and other educational institutions.

For thirty-five years, Schiff was president (and a major supporter) of Montefiore Hospital in New York. His assistance allowed both the Library of Congress and the JTS's library to acquire major book and manuscript collections. He was a supporting member of the Hebrew Free Society, the Young Men's Hebrew Association, the Jewish Publication Society, the Home for Aged and Infirm Hebrews, the Hebrew Technical School, and virtually dozens of other social organizations. In 1906 he was a founding member of the American Jewish Committee and in 1914 was instrumental in creating the American Jewish Relief Committee (later the Joint Distribution Committee). He donated $100 thousand to the Technion (the Haifa Institute of Technology).

Schiff's financial contributions, however, were not limited to Jewish organizations. He also gave generously to the American Red Cross, Tuskegee Institute, Harvard University, and Frankfurt University (Germany) and contributed $1 million to Barnard College. His list of contributions was endless.

Schiff died in 1920 at the age of 73. It was said that "nothing Jewish was alien to his heart." His philanthropic contributions and love for his fellow Jew have ensconced him in the history of the Jewish people.

שלום פערלמוטער
טעאטער-ארכיוו

JACOB R. SCHIFF
270 MADISON AVENUE
NEW YORK 16, N. Y.

April
23rd
1947

Mr. Salon J. Perlmutter,
152 West 42nd Street, - Suite 903
New York City

Dear Mr. Perlmutter:

I am enclosing my check to the order of Isidor Lash.

I wish it could have been for a larger amount, but many demands are made upon me and I must try to be just to all causes.

Faithfully yours,

Jacob R. Schiff

JRS:SLD

ENC.

Typed letter sending a charitable contribution, signed by Jacob Schiff.

ISAAC MAYER WISE

"It is not our duty to reform the orthodox, nor is it the duty of the orthodox to reclaim the reformers. Let each worship as he thinks proper, and build up Judaism."

The son of European tradition, Isaac Mayer Wise is generally considered the leading Reform personality of American Judaism. It was Wise who envisioned, planned, and constructed the framework for Reform Judaism, which flourishes today.

Wise was born in the village of Steingrub, Bohemia (then part of Austria and later Czechoslovakia), on March 29, 1819. His father was his first teacher at the *cheder* that he conducted, and at age 6 Wise was already beginning Talmud. At age 9, Wise was sent to live with his grandfather to continue his learning. Three years later, upon his grandfather's death, Wise went to Prague, the seat of learning in Bohemia. There he continued his education and at age 23 received his ordination. He further expanded his education by taking secular courses at the universities of Prague and Vienna. He took a pulpit in the small town of Radnitz for several years, but between the local and official government anti-Semitism and his conflicts with the neighboring Orthodox community, Wise felt pressured and in 1846 left with his wife and first child for the United States.

America opened up new vistas for Wise. He saw there an unrestricted land and

people with a new spirit. He took the pulpit in Albany, New York, at Congregation Beth-El, beginning his efforts to modify and reform the generally Orthodox Judaism in practice. His changes were considered radical by the mostly German-speaking immigrants who made up the congregation. They were comfortable with and receptive to traditional ways. Wise's introductions included establishing a choir, installing an organ, allowing family pews and doing away with the separate women's section, abridging some of the traditional prayers, discontinuing the sale of *aliyahs*, substituting a confirmation ceremony for boys and girls in lieu of the traditional male *bar mitzvah*, and beginning weekly sermons.

These changes did not come overnight; some were demonstrably resisted. In 1850 the internal conflicts came to a head when Wise assertively acknowledged in a debate that he did not believe in a personal messiah or in *t'chiat ha-meitim*, resurrection. His congregation split, and Wise and his followers formed a new synagogue, *Anshe Emes* (Men of Truth).

Wise continued his efforts in Albany until 1854, when he accepted a position in Cincinnati at Bene Yeshurun. Here Wise was to find a receptive, malleable congregation and in their rabbi, the congregation found a leader of the first order. The match was a good one; Wise remained there for forty-six years, until his death. In his first year there, he founded *The Israelite* (later *The American Israelite*), an English weekly Jewish newspaper. In it, he presented his philosophy for a changing Judaism. He also defended attacks on Jews and pioneered Jewish journalism in English. Wise founded a second publication, *Die Deborah*, a German weekly. At Bene Yeshurun he continued modifications of the traditional service that he had begun at Beth-El. Wise removed the liturgical poetry known as *piyyutim*, and discontinued the second day of the three major holidays of Pesach, Shavuout and Sukkot (Passover, the Feast of Weeks or Pentecost, and Tabernacles). A wise man who recognized that people need time to accommodate themselves to change, he waited fourteen years (until 1873) to introduce two more major changes: eliminating the second day of Rosh Hashanah and worshiping with uncovered heads. Other changes at Bene Yeshurun included increased English in the service (with a corresponding decrease in Hebrew), Friday-evening lectures and sermons, and new rituals. Under Wise, Bene Yeshurun became what has been called "the First Temple of Reform."

An energetic man, Wise is credited with establishing the major institutions of Reform Judaism: he was foremost in establishing the Union of American Hebrew Congregations (the UAHC, in 1973), the Hebrew Union College (1875), and the Central Conference of American Rabbis (1889). Wise had the vision and wisdom to recognize that America provided what he considered a fresh start for the Judaism of Europe. There were no yokes in the United States such as Europe had developed over centuries. New generations of American-born Jews, inculcated with the nation's Pioneer spirit and led by American-born rabbis of the same ilk and background, could flourish in this new world.

For all his innovations and changes, Wise had strong feelings about traditional ways. He resisted any movement to change the Sabbath from Saturday to Sunday. He advocated Hebrew as the language of prayer: *"It is that which our prophets spoke . . . furthermore our brethren in all parts of the world are familiar with the Hebrew service, and no Israelite would feel himself a stranger in the house of the Lord."* Wise advocated and believed in the *halachah*, recognizing its strength in sustaining its people and providing the nation of Israel with a rich quality of life no matter where Jews were found. Wise believed in the direct divinity of the Ten Commandments, although he felt that the rest of the Torah was composed by Moses, not merely written down by him. Wise advocated

a moderate Reform Judaism and believed that Judaism was truly the universal religion. He saw Reform as an evolutionary, not revolutionary, development of Judaism.

Wise died on March 26, 1900, having suffered a major stroke on the Sabbath two days before. His impact and legacy were significant. Rabbi Isaac Mayer Wise is credited with establishing the character and content of Reform Judaism in America.

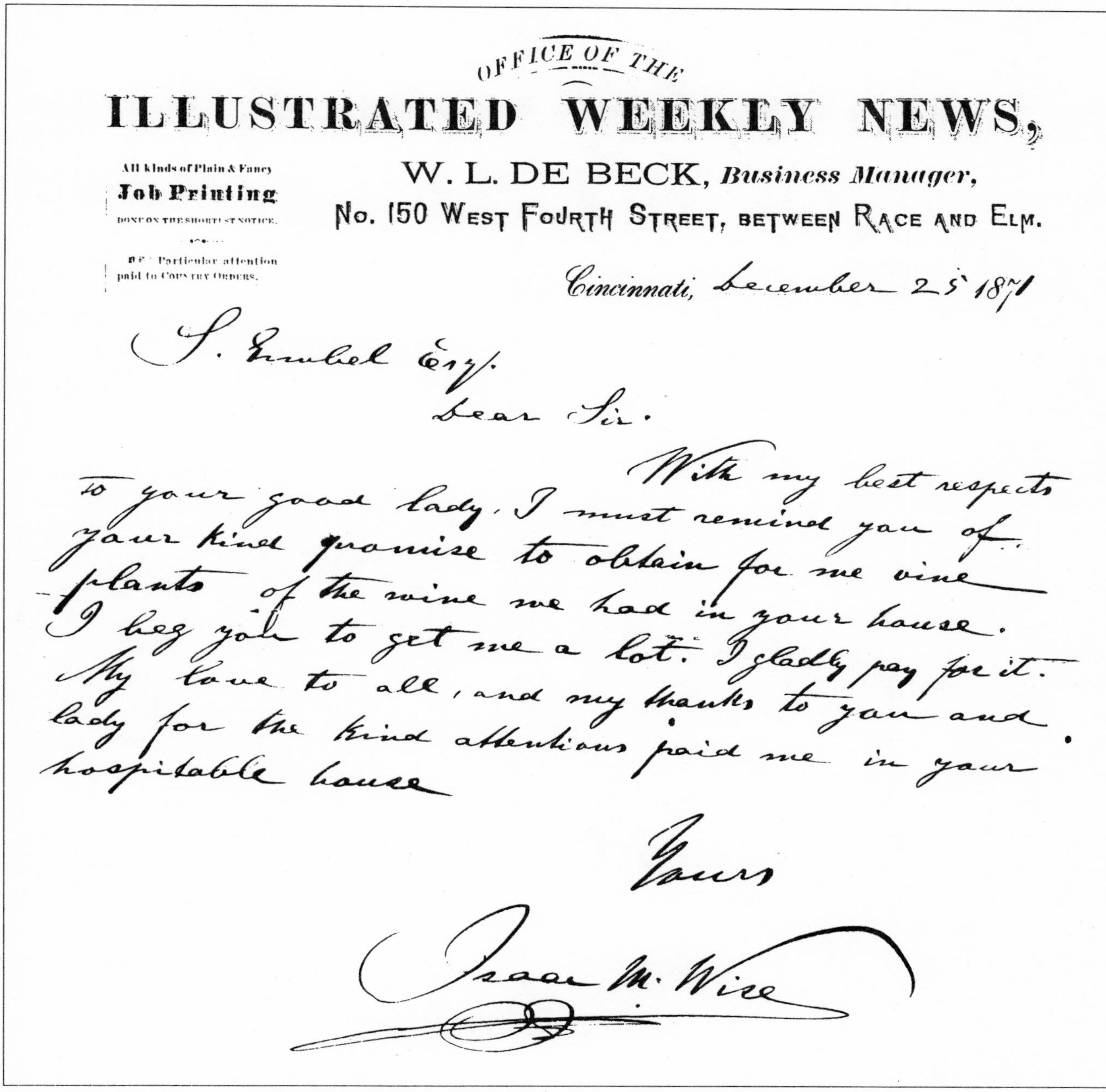

OFFICE OF THE

ILLUSTRATED WEEKLY NEWS,

All kinds of Plain & Fancy **Job Printing** done on the shortest notice. Particular attention paid to Country Orders.

W. L. DE BECK, *Business Manager,*

No. 150 West Fourth Street, between Race and Elm.

Cincinnati, December 25 1871

S. Knubel Esq.

Dear Sir.

With my best respects to your good lady, I must remind you of your kind promise to obtain for me vine plants of the wine we had in your house. I beg you to get me a lot. I gladly pay for it. My love to all, and my thanks to you and lady for the kind attentions paid me in your hospitable house

Yours

Isaac M. Wise

Handwritten letter about obtaining vine plants dated December 25, 1871, by Isaac Mayer Wise on Illustrated Weekly News *letterhead. (Courtesy of the American Jewish Archives, Cincinnati Campus, Hebrew Union College, Jewish Institute of Religion.)*

VII

ONE OF A KIND

God needs me as I am, and He needs you otherwise! Only because you are Edom may I be Jacob.

—Richard Beer-Hoffman

ELIEZER BEN-YEHUDA

"In every new event, in every step, even the smallest in the path of progress, it is necessary that there be found one pioneer who will lead the way without leaving any possibility of turning back."

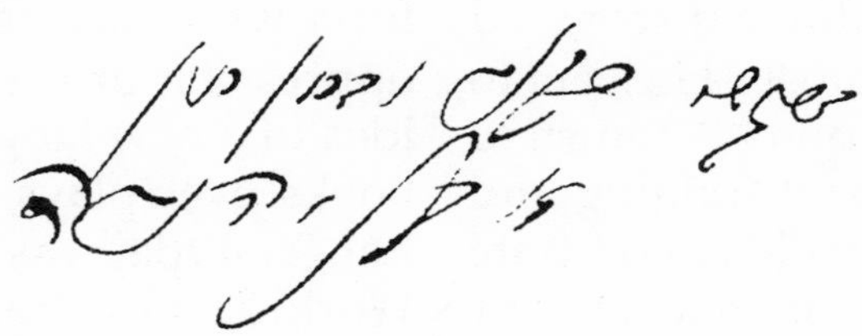

Even though these words of Eliezer Ben-Yehuda were written about a different issue, they can well define who Ben-Yehuda was: the father of modern spoken Hebrew.

For the nearly 2,000 years of the Diaspora, Jews spoke three primary languages: Aramaic, Ladino, and Yiddish. Hebrew itself had ceased to be an everyday spoken language after c. 200 C.E., and among the masses of Jews, it was *lashon kodesh*, the holy tongue. Although it was estimated that at least half of all Jews could read and write Hebrew with sufficient fluency to understand one another or read a Hebrew book of medium difficulty, Hebrew itself was not a spoken language. Not until Eliezer Ben-Yehuda.

Eliezer Yitzchak Perlman was born in Luzhky, Lithuania, in 1858. His father was a *Chabad chasid*. As a child, he attended a *yeshivah* and received a traditional education, but he was also secretly introduced to a Hebrew translation of *Robinson Crusoe*. This proved to be a turning point in his life. Although removed from the *yeshivah* by his family when they learned that he was reading secular material, he continued doing so and was eventually sent away from his home. He was fortu-

nate to be taken in by another *Chabad chasid*, Samuel Naftali Herz Yonas, who not only was not opposed to secular material but loved the Hebrew language and wrote for Hebrew periodicals.

For two years under the tutelage of Yonas and his daughter Deborah, Perlman read secular material and learned German, Russian, and French. Although emotionally tied to the family, he nonetheless left them to study in a larger town at a *gymnazium*, after which he left for Paris, where he planned to study medicine. It was Perlman's hope that this move would bring him in contact with fellow Jews who shared his dream: to live in a Jewish homeland where Hebrew was the everyday spoken language.

A Zionist, he wrote an article for a Viennese Hebrew journal in which he advocated settlement in the land of Israel (he preferred the name *Israel* to *Palestine*). He signed the article with his hebraized surname, Ben-Yehuda, son of Judah.

While in Paris, Ben-Yehuda discovered that he suffered from tuberculosis. He went to Algeria for his health, and upon his return to Paris decided to forgo medical training and move to Palestine, where he could concentrate on developing the Hebrew language. In 1881 he married Deborah Yonas, and together they left for Palestine. On the way, he began teaching her Hebrew.

Ben-Yehuda's idea of revitalizing Hebrew was not a popular one. Religious Jews felt that Hebrew was too sacred to be the common, everyday language. European Jews were satisfied with Yiddish as the national Jewish vernacular. Only a handful of people agreed with Ben-Yehuda's ideas of a Jewish homeland, with Hebrew as its mother tongue.

In Jerusalem, Ben-Yehuda started a Hebrew newspaper, *Ha-Tzvi* ("The Deer"), campaigned for Hebrew as the national language, began his life's work of a contemporary Hebrew dictionary, taught Hebrew, wrote Hebrew schoolbooks, and formed a society—Defenders of the Language—whose members spoke only Hebrew among themselves and taught their families Hebrew.

The strict, nonviolated rule of the Ben-Yehuda household was only Hebrew could be spoken, no other language. To maintain this, he had to research, develop, and create words for a language that had stopped growing 2,000 years before. His knowledge of the languages Deborah had taught would serve him well.

In 1891 Deborah died, leaving him with five young children. Within three months, three of the children died. Several months later Ben-Yehuda married Deborah's younger sister, Pola, who changed her name to the Hebrew *Chemdah* ("Cherished"). She became his constant companion and aide in his work, publishing translations and original Hebrew stories.

By 1897 the use of Hebrew had begun to spread through the country. It was a constant battle, with not only fellow Jews but also the Turkish authorities. Nonetheless, his efforts were paying off. Settlers escaping the oppression of Eastern Europe embraced the idea of a new language with a new life. More books, even plays, were appearing in Hebrew. Ben-Yehuda was elected a member of the World Zionist Organization executive committee, and the Jewish Colonization Association voted him a significant financial grant.

In 1901, at the age of 43, Ben-Yehuda began focusing on a dictionary, which eventually would become a seventeen-volume work. He traced lost Hebrew words; created new ones; examined the roots and development of words that would become part of a modern, living Hebrew; translated each word into French, German, and Russian; and gave cross-references to sources in literature. Ben-Yehuda's knowledge of English, French, German, and Russian was expanded by his learning Arabic, Aramaic, Assyrian, Coptic, ancient Egyptian, and Ethiopian. Indicative of the degree of Ben-Yehuda's task to create a dictionary was the

fact, as he explained to his wife, that the Hebrew of his time had no word for *dictionary*.

In 1904 Ben-Yehuda's efforts on the dictionary suffered a setback with Theodor Herzl's death; this threw him into a depression. Chemdah encouraged him to continue, and she borrowed funds to travel to England, where she persuaded Baron Edmund de Hirsch to help underwrite the project. In 1905 the first volume was ready for publication.

Ben-Yehuda continued his work on the dictionary throughout his life. He spent several years during the World War I in the United States because his pro-Zionistic views had placed him in jeopardy with the ruling Turkish authorities. In New York, he gave lectures and organized fund-raising campaigns for his project. He returned to Jerusalem in 1919.

By 1922, the year in which he died, Ben-Yehuda had finished the fifth volume of the dictionary. Under the British mandate, Arabic, English, and Hebrew were all official languages of Palestine. The strong objections from those favoring German, English, Yiddish, and other languages were all overridden. In a census taken before Ben-Yehuda died, the majority of Jews in Palestine listed Hebrew as their native tongue. As noted historian Cecil Roth observed, "Before Ben-Yehuda . . . Jews *could* speak Hebrew; after him they *did*."

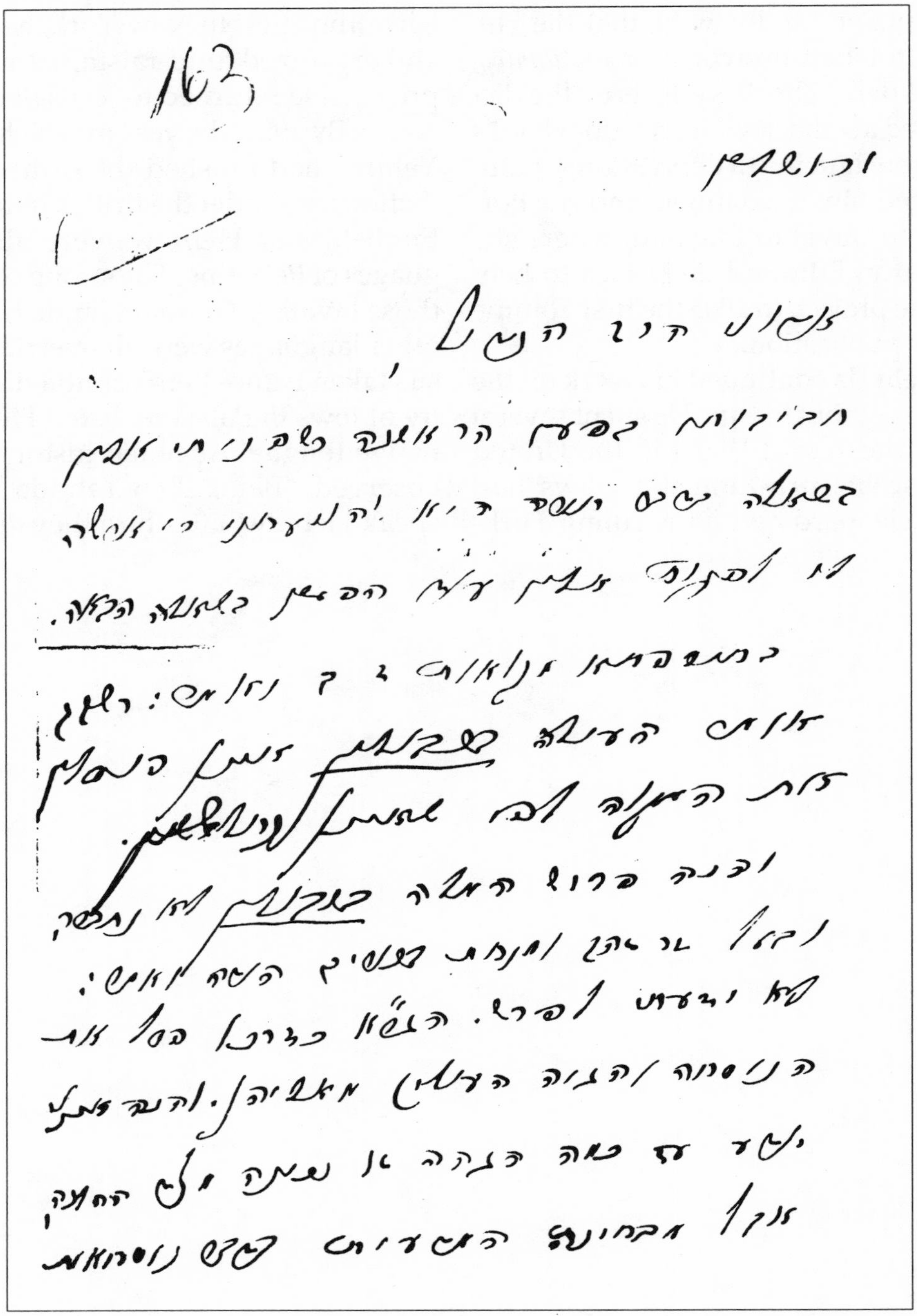

Undated handwritten letter from Eliezer Ben-Yehuda to Rabbi Abraham Kook regarding technical terms and words used in the construction of mikvahs (*ritual baths*).

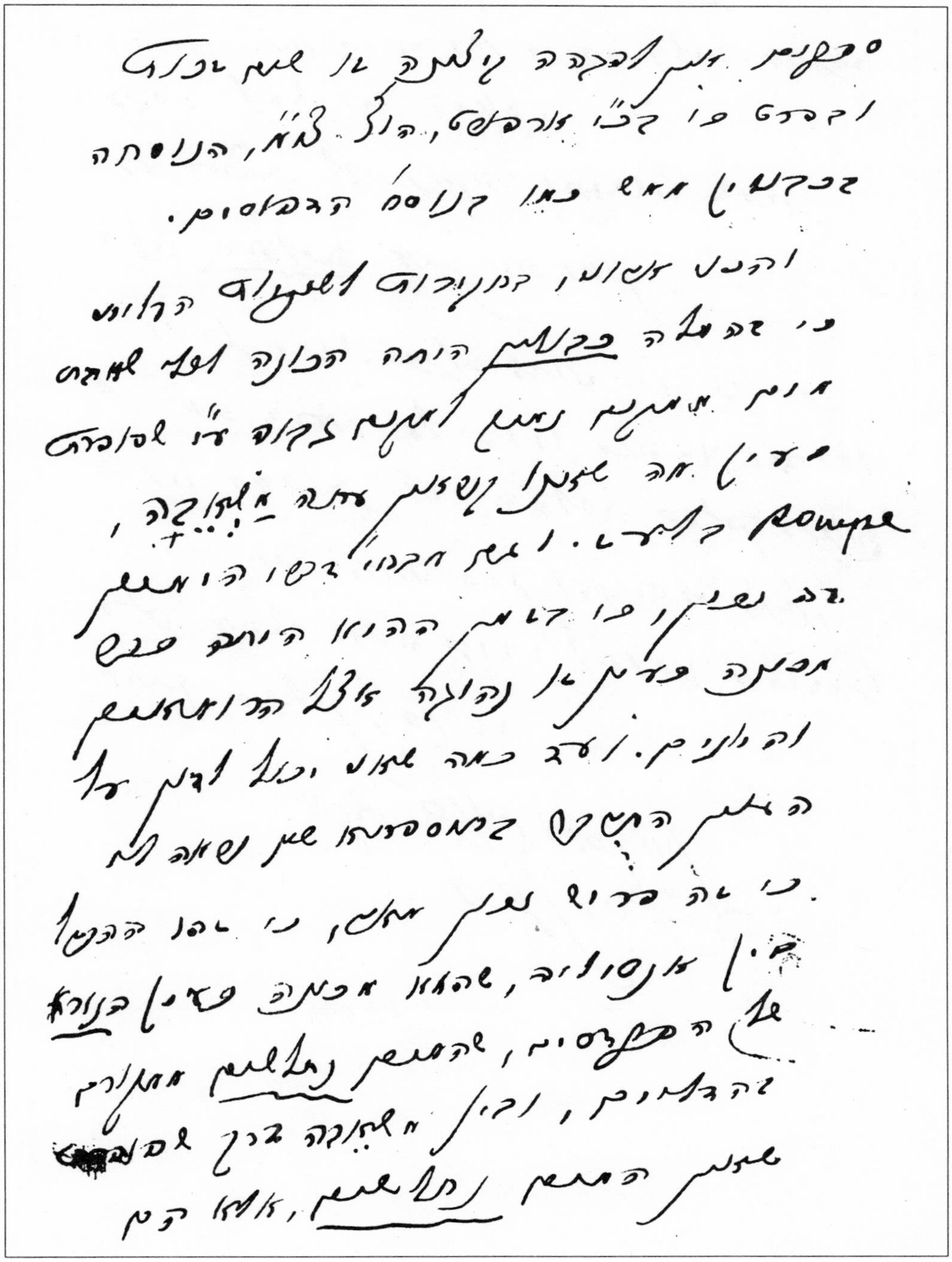

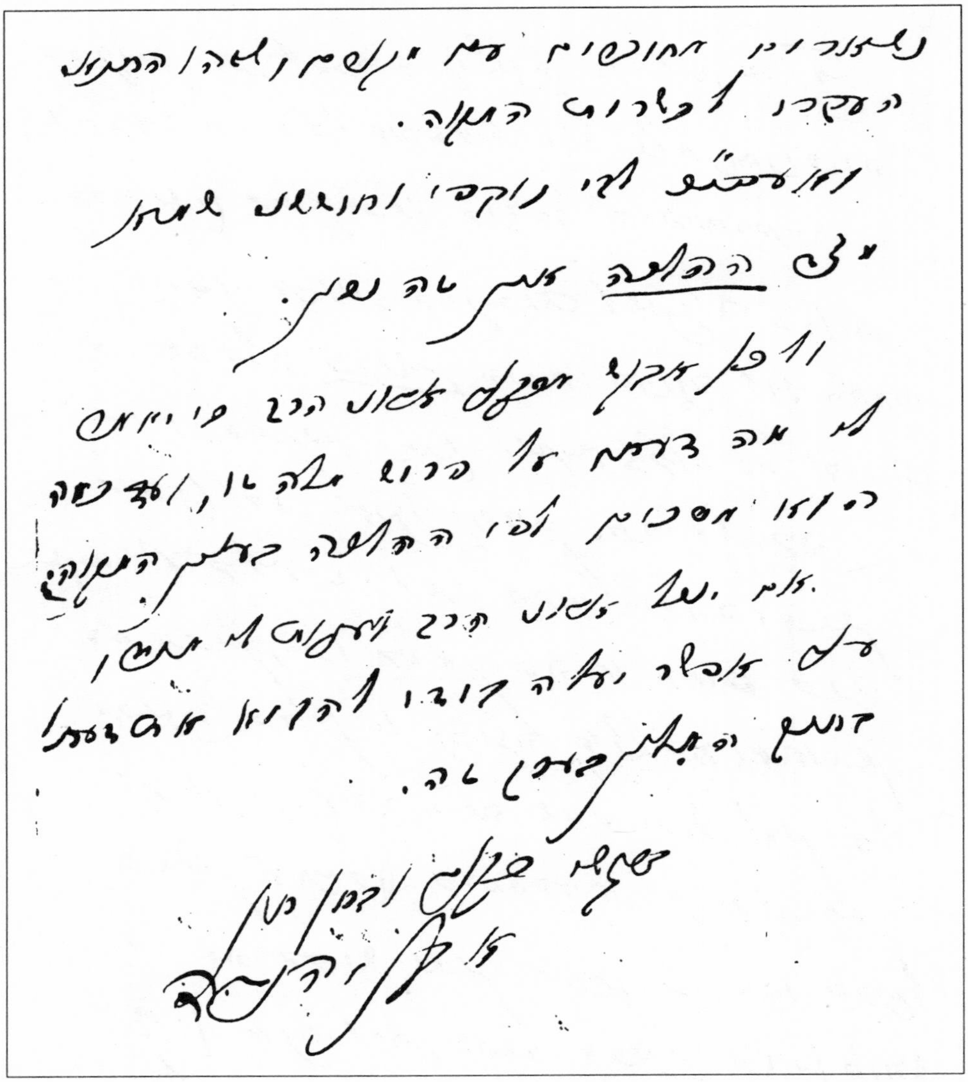

ROBERT BRISCOE

"I was drawing my own Coat of Arms. . . . So I drew the Arms of of Dublin, the three gates which look like three small castles. Now I recollected that in the time of Hitler my co-religionists had been forced to wear on their left arms the Star of David as a badge of contempt. Because of my pride in my heritage and my devotion to my faith, I decided to adopt this badge voluntarily. So I superimposed on the Arms of Dublin a large double triangle—the Star of David. That is my crest and both Jew and Gentile admire and praise it. . . ."

—For the Life of Me

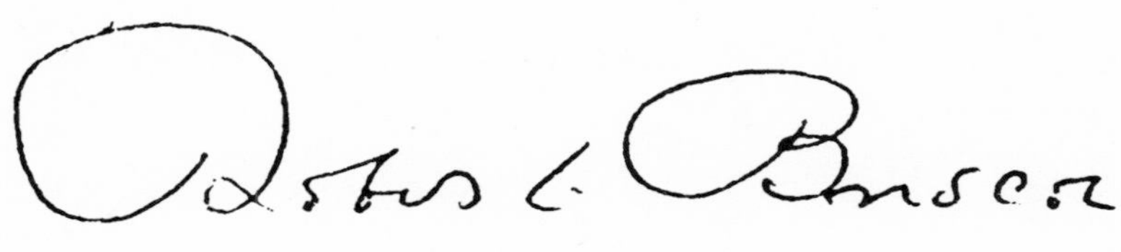

Irish patriot, politician, and businessman Robert Briscoe is best remembered as the first Jewish Lord Mayor of Dublin: a Jew in a staunchly Catholic nation.

The child of immigrant parents (his father was Lithuanian, his mother German), Briscoe was born September 25, 1894, in Dublin and educated in Ireland and England. Academically founded in electrical engineering, he worked in the import–export business in Germany. When World War I broke out, his parents were vacationing in Austria. Upon attempting to join them, he was captured by the Austrians and briefly jailed. In a prisoner exchange agreement, he and his parents were returned to Ireland under the condition they not fight for the British. Patriotic Irishmen, they readily agreed.

Briscoe's father sent him to the United States, where he felt his son would be safe from the escalating horrors of the war. But Briscoe returned in 1916, upon the Easter Rising of Irish patriots for independence from England. He soon joined the Irish Republican Army.

Over the next five years, "Captain Swift" (as he was nicknamed for his speediness in handling assignments) ardently fought for his country's independence. Educated and polished, he was successful in many assignments since he did not fit the traditional image

of a rebel. He was involved in smuggling not only diplomatic communiques but also shiploads of weapons and ammunition. The British circulated a broadside about Briscoe, describing him as "unlike most Irish rebels" and having "a gentlemanly appearance, which makes him most elusive." The uprising saw a temporary respite in 1921, ending permanently in 1923. Briscoe was involved until the end and his name was well established among his countrymen as an ardent patriot.

After the Irish war for independence, Briscoe turned to the family's import business. In 1927 he won a seat in the Dail Eireann, the Irish parliament, its first Jewish member. He held this seat for the next thirty-eight years.

Politically active throughout his life, in 1956 Briscoe was appointed Lord Mayor of Dublin, the first Jew to ever be so honored. As Lord Mayor that year, Briscoe traveled to New York City as the guest of honor in the annual St. Patrick's Day Parade. He brought with him green yarmulkes and called himself "an Irish Jew—one of the lepre-cohens."

Always an ardent and proud Jew, Briscoe was an equally proud Zionist. With the rise of the Nazis to power, Briscoe met with Vladimir Jabotinsky, who came to visit Briscoe to learn about tactics employed by the IRA in fighting the British. By the war's end, Briscoe had helped arrange for European survivors to make their way to Palestine. He again traveled to the United States, seeking U.S. government support for the creation of a Jewish state.

In 1961 Briscoe was appointed for a second term as Lord Mayor of Dublin. He died in 1969. The Briscoe family crest, awarded to him, featured a blue Star of David draped with a red band bearing the Irish words for freedom, equality, and fraternity. Briscoe's patriotism won him, an unabashed Jew, the honor and respect of a Catholic country.

IRVING BERLIN

"Everybody ought to have a lower East Side in their life."

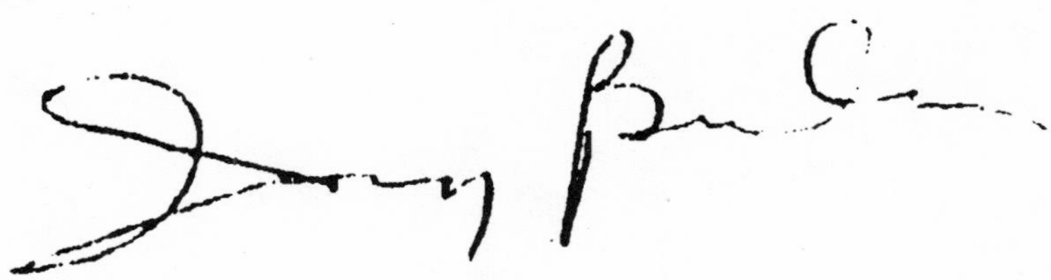

One of America's greatest composers and popular lyricists, Irving Berlin brought to the American musical scene hit after hit, so much so that his name is synonymous with twentieth-century show, stage, movie, and popular songs. Along with a handful of other composers and lyricists, he helped to set the standard for American music.

Irving Berlin was born Israel Baline in Temouyn, Siberia, in 1888. Fleeing pogroms, his family came to the United States when he was 6 and settled on New York's famous Lower East Side. *"Everybody,"* Berlin remarked later in life, *"ought to have a Lower East Side in their life."* His father died when he was 8, and Berlin went to work to help support his family.

Berlin got his musical start working as a singing waiter in restaurants in New York's Chinatown and Bowery. His first song—"Marie of Sunny Italy"—was published in 1907, when he was 19. At this time, he changed his name from Israel Baline to Irving Berlin. Berlin's first hit came in 1911, when his "Alexander's Ragtime Band" became the song of the day. With "Alexander," Berlin became a household name. From single songs, Berlin progressed to writing complete stage scores,

and by 1921 he was writing for his own theater and functioning as his own publisher.

Berlin's career spanned the greater part of the twentieth century, during which he wrote songs for plays and movies. Some of his most famous include "Blue Skies" (sung by Al Jolson in the first talking movie, *The Jazz Singer*), "Easter Parade," "Anything You Can Do (I Can Do Better)," "Oh, How I Hate to Get Up in the Morning," "There's No Business Like Show Business," "God Bless America" (which has become an unofficial second national anthem), and his most famous, "White Christmas." Associated with and immortalized by Bing Crosby in the movie *Holiday Inn* in 1942, "White Christmas" has sold tens of millions of copies.

Berlin died in 1989 at the age of 101. He was the recipient of many awards and honors, including a special Tony Award in 1962, and seven years earlier, a special congressional gold medal for his composition "God Bless America." Berlin was in the forefront of creating music that entertained and uplifted a nation.

IRVING BERLIN
1650 BROADWAY
NEW YORK 19, N.Y.

IRVING BERLIN

August 16th, 1954

Mr. Jacob R. Marcus
American Jewish Archives
Clifton Avenue
Cincinnati 20, Ohio

Dear Mr. Marcus:

I have your letter of July 28th.

The medal which was approved by President Eisenhower is being struck by the Treasury Department and the chances are I will not receive it until sometime late in the Fall. When I do, I will be glad to send you a photograph of it for your Archives.

With my best wishes, I am

Sincerely yours,

I
B
:
h
s

Typed letter on personal letterhead signed by Irving Berlin.

MARC CHAGALL

"When I am finishing a picture I hold some God-made object up to it—a rock, a flower, the branch of a tree or my hand—as a kind of final test. If the painting stands up beside a thing a man cannot make, the painting is authentic. If there's a clash between the two, it is bad art."

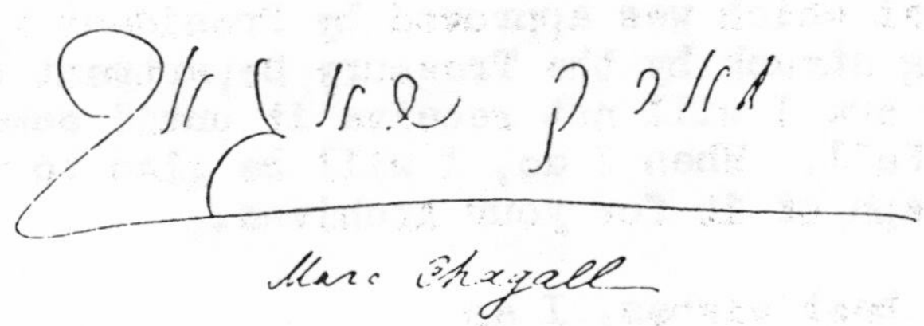

The name of Marc Chagall is recognized around the world. Although his works have been considered hard to classify, Chagall is indelibly known as a Jewish painter.

Born in Vitebsk, Russia, in 1887, Chagall (whose family name was Segal, *Chagall* being his own variant spelling) spent his early years in both Vitebsk and Liozno, a neighboring village where his grandfather lived. Chagall attended *cheder* as a child and then public school, where his talents were discovered. His parents disagreed greatly about developing his gifts, but his mother's support allowed him to attend a local art school. Later he studied in St. Petersburg where, at the age of 19, he won a scholarship to the school sponsored by the Imperial Society for Furtherance of the Arts. As a Jew, he was forced to live outside the city.

In 1910, due to the monthly stipends of Max Vinaver, a lawyer who admired the budding painter's talent, Chagall moved to Paris, the artistic capital of the world. He worked, lived, breathed in the city, and painted there from 1910 to 1914. His canvases soon exhibited a change. Previously, they had been dark, a residue of his life and experiences in Russia. But in Paris, the "City of Lights," Chagall moved toward brighter, more intense colors and patterns. In 1914 a one-man show of his in Germany featured over 200 pieces. Chagall

then returned to Vitebsk, where World War I trapped him.

Drafted into the army, he was given a desk job, which allowed him time to paint after his official duties. The following year he married Bella Rosenfeld and began a series of canvases featuring her. When the Bolsheviks came to power in 1917, Chagall was appointed commissar for fine arts in Vitebsk and the director of the Vitebsk Free Academy of Art. But eventually his concept of art clashed with the party's, and in 1922 he left Russia. After a stopover in Germany, Chagall returned to Paris in 1923. He worked on etchings there for Gogol's *Dead Souls* and La Fontaine's *Fables*, circus scenes, and other projects.

In 1931 Chagall made his first visit to Palestine, also touring Egypt and Syria. Heavily impressed by what he saw, he was inspired to create 105 biblical etchings, considered some of the finest examples of the art. By the mid-1930s Chagall had gained recognition in France, Germany, and Switzerland. But in 1937, with the Nazi rise to power, fifty-seven pieces of his were confiscated from public collections. A number of these were displayed by the Nazis as "degenerate art" in Munich. After France fell to the Nazis in 1940, Chagall, seeing the future, left for the United States, arriving in 1941.

Besides being a citizen of Europe for three decades, Chagall was also a Russian Jew, and his national ethnic identities were a backbone of his work. The war years took a heavy toll on Chagall. His canvases from this period are said to reflect his depression over the horrors in Europe. Adding to his distress was the death of his wife in 1944. For nine months, he was unable to work. When he did resume, it was to illustrate her memoirs, *Burning Lights*.

Chagall returned to France in 1948 and remarried in 1952. He was honored with several important exhibitions, a retrospective at the New York Museum of Modern Art, and the opening show of the National Museum of Modern Art in Paris. He went on to create a number of world-renowned works: the famous Twelve Tribes stained glass windows for the Hadassah Hospital in Jerusalem, the stained glass windows for a cathedral in Metz, a stained glass window for the audience hall in the Vatican, and the Peace Window for the United Nations Secretariat. In addition, he painted two large murals for the Lincoln Center in New York, repainted the ceiling of the Paris Opera, and designed the mural, floor mosaics, and curtains for the Israeli Knesset in Jerusalem.

A definition of Chagall's work is not easily derived. His art has been explained thus: "In a period when art was becoming increasingly obscure, the public appreciated the art of Chagall, which did not challenge them, and were happy to participate in the world he created."

Chagall died at the age of 98 in 1985. His overt expressions of Judaism brought a new dimension of art to Jews and non-Jews alike.

ELI COHEN

"I am an Israeli operative employed by the Mossad. My name is Eliahu ben Shaul Cohen, and I live with my wife and three children in Bat Yam, near Tel Aviv. All I will add is that I operated in the best interest of my country."
—Confession under torture

Kamel Tabet Amin was a Syrian businessman. A prosperous merchant, philanthropist, eligible bachelor, political contributor, and staunch patriot, he was a popular member of Syrian society. At the time of his death, his favored-son status and social success had elevated him to consideration for appointment as deputy minister of defense.

He was also Israel's most successful spy.

Eli Cohen was born in Alexandria, Egypt, in 1924, the son of a Jewish-Syrian shopkeeper. He attended secular high school and the Institute of Higher Hebraica Studies. As a youth, he worked for a free Egypt—free from British rule—and participated in public anti-British demonstrations.

Cohen studied electrical theory at Farouk University, but when the State of Israel was founded in 1948, overt anti-Semitism increased and eventually all Jewish students were expelled. He then joined an underground Zionist group. Cohen received three months' basic intelligence training in Tel Aviv and returned to Egypt to assist in diversionary tactics. Arrested twice and imprisoned for several months, but never convicted of a crime, in late 1956 he was expelled from Egypt. He arrived in Israel in early 1957.

Cohen initially worked in the Ministry of Defense as a translator but later accepted a position with the Mossad, Israel's espionage service. After appropriate training, Cohen, married and with a family, was sent to infiltrate Syrian society and obtain military information.

Posing as importer-exporter Kamel Tabet Amin, Cohen first went to Argentina as a Syrian expatriate. He spent several months there, establishing his name and presence and becoming friends with a number of influential Syrians, not least among them the military attaché Amin al-Hafez. Al-Hafez would later return to Syria to become the chief of staff and eventually president of Syria. When Cohen "returned" to Syria, he carried with him valuable contacts and letters of introduction.

Over the three years he worked and lived in Syria as a foreign agent, he developed the cover of being a devoted Marxist and a member of the Socialist Baath Party. A patriot, he often complained to his social/political friends about the state of Syrian military readiness, or, from his perspective, unreadiness. The ruse worked, and Cohen was frequently taken on tours of military installations adjacent to the Israeli border to observe the deployment of troops and the latest Syrian military and communications technology. With a hidden camera, he took photographs. He assisted in obtaining information about the new Soviet MiG-21 fighter planes. When Syria developed a plot to divert water from the Jordan River, thus endangering Israeli agricultural and general water supplies, Cohen, faking interest in buying property, got a tour of the area. With the information he supplied, the Israeli air force bombed and destroyed the project.

Cohen's espionage activities were finally detected in January 1965 by new Syrian communications tracking equipment. His arrest shocked Syrian military, diplomatic, and society people. He was initially taken for an Arab spy, but under in-depth interrogation, with torture, he finally revealed he was an Israeli. Requests for clemency poured in from many nations and leaders, including Charles de Gaulle and the pope, but an angry and embarrassed Syrian tribunal handed down a sentence of death. In Damascus's public square, Cohen was hanged. The Syrians left his body on the gallows for seven hours. All Israel mourned his death. His body was never returned.

Cohen's activities proved to be of inestimable value to Israel. When the 1967 Six-Day War broke out, two years after his execution, Syrian forces were defeated in a matter of hours. Numerous lives were saved by the information for which Eli Cohen gave his life.

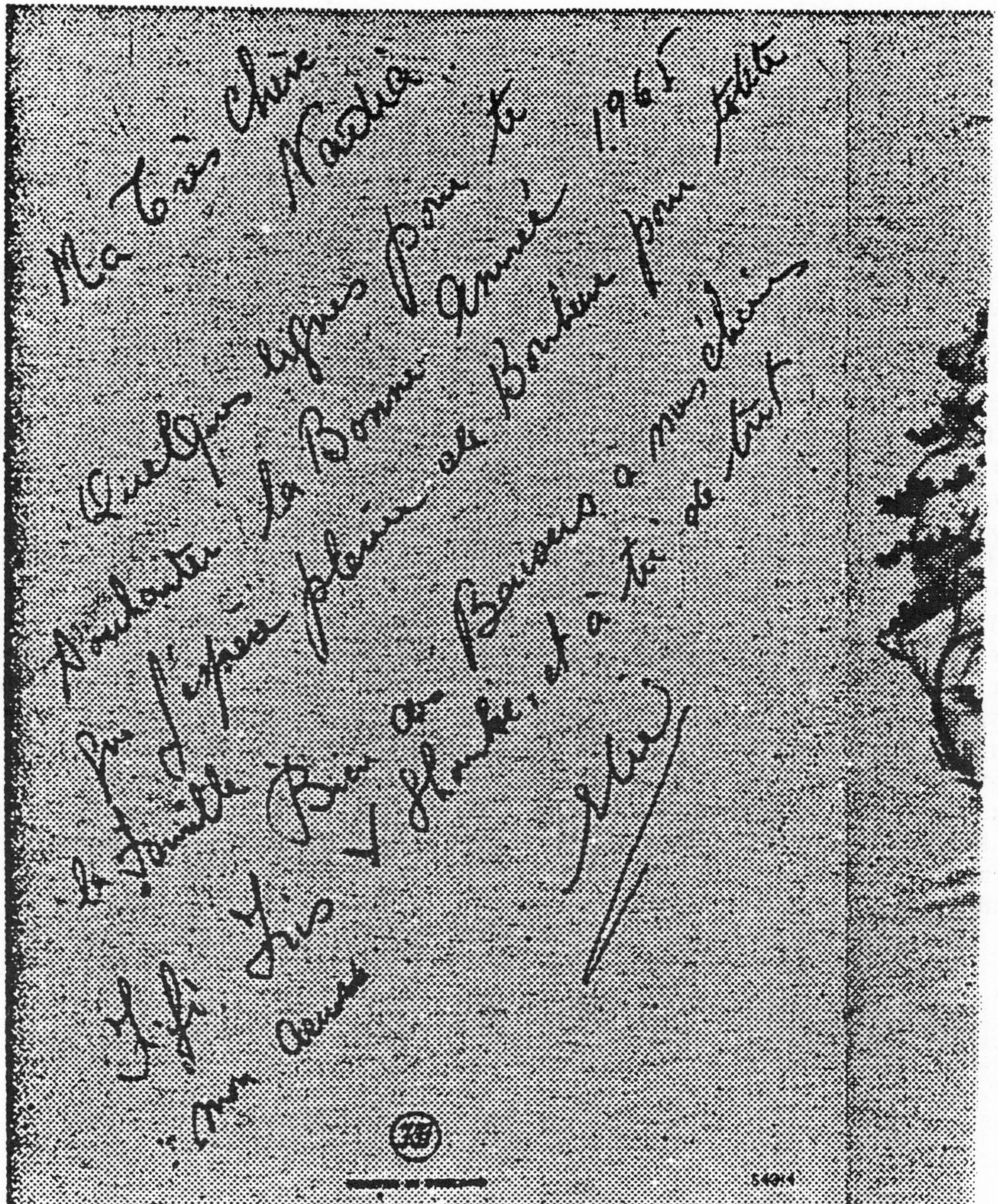

Ma très chère Nadia
Quelques lignes pour te souhaiter la Bonne Année 1965 pour je l'espère pleine de Bonheur pour toute la famille. Bien des Baisers à mes chères Fifi, Iris et Shaul, et à toi de tout mon cœur
Eli

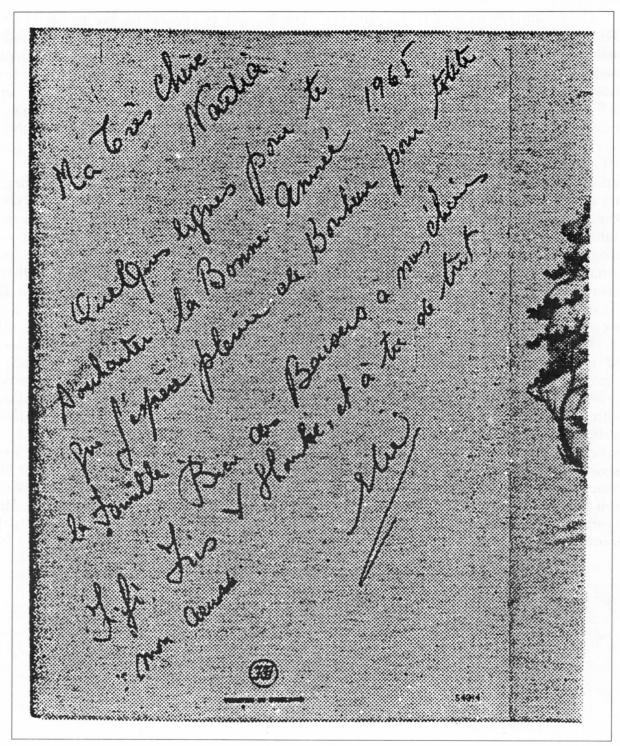

Note signed by Eli Cohen.

Dearest Nadia, only a few lines to wish you a happy 1965. I hope it will be a year of abundance for the entire family. Lots of kisses to Fifi, Iris and Shaul and you with all my heart.

Translation of note from the French.

AARON COPLAND

"I think of my music as Jewish because it's dramatic, it's intense, it has a certain passionate lyricism in it. I can't imagine it being written by a goy."

Leonard Bernstein called him "the leader to whom all young composers brought their compositions." The *New York Times* categorized him as "America's best known composer of classical music, and a gentle yet impassioned champion of American music in every style." He was titled "the dean of American composers."

Aaron Copland was an American original. He wrote music for every style: jazz, theater, chamber music, ballet, popular. An iconoclast, Copland was a composer who created and personified an American class of music. His originality and uniqueness put him in a class by himself.

This American original was born in what some consider the American heartland: Brooklyn, New York, on November 14, 1900. His parents were Russian Jews. Until 1921, he studied music, composition, theory, and orchestration under the noted Rubin Goldmark. He then moved to France, where he observed that the native music seemed to reflect the national character of French life. America had no such relationship in its formal music. Upon his return in 1924, Copland began to compose music that reflected America's culture, history, environment, and legends. His early works still bore the names of classical works: *Symphony for Organ and Orchestra, Music for Theater,*

Symphonic Ode, Short Symphony, and *Piano Sonata.* A daring composer, he also produced nonconventional pieces based on jazz, tone, and nontraditional instrumental combinations.

Drawing from popular American melodies, common folk tunes, and cowboy themes, Copland began to write the music he hoped would have broad appeal. The years 1938, 1942, and 1944 saw the premieres of his ballet works *Billy the Kid, Rodeo,* and *Appalachian Spring.* For the last, Copland won a Pulitzer Prize. In 1942, there was his *Lincoln Portrait,* for both orchestra and speaker. These compositions were all richly received and popularly accepted.

Like many composers, Copland was approached by Hollywood to write for the movies. His screen scores include *Of Mice and Men, Our Town, The Red Pony,* and *The Heiress.* Copland also authored several books on music. In 1964 he was awarded the Presidential Medal of Freedom.

Copland held a number of positions in the American music scene throughout his life. From 1937 to 1945 he was president of the American Composers' Alliance. He was a director of the League of Composers and for twenty-five years (1940–1965) headed the composition department at the prestigious Berkshire Music Center in Tanglewood, Massachusetts. Copland retired from composing in 1970 to concentrate on lecturing and conducting. He died in 1990.

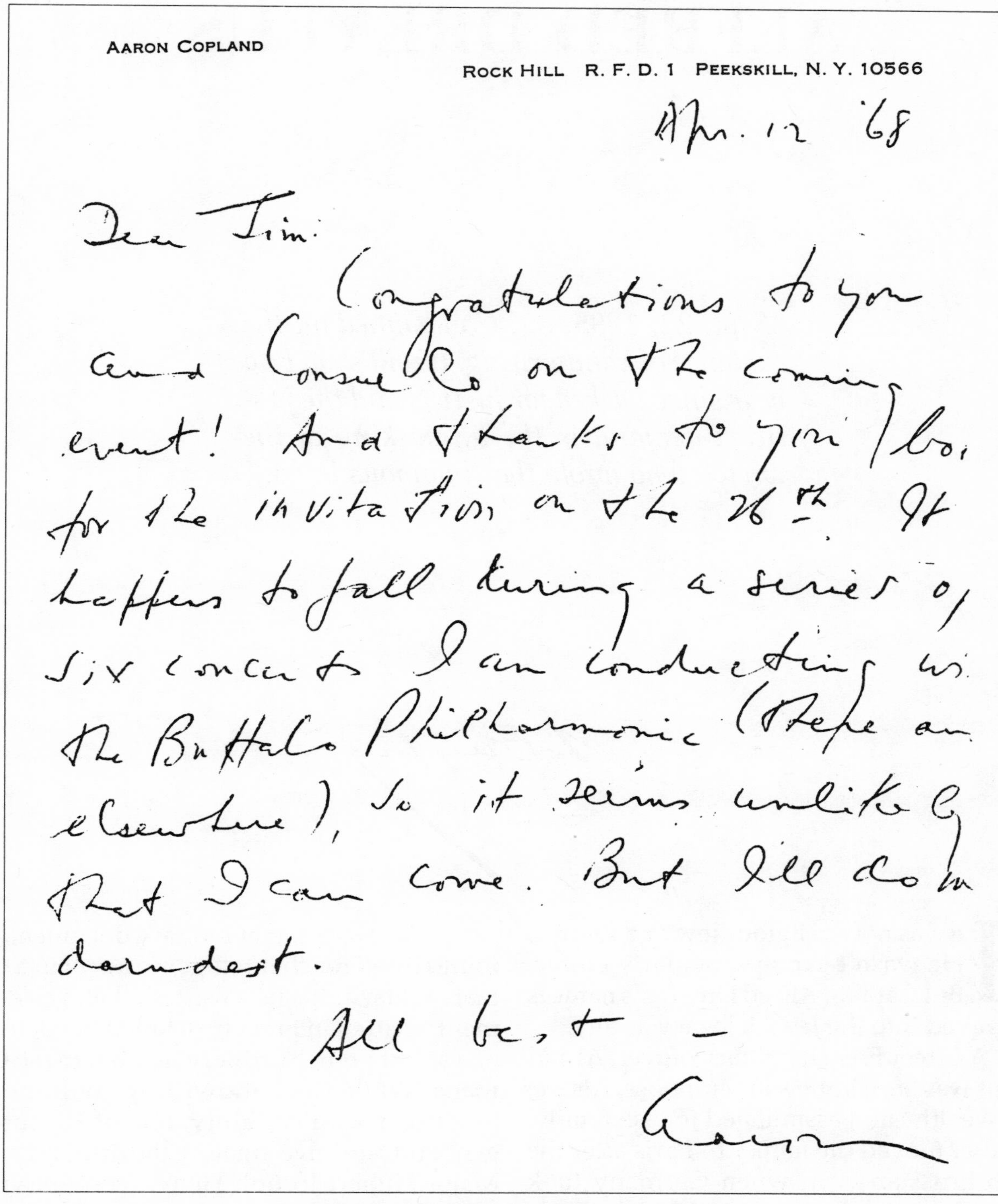

AARON COPLAND

ROCK HILL R. F. D. 1 PEEKSKILL, N. Y. 10566

Apr. 12 '68

Dear Jim:

Congratulations to you and Consuelo on the coming event! And thanks to you both for the invitation on the 26th. It happens to fall during a series of six concerts I am conducting with the Buffalo Philharmonic (here and elsewhere), so it seems unlikely that I can come. But I'll do my darndest.

All best —

Aaron

Handwritten letter by Aaron Copland.

ALFRED DREYFUS

"Sept. 22, 1895. . . . Condemned on the evidence of handwriting, it will soon be a year since I asked for justice; and the justice I demand is the unmasking of the wretch who wrote that infamous letter."

He was not a religious Jew or a Zionist. He wasn't even particularly ethnic. But Captain Alfred Dreyfus's name is as engraved into the Jewish legacy as any.

A career French military officer, Alfred Dreyfus was born in 1859 in Mulhouse, Alsace, into a wealthy and assimilated Jewish family. His father moved the family to Paris after the Franco-Prussian War, when Germany took control of the area. Dreyfus attended the Ecole Polytechnique and entered the army as an engineer with the rank of lieutenant. Overcoming anti-Semitic sentiments and pressures, in 1892 he was promoted to captain as a member of the general staff. He was the only Jew.

In 1894 a secret military document was found by a French intelligence agent in a German military attaché's wastebasket. The document, written in French, detailed the delivery of a secret French artillery manual to the Germans. While the handwriting could not be identified with certainty, one of the intelligence officers investigating the discovery, one Major Hubert Joseph Henry, convinced his senior ranking officers that, due to a similarity in penmanship, the "outsider" Dreyfus was the author of the treasonous document. Dreyfus, protesting his innocence, was arrested and imprisoned, awaiting court-martial.

At the military trial, Henry told the military court that he had secret information, which he could not reveal, that Dreyfus was the guilty party. With intense public anti-Semitism, a virulent anti-Semitic press, religious Catholic and royal demands, and improper due process of military law and outright illegalities—the French Ministry of War had provided the military court with a folder of secret documents (some forged), and Dreyfus's attorney was not informed of the presentation of this "evidence"—Dreyfus was convicted. His sentence was expulsion from the army and life imprisonment in solitary confinement in exile. In a public ceremony witnessed by mobs shouting anti-Semitic slogans, Dreyfus's military epaulets were torn off and his sword broken, and he was transported in chains to the infamous Devil's Island off the coast of Guiana, South America. Even while he was en route, the German ambassador made a formal statement that Germany had had no contact with Dreyfus.

Thus began the Dreyfus affair.

Dreyfus's family and supporters continued to protest the kangaroo-court verdict. Within the next two years, damning evidence and admissions would come to light proving that Dreyfus had been framed. Yet, when the French military was presented with the evidence, it was rejected with the response that the French army could not admit a mistake without impugning its reputation. The general staff and the government would not admit that a miscarriage of justice, at the highest levels, had taken place.

The Dreyfus affair split French society in two. The brazenness of the government in failing to acknowledge illegalities and mistakes went against the moral fiber of many. The novelist Emile Zola, who was not Jewish, wrote his famous open letter of January 3, 1898—*J'Accuse* ("I Accuse")—to the president of France, defending Dreyfus's innocence and accusing his prosecutors of malicious libel. Two hundred thousand copies were sold in Paris. The letter caused a sensation. Anti-Semitic riots broke out. Officers of the general staff threatened mass resignation if Dreyfus was acquitted. Zola himself was indicted for libel, tried by a court, and found guilty. (He fled to England.)

In the summer of 1898, a new minister of war reopened the case. The forgeries were validated as such. Henry was arrested and later committed suicide in jail. The court of appeals ordered a new trial and Dreyfus, who had been languishing in solitary confinement and was unaware of the tumultuous events taking place, was returned to France. The second trial brought to light the forgeries and anti-Semitic plotting, but even so, Dreyfus's original conviction on charges of treason was upheld. Because of "extenuating circumstances," however, Dreyfus was sentenced to only ten years' imprisonment, five of which he had already served. Again there was an uproar, and within a few days the new president of France, Emile Loubet, a liberal who was incredulous at the verdict, granted Dreyfus a pardon.

Seven more years would pass before Dreyfus would receive a full exoneration by still another court of appeals. Dreyfus was reinstated in the French army and promoted to major. He would retire a year later. He rejoined the army with the outbreak of World War I, was promoted to lieutenant colonel, and received the Legion of Honor. After the war, he lived in Paris in retirement until his death in 1935.

The Dreyfus affair caused major repercussions in the lives of individuals and governments. Theodor Herzl was heavily influenced by the public displays of anti-Semitic mobs and their cries of death to Jews; he considered it in his embracing the philosophy of Zionism. The Dreyfus affair has been seen as a turning point in the history of the French Third Republic. Anticlerical legislation was passed, separating church and state. Old government gave way to new.

Alfred Dreyfus is part of the history of Judaism for the symbol he became. Not notably religious, ethnic, or associated strongly with the People of Israel, he nevertheless became a symbol of the blatant, virulent, and completely irrational anti-Semitism so pervasive in Europe at that time. Equally, he became the symbol of the iron-willed Jew who would not give up his name, his honor, or his identity, no matter what the pressures.

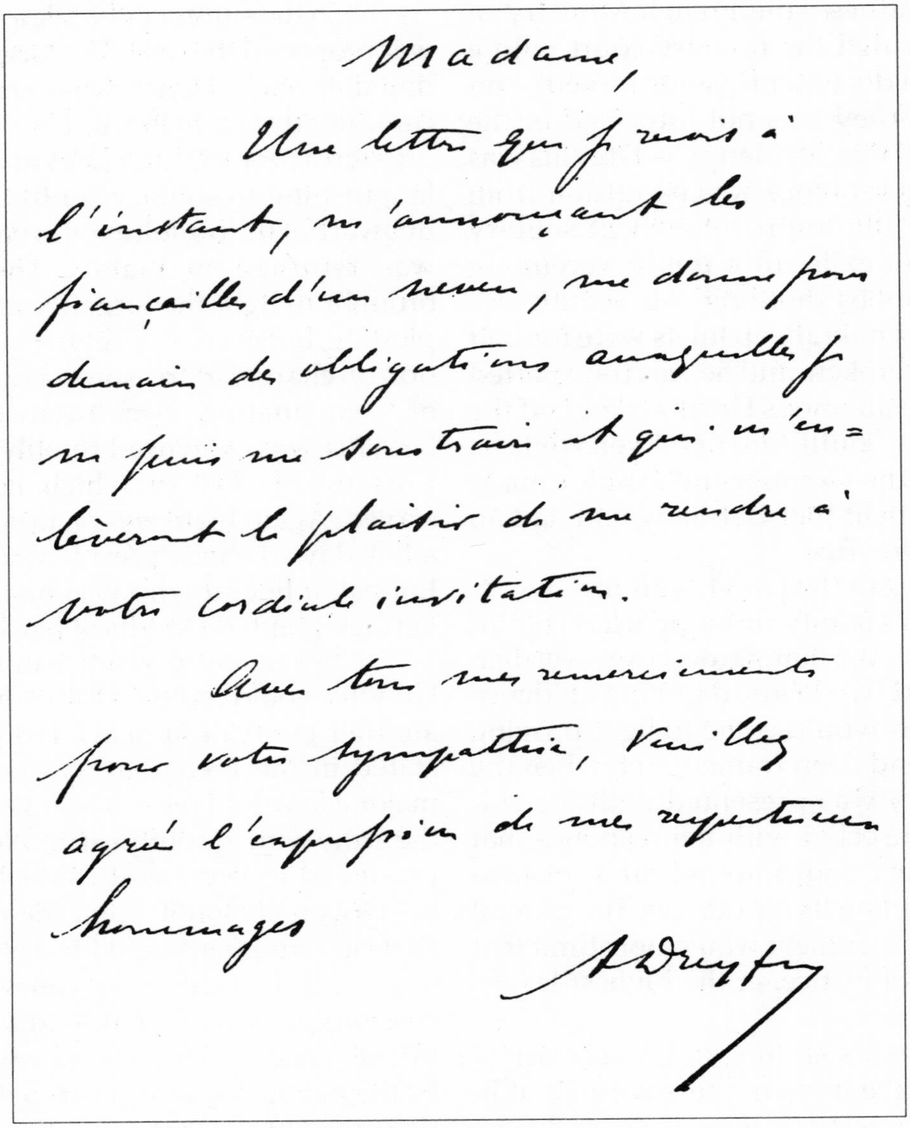

Madame,

Une lettre que je reçois à l'instant, m'annonçant les fiançailles d'un neveu, me donne pour demain des obligations auxquelles je ne puis me soustraire et qui m'enlèvent le plaisir de me rendre à votre cordiale invitation.

Avec tous mes remerciements pour votre sympathie, veuillez agréer l'expression de mes respectueux hommages

A Dreyfus

Note signed by Alfred Dreyfus.

Madame,

I just received a letter telling me about the engagement of one of my nephews. So I will have to be there tomorrow and it deprives me of the pleasure to go to your cordial invitation.

Thank you so much for your kindness, please accept my best regards.

A. Dreyfus

Translation of note.

NAFTALI HERZ IMBER

"What will a paean help me in my tomb?
. . . Give me bread and clothes now."
—The New Dawn, *1899*

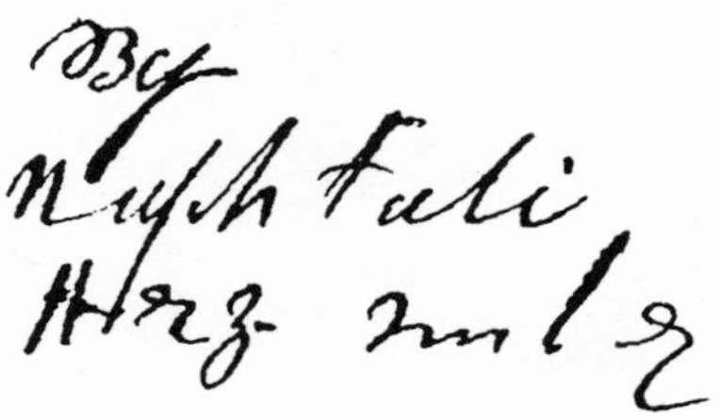

Writing sample.

Naftali Herz Imber's plaintive cry well capsulizes his life. The composer of "Hatikvah," the Jewish and Israeli national anthem, Imber suffered the fate of many a national poet: fame accompanying a life of suffering and unhappiness.

Born in Galicia in 1856, Imber received an in-depth traditional education without any secular knowledge. He first visited Palestine in 1882 as the personal secretary and adviser on Jewish affairs to Laurence Oliphant, a Christian Zionist. In 1888 he returned to Europe but shortly thereafter again returned to Palestine and the Far East, including Bombay. Pursued by missionaries in India as well as Palestine, rumors developed that he had converted to Christianity. The rumors were not proven, but the stigma remained.

A wandering, restless individual, Imber went to America, back to England, then back to America, where he spent the remainder of his life. He married Dr. Amanda Katie, a Protestant physician who converted to Judaism, but the marriage was short-lived. In his life,

Imber published two volumes of poetry, *Dawn* (1884) and *The New Dawn* (1899) and in 1905 produced a Hebrew translation of *The Rubiyat of Omar Khayyam*. He also wrote some monographs of talmudic literature. In reality, however, Imber was unsuccessful in his writing and eventually succumbed to alcoholism. He spent the end of his life in poverty and squalor and died in 1909.

Imber's masterpiece, "Hatikvah" ("The Hope"), first appeared in print in 1886, although it was written in 1878. It was motivated by the founding of the settlement Petach Tikvah in Palestine. Literary and musical analysis shows "Hatikvah" to have been influenced by German and Polish patriotic songs, and the melody is based on the Moldavian-Romanian folk tune "Carul cu Boi" ("Cart and Oxen"). Its adoption by the Jewish people began almost immediately. It was sung at the Fifth Zionist Congress in 1901, but it was not until the eighteenth Congress in 1933 that it was formally declared. Two versions of "Hatikvah" exist, with the change in the second stanza:

As long as deep in the heart
The soul of a Jew yearns
And towards the East
An eye looks to Zion

Our hope is not yet lost
The hope of two thousand years
To be a free people in our land
The land of Zion and Jerusalem.

(*Former Version*)

Our hope is not yet lost
The age-old hope
To return to the land of our fathers
To the city where David dwelt.

"Hatikvah" is sung at almost every Jewish function, either at the opening or closing ceremonies. In the United States, it generally follows the singing of "The Star-Spangled Banner." Naftali Herz Imber produced an anthem not only for a country but for a people.

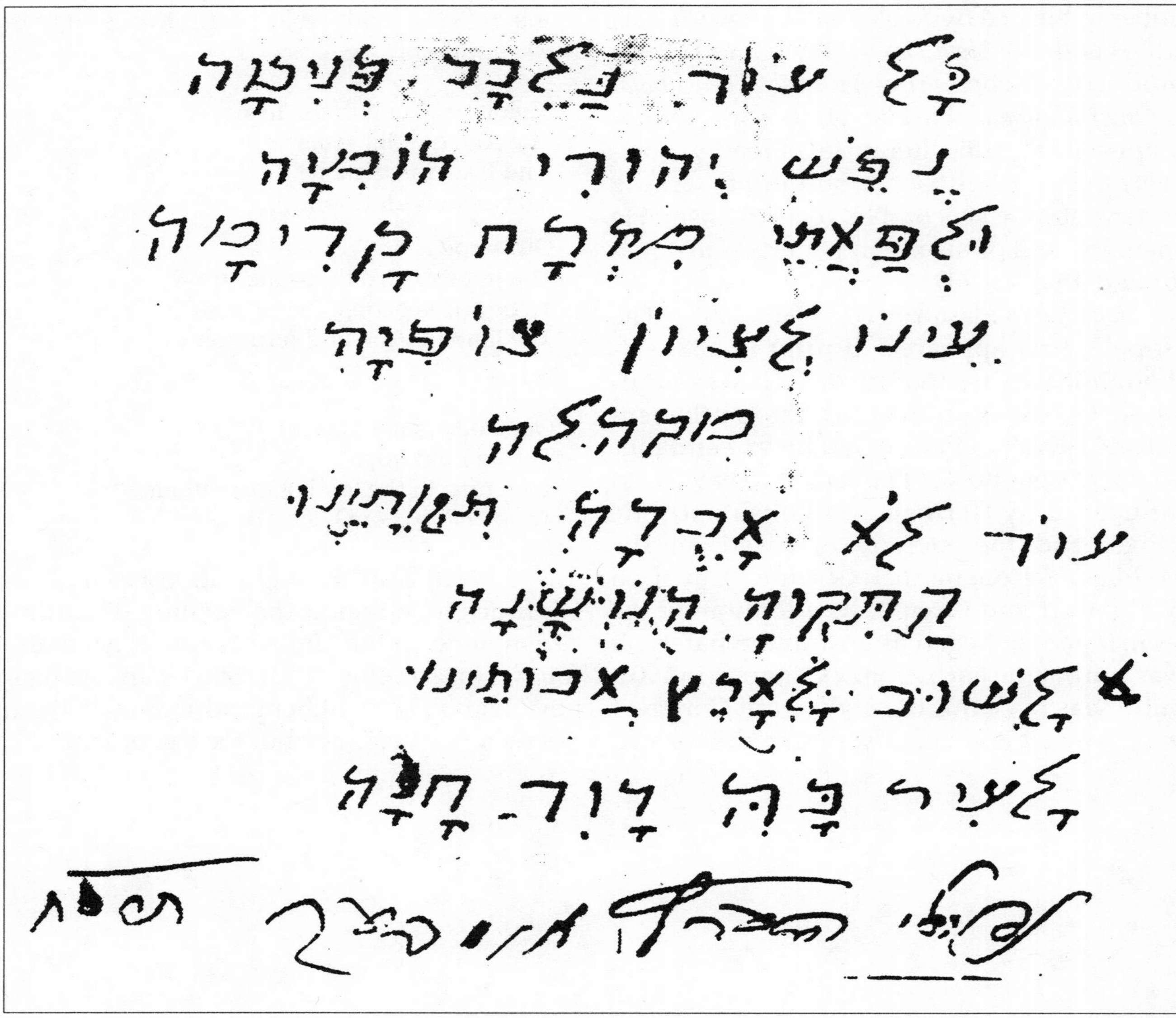

כל עוד בלבב פנימה
נפש יהודי הומיה
ולפאתי מזרח קדימה
עינו לציון צופיה
[illegible]
עוד לא אבדה תקותינו
התקוה הנושנה
לשוב לארץ אבותינו
לעיר בה דוד חנה
נפתלי הערץ אימבער

Text of "Hatikvah" written and signed in Hebrew by Naftali Herz Imber.

THEODORE "TEDDY" KOLLEK

"The first principle is that this must remain one city."

Jerusalem, home to three major religions and historically rife with strife, has been fought over for virtually centuries. Only one person has seemingly ever brought the city together. That person is Teddy Kollek, who was mayor of Jerusalem for twenty-eight years.

Kollek was born in Vienna on May 27, 1911. As a youth, he was involved with several Zionist groups, including T'chilat Lavan and Hehalutz and other youth movements in Czechoslovakia, Romania, England, Austria, and Germany. He made *aliyah* in 1935 and in 1937 was a founding member of Kibbutz Ein Gev.

From 1940 on, Kollek worked with David Ben-Gurion and the Jewish Agency in a variety of capacities: in the early war years he worked with Allied intelligence agencies and Jewish underground contacts in Nazi-held Central and Eastern Europe. In 1943 Kollek opened the Jewish Agency office in Istanbul. He later worked with the U.S. Office of Strategic Services and British military intelligence. After the war, he headed the *Haganah*'s operations in the United States, and served as Israel's first defense minister in America. In 1949 he headed Israel's Foreign Ministry in the United States and from 1950 to 1952 was Israel's min-

ister plenipotentiary to the U.S. In 1952 he returned to Israel and was appointed by Ben-Gurion as director general of the prime minister's office. In that capacity Kollek worked for twelve years, dealing with wide-ranging issues and organizations.

Kollek was elected for his first term as mayor in 1965, as a candidate from Ben-Gurion's Rafi Party. With the Israeli victory in the 1967 Six-Day War, the concrete and barbed-wire walls were torn down and a divided Jerusalem was opened up. Kollek's job as mayor began in earnest. He strove to normalize life in a city that was a stranger to itself. To deal with the problems facing a unified Jerusalem, Kollek founded the Jerusalem Committee to help citizens plan for the future. It was an international body comprised of religious leaders, scholars, artists, architects, and more.

Kollek's contributions have sometimes been controversial. Arguing with Jews, Arabs, Christians, Muslims, chasidim, Greek Orthodox Armenians, and other centuries-old communities, Kollek helped to make Jerusalem a vibrant international city with parks, theaters, new neighborhoods, museums—all that encompass a twentieth-century leading cultural center. At the same time, he has fought to preserve the historical and architectural flavor of Jerusalem.

Beyond the physical aspects, Kollek fought to maintain an open, unified city. He is well known (and often criticized) for his ability to compromise. He has frequently befriended the Arabs, sometimes in the face of heavy Israeli criticism. His mayoral terms were always marked by a vision of a city at peace.

After twenty-eight years, Kollek left office in 1993. He has been honored by organizations worldwide and been granted eleven honorary doctorate degrees from such universities as Notre Dame, Harvard, Yale, and Yeshiva University. He continues to serve as chairman of the Jerusalem Foundation and of the Israel Museum and is head of the planning committee for the 1996 Jerusalem Trimillennium celebration. As much as the ancient Roman walkways beneath the modern streets, Teddy Kollek is part of the eternal city of Jerusalem.

ראש העיר
رئيس البلدية
MAYOR OF JERUSALEM

July 12, 1984

Dr. Michael L. Klein
Office of the Dean
Hebrew Union College
13 King David Street
Jerusalem

Dear Dr. Klein:

Thank you for your letter and your kind words.

The particular importance of the Harvard degree was that it gave widespread recognition to our efforts in Jerusalem - from a neutral but important quarter not especially known for pro-Israel leanings.

I trust this finds you well and send you every good wish.

Yours,

Teddy Kollek

Teddy Kollek

TK:he

Typed letter on trilingual (Arabic, Hebrew, and English) letterhead dated July 12, 1984, regarding a recently conferred honorary doctorate degree awarded to Teddy Kollek by Harvard University. (Courtesy of the American Jewish Archives, Cincinnati Campus, Hebrew Union College, Jewish Institute of Religion.)

SIR MOSES MONTEFIORE

"Should my presence in Constantinople or Adrianople be deemed in any way beneficial to the sufferers, I shall be ready to proceed there without delay."
—Telegram to a refugee relief committee, at age 98

To Sir Moses Montefiore go the appellations philanthropist, master of good deeds, and *Guter Yid*, one who crusades for the Jewish cause. He proved to be a landmark figure not only in the Jewish world but in the secular one as well.

Montefiore was born in 1784 in Leghorn (Livorno), Italy, while his family was visiting there from London; the Montefiore family had emigrated to Italy from Spain in the sixteenth century. Raised in London, he received a traditional education and at age 13 was apprenticed to wholesale tea merchants. Having a natural flair for business, and benefiting from affluent relatives and good contacts, by age 20 Montefiore was one of only twelve licensed Jewish stock exchange brokers. In 1812 he married Judith Cohen, daughter of Levi Barent Cohen, and became through marriage a brother-in-law to Nathan Mayer Rothschild. In Rothschild he found a kindred spirit who shared and furthered Montefiore's business and Jewish interests. Montefiore continued to succeed in business and became president of the Alliance Insurance Company (which he founded) and the Imperial Gas Company. The latter pioneered the use of gaslighting in England and throughout Europe.

At the age of 40 and at the urging of his wife "to quit business and thank God and be

content," Montefiore effectively retired from business and turned his attention to philanthropy and Jewish causes. Childless and independently wealthy, he and his wife had the resources and convictions to devote to their interests and activities, which were seemingly limitless. Throughout his life and countless involvements, Montefiore credited his wife as his constant inspiration.

Even as a young man Montefiore was destined for firsts. He was the first member of London's Sephardic Bevis Marks synagogue to be received as a member under the statutory age of 21. In 1835 he was voted president of the Board of Deputies of British Jews, the foremost group representing British Jewry. Montefiore broadened the group's involvement in both British and international Jewish affairs. He held the presidency for forty-four years. In 1837 Montefiore was elected as a sheriff of London, the first Jew to be so voted. As a result of his position, he was knighted by Queen Victoria. (In 1846 he received the additional honor of being named a baron.) As one of London's sheriffs, Montefiore distinguished himself by his attention to the poor, his concern for the welfare of prisoners, and, for those times, his strong opposition to the death penalty.

An imposing figure (6′ 3″ tall) blessed with good health (he lived to be 101), Montefiore traveled virtually around the civilized world to come to the aid of his fellow Jews. He visited Palestine seven times between 1827 and 1874, the first time traveling five months to get there, then spending but three days in Jerusalem. An observant Jew, Montefiore kept the Sabbath, the laws of *kashrut*, and daily prayer. On extended trips, he took with him his own *shochet*, or ritual slaughterer, to prepare his food. Based on what he saw—both the poverty and extreme need in Palestine and the potential of the people and the land—Montefiore became committed to the idea of a Jewish homeland. He not only gave of his own funds but also persuaded others to give of theirs. In 1855 the American philanthropist Judah Touro willed $50,000 to the Jews of the Holy Land, the spending of which was to be administered by Montefiore. Montefiore himself gave funds for the building of community housing outside the walls of old Jerusalem, secured a permit from the Sultan to rebuild the old Hurvah synagogue, began the development of a girls' school, and even sent a physician and printing press to help establish a viable and modern Jewish community. The area known as Yemin Moshe outside the walled area is named after him.

Montefiore traveled to other nations as well, always seeking to improve the living conditions of the local Jewish community and combat anti-Semitism. His position as a leading citizen of England made him a politically distinguished figure, and his credentials carried in them the stature of the British Empire. In 1840 he traveled to Constantinople, Turkey, and Alexandria, Egypt, meeting with the Turkish sultan and the Egyptian viceroy, arguing against the centuries-old Passover blood libels, and securing the release of Jewish prisoners. Over the decades, Montefiore traveled to Russia, Italy, Palestine, Romania, Morocco, Egypt, and Hungary, among other countries, all for the Jewish cause. He helped not only Jews but Christians as well and developed a reputation as a humanitarian. Rarely did he return from a mission unsuccessful. Jews the world over looked to "Sir Moses" as their international representative. In 1865, on the grounds of his private estate, he established the Judith Lady Montefiore College for retiring rabbinic scholars.

On the occasion of his hundredth birthday in 1874, Montefiore received greetings from royalty and heads of state. Public holidays were held even as far away as Dutch-ruled Curacao. Queen Victoria congratulated him on "a century of loyalty and philanthropy." Sir Moses Montefiore died in 1885 at the age of 101. Memorial services were held worldwide. The Jewish world had lost a spokesman, defender, and leader.

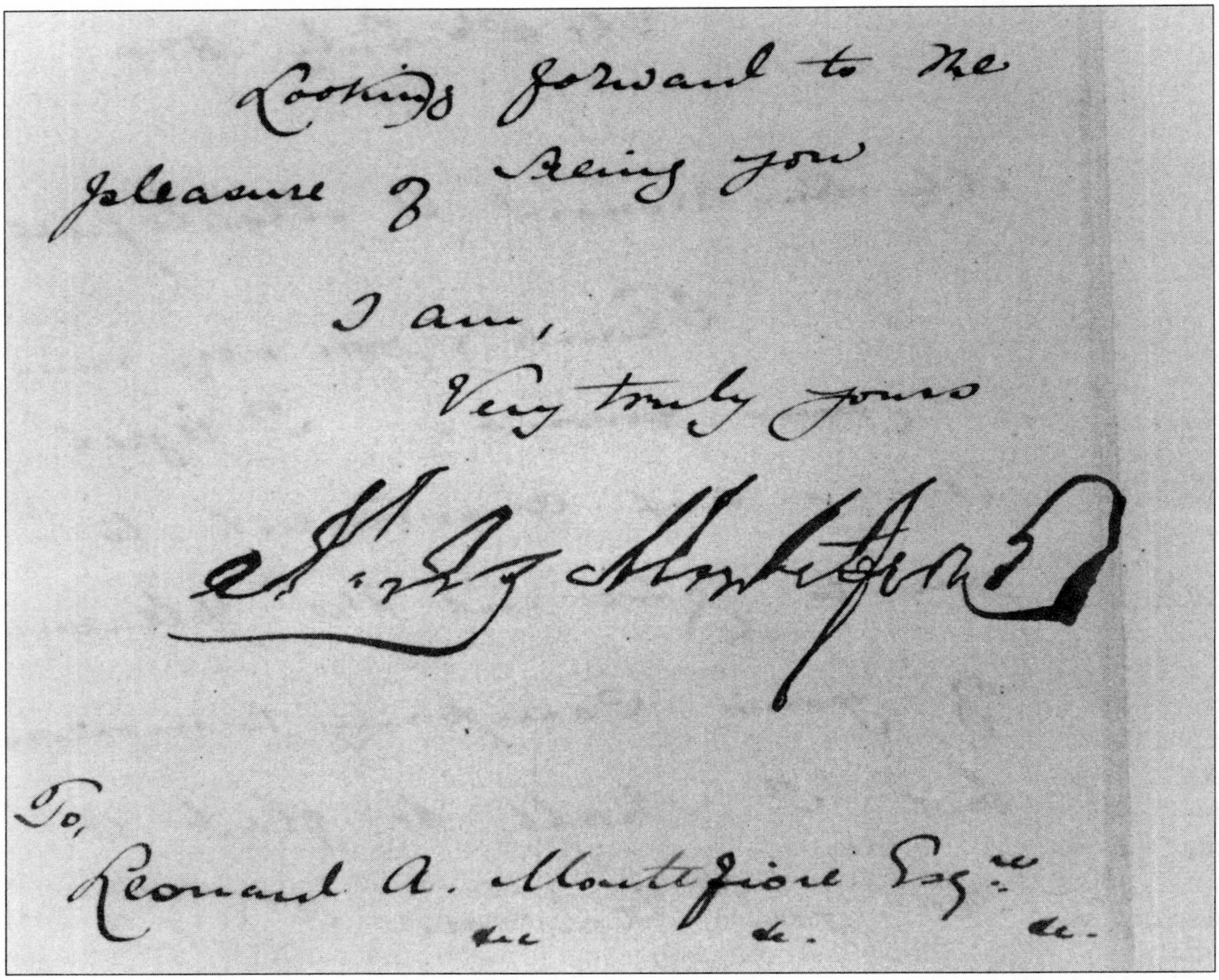

Looking forward to the
pleasure of seeing you

I am,
Very truly yours

To,
Leonard A. Montefiore Esq.re
&c &c &c

Undated secretarial written note signed by Moses Montefiore to a relative, "Leonard A. Montefiore, Esq."

ROMAN VISHNIAC

"I read the book by Hitler, Mein Kampf *. . . I wanted only, if I cannot save the people, I should save their memory."*

Photography has irrevocably changed our world. It has taken us to places never seen before, through microphotography and space photography. But most important, it has preserved people, places, and things that once were and will be no more. Of the civilization that the Jews developed in Europe and Russia over one thousand years but that was destroyed by the Nazis, a portion was saved by Roman Vishniac.

A noted zoologist and physician, Vishniac was born August 19, 1897, near St. Petersburg, Russia. He came from a well-to-do family and grew up in Moscow, where his grandfather had a permit to live. Vishniac was educated at home until he was 10, then attended private schools and Shanyavsky University in Moscow. There he studied medicine and zoology, receiving his M.D. and Ph.D. in medicine and zoology. Increasing anti-Semitism forced Vishniac to leave Russia for Latvia, then Berlin, where his family had moved in 1918. In Berlin, he worked to help support his family and took postgraduate courses in endocrinology, optics, and oriental art. However, upon completion of his studies in art, he was refused his doctorate by

university authorities under Nazi pressure. He thus set out to capture Eastern European Jewish life on film.

His interest in photography began in childhood, when his grandmother had given him a microscope. With new worlds open to him, Vishniac had developed a box system to photograph what was under his lens. At the age of 7, he had microphotographed a cockroach's leg. Now, compulsively, he was to macrophotograph a soon-to-be obliterated culture and way of life. Over the course of eight years, Vishniac wandered through Poland, Russia, Lithuania, Latvia, Hungary, and Czechoslovakia. He took more than 16,000 photographs, of which 2,000 survived. Vishniac took photos of village and city life, plain people and aggrandized ones, synagogues, *yeshivot*, people in the marketplace and in the street, young children, simple old folks, rabbis, cobblestoned streets and byways, courtyards, poignant cemetery scenes—the width and depth of a centuries-old but vibrant culture.

Vishniac's work was done at great risk. He was arrested several times. On at least two occasions he dressed in Nazi uniform to capture historic moments of horror—the 1933 book burning by Nazis and the aftermath of the infamous Kristallnacht. Twice he was taken to concentration camps. Upon his release in 1940, he joined his family in Sweden. The entire family then immigrated to the United States.

Vishniac's photos, frequently taken under adverse conditions (many of his subjects refused to be photographed; thus he often took hidden photos under less than optimum conditions), have preserved the life of pre–World War II Eastern European Jewry. His photographs are neither glamorous nor romanticized. His books include *Polish Jews: A Pictorial Record* (1947, and reprinted), *Life of the Six Millions* (1969), and *A Vanished World* (1983).

Upon arrival in the United States, Vishniac began a new life, although with great difficulty. Speaking eight languages but knowing no English, he was forced to pursue portrait photography in order to make a living. In 1950 he became a full-time free-lance scientific photographer. He did both medical and natural photography: "Cytoplasmic Circulation in Microscopic Algae as Related to Photosynthesis" and "Frost on Leaves" demonstrate the range of his work. His scientific background combined with his technical skills led to positions as professor of humanities at the Pratt Institute and professor of biological education at Yeshiva University. Vishniac lectured often on both scientific topics and his multiranged photography.

Vishniac died on January 22, 1990. As a scientist, ethnographer, and photographer, he preserved for future generations the life and history of a benign and peaceful people who were brutally murdered for no fathomable reason. He saved their memory.

זכור!
REMEMBER!
R Vishniac
a community-wide observance commemorating the Holocaust
renowned photographer Roman Vishniac will present "The Vanished World"
SATURDAY, APRIL 12, 1980 • 8:30 PM
BETH JACOB CONGREGATION
9030 West Olympic Boulevard, Beverly Hills
Admission Free/For information call 852-1234 ext. 2813
Sponsored by (partial list): Jewish Federation Council; the Simon Wiesenthal Center for Holocaust Studies; Beth Jacob Congregation; the Board of Rabbis; the Council of Postwar Jewish Organizations Survivors of the Nazi Holocaust; the American Congress of Jews from Poland and Survivors of Concentration Camps; the Martyrs Memorial; the Anti-Defamation League; the American Jewish Congress; the Jewish Labor Committee; the National Conference of Synagogue Youth

Roman Vishniac signed poster from an April 12, 1980, lecture in Los Angeles. Photograph is "Granddaughter and grandfather. Warsaw, 1938."

VIII

HOLOCAUST VOICES

I did not forget you.

—Simon Wiesenthal

ANNE FRANK

"I still believe that people are really good at heart."

Anne Frank was the conscience of a horrific world. Murdered at the age of 14, a victim of Nazi concentration camps, she left behind an immortal legacy.

She was born June 12, 1929, in Frankfurt, Germany. Her parents fled to Holland when she was 4 years old. As the Nazis tightened their stranglehold on the Netherlands, Anne's father, Otto Frank, began preparing, as did thousands of other Dutch Jews, for the family to go into hiding. On July 5, 1942, Anne's 16-year-old sister Margot received her order from the Central Office for Jewish Emigration for *Arbeitseinsatz*, or forced labor. The next day, with the knowledge and help of four of Frank's employees—Miep Gies, Johanes Kleiman, Victor Kugler, and Elii Voskuijl—the family moved into the vacant annex of Otto Frank's business. A week later they were joined by the family of Otto Frank's partner, Hermann van Pels. On November 16, an eighth person came to be hidden in the annex, Dr. Fritz Pfeffer, a dentist.

For over two years, as war raged and Nazi oppression intensified, the eight people hid in the small annex. Obtaining food and clothing, as well as maintaining their sanity, were ongoing challenges for the occupants.

On her thirteenth birthday Anne had been given a diary, in which, to her imaginary friend Kitty, she kept a record of her observations, thoughts, and emotions. With a talent for writing, she dutifully and beautifully recorded

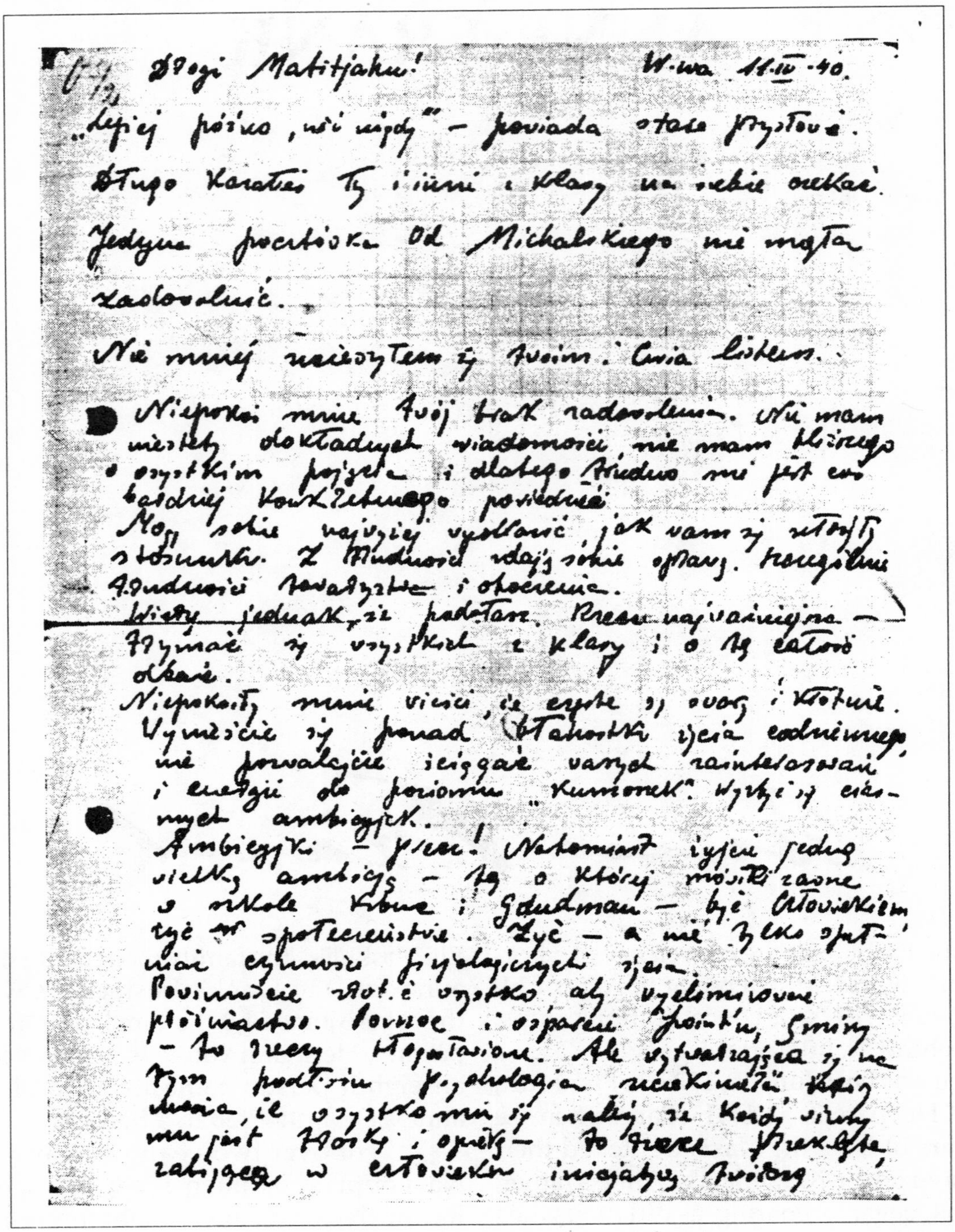

Drogi Matitjahu! W-wa 11.IV.40.

„Lepiej późno, niż nigdy" – powiada stare przysłowie.

Długo kazałeś Ty i inni z klasy na siebie czekać.

Jedyna pocztówka od Michalskiego nie mogła zadowolić.

Nie mniej ucieszyłem się Twoim i Ewa listem.

Niepokoi mnie Twój brak zadowolenia. Nie mam niestety dokładnych wiadomości, nie mam bliższego o wszystkim pojęcia i dlatego trudno mi jest coś bardziej konkretnego powiedzieć.
Mogę sobie najwyżej wyobrazić, jak wam się ułożyły stosunki. Z trudności zdaję sobie sprawę. Szczególnie trudności towarzystwa i otoczenia.
Wiesz jednak, że podstawa. Rzecz najważniejsza – trzymać się wszystkich z klasy i o tę całość dbać.
Niepokoi mnie wieść, że często się swarzycie i kłócicie.
Wznieście się ponad błahostki życia codziennego, nie pozwalajcie ściągać waszych zainteresowań i energii do poziomu „kumorek". Wyzbądźcie się ciasnych ambicyjek.
Ambicyjki – precz! Natomiast żyjcie jedną wielką ambicją – tą o której mówiłem zawsze w szkole, Kibuc i Gordonii – być człowiekiem, żyć w społeczeństwie. Żyć – a nie tylko spełniać czynności fizjologicznych życia.
Powinniście zrobić wszystko aby wyeliminować plotkarstwo. Pomoc i oparcie [illegible] – to rzeczy [illegible]. Ale wytwarzająca się na tym podłożu psychologia niewolnicza, świadomość, że wszystko mi się należy, że każdy winny mi jest troski i opieki – to rzecz przeklęta, zabijająca w człowieku inicjatywę twórczą

Letter in Polish by Mordecai Anielewicz.

occupied areas of the Soviet Union, he moved to establish an armed Jewish underground. These efforts never took root.

In the summer of 1942 he returned to Warsaw from Bedzin, Poland, and again began to work with armed Jewish resistance groups, notably the Zydowska Organizacja Bojowa (Z.O.B.), Jewish Fighting Organization. He began restructuring it and in November was named its commander.

The first armed engagements between the Germans and the Warsaw ghetto Jews occurred on January 18, 1943, during attempted mass deportations. A number of Jewish fighters were killed. The Germans, surprised by the resistance, quickly halted the deportations and temporarily withdrew. The ghetto's inhabitants established what bunkers and fortifications they could and, with what small arms they had been able to obtain and smuggle in, prepared for the inevitable. The Germans renewed their deportation drive in Warsaw on April 19, 1943—the eve of Passover. For nineteen days, the Warsaw ghetto resisted, fighting in the streets and then from the bunkers. On May 8, with most of his staff, Mordecai Anielewicz was killed in the bunker at 18 Mila Street. In a bizarre world where he knew his unescapable fate, he realized his ideal to die as a Jew fighting against Jewish enemies.

Kibbutz Yad Mordecai in Israel was named after him.

MORDECAI ANIELEWICZ

"What happened is beyond our wildest dreams. Twice the Germans fled from our ghetto. One of our companies held out for forty minutes and the other for over six hours. . . . I have no words to describe to you the conditions in which the Jews are living. Only a few chosen ones will hold out; all the rest will perish sooner or later. The die is cast. In the bunkers in which our comrades are hiding, no candle can be lit for lack of air. . . . The main thing is: My life's dream has come true; I have lived to see Jewish resistance in the ghetto in all its greatness and glory."

—Last letter, April 23, 1943

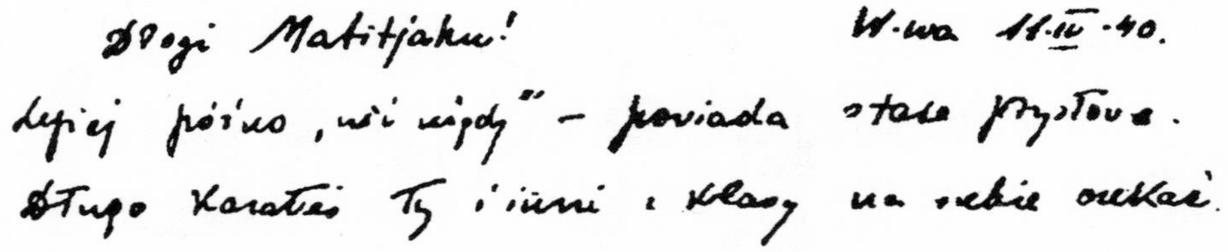

Writing sample.

One of the outstanding heroes of the Holocaust, Mordecai Anielewicz was the commander of the Warsaw ghetto uprising. He was killed at the age of 24 when the Warsaw ghetto finally fell.

Born to a poor family in Warsaw, as a youth Anielewicz joined the Ha-Shomer Ha-Tzair Socialist Zionist movement. In the same week that the Germans invaded Poland, Anielewicz fled east, reaching Soviet-occupied areas of Poland. It was his intent to go to Romania and from there to Palestine. He was captured, however, by Soviet authorities and jailed.

Upon his release, he returned to Warsaw, then went to Vilna, observing the situation of other Jewish communities. Meeting other Zionist-oriented young men and women, he volunteered to return to Poland to assist in the underground resistance.

Once back in Warsaw, he organized seminars and helped develop an underground press. In the summer of 1941, when reports reached him of the murder of Jews in German-

her life. The diary has been described as possessing "sharp observation, introspection, and clear formulation." The entry from April 11, 1944, reads in part:

> Surely the time will come when we are people again, not just Jews. Who has inflicted this upon us? Who has made us Jews different from all other people? Who has allowed us to suffer so terribly up till now? It is God that has made us as we are, but it will be God, too, who will raise us up again. If we bear all this suffering and if there are still Jews left, when it is over, then Jews, instead of being doomed, will be held up as an example. Who knows, it might even be our religion from which the world and all peoples learn good and for that reason and that reason only do we have to suffer now.

Later in that same entry she wrote:

> I don't believe that the big men, the politicians and the capitalists alone are guilty of the war. Oh, no, the little man is just as keen . . . there is an urge and rage in the people to destroy, to kill, to murder, and until all mankind, without exception, undergoes a great change, wars will be waged.

Following an act of betrayal by an informer, Anne and her companions were arrested by members of the Nazi SS on August 4, 1944. Johanes Kleiman and Victor Kugler were also arrested and interred in the Netherlands. The eight Jews were deported to various concentration camps. Anne's mother died in Auschwitz. In October, Margot and Anne were sent to Bergen-Belsen where, in March 1945, as a result of starvation, exposure, and lack of medical attention, they both died of typhus. The camp was liberated in April.

After the occupants of the annex had been arrested, Miep Gies recovered the diary and other papers. Only Anne's father, Otto, survived the extermination camps, and upon his return from Auschwitz, Gies returned them to him.

Early attempts to have Anne's diary published were rebuffed, but under the title *The Annex*, the diary was published in 1947. It has since been published in more than fifty languages and has sold some twenty million copies. The diary has served as the basis and inspiration for plays, movies, and musical compositions. In 1960 the annex was made into a museum on anti-Semitism and racism. Anne's original diary is on loan there from her father. The Anne Frank Foundation is a combination archive and educational / documentation center.

Anne Frank became the symbol of the martyred Jewish child and the voice of innocence.

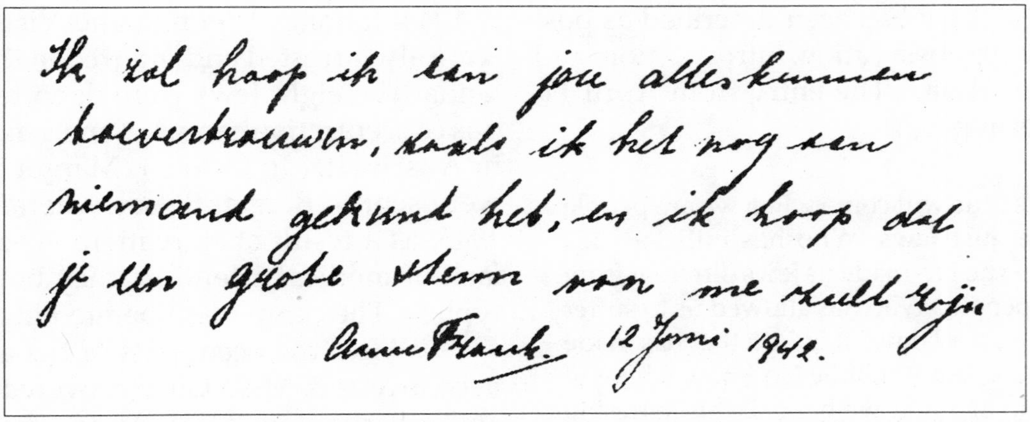
Ik zal hoop ik aan jou alles kunnen toevertrouwen, zoals ik het nog aan niemand gekund heb, en ik hoop dat je een grote steun voor me zult zijn.
Anne Frank. 12 Juni 1942.

Anne Frank's first diary entry.

I hope I shall be able to confide in you completely, as I have never been able to do in anyone before, and I hope that you will be a great support and comfort to me.

Anne Frank (June 12, 1942)

Translation of diary entry.

JANUSZ KORCZAK

"Don't ever forget this sight. Always remember what a child's frightened heart looks like."

—Lecture to fellow physicians, wherein he exposed a frightened child's heaving chest

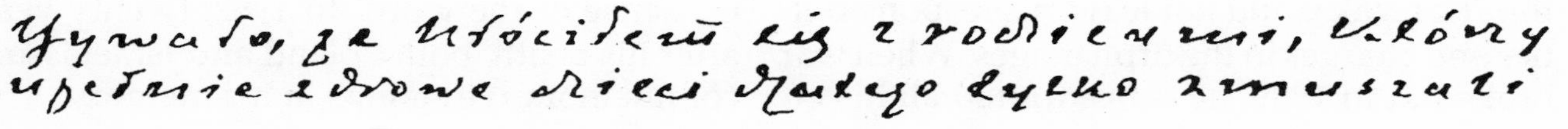

Writing sample.

The name of Dr. Janusz Korczak has not received the same eminence as those of Drs. Albert Schweitzer and Tom Dooley. Yet, it should. Korczak was still one more example of a doctor who gave his life selflessly for his patients. In his case, they were children.

Korczak (Henryk Goldszimdt) was born in Warsaw in 1879 into a wealthy and assimilated Polish Jewish family. After completing his studies in medicine at Warsaw University, he became professionally involved with poor and underprivileged children. He treated children free of charge, did volunteer work in summer camps for the poor, and wrote. His first book, *Children of the Street* (1901), described the living conditions and desperate existence of homeless orphans. His 1911 *A Child of the Salon* dealt with a pampered and spoiled middle-class boy whose focus was control of money. Both books evoked controversy and criticism, especially in response to Korczak's own social criticisms.

In 1911 Korczak was appointed director of a new Jewish orphanage in Warsaw, a post he held for the rest of his life. In this position, he introduced some revolutionary ideas on administering orphanages. He allowed the children to participate in addressing the problems of the orphanage, let them produce their own newspaper, encouraged self-government among the children, and gave each child individual respect and understanding. His success

was such that Korczak was solicited to assist in developing a non-Jewish orphanage for Polish children.

World War I interrupted his activities, and during the war he served as a military medical officer. Upon his return to civilian life, he resumed his activities, becoming a popular radio broadcaster ("Old Doc"), publishing a children's newspaper, and on the adult level lecturing at the Free Polish University. During one such lecture, Korczak brought a child up onto the dais. He removed the child's shirt and placed him behind a fluoroscope, with the boy's racing heart clearly visible. With the love and dedication he felt toward children, Korczak admonished his audience: "Don't ever forget this sight. Always remember what a child's frightened heart looks like."

As anti-Semitism grew progressively stronger in 1930s' Poland, Korczak twice visited Palestine and was impressed by what he saw. Yet he was torn between his loyalties as a Polish Jew and a Polish national. On top of this, Korczak could not leave his responsibilities and charges in the orphanages. When war broke out in 1939, he concentrated all his efforts on Jewish children. In 1940 the orphanage he directed was moved into the Warsaw ghetto. Although offered the opportunity by non-Jewish friends to leave the ghetto, he refused. In the summer of 1942, amid mass deportations, the children in the orphanage were ordered to report to the deportation center. Knowing what the immediate future was, Korczak accompanied his children to the trains. German officials, recognizing the embarrassment his death could bring, offered Korczak a last-minute opportunity of release and freedom. Korczak refused and stepped into the cattle cars with his charges, reportedly holding one child with each hand. The train was bound for the death camp of Treblinka. Nothing further was ever reported of Korczak or the children.

Korczak was many things: a groundbreaking pediatrician, a children's rights reformer and activist long before there was an organized cause, a social worker, a writer about and for children, and a martyr in the truest sense of the word. In 1962, twenty years after his death, both Poland and Israel issued commemorative stamps in his memory.

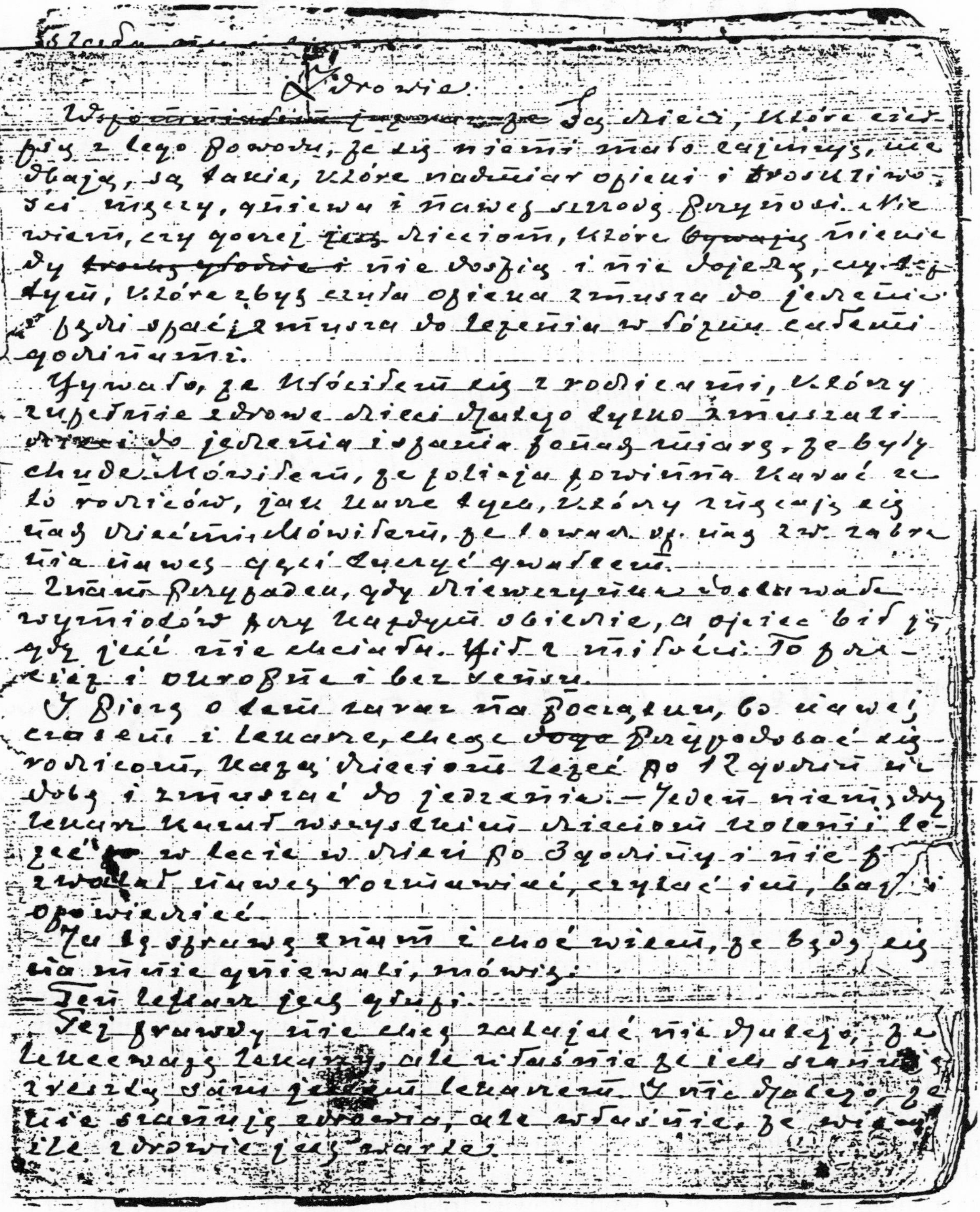

Handwritten diary entry of Dr. Janusz Korczak.

HANNAH SENESCH

"My God,
May there never be an end
To the sand and the sea,
To the whispering of the water,
To the glistening of the skies
To the prayer of man."
—"Blessed Is the Match"

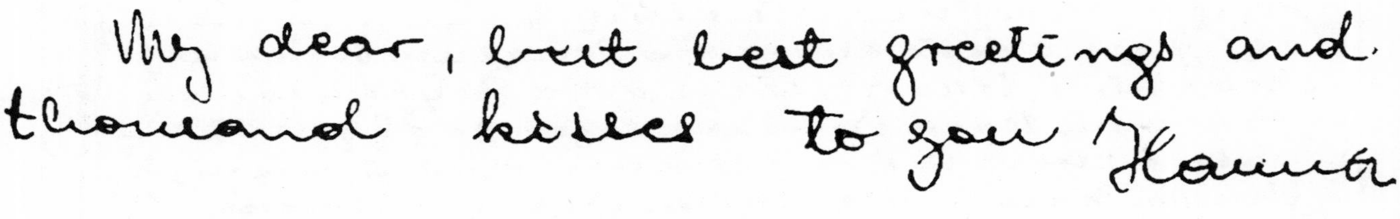

Writing sample.

Twenty-three-year-old Hannah Senesch was a heroine not only in the romantic mold but in the truest sense: a Zionist and gifted poet who gave her life for her people.

Hannah Senesch (Szenes) was born in Budapest in 1921. Her family, middle class and assimilated, sent her to a Protestant school instead of a Jewish one. Senesch showed promise as a child. The daughter of well-known Hungarian journalist and playwright Bela Senesch, she herself began writing, and keeping a diary, at age 13. The diary was begun in Hungarian, but later she wrote in both Hungarian and Hebrew. At age 17 she became involved with Zionism and Judaism and began learning Hebrew and receiving religious instruction under the chief rabbi of Buda, Imre Benoschofsky. Her burgeoning sense of Jewish identity coincided with the approach of World War II and increasing public anti-Semitism.

Originally a youthful and strongly patriotic Hungarian, she threw off her national identity when, at 17, having been elected president of her high school's literary society, she was informed that, as a Jew, she could not hold

office. She quit the society. Her brother was denied admission to the local university and left Hungary for France. Senesch then joined Maccabea, the oldest Zionist organization in Hungary, and daily became more and more a Zionist and a Jew. In October 1938, she wrote: *"I've become a Zionist. This word stands for a tremendous number of things. To me, it means, in short, that I now consciously and strongly feel I am a Jew, and am proud of it. My primary aim is to go to Palestine, and to work for it."*

Before graduating from high school in 1939, she had written to the Girls' Agriculture School at Nahalal, Palestine, applying to attend there. She was accepted and arrived there in September 1939, where she was swept up in her feelings of Zionism, Judaism, and destiny. Enamored of the land and its people, her own people, her poetry flourished. She wrote home to her mother: *"I am in Nahalal . . . I am home. . . . This is where my life's ambition—I might even say my vocation—binds me, because I would like to feel that by being here I am fulfilling a mission. . . ."*

In 1941 Senesch joined Kibbutz Sedot Yam and the *Haganah,* the underground Jewish paramilitary organization. In 1943 she enlisted in the British army. Senesch volunteered for paratrooper training and in January 1944 was sent to Egypt. In March 1944 she parachuted behind Yugoslavian lines on a mission to rescue Allied POWs and help oragnize Jewish resistance. Crossing the Hungarian border in June, Senesch was arrested by Hungarian police and turned over to the Germans. She was sent for interrogation to Budapest where she was tortured by both the Gestapo and Hungarian counterespionage agents. Even during her prison days, she continued writing, both letters and poetry. Tried by a secret court on October 28, Senesch was executed by a firing squad on November 7, 1944. Along with six other paratroopers who were similarly executed, she was reburied in the military cemetery on Mount Herzl in Israel in 1950.

Although Hannah Senesch's life was brief, her fervor, sense of dedication, and ultimate sacrifice caused her to become a symbol of Jewish spirit and inspiration. She has been called the Jewish Joan of Arc.

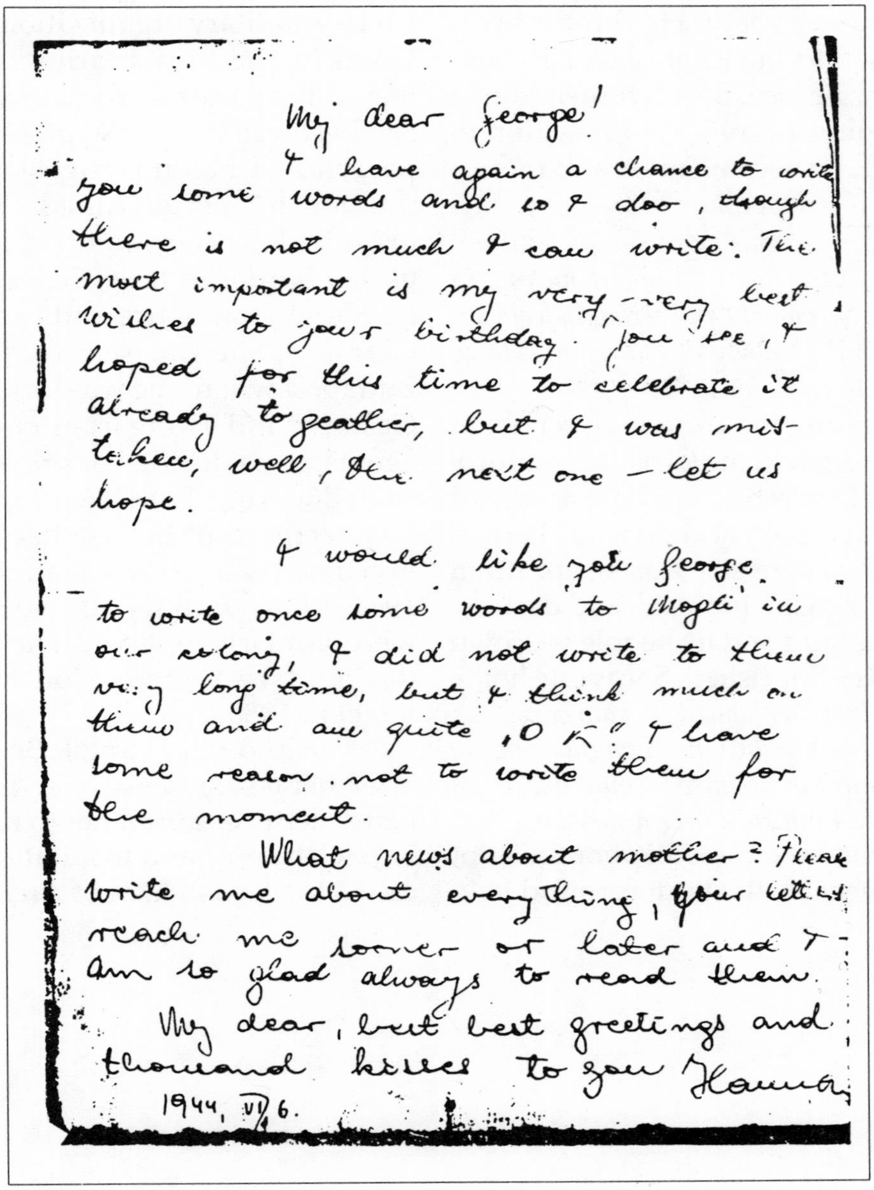

My dear George!
I have again a chance to write you some words and so I doo, though there is not much I can write. The most important is my very-very best wishes to your birthday. You see, I hoped for this time to celebrate it already together, but I was mistaken, well, the next one — let us hope.

I would like you George, to write once some words to Mogli in our colony, I did not write to them very long time, but I think much on them and am quite „O.K." I have some reason not to write them for the moment.

What news about mother? Please write me about everything, your letters reach me sooner or later and I am so glad always to read them.

My dear, best best greetings and thousand kisses to you Hanna,

1944, VI/6.

English letter from Hannah Senesch to her brother George.

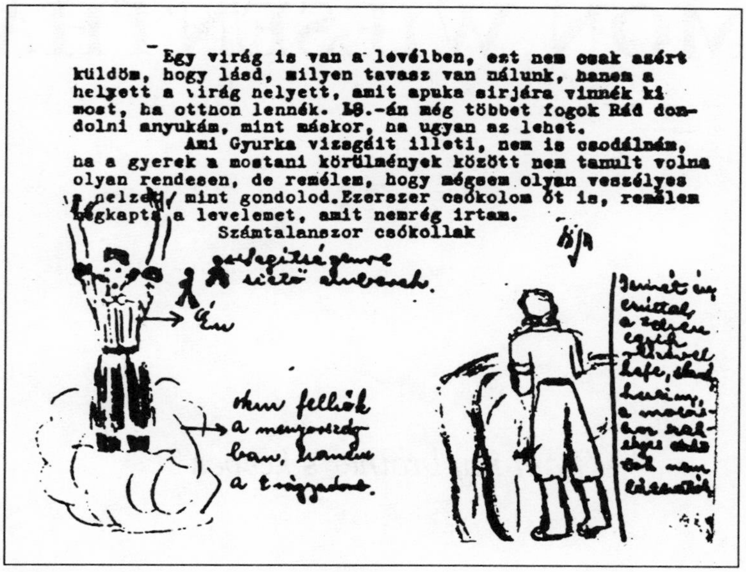

Egy virág is van a levélben, ezt nem csak azért küldöm, hogy lásd, milyen tavasz van nálunk, hanem a helyett a virág helyett, amit apuka sirjára vinnék ki most, ha otthon lennék. 18.-án még többet fogok Rád gondolni anyukám, mint máskor, ha ugyan az lehet.

Ami Gyurka vizsgáit illeti, nem is csodálnám, ha a gyerek a mostani körülmények között nem tanult volna olyan rendesen, de remélem, hogy mégsem olyan veszélyes a helyzet, mint gondolod. Ezerszer csókolom őt is, remélem megkapta a levelemet, amit nemrég irtam.

Számtalanszor csókollak

Typed letter with handwritten notes and sketches by Hannah Senesch.

SIMON WIESENTHAL

"I am my brother's keeper."

If anybody can be considered the conscience of the Holocaust, surely it is Simon Wiesenthal. A survivor who has dedicated himself to the pursuit of justice for crimes against humanity, he has been responsible for the prosecution of more than 1,100 Nazi war criminals, including Adolf Eichmann and Karl Silberbauer, the Gestapo officer who arrested Anne Frank.

An architect by training, Wiesenthal has become a hunter by conscience. He was born December 31, 1908, in Buczacz (near Lvov), Galicia. He attended public high school in Vienna, but after rejection from the Technical University at Lvov because of the Jewish quotas, he studied and received his degree as an architectural engineer at the University of Prague. When the Germans invaded Russia in 1941, Wiesenthal and his wife, Cyla, were arrested by Ukrainian police and assigned to forced labor camps. Through bribes, Wiesenthal was able to get his blonde, Aryan-appearing wife out of the camp. For two years, she passed as an Aryan and lived in Warsaw. Wiesenthal, however, remained in the camps. By the end of 1942, the majority of their two families had been murdered; eighty-nine family members were eventually killed. Wiesenthal labored at the Ostbahn camp, a railroad-repair facility. With the assistance of the deputy director of that

camp, he escaped from there in October 1943, shortly before the Germans began organizing mass murders of the prisoners.

Wiesenthal stayed free until June 1944, when he was recaptured. Returned to Janowska, the first concentration camp to which he had been sent, Wiesenthal was kept alive by fate for selfish German motives: the soldiers there knew if they had no prisoners to guard, they would be sent to fight on the advancing Russian front. To avoid that, the SS guards joined in the flight west away from advancing Russian armies, keeping 34 Jews alive to guard: 34 of the original 149,000 Jews of Lvov. They, plus the inhabitants of the village of Chelmiec, were marched across Poland through fields and forests in winter snows to Mauthausen, in upper Austria. People died hourly. Arriving at Mauthausen, 180 people died on the four-mile march from the train depot to the concentration camp.

By this time (February 1945) Wiesenthal was close to death. His weight was down to 100 pounds. At Mauthausen, he was placed in Room A, Block VI, the death block. The daily ration was 200 calories—one bowl of watered-down, foul soup. Most people in his block lay all day on their bunks, two or three to a bunk, too weak to sit up or walk. At times, Wiesenthal awoke to find the bunkmates next to him dead. Wiesenthal ascribed his survival to a Polish trustee he had known earlier, one Eduard Staniszewski, who occasionally brought him small pieces of bread. Although the war would soon be over—the prisoners knew about the Russian assault and heard the sounds of American aircraft in the skies—there was grave doubt who would survive: *"Sometimes we in Room A thought we were the last men alive on earth,"* Wiesenthal later wrote. *"We had lost touch with all reality. We didn't know whether anybody else was still alive."* Mauthausen was liberated by the Americans on May 5, 1945. Even after liberation, 3,000 prisoners in Mauthausen died. A survivor, Wiesenthal had been in four camps: Janowska, Plaszow Grossrossen, Buchenwald, and Mauthausen.

With his health slowly returning, Wiesenthal went to work for the Americans to collect evidence and testimony on Nazi atrocities. He worked for the U.S. Army War Crimes Section, the Office of Strategic Services, and the Counter-Intelligence Corps. He also headed the Jewish Central Committee of the United States Zone of Austria, a welfare and relief organization. The information Wiesenthal gathered was used to prosecute war criminals.

Wiesenthal worked for the U.S. Army until 1947. (He and his wife, each of whom heard from witnesses that the other was dead, were reunited at the end of 1945.) When his work for the army was done, Wiesenthal and some thirty volunteers opened the Jewish Historical Documentation Center in Linz, Austria. There they gathered and preserved testimony, documents, information, and data for future trials. The center stayed open until 1954. By then, Nazi "hunting" was no longer a major issue: the Cold War occupied much of the world powers' time. Wiesenthal sent all his files but one to the Yad Vashem Archives in Israel.

Although Wiesenthal continued with other pursuits, he never gave up his search to locate war criminals. The one dossier he kept when the center closed was that of Adolf Eichmann. Eichmann was the chief of the Gestapo's Jewish Department, and it was Eichmann who supervised the actual implementation and machinations of the "Final Solution." From leads, whispers, and rumors, Wiesenthal and Israeli agents located Eichmann in Argentina, and it was there that Israeli agents captured Eichmann in 1961 and brought him to Israel. His trial drew worldwide attention. Eichmann was eventually found guilty of mass murder and crimes against humanity and was executed in May 1962.

Heartened by this, Wiesenthal reopened the Jewish Documentation Center in

Vienna and renewed his search for war criminals. Over the decades he has located and successfully seen prosecuted Franz Stangl, commandant of Treblinka and Sobibor; Hermine Braunsteiner, who supervised the murders of several hundred children at Majdanek; and hundreds of other Nazis, Nazi collaborators, and SS soldiers and camp guards. By its nature, Wiesenthal's work is confidential and at times furtive. It is always painstaking, for Wiesenthal must produce evidence that will stand up in court. This has proven particularly difficult with the passage of time, when physical characteristics and memories change. Wiesenthal still gets leads from Jews, non-Jews, ex-soldiers, civilians, and even some ex-Nazis who have grudges against other ex-Nazis.

Wiesenthal has been honored worldwide. Although he does his work for justice and not personal gain, he has been honored by the United Nations, the United States, Holland, Austria, France, and Luxembourg. President Jimmy Carter presented him with the U.S. Congressional Gold Medal. He continues his work today, although he is in his late eighties, and even though both the victims and the criminals are dying off. He will continue until he himself dies.

Wiesenthal was once asked by a *New York Times* reporter to explain why he does what he does. The reporter noted the following:

> Wiesenthal once spent the Sabbath at the home of a former Mauthausen inmate, now a well-to-do jewelry manufacturer. After dinner his host said, "Simon, if you had gone back to building houses, you'd be a millionaire. Why didn't you?"
>
> "You're a religious man," replied Wiesenthal, "you believe in God and life after death. I also believe. When we come to the other world and meet the millions of Jews who died in the camps and they ask us 'What have you done?' there will be many answers. You will say 'I became a jeweler.' Another will say 'I have smuggled coffee and American cigarettes.' Another will say 'I have built houses.' But I will say, 'I didn't forget you.'"

IX

SIGNERS OF THE ISRAELI DECLARATION OF INDEPENDENCE

SIGNERS OF THE ISRAELI DECLARATION OF INDEPENDENCE

"The Land of Israel was the birthplace of the Jewish people. Here their spiritual, religious, and national identity was formed. Here they achieved independence and created a culture of national and universal significance. Here they wrote and gave the Bible to the world. . . . With trust in Almighty God, we set our hand to this Declaration, at this session of the Provisional State Council, on the soil of the Homeland, in the city of Tel Aviv, on this Sabbath eve, the fifth of Iyar, *5708, the fourteenth day of May, 1948."*

—Opening and closing paragraphs of the Israeli Declaration of Independence

If ever individuals held history in their hands, it was the men and women who signed the Israeli Declaration of Independence: people who risked their lives, the lives of their families and loved ones, and the lives of their fellow countrymen by signing their names to, at best, an ephemeral piece of paper and a universal dream.

Israel's signers, thirty-seven in all, included men, women, conservatives and liberals, a Communist, two rabbis, and a host more of the spectrum that *Klal Yisrael*, the collective community of Israel, has always been. Several parties not included in the separate National Administration were represented in the Provisional Council. The breakdown of the parties was as follows:

Party	Number of Representatives
Mapai	10
General Zionists	6
Mizrachi	5
Ha-Poel Ha-Mizrachi	5
Mapam	5
Agudat Yisrael/Poale Agudat Yisrael	3

Aliyah Chadasha	1
Yemenites	1
Sephardim	1

The signers have been known as both the National Council and the Provisional Council of Israel. The actual wording of the declaration was drafted by five members: David Remez, Felix Rosenblueth, Moshe Shapira, Moshe Shertok, and Aharon Zisling. Politics being what they are, the final wording was selected by David Ben-Gurion, Rabbi Y. L. Fishman, and Aharon Zisling. The declaration was publicly read, by Ben-Gurion, to the Provisional Council in the Tel Aviv Museum Hall on May 14, 1948. Following the reading, Ben-Gurion was the first to sign it. The secretary, Ze'ev Schaerf, then called out the names of the council members alphabetically (in Hebrew). Each came forward to sign it. Room was left for their fellow delegates who, because of armed fighting already in progress, were unable to come from Jerusalem. Following all council members' signing, Ben-Gurion announced: "The State of Israel has arisen. This session is closed."

Most signers are not well known. They were unsung patriots with little claim to fame. The David Ben-Gurions are readily known. But how many people have heard of Saadia Kobashi or Herzl Vardi? As individuals, their influence was limited; as a body, they represented a people declaring political statehood. It was the Kobashis and the Vardis who founded a new country. And because of this, their names will not be forgotten.

David Ben-Gurion

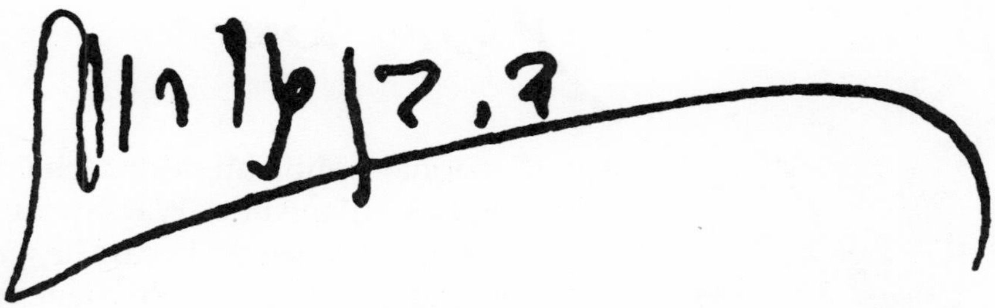

See separate entry.

David Auster

Born in Stanislav, Galicia, in 1893, Auster was the first mayor of Jerusalem in the new State of Israel. A lawyer by profession, he studied law in Vienna. Following his graduation in 1914, he moved to Palestine. After serving with the Austrian Expeditionary Forces in World War I, he established a law practice in Jerusalem. He served as secretary of the legal department of the Zionist Commission from 1919 to 1920. In 1934 he was elected a Jerusalem councillor and the next year was appointed deputy mayor. He served as acting mayor from 1936 to 1938 and again from 1944 to 1945. In 1947 Auster represented the Jewish cause to the United Nations against the internationalizing of Jerusalem. Auster served as mayor of Jerusalem in the State of Israel from 1948 to 1951. He was also the head of the Israel United Nations Association from its creation until his death in 1962.

Mordechai Bentov

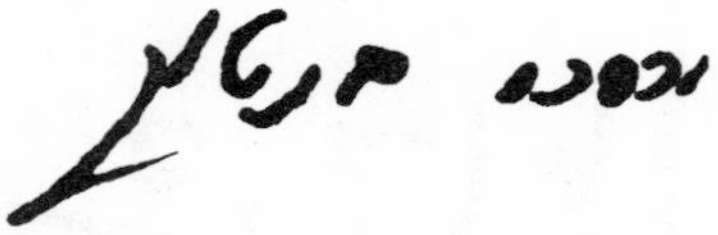

A professional politician, Mordechai Bentov (originally Gutgeld) was born in a village near Warsaw in 1900. He settled in Palestine at the age of 20. For several years he was a laborer, helping to drain swamps and build roads. He then studied governmental law in Jerusalem and became a member of Kibbutz Mishmar Ha-Emek. Bentov was a member of several political parties and movements. In 1939 he was a member of the Jewish delegation to the Round Table Conference with the British government to discuss the future of Palestine. He was a member of the Mapam political party, serving as editor of its daily newspaper, *Al Ha-Mishmar*, from 1943 to 1948, and was a member of the Knesset for the Mapam from 1949 to 1965. As a member of the provisional government, Bentov acted as minister of labor and reconstruction. He later served as minister of development (1955–1961) and minister of housing (1966–1969). Bentov was also the author of several books and numerous articles and essays on political and economic subjects.

Yitzchak Ben-Tzvi

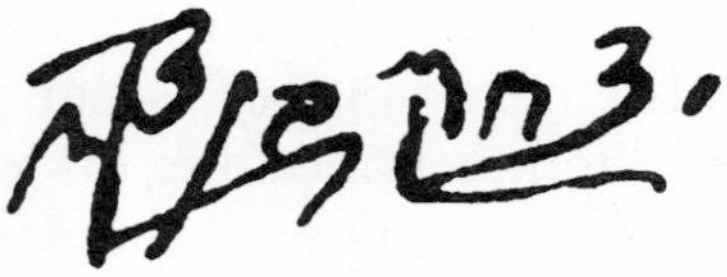

See separate entry.

Eliahu Berligne

One of the founders of Tel Aviv, Eliahu Meir Berligne moved to Palestine in 1907 at the age of 41. A Russian Jew, he was a delegate to several Zionist congresses. As a founder of Tel Aviv, he served on its first administrative committee and was appointed its chairman in 1909. In 1919 he was a member of the *yishuv* delegation to the Paris Peace Conference. He was also a member of the Provisional Council of Palestinian Jewry from 1920 to 1948, serving as its treasurer, and of the General Zionists, which later became the Progressive Party. In 1946 he was named an honorary citizen of Tel Aviv. He died in 1959.

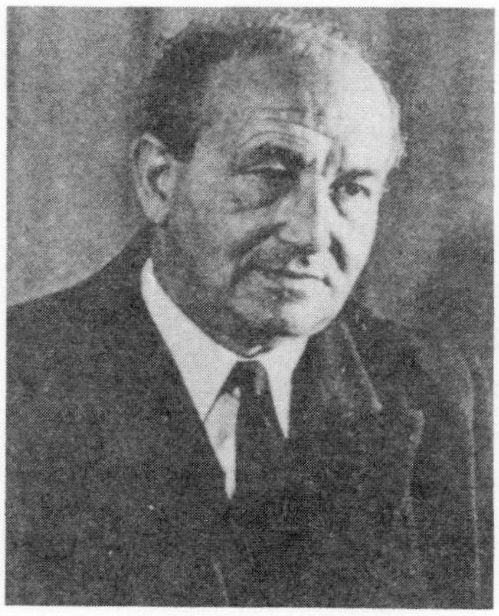

Peretz (Fritz) Bernstein

Bernstein was multifaceted: a journalist, industrialist, politician, and Zionist. He was born in Meiningen, Germany, in 1890. After studying commerce there, he moved to Rotterdam, Holland, where he went into business. He joined the Dutch Zionist organization, and later served as secretary and president of the Dutch Zionist Federation. From 1930 to 1935, he was editor of the Dutch Zionist weekly. In 1936 he settled in Palestine and became editor of the General Zionist newspaper *Ha-Boker*. He also became the chairman of the Union of General Zionists. Bernstein held the position of minister of commerce and industry from 1948 to 1949 and again from 1952 to 1955. He was a member of the Knesset from 1948 to 1965. In his writings he argued against left-wing positions and advocated business-oriented policies. In his key work, *Anti-Semitism as a Sociological Problem*, he tried to show that anti-Semitism as a phenomenon would not be solved by either better education or persuasion. Bernstein died in 1971.

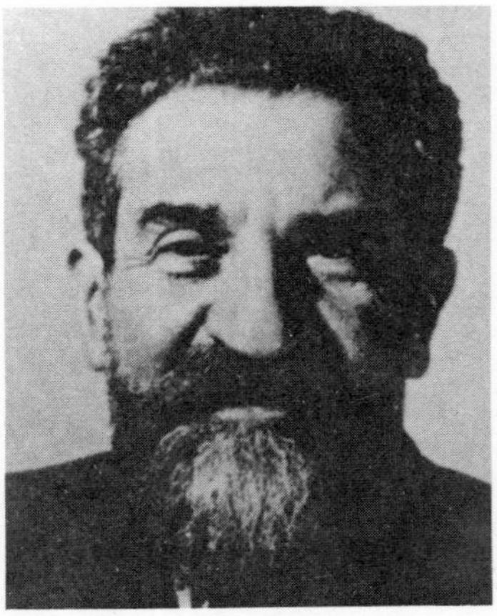

Wolff Gold

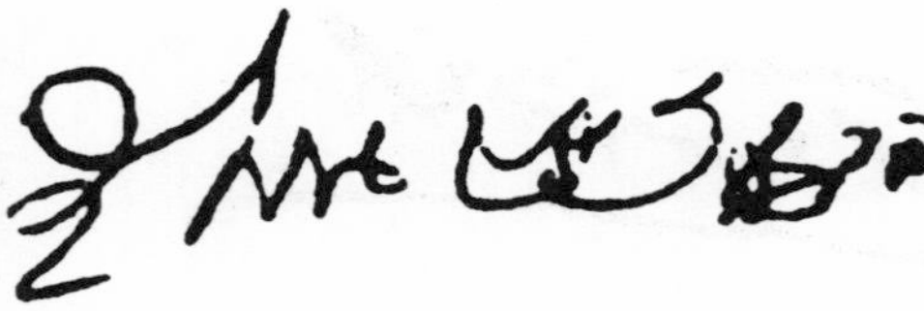

One of two "official" rabbis in the group of signers, Wolff Gold was a leader of religious Zionism. A community organizer and educator, he was a Zionist all his life. He was born in Sczcyczyin, Poland, in 1889 into a rabbinical family. He received his *s'michah* at 17 and replaced his father-in-law as town rabbi in Juteka before coming to the United States in 1907. He served in a variety of posts in several communities, including Chicago, Scranton, Williamsburg, San Francisco, and New York, where he was a founder of the *yeshivah* Torah v'Da'as. Gold was a delegate to all the Zionist congresses and a member of the Zionist General Council from 1923. He first visited Palestine in 1924. He was also active in the Mizrachi movement and served as the president of the American Mizrachi from 1932 to 1935. He settled in Palestine in 1935. He represented the Mizrachi in the Jewish Agency and was a member of the Jewish delegation to the United Nations in 1946. Following Israel's establishment, he headed the Jewish Agency's Department for the Development of Jerusalem and in 1951 headed up the Department for Torah Education and Culture. In that position, Gold was influential in the establishment of schools and other educational facilities in the Diaspora. After his death, an institute for Jewish studies and a teachers' seminary were named for him. He died in 1956.

Meir Grabovsky

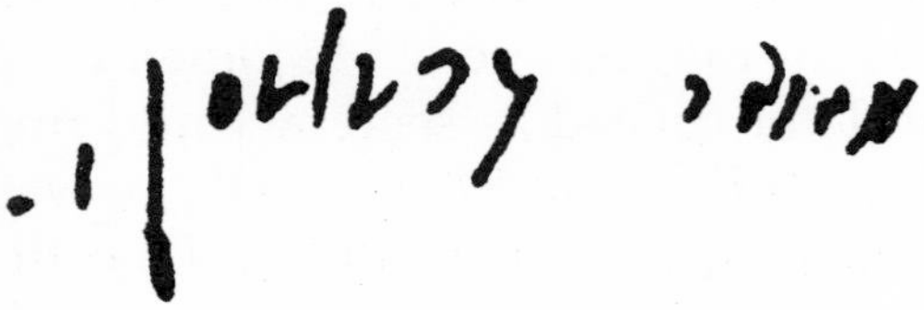

Also known as Meir Argov, after hebraizing his name, Grabovsky was one of the leading members of the Mapai Party. Born in Russia in 1905, he moved to Palestine in 1925. He was a member of the Vaad Leummi and a representative of the Mapai Party, and held a number of posts in the government and within his own party. During the drafting of the declaration, Grabovsky proposed the addition of the word *language* to the clause addressing freedom of religion, conscience, education, and culture, a change to which Ben-Gurion agreed.

Yitzchak Gruenbaum

First minister of the interior for the State of Israel, Yitzchak Gruenbaum was one of several signers who were not present for the official ceremony; he was in Jerusalem, which was under siege, at the time. Leader of the radical faction in General Zionism, Gruenbaum was born in Warsaw in 1879, first studying medicine, then switching to law. He began his Zionist activities during his student days. He was a delegate to all the Zionist congresses from the seventh congress on. Extremely active in the fight for the rights of Polish Jewry from 1900 through the 1930s, he was elected a member of the Polish parliament. His concepts of combining minorities for a stronger voice angered both Jews and Poles. He left Poland in 1932 for Paris and in 1933 was voted a member of the executive committee of the Jewish Agency. He then settled in Palestine. As a member of the executive committee, he was in charge of the *aliyah* department and later, for thirteen years, the labor department. He was also treasurer of the Jewish Agency and acted for a time as its commissioner. From 1935 to 1948 he headed the publishing house Mosad Bialik. After the founding of the state, he was responsible for organizing the country's first elections. He submitted his own party list but won no seats. He nonetheless remained active for many years in journalism and ongoing Zionist affairs. Gruenbaum's extremism in his views won him both enemies and admirers. He died in 1970.

Avraham Granovsky

Head of the Jewish National Fund (JNF), economist Avraham Granovsky (Granott) was born in 1890 in Folesti, Bessarabia. He settled in Jerusalem in 1922 as the fund's managing director. He spent virtually his entire life with the JNF, holding a variety of positions, including president and chairman of the board of directors. Granott was cofounder and chairman of the Progressive Party and was elected to the first Knesset, serving as chair of the finance committee. He is credited with establishing Israel's principles for a progressive agrarian policy.

Eliahu Dobkin

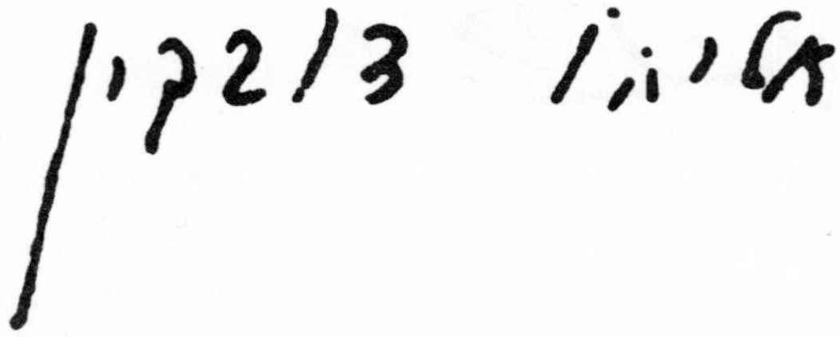

A Labor Zionist leader who held numerous positions in Jewish organizations, Eliahu Dobkin was born in 1898 in Bobruisk, White Russia (Belorussia). He founded the student organization *He-Chaver* and became general secretary of the *He-Chalutz* movement in Warsaw in 1921. He arrived in Palestine in 1932 and served on the executive committee of the Jewish Agency. During World War II, he was in charge of the Jewish Agency's immigration department, dealing with rescues from Europe. From 1951 to 1968 Dobkin served as head of the Jewish Agency's Youth and He-Chalutz Department and as chairman for eleven years of the United Israel Appeal (*Keren Hayesod,* 1951–1962). He was also chairman of the Bezalel National Museum in Jerusalem.

Meir Wilner-Kovner

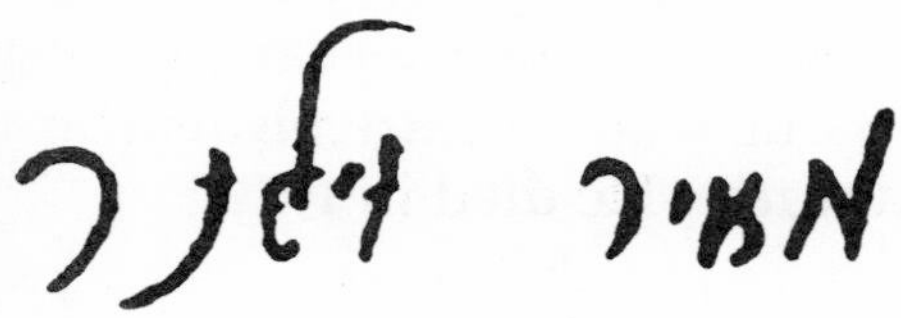

A native of Vilna, Meir Wilner settled in Palestine in 1938. He holds the distinction of being the sole representative of the Communist Party. During the drafting of the declaration, he suggested the addition of articles denouncing the British mandate and opposing military bases, but his suggestions were rejected as inappropriate and out of place.

Zerach Wahrhaftig

Also a lawyer, Zerach Wahrhaftig was the leader of the National Religious Party in Israel. He was born in 1906 in Volkovysk, Belorussia. He was a member of the Mizrachi Party and with the onset of World War II fled through the Soviet Union and Japan, coming to the United States. He settled in Palestine in 1947, joining the Vaad Leummi. He was elected to the Knesset repeatedly on the Ha-Po'el Ha-Mizrachi ticket (later the National Religious Party) and served as minister of religious affairs for several years. He was also associated with Bar-Ilan University. A prolific author, he wrote several books while in the United States and Israel.

Herzl Vardi

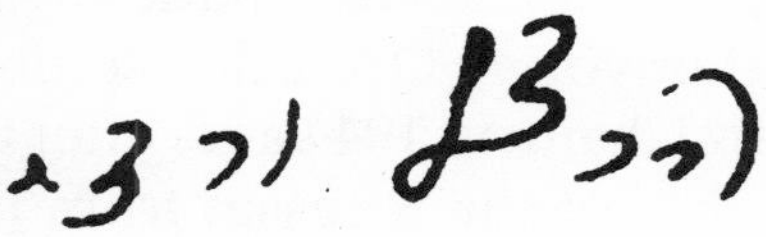

Veteran political activist, journalist, and newspaper editor, Herzl Vardi (Rosenblum) was born in Kovno, Lithuania, in 1903 and settled in Palestine when he was 32 years old. He was a representative of the Revisionist Party.

Rachel Cohen

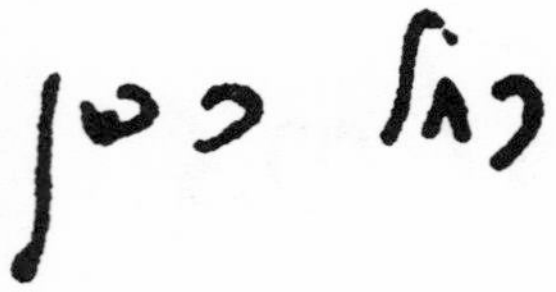

Rachel Cohen (Kagan) was one of only two women signers. Born in Odessa in 1888, she settled in Palestine in 1919. She was a member and representative of the Women's International Zionist Organization (WIZO) and was elected to the Knesset on the WIZO ticket from 1949 to 1951.

Kalman Kahana

Leader of the Poalei Agudat Yisrael movement, Kalman Kahana was one of the four rabbis in the group of signers. He was born in 1910 in Brody, Galicia, and made *aliyah* to Palestine in 1938 with a group of other young Orthodox settlers. He was a founder of Kibbutz Chofetz Chaim in 1944 and, after the establishment of the state, was a member of the Knesset from its inception. A scholar who wrote on the Rambam (Maimonides) and published several rabbinic studies, he served as deputy minister of education from 1962 to 1969 and eventually served as president of the Poalei Agudat Yisrael.

Saadia Kobashi

The voice of the Yemenites in Palestine and Israel, Kobashi was born in Yemen in 1904 and was brought to Palestine when he was 5. He was a member of the Vaad Leummi and the representative of the Yemenite Party.

Yitzchak Meir-Levin

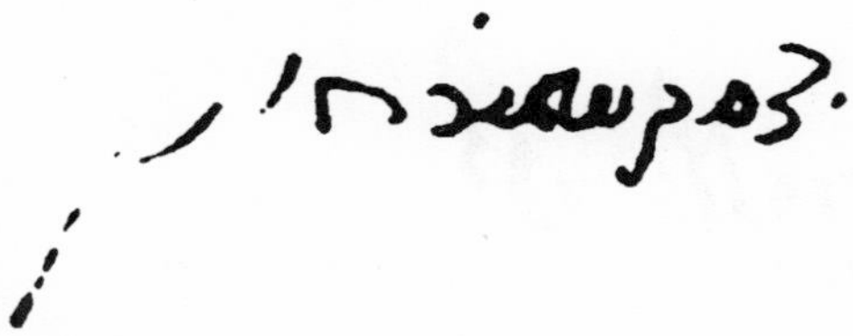

Rabbi Yitzchak Meir-Levin was the leader of the Agudat Yisrael Party. Born in Gor (Gur, Gora), Poland in 1894, he came from a distinguished family: he was a grandson of the former Gerer Rebbe, Yehuda Leib Alter (the S'fas Emes) and a son-in-law of the Gerer Rebbe of his time, Abraham Mordechai Alter. Politically active in the Agudat Yisrael Party from its inception, he rose to its leadership. He represented the powerful and influential party at a number of world political gatherings. Meir-Levin escaped Poland in 1940 and settled in Palestine, which he had first visited in 1935. Throughout the war he was involved in rescue operations. After the war, Meir-Levin was elected to the first Knesset and was Israel's first minister of social welfare. He died in 1971.

Meir David Loevenstein

Loevenstein was born in Copenhagen in 1901 and brought to Palestine as a toddler in 1904. He was a member of the Agudat Yisrael Party.

Tzvi Luria

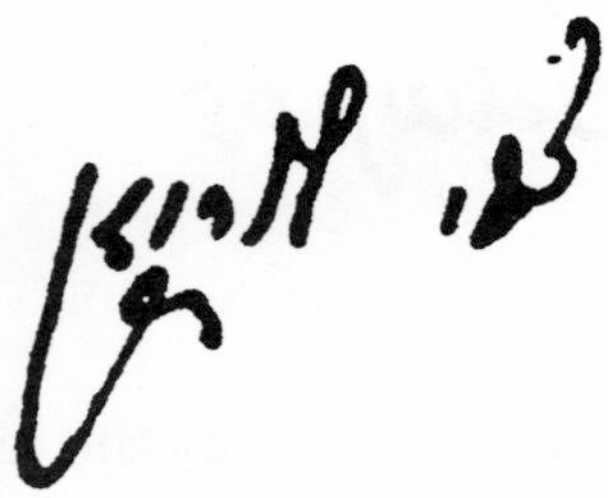

A member of the Mapam Party, as well as the Vaad Leummi, Tzvi Luria was another labor-oriented leader. He was born in Lodz, Poland, in 1906 and settled in Palestine in 1925. Originally an agricultural worker at Petach Tikvah, he joined the HaShomer HaZair movement and was involved with them for eight years, two as secretary of the world leadership in Warsaw. Luria served on the Vaad Leummi and was on its executive from 1946 to 1948 as director of its information department. From 1948 on, he was a member of the executive council of the Jewish Agency in both New York and Jerusalem. He died in 1968.

Golda Myerson (Meir)

See separate entry.

Nachum Nir

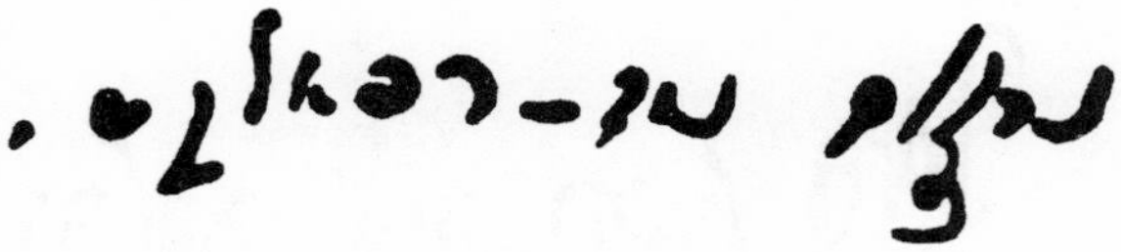

Nachum Nir (Rafalkes) was an attorney, a labor leader, and the second speaker of the Knesset. Born in Warsaw in 1884, he studied law and practiced in St. Petersburg. He joined the political party *Poale Zion* in 1905, remaining a member throughout its existence. In 1918 he returned to Warsaw and was elected a member of the city council. In 1925 Nir settled in Palestine, where he practiced law and represented his party in the Histadrut and the Vaad Leummi. He later held the position of deputy chairman of the pre-state People's Council. After statehood, Nir was a member of the Knesset from its founding until 1965, and served as its deputy speaker. He died in 1968.

Tzvi Segal

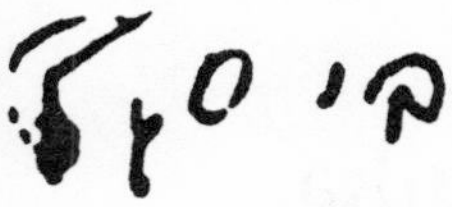

A native of Poland (born in 1901), Segal made *aliyah* to Palestine in 1938. A member of the Revisionist Party, he spoke on behalf of the members of the Hatzohar in the provisional government's first meeting on May 16, objecting to Israel's cooperation with the United Nations since the UN favored partition.

Yehuda Leib HaCohen Fishman (Maimon)

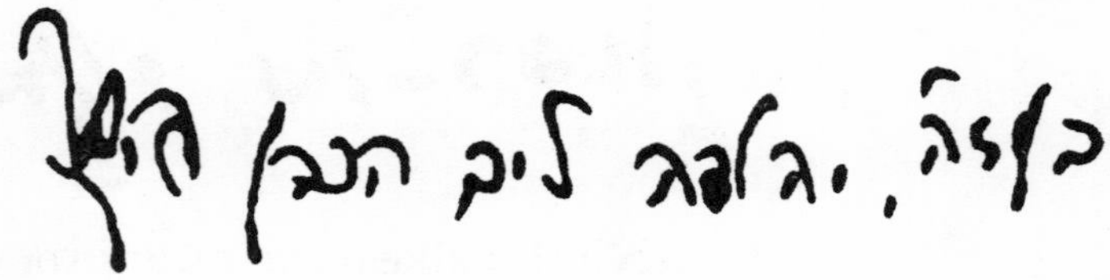

Active for many years in the rabbinate before becoming politically active, Rabbi Yehuda Leib Fishman was a leader of religious Zionism. He was born in 1875 in Marculesti, Bessarabia (Romania), and studied in Lithuanian *yeshivot*. After ordination, he was both a preacher and town rabbi. He became politically active in 1900 and attended all the Zionist congresses from the second one on. He was a member of the Zionist General Council. Fishman was also a lifelong member of the Mizrachi Party, holding a number of positions within it over the years. He was appointed minister of religions and minister in charge of war casualties, both in the provisional government and in the first elected one. Active in political and religious circles, and the author of a number of religious works, he died in 1962.

David Tzvi Pinkas

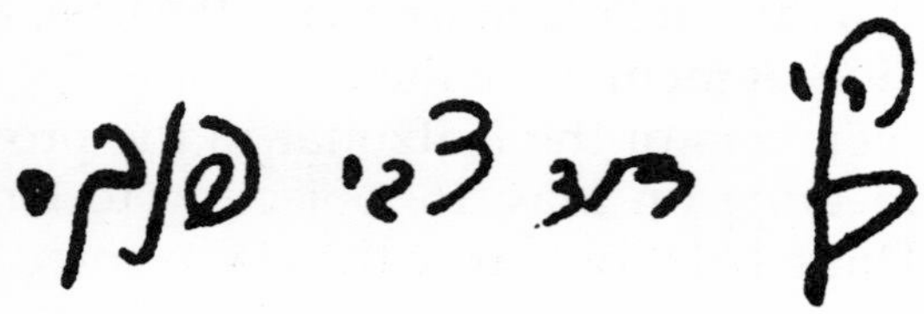

David Pinkas was born in Hungary in 1895 and settled in Palestine when he was 30. In Israel's first government, among other positions held, he was the chairman of the State Council's Committee on Committees. He was a member of the Vaad Leummi and a representative of the Mizrachi Party.

Aharon Zisling

One of the four members of the council who crafted the final draft of the declaration, Aharon Zisling was a lifelong labor leader in Palestine and Israel. Born in 1901 in Minsk, his family moved to Tel Aviv in 1914. His philosophy was that of labor, and he was a founding member of the workers' collective Chavurat Ha-Emek. He served on a number of workers' councils and organizations, was a founder of the Youth Aliyah, and was actively involved in several political parties and offshoots, including Histadrut and the Jewish Agency. After the founding of the state, he served as minister of agriculture from 1948 to 1949. From 1961 to 1963 he was a member of the Zionist executive council, heading up its absorption department. He was a member of the *Haganah's* command and helped found the Palmach. Zisling died in 1964.

Moshe Kolodny

Moshe Kolodny, who adopted the surname Kol, settled in Palestine in 1932 at the age of 21. A native of Pinsk, he was politically active even as a youth. Throughout his life, Kol served in a number of political positions, including with the Histadrut and Jewish Agency executive councils. He was head of the youth *aliyah* department (a position he held for eighteen years) and founder of the Progressive Party. He served several times in the Knesset and was also the minister of tourism and development.

Eliezer Kaplan

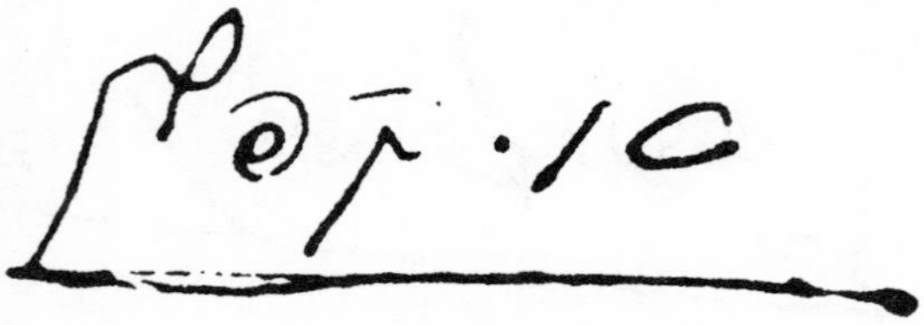

Eliezer Kaplan was born in Minsk in 1891. An engineer by education, he received his diploma in Moscow in 1917. He was one of the founders of the Socialist Zionist movement Zeirei Zion in Russia. He also founded, in 1920, the HaPoel HaZair and Zeirei Zion organization known as Histachadut, whose philosophy was "pioneering and labor in *Eretz Yisrael* and popular socialism." Kaplan settled in Palestine in 1920 and was an administrator for the Public Works Office. He held numerous political positions and was a member of the executive council of the Jewish Agency. With the establishment of the state, Kaplan was elected to the Knesset and served as Israel's first minister of finance. It was Kaplan who laid the foundation for Israel's financial and fiscal policies and was extremely influential in shaping Israel's first budgets, tax structure, and economic policy. Shortly before his death in 1952, he was appointed deputy prime minister, dealing mainly with economic matters. The Eliezer Kaplan School of Politics and Social Sciences at Hebrew University was named after him.

Abraham Katznelson

Also known as Abraham Nissan. Born in Bobruisk, White Russia, in 1888, Katznelson was both a labor politician and Israeli diplomat. He settled in Palestine in 1924, following service in the Russian army during World War I as a medical officer. He was a key member of the Mapai and HaPoel HaZair parties. From 1950 until his death in 1956, he served as Israel's minister to the Scandinavian countries.

Felix Rosenblueth (Pinchas Rosen)

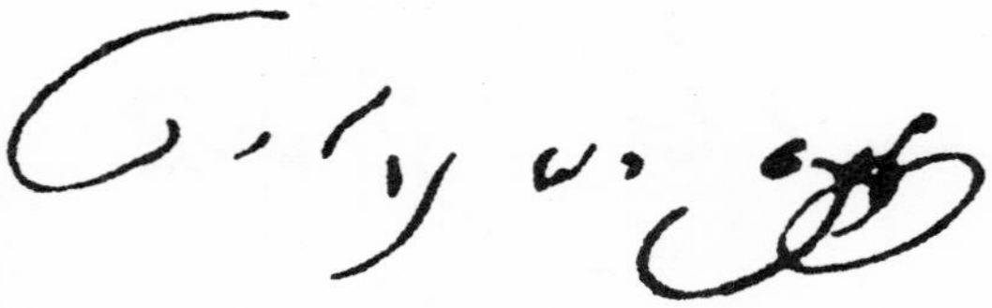

A lawyer by training, Pinchas Rosen was an Israeli and Zionist leader. Born in Berlin in 1887, he was a cofounder of the youth movement Blau-Weiss and was later chairman of the Zionist Organization of Germany from 1920 to 1923. He lived in Palestine from 1923 to 1925, after which he became a member of the Zionist executive council in London from 1926 to 1931. He returned to Palestine permanently in 1931 and, while practicing law for the next sixteen years, he held a variety of positions and was active in a number of civic and community organizations. In the struggle for statehood, he opposed Jewish terrorism and favored the United Nations' partition plan. Following statehood, Rosen was a member of the Knesset for the Progressive Party from 1949 to 1968 and served as minister of justice from 1948 to 1961. He was highly involved in organizing Israel's legal and judicial system.

David Remez

Moshe David Remez (Drabkin) was an early labor leader. Born in Kopys, White Russia (Belorussia), in 1886, he was a member of the Poalei Zion movement in his youth. He studied law in Constantinople and settled in Palestine in 1913, where he was an agricultural worker/laborer for five years. After World War I, he became politically active, involving himself with Achdut Ha-Avodah, Mapai, and the Histadrut. He was chairman of the Vaad Leummi from 1944 to 1948 and was one of the Jewish leaders arrested by the British on "Black Saturday." He spent several months in a British detention camp. In 1948 he was appointed minister of transport as a member of the provisional government, and in 1950 he was appointed minister of education. He died in 1951.

Berl Repetur

Berl Repetur was born in Beruzin, Russia, in 1902. He settled in Palestine in 1920 and held a number of positions as a member of the Mapam Party and the Vaad Leummi.

Mordechai Shattner

Hungarian by birth, Shattner made *aliyah* to Palestine in 1924, at the age of 20. Like others, he was a member of the Mapai Party and the Vaad Leummi.

Ben-Zion Sternberg

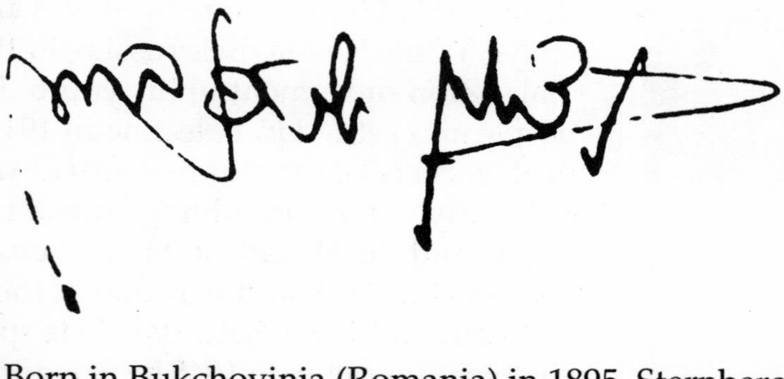

Born in Bukchovinia (Romania) in 1895, Sternberg made *aliyah* to Palestine in 1940, at the age of 45. He was a representative of the Revisionist Party.

Bekhor Shitreet

Another of the Sephardic signers of the declaration, Shitreet was born in 1895 in Tiberias. He was an organizer of the police force in Tiberias and was police commander in Lower Galilee. After formal training, he handled criminal investigations in a number of towns and held the position of magistrate in several communities. After statehood, Shitreet became a member of the government, representing Sephardic and oriental Jews, and held the position of minister of police and minorities. He became a member of the Knesset for the Mapai Party and served as minister of police. He died in 1967.

Moshe Shapira

A lifelong religious Zionist, Moshe Shapira was the leader of the National Religious Party. He was born in 1902 in Grodno, Belorussia. As a youth, he was active in the *aliyah* of religious pioneers to Palestine. He attended the Hildesheimer Rabbinical Seminary in Berlin and continued his activities in the Ze'ieri Mizrachi movement; he was a delegate to several Zionist congresses. In 1925 he settled in Palestine and became a central political figure in the Mizrachi. In 1935 he became an alternate and then full member of the Zionist executive council and, when statehood was declared, Shapira was appointed head of the immigration department. His name was changed to Chaim Moshe Shapira after he was seriously wounded in an attack at the Knesset. Shapira served in numerous Israeli governments in a variety of roles: as minister of immigration, health (1948–1949 and 1961–1965), interior (1949–1952 and 1959–1970), and religious affairs and social welfare (1952–1958). He died in 1970.

Moshe Shertok (Sharett)

See separate entry.

GLOSSARY

Chasidut The philosophy of Chasidism, as generally pertains to the movement founded by Israel ben Eliezer, the Baal Shem Tov, of the eighteenth century.

Chillul Ha-Shem Profanation of the name of God; any act that brings God's name, and by extension the Jewish name, into disrepute.

Halachah Jewish law.

Haskalah The movement active between 1750 and 1880 that sought to spread general European culture among Eastern European Jews.

Ilui A youthful genius or child/teenage prodigy in talmudic study.

Kedushah Holiness; sanctity.

Kiddush Ha-Shem Sanctification of the name of God; any act that brings merit or positive image to the Jewish name.

Maskil An advocate of the Enlightenment, or *Haskalah,* movement.

Mitnaggdim Originally, the Eastern European Jewish opponents of Chasidism.

Pilpul In talmudic and rabbinic literature, casuistry as developed in Poland in the sixteenth century. Often considered "hairsplitting."

Posek A rabbinic scholar or codifier who makes decisions relating to Jewish law.

Rebbe In chasidic circles, the leader of the community or group. In nonchasidic circles, a teacher.

Responsa Written opinions to questions on aspects of Jewish law by qualified authorities. These are frequently in book form of questions and answers, called in Hebrew *sh'elot u-teshuvot.*

S'michah Orthodox rabbinic ordination.

Vaad Leummi The national council of the Jewish community in Palestine during the period of the British mandate.

Yeshivah A traditional Jewish academy or school devoted primarily to the study of the Talmud and rabbinic literature.

Yishuv Settlement; more specifically, the Jewish community of *Eretz Yisrael* in the prestate period. The pre-Zionist community is generally designated the "old *yishuv,*" the community evolving from 1880, the "new *yishuv.*"

CREDITS

I would like to thank the following individuals and institutions for their gracious assistance in providing the majority of autographic materials in this book. In a number of cases, I was fortunate to receive several examples of the same individual's autograph and thus had overlapping samples from which to choose. Likewise, I would like to thank those benefactors who, through modesty and for privacy and security reasons, asked to remain anonymous. I apologize for any errors or oversights.

ADM Publishing House: pp. 256, 258—Eli Cohen.

American Jewish Archives: pp. 31, 106, 108, 111, 113, 114, 116, 237, 239, 269, 271—Alexander Goode, Louis Ginzberg, Mordecai Kaplan, Judah Magnes, Isaac M. Wise, Teddy Kollek.

ANNE FRANK-Fonds (AFF): pp. 284, 286—Anne Frank.

Reuben Brennan Archives, Jewish Folk Library: pp. 191, 193—Mendele Moicher Seforim.

Blumenthal Library, Judah Magnes Museum: pp. 170, 213, 215, 272, 274—Chaim Weizmann, Louis D. Brandeis, Moses Montefiore.

Central Zionist Archives: pp. 141, 143, 145, 147, 151, 153, 161—Theodor Herzl, Vladimir Jabotinsky, Max Nordau, Joseph Trumpeldor.

Sylvia Ettenberg: pp. 109, 136, 137—Abraham Joshua Heschel, Abba Eban.

Farrar, Straus & Giroux Publishers: p. 277—Roman Vishniac. Photograph "Granddaughter and grandfather. Warsaw, 1938" from A VANISHED WORLD by Roman Vishniac. Copyright © 1969, 1973, 1983 by Roman Vishniac. Reprinted by permission of Farrar, Straus & Giroux, Inc.

Abraham Finkel: pp. 28, 30, 57, 59—Yitzchak Meir Alter of Ger, Shneur Zalman of Liadi.

Menachem Glenn: pp. 54, 56—Yisroel Salanter.

Giora Senesch, Peter Hay: pp. 290, 292, 293—Hannah Senesch.

Charles Hamilton: pp. 133, 189, 225, 228—Moshe Dayan, Emma Lazarus, Uriah P. Levy, Mordecai M. Noah.

The Huntington Library: pp. 209, 211, 212, 227, 230—Judah Benjamin, Uriah P. Levy, Mordecai M. Noah.

Israeli Government Printing Office: pp. 129, 131, 135, 301–318—Yitzchak ben Tzvi, Menachem Begin, Moshe Dayan, Moshe Shertok, David Ben-Gurion, David Auster, Mordechai Bentov, Eliahu Berligne, Peretz Bernstein, Wolff Gold, Meir Grabovsky, Yitzchak Gruenbaum, Avraham Granovsky, Eliahu Dobkin, Meir Wilner-Kovner, Zerach Wahrhaftig, Herzl Vardi, Rachel Cohen, Kalman Kahana,

Saadia Kobashi, Yitzchak Meir-Levin, Meir David Loevenstein, Tzvi Luria, Golda Meir, Nachum Nir, Tzvi Segal, Yehuda Fishman, David Pinkas, Aharon Zisling, Moshe Kolodny, Eliezer Kaplan, Abraham Katznelson, Felix Rosenbleuth, David Remez, Berl Repetur, Mordechai Shattner, Ben-Zion Sternberg, Bekhor Shitreet, Moshe Shapira.

Schwadron Collection, Jewish National University Library: pp. 3, 4, 50, 148, 173, 176, 178, 180, 187, 254, 266, 268—Israel Ben Eliezer, Levi Yitzchak of Berditchev, Moses Ben Maimon, Golda Meir, Chaim Weizmann, S. Y. Agnon, Sholom Aleichem, Sholom Asch, Chaim Nachman Bialik, Ahad Ha'am, Marc Chagall, Naftali H. Imber.

Jewish Theological Seminary of America: pp. 8, 10, 15, 17, 18, 20, 21, 23, 33, 35, 36, 38, 39, 42, 45, 47, 48, 49, 60, 61, 62, 64, 65, 67, 71, 73, 97, 99, 100, 102, 103, 104, 105, 117, 120, 122, 231, 233—Naftali Tzvi Yehuda Berlin, Moses Sofer, Akiva Eiger, Jacob Emden, Yehudah Ha-Levi, Samson Raphael Hirsch, Joseph Karo, Abraham Isaac Kook, Moses Chaim Luzzatto, Meir Leib Ben Yechiel Michael, Chaim Soloveitchik, Joel Sirkes, Ezekiel Landau, Isaac Elchanan Spektor, Leo Baeck, Simon Dubnow, Abraham Geiger, Solomon Schechter, Leopold Zunz, Haym Salomon.

Sholom Katz, Esq.: pp. 24, 26, 27, 68—Moshe Feinstein, Menachem Mendel Schneerson.

Kibbutz Ha-artzaa Hashomer Hatzair: pp. 281, 283—Mordecai Anielewicz.

Ktav Publishing House, Inc.: p. 11—Israel Meir Kagan.

David Schulson Autographs: pp. 79, 81, 83, 85, 138, 140, 156, 159, 182, 216, 218, 219, 221, 222, 224, 251, 253, 259, 261—Albert Einstein, Levi Eshkol, Henrietta Szold, Chaim Nachman Bialik, Benjamin Cardozo, Felix Frankfurter, Samuel Gompers, Irving Berlin, Aaron Copland, David Ben-Gurion.

YIVO: pp. 164, 184, 186, 234, 236, 287, 289—Menachem Ussishkin, Abraham Cahan, Jacob Schiff, Janusz Korczak.

In addition, I gratefully acknowledge permission to quote from the following sources:

Responsa by Akiva Eiger, Moshe Feinstein, Joel Sirkes, and Ezekiel Landau from *The Responsa Anthology* by Avraham Yaakov Finkel. Copyright © 1990 by Avraham Yaakov Finkel. Published by Jason Aronson Inc. Used by permission.

Translations of Yehudah Ha-Levi by Louis Minkin from *Great Jewish Personalities in Ancient and Medieval Times*. Used by permission of B'nai B'rith, Department of Adult Jewish Education.

Translation of Hannah Senesch's "Blessed Is the Match" by Dr. Marie Syrkin. Used by permission of the Jewish Publication Society.

About the Author

Harvey Lutske was born in Chicago and grew up in Los Angeles, where he is the chief claims agent for the Los Angeles Department of Water and Power, the largest public utility in the United States. He was a paratrooper with the United States Army's renowned 82d Airborne Division, after which he returned to school to finish his education. He has a bachelor's degree in journalism and a master's degree in business administration. His work has appeared in American and Canadian magazines and newspapers, and he is the author of *The Book of Jewish Customs*. He and his wife, Dr. Sharon Korr, live in Southern California with their three sons.